WordPerfect®
in the Law Office

BUSINESS
COMPUTER
LIBRARY

WordPerfect®
in the Law Office

Written by
Kenneth D. Chestek

WordPerfect in the Law Office

Library of Congress Catalog No.: 95-06131-9

ISBN: 0-7897-0613-x

98 97 96   6 5 4 3 2 1

Interpretation of the printing code: the rightmost double-digit number is the year of the book's printing; the rightmost single-digit number, the number of the book's printing. For example, a printing code of 96-1 shows that the first printing of the book occurred in 1996.

Screen reproductions in this book were created using Collage Plus from Inner Media, Inc., Hollis, NH.

Composed in *Stone Serif* and *MCPdigital* by Que Corporation

Credits

President
Roland Elgey

Vice President and Publisher
Marie Butler-Knight

Associate Publisher
Don Roche Jr.

Editorial Services Director
Elizabeth Keaffaber

Managing Editor
Michael Cunningham

Director of Marketing
Lynn E. Zingraf

Senior Series Editor
Chris Nelson

Title Manager
Kathie-Jo Arnoff

Acquisitions Editor
Elizabeth South

Product Director
Forrest Houlette

Editors
Linda Seifert
Geneil Breeze

Assistant Product Marketing Manager
Kim Margolius

Technical Editor
Richard Belthoff

Acquisitions Coordinator
Tracy Williams

Operations Coordinator
Patty Brooks

Editorial Assistant
Carmen Krikorian

Book Designer
Ruth Harvey

Cover Designer
Barbara Kordesh

Production Team
Brian Buschkill
Jason Carr
Bryan Flores
Trey Frank
Jason Hand
John Hulse
Stephanie Layton
Michelle Lee
Kaylene Riemen
Bobbi Satterfield
Michael Thomas
Scott Tullis
Kelly Warner
Karen York

Indexer
Cheryl Dietsch

About the Author

Ken Chestek is a partner in the law firm of Agresti & Agresti in Erie, PA. He has been practicing law for 16 years and has a general practice with a concentration in litigation. He served as Editor-in-Chief of the University of Pittsburgh Law Review and is currently chief counsel for Erie County, Pennsylvania.

Chestek is the author of *WordPerfect Power Macros for Windows* published by Que and has written chapters in several other Que titles about WordPerfect products. He is currently an assistant sysop in the WordPerfect Users Forum on CompuServe. He has used WordPerfect since version 4.1 and has served as a beta tester for several versions of WordPerfect.

Acknowledgments

Somebody once said, "No book is an island" (or something like that). Although my name gets to go on the spine of the book, it wouldn't be fair for me to take all the credit when so many others inhabit this "island" with me.

I'd like to thank **Kathie-Jo Arnoff** and **Michael Cunningham** at Que for their hard work in getting this book into print. As with any book project, the last few hectic weeks presented us with a few technical challenges, but their dedication to the project made it easy to overcome them. Thanks also to **Forrest Houlette** for offering constructive suggestions.

This book had its origins in cyberspace. I've been hanging around in the WordPerfect Users forum on CompuServe so long that they finally made me a sysop so I could give back a small part of the tremendous assistance I've gotten there over the years. I learned so much about the program in general, and macros in particular, from the "regulars" in the forum that I finally decided to write it all down, and this book is the result. Special thanks go to **Gordon McComb** and **John Filshie**, both sysops on the forum, who taught me everything I know about macros; thanks also to wizop **Guerri Stevens** who, along with John and Gordon, helped me work out some bugs in early versions of my macros. John also wrote a couple of the macros which are included on the disk, and gave me permission to include them here.

Rich Belthof of the law firm Grier and Grier in Charlotte, N.C. provided the technical editing for the book. He tested each macro and form on the disk (and in some cases more than one version as he discovered errors in the early drafts), as well as checking the text for accuracy. Several other lawyers, including **Eric Levine** from New York City, also tested early versions several of the macros and forms and provided helpful suggestions for improvements.

Thanks also to **Elden Nelson** for his help early on in getting this project off the ground. Elden helped champion this book while he was with Que Corporation and also when he returned to WordPerfect Corporation.

Finally, and most importantly, I want to dedicate this book to my wife **Ginny** and my children **Cindy** and **David** who kept me human throughout the process. They put up with a lot of "absentee husband/father" for a few months while I was writing, and this dedication won't make up for that, but it will help them to know how much I appreciate their support.

We'd Like to Hear from You!

As part of our continuing effort to produce books of the highest possible quality, Que would like to hear your comments. To stay competitive, we *really* want you, as a computer book reader and user, to let us know what you like or dislike most about this book or other Que products.

You can mail comments, ideas, or suggestions for improving future editions to the address below, or send us a fax at (317) 581-4663. For the online inclined, Macmillan Computer Publishing has a forum on CompuServe (type **GO QUEBOOKS** at any prompt) through which our staff and authors are available for questions and comments. The address of our Internet site is **http://www.mcp.com** (World Wide Web).

In addition to exploring our forum, please feel free to contact me personally to discuss your opinions of this book: I'm **76507,2715** on CompuServe, and I'm **kjarnoff@que.mcp.com** on the Internet.

Thanks in advance—your comments will help us to continue publishing the best books available on computer topics in today's market.

Kathie-Jo Arnoff
Title Manager
Que Corporation
201 W. 103rd Street
Indianapolis, Indiana 46290
USA

Contents at a Glance

Contents

4 Footnotes, Tables, and Compare   141

5 Automating With Macros   181

9 Correspondence Systems   291

10 Litigation Documents   321

11 Real Estate Documents   349

12 Commercial Law Practice   373

Introduction

OK. You've finally given in. Technology marches on and you've finally decided it's time to automate. You are now the proud owner of a shiny new 486 computer (whatever that is), sitting there on the floor next to your desk. There's this little thing, looks like a bar of soap, sitting next to the keyboard. People in the office have been talking about "Windows," in the singular, as if it were something other than panes of glass.

Even your colleagues are talking about computers these days. You know them. The ones who throw around draft after draft of contracts, each one redlined to mark changes from the last version; or the ones whose briefs, even for a simple case, look like they were professionally typeset and printed. They are starting to ask you now if you can give them your pleadings "on disk," and you're pretty sure they don't want you to deliver them by Frisbee.

The office automation experts are telling you that computers are the wave of the future in law offices. They say you can increase productivity and improve the quality of your work product at the same time by using computers. So you gave in and bought yourself this computer. The guy who sold it to you says that all the lawyers in town use WordPerfect, so you bought that too.

Now what?

If you are a lawyer or work in a law office and are a new user of WordPerfect for Windows, or if you are an old user who suspects that you are not getting the most out of that powerful program, then this book is for you.

Who This Book Is For

This book is for anybody who works in a law office. Yes, that includes the lawyers too! The days when only secretaries were allowed near the computer are long since passed, and more and more attorneys now have computers at their desks too. Anybody who uses WordPerfect to create documents can benefit from the tips and strategies in this book to make his or her time at the computer far more productive.

Even attorneys who prefer to have a secretary do all of the typing can learn from this book. All lawyers, whether they have a computer at their desk or not, want to be sure that the work of the office is completed quickly and efficiently. This book contains numerous tips and suggestions about how documents can be assembled quickly and easily, either from complete form documents or from "building blocks" such as standard paragraphs. Understanding how these techniques work will enable the lawyer to help create the form documents that will make the system work smoothly. (And don't forget—the lawyer is going to end up *using* all those form documents later on!)

What This Book Is About

Law offices are heavy users of word processing. Let's face it; this is what we do for a living. We're wordsmiths. We write wills; we draft contracts; we plead our cases on paper many times over before we ever enter a courtroom. Words are our livelihood. So it makes sense that lawyers want the most powerful word processing program available. And, because WordPerfect is just that, it also makes sense that WordPerfect has become, far and away, the most widely used word processing program in law offices all around the country.

Yet, as powerful as WordPerfect is, many of its features remain a mystery to most users. Hidden within its rich feature set are little shortcuts and tricks that can make any user, from lawyer to secretary, far more productive than he or she could imagine. Some of these features were added specifically for law offices. But many users simply don't know about them. In a sense, WordPerfect has become a victim of its own power: there is just so much there that it is difficult for a user to grasp it all, without attending a two-week training seminar. And who has the time or money for that?

This book provides tips on how to use the WordPerfect features most useful in a law office. It provides step-by-step instructions for all of these features. It also provides tools like macros, templates, and other documents that can help lawyers and their support staffs get the most out of WordPerfect.

There are a lot of "document assembly" software packages on the market, aimed at legal users. Although they all work, each of them has several inherent drawbacks: (a) they require you to purchase another program in addition to your word-processing program; (b) they require you to learn a new program, and (c) most of them need to be run alongside your word-processing program, taking up computer memory and adding one more level of complexity to an already taxed system. By contrast, WordPerfect for Windows is powerful enough by itself to handle almost all of your document assembly needs.

This book is designed to help you get the most out of your investment in WordPerfect. It will first describe for you some of the special features that are most useful to lawyers and legal secretaries. It will then take a "real world" look at how WordPerfect can be used to greatly speed up the production of the varied documents that are an important part of our work product.

How This Book Is Organized

This book consists of two parts, plus a disk.

Part I, "Special Features," is a description of some of the specialized features built in to WordPerfect. It is, of course, impossible to cover all of WordPerfect for Windows in a book this size. The official WordPerfect for Windows 6.1 printed manual is more than 800 pages long and does not cover any of the features in as much depth as this book does. Only a handful of the features that are built in to WordPerfect that are of the greatest use in law offices are covered, including a number that probably have no use to anybody else. (What other profession, for example, will ever need to create a Table of Authorities?)

This means, of course, that we must assume the reader has a basic understanding of how the program works. We assume, for example, that you already know how to open and close documents, enter and format text, and perform simple editing operations such as cut-and-paste and other basic word processing functions. We will devote our attention to the more sophisticated features like Templates, Merge, Macros, Outlines, and so forth, because this is where the real treasures are buried.

Part II, "Assembling Documents," takes a different approach. Rather than describing features, it describes tasks that you typically run into in a law office and then show you various combinations of features that you can use to complete those tasks efficiently. For example, it will describe methods of setting up form documents so that you can create custom documents for specific clients very quickly using Templates, or Merge, or a combination of both.

The Companion Disk at the back of the book includes a number of macros, templates, and other form documents. However, keep in mind that this is *not* a "form book." The form documents and templates are provided to show you how you can set up a document to automate your work. The text describes for you, step-by-step, how you can take your own documents and put them into this form. Expect to devote some time to working your existing form documents into the format shown in the text.

On the other hand, the macros on the Companion Disk are extremely useful tools that can be used "right out of the box." Some provide you with editing tools. Others help you maintain phone lists, or address lists, and other compilations. An installation program is provided on the Companion Disk.

A note about formatting: All of the templates and form documents use a proportional-spaced font as the default font. I have selected the TrueType Times New Roman font as the initial document font for all files, simply because that font should be available on any computer you may use. If it is not available, WordPerfect will automatically select a compatible replacement font that is installed on your computer. You may want to change the default fonts on any of the forms you decide to use, however.

The same holds true for some "special" fonts used by several of the documents on the Companion Disk. I have tried to stick with either TrueType fonts or fonts supplied with WordPerfect; again, if you do not have those fonts installed on your computer, or if your printer does not support them, WordPerfect should make substitutions automatically.

Conventions Used in This Book

It has been said that "consistency is the hobgoblin of small minds." If that is true, then I'm going to make an effort to be small-minded about the presentation of this book. As much as possible, this book tries to adhere to a few stylistic points:

- A reference to a computer filename is in all capital letters. For example, the Letter Maker macro is referred to as LETRMAKR.WCM.
- Whenever I refer to a message that you may see on your computer screen, a special monospace font—Press Enter to Continue—is used.

- Whenever you have to type something on your keyboard, the exact words to be typed are shown in boldface: **copy a:\macros*.* c:\wpwin60\macros**.

- Keys on your keyboard or combinations of keystrokes are shown as Alt+F10.

- When describing menus, dialog boxes, or other parts of the WordPerfect program, or a dialog box from one of the macros on the Companion Disk, the complete menu or dialog box title is used, initial capitalized. For example, Template refers to the Template feature found on the File menu; the word "template," not capitalized, refers to a template document in the generic sense.

- WordPerfect formatting codes are inside of square brackets: [HRt]. When a paired code is described (such as an appearance attribute that can be turned on or off), an angle bracket to distinguish between the two parts is included: For example, [Bold>] means that the Bold attribute is turned on, while [<Bold] means the attribute has been turned off.

You will also see various icons in the book from time to time (after all, it is a graphical program, and I may as well practice what I preach). When a macro, form document, or template that is included on the Companion Disk at the back of the book is used, you'll see the icon to the right of this paragraph:

Some of the keystrokes or menu selections for features have been revised between version 6.0 and 6.1. Where there is a difference, the 6.1 keystrokes or menu selections are given first, followed by the 6.0 keystrokes or selections, flagged by the icon to the right of this paragraph:

Note

This paragraph format indicates additional information that may help you avoid problems or that should be considered in using the described features.

Tip

This paragraph format suggests easier or alternative methods of executing a procedure.

> **Caution**
>
> This paragraph format warns the reader of hazardous procedures (for example, activities that delete files).

Many features of WordPerfect for Windows are easiest to use with a mouse. Thus, when describing how to do something, more often than not I describe either the mouse clicks necessary to accomplish the task, or describe the route through the menus. For example, to describe how to search for a specific code (such as a hard page break), you would follow these steps:

1. Choose **E**dit, **F**ind, **M**atch, **C**odes.
2. From the dialog box, double-click Hpg.
3. Choose **F**ind Next.

Note that the boldface letters in these steps correspond to the mnemonic equivalents of the command (the letters underlined in each menu or dialog box). Thus, you can access those menus either by clicking the mouse or from your keyboard.

If you are moving to WordPerfect for Windows from any version of WordPerfect for DOS, you are probably quite comfortable with what has become known as the "DOS keyboard." That is, when you press F7, you expect to exit from the document on your screen. You'll probably be surprised, and then annoyed, when pressing F7 simply indents the text; you thought that's what F4 was for. The reason for the dilemma is this: WordPerfect created keyboard assignments for its program long before Windows was invented. But one of the benefits of Windows is that programs for Windows are easier to learn if they all look and act alike. One way to do this is to standardize the keyboard for all programs, using what is known as the Common User Access keyboard (also known as CUA).

WordPerfect for Windows allows you to use either the CUA keyboard or a keyboard that is (almost) exactly like the WordPerfect for DOS keyboard. If you are new to WordPerfect, you should probably use the CUA keyboard. But long-time DOS users who are converting to the Windows version will feel grumpy for a while if they try to relearn the new keyboard. To make the book as useful as possible to all readers we will describe all actions with reference to the menus and dialog boxes; you can decide which keyboard to use to get to them.

However, we will use Windows lingo to describe how things work. For example, we will use the words "insertion point" instead of "cursor;" you will "play" a macro, not "run" it. Like it or not, Windows is here to stay.

Hardware Requirements

Let's get technical for a few minutes and discuss the type of system you need.

To run WordPerfect for Windows 6.0 or 6.1 adequately, you need a fairly competent computer. Although theoretically WordPerfect for Windows will run on a computer equipped with an 80386 or equivalent microprocessor and 4M of RAM, life is too short to have to wait around for things to get done this way. Most users find that a 486 chip (preferably with a 50Mhz or faster clock speed) and a minimum of 8M of RAM are really required to run the program adequately. Obviously, the faster the chip and the more memory available, the happier you will be.

WordPerfect is famous for its support for every oddball printer ever manufactured, from low-end dot matrixes to high-speed lasers. However, if you want your documents to look crisp and professional, we recommend an ink-jet or a laser printer. Chapter 3 discusses using typography and other methods to make your documents sparkle; you will need a good printer to pull this off.

Software Requirements

This topic is not as obvious as it would seem. The obvious answer is, to use this book you need WordPerfect for Windows, version 6.0 or 6.1. But that is not quite a complete answer.

WordPerfect periodically releases *interim* versions of its programs, also known as *maintenance releases*. Although these interim releases maintain the same version number (*i.e.,* they're all called "WordPerfect for Windows, version 6.0"), there are subtle differences between the versions. Usually the interim releases correct problems with earlier releases; occasionally they add new features.

With WordPerfect 6.0 (both for DOS and for Windows), WordPerfect Corporation has taken to adding a lowercase letter after the version number to indicate an interim release. Thus, the first interim release of WordPerfect for Windows 6.0 was version 6.0a. At the time this book went to press, the most recent version of the program was version 6.1.

Version 6.0a of the WordPerfect for Windows program corrected a number of problems with the initial release, but more importantly it added a number of new features to the program. Most relevantly to this book, version 6.0a added many new commands to the macro language, many of which are used in the macros included on the Companion Disk at the back of this book. Therefore, if you want to use the macros on the Companion Disk, it is highly recommended that you obtain version 6.0a if you do not already have it. You can't beat the price: WordPerfect Corporation will ship it, free, to all registered users of version 6.0 who request it.

To check and see if you have the updated version, do the following:

1. Choose **H**elp, **A**bout WordPerfect...

2. The version number should appear in the graphic box near the upper-left corner. In addition, the Program Release date in the dialog box should be April 20, 1994, or later.

3. Choose OK to dismiss the box.

If the Program Release date is after April 20, 1994, you should be able to use all of the macros and templates on the Companion Disk. (Our version 6.0 icon refers to steps compatible with 6.0a.)

Most of the features described in this book are available both in version 6.0 and 6.1. Where the keystrokes or menu structure differs between the two programs, we have attempted to identify the differences. Also, this book refers to a few features that are unique to version 6.1, and it clearly identifies them as available only in that version.

Also, note that most of the screen pictures you will see throughout this book are of screens appearing in version 6.1. Some of the version 6.0 screens may be slightly different, but the variations are minor. These screens have not been reproduced, in the interest of saving space.

What about the future? Historically, WordPerfect files have been "forward-compatible." That is to say, WordPerfect 6.0 and 6.1 can read and use WordPerfect 5.1 or 5.2 files without conversion (although this is not always true of the macros). There is no guarantee that this will continue in the future, but when WordPerfect is upgraded to the next level, chances are excellent that the form documents and templates in this book will work in it. The macros may need some tinkering, but WordPerfect may also provide a conversion utility to help out there, too.

A Final Word

There are many ways to solve most word processing problems. This book suggests a number of solutions to common problems; but this is not to say that these solutions are the "only" or the "best" solutions. If you have already devised a different technique that works for you, stick with it. Hopefully this book will suggest to you better or faster ways of doing things, or provide you with answers to some problems you haven't yet solved.

I hope this book is useful to you and increases your productivity.

Part I

Special Features

1 Making WordPerfect Work the Way You Do

2 Outlines, Numbers, and More

3 Tricks with Typography

4 Footnotes, Tables, and Compare

5 Automating with Macros

6 A Merge Primer

7 Using Templates

Making WordPerfect Work the Way You Do

WordPerfect is a powerful and feature-rich program. It's almost too rich—there are so many tricks and shortcuts that they tend to get lost. Even the manual that comes with the program can't do them all justice.

This chapter focuses on just a few of the WordPerfect features that can help make you more productive in a law office. It also describes a few files contained on the Companion Disk, designed for lawyers and legal assistants that will help to customize WordPerfect.

Take time to look at this chapter, even though some of the topics may seem elementary to you. Even the most experienced WordPerfect user can usually find a hidden gem in the program—a new trick or feature that can make him or her more productive. Use this chapter as a jumping-off point to think about ways to solve some of the word processing problems you run into frequently. Even if the answer to your problem is not in this chapter, you may be able to hitchhike on some of the ideas to find your own route to the best solution.

This chapter provides help for the following:

- Using special legal characters in documents
- Creating a custom keyboard to quickly insert special characters, activate features, or play macros by using hot keys
- Creating special toolbars to provide one-click access to features and macros
- Using the Replace feature to modify documents
- Using the Quick Correct feature to modify documents
- Using Bookmarks to move around in a document

Creating Special Legal Characters

Even though almost every law office in the country these days has a computer with a word processor and even though most of those computers sport WordPerfect and laser printers too, it is still surprising how often one sees briefs, correspondence, and other legal writings that don't take advantage of the availability of even the most common legal symbols. Many users still type abbreviations like "Sec." for "section" and "Par." for "paragraph," when the § and ¶ symbols are just a few keystrokes away. Some users may admit that they don't know how to get those symbols into their documents; others may think that it is just as fast to type "Sec." as it is to locate that symbol in the WordPerfect Characters dialog box and enter it that way.

If you fall into either of those groups, you just ran out of excuses. In this section you learn how to create those characters (and many more) manually. In the next section, you learn how to assign those characters to hot keys so that you can insert them into your document just as quickly and easily as you type a capital letter.

The WordPerfect Special Character Sets

WordPerfect, as befits the most powerful word processing program on the market, has a staggering array of characters available. You are not limited to the 26 letters (upper- and lowercase), numerals, punctuation marks, and the few special symbols that appear on a standard keyboard. WordPerfect can create more than 1,500 characters, icons, and symbols. You can use the Greek, Hebrew, Cyrillic, and Arabic alphabets, among others. Plus, if your printer can print graphics (and almost all of them on the market today can), it can print every one of those special characters.

The program ships with 14 predefined *character sets*. It also includes a blank character set that allows you to define your own set of characters (although with more than 1,500 characters built in, it is hard to imagine what else you would ever need). The character sets are based on logical groupings of characters listed in table 1.1.

Table 1.1	WordPerfect Character Sets
Set No.	**Character Set**
0	Standard ASCII (keyboard) characters
1	Multinational characters
2	Phonetic symbols
3	Box Drawing lines

Set No.	Character Set
4	Typographic symbols
5	Iconic symbols
6	Math/Scientific symbols
7	Math/Scientific Extensions symbols
8	Greek characters
9	Hebrew characters
10	Cyrillic characters
11	Japanese characters
12	User-defined
13	Arabic characters
14	Arabic Script characters

Each special character has a unique name, dependent on its position in the character set. For example, the name of the section marker § is Character 4,6 because it is located in Character Set 4 (Typographic symbols) and is the sixth character in that set.

The WordPerfect Characters Dialog Box

You can view all of the available characters on-screen and insert them via the WordPerfect Characters dialog box, shown in figure 1.1.

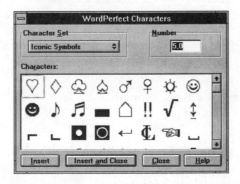

Fig. 1.1
The WordPerfect Characters dialog box, showing just a few of the special characters available.

Because this dialog box is so useful, there are two quick ways to get to it (three if you're using the DOS keyboard):

- From the **I**nsert menu, choose **C**haracter.
- Press Ctrl+W (unless you have redefined that key combination in a soft keyboard layout).

■ If you're using the DOS keyboard layout, Shift+F11 will also bring up the WordPerfect Characters dialog box.

> **Note**
>
> The number of characters displayed inside the box depends on how you size the box. If you want to view more characters at one time, just increase the size of the box. Move the mouse pointer to the edge of the box; when it changes its shape from a single diagonal arrow to an arrow pointing in both directions, press the left mouse button. Without releasing the button, drag the edge in the direction of the arrow (up and down, right or left, or diagonally) to increase or decrease the size of the box. When it is as large or small as you prefer, release the button. (Note that there is a minimum size for the box; you cannot make the box any smaller than the minimum size.)

To insert a character from the WordPerfect Characters dialog box, you must first mark it in the display window. If you know the character set and number for the symbol you want to insert, you can simply type this information into the **N**umber entry box in the upper right corner, separated by a comma (for example, type **4,6** to insert a section marker). Then press the **I**nsert button to place this character into your document.

More likely, however, you will not have the character name readily available to you, and you will have to search through the WordPerfect Characters dialog box to find the character you're looking for. To do this, follow these steps:

1. First, determine which character set contains the character you want. For example, let's say you want to insert the section marker §. By referring to Appendix A of the Reference manual, you can see that this symbol appears in Character Set 4.

2. Next, use the Character **S**et pop-up button in the upper-left corner to highlight the name of the character set you're looking for (see fig. 1.2). When the name of the correct character set appears inside of that button, the characters in that set will appear in the Characters window. (You may have to use the scroll bar at the right edge of the window to actually see the entire character set.)

3. Next, highlight the character you want to insert. Although you can use the keyboard to do this (simply press Alt+R, then use the arrow keys), it is usually easier to click on the desired symbol or character with the left mouse button. A flashing box appears around the currently selected character.

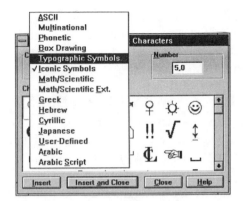

Fig. 1.2
Finding the correct character set.

Special Features

4. After you've selected the character you want, press the Insert button to place the character in your document; then press **C**lose to dismiss the dialog box. (You can combine these two steps into one by choosing the Insert and Close button instead.)

Tip

You can also insert any character quickly by double-clicking it.

If all of that seems like a lot of work just to insert a single character into your document, read on. Next you'll look at how to combine all of those steps into single key combinations, one for each special character you use frequently, so that you can type these characters in your document just as quickly as you can type any letter of the alphabet. You'll do this by assigning these special characters to keystroke combinations of your choice.

Customizing Your Keyboard

WordPerfect is probably the most flexible word processing program ever made. You can change nearly every element of the screen to suit your own needs and tastes, including all of the menus, the Power Bar, the Button Bar/ Toolbar, the status line, and just about anything else. You can also customize your keyboard—that is, change it so that virtually any key or combination of keystrokes (known as hot keys) perform some special task assigned by you.

Although it is possible to program your boss's keyboard so that, when he types his name, the words "Give me a raise" appear on his screen, the customizing feature is extremely valuable for tasks far more important than April Fool's jokes. By customizing your keyboard to fit your particular needs, you can assign any number of special characters to hot keys. Need to type a paragraph marker? Assign the ¶ symbol to the key combination Ctrl+P, then just press those two keys at the same time to insert the symbol wherever and whenever you need it.

The Keyboard Preferences Dialog Box

Redefining what keys or what key combinations do is called defining a soft keyboard. To do this, you must use the Keyboard Preferences dialog box. Display this dialog box by choosing **E**dit (or **F**ile in version 6.0), **Pr**eferences, then **K**eyboard. Figure 1.3 shows this dialog box.

> **Note**
>
> The keyboard is called "soft" because it is software based, that is the software intercepts the keystroke and makes the program do something different than the hardware was designed for.

Fig. 1.3
Creating a new soft keyboard definition.

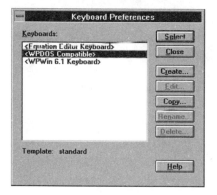

The first time you display this dialog box, you should see three or four keyboard options: the Equations Editor keyboard, the WPDOS Compatible keyboard, the WPWin 6.0 keyboard (or if you're using version 6.1, the WPWin 6.1 keyboard). These are the standard selections which you cannot change or delete. The keyboard you currently use is highlighted when you display the dialog box.

Before you define a personalized soft keyboard, you should decide which of the standard keyboards you should use as a base. (There are really only three significant choices: WPDOS Compatible, WPWin 6.0, and WPWin 6.1, because few lawyers really need to write equations.) If you're moving up to WordPerfect for Windows from an earlier DOS-based version of WordPerfect, you may want to stay with the WPDOS Compatible keyboard, because it will feel more normal to you. But if you are a new user of WordPerfect, or if you use a lot of other Windows products, you should choose either the WPWin 6.0 or WPWin 6.1 keyboard, since that will make all Windows products seem to work in similar ways.

To define a soft keyboard, do the following:

1. From the Keyboard Preferences dialog box, highlight the keyboard you want to use as a base.

2. Choose Create.

3. In the Create Keyboard dialog box, enter a unique filename for the keyboard you are creating. For example, if you're creating a keyboard to contain special legal symbols, you may want to name your keyboard "LEGAL." Choose OK when done.

You now see the Keyboard Editor screen (see fig. 1.4), along with the name of the keyboard you typed in the previous step. This is the screen you will use to make all special key assignments.

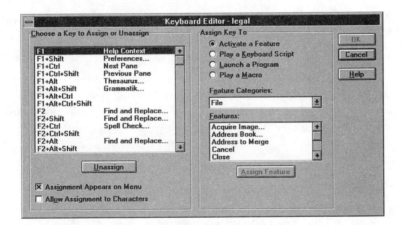

Fig. 1.4
Selecting key assignments in the Keyboard Editor.

Note

The Keyboard Editor screen is set up differently in versions 6.0 and 6.1, although they accomplish the same functions. In the interest of space, only the 6.1 screens are shown throughout this section of the chapter.

This dialog box has two parts. The left side shows what each keystroke and key combination currently do. The right side is where you can make changes and specify new functions for each key. You're likely to need three of the four available options: Activate a Feature (such as the Date Text feature), Play a Keyboard Script (for quick insertion of frequently used characters or text), and Play a Macro. You will not often want to launch a new program from the keyboard, which is the fourth option available.

Rearranging Features in a Soft Keyboard

The first major task you can accomplish using the Keyboard Editor is to change the keystrokes that activate various WordPerfect features. For example, on the WPDOS Compatible keyboard the F7 key activates Close. You can, if you want to, assign another feature (such as Play Macro) to F7, and then assign Close to any other key you choose.

Suppose you're using the WPDOS Compatible keyboard, and seldom use the Tab Hard Decimal feature assigned to Ctrl+F6. You do, however, frequently use Date Text to insert the current date into your document, so you want to assign that feature to Ctrl+F6. To do this, follow these steps:

1. Be sure the Keyboard Editor is on your screen and the name you gave your soft keyboard shows in the title bar. Next, in the right half of the Keyboard Editor dialog box, check to be sure that the Activate a Feature radio button is selected under Assign Key To.

2. On the left side of the screen, in the Choose a Key to Assign or Unassign group box, find the Ctrl+F6 key combination; do this by using the scroll bars or by clicking the mouse in that list box and typing the name of the key.

   The list of key assignments in the window shows that the Tab Hard Decimal feature is currently assigned to that key.

3. To tell WordPerfect to assign the Date Text feature to that key, you need to find it in the Features box on the lower-right half of the dialog box. The Features box lists all of the features available under each of the main menu bar categories (notice in fig. 1.4 that the Feature Box defaults to the features found under the File menu). Because the Date Text is an option under the Insert menu, click the drop-down arrow to the right of the Feature Categories entry field; then locate the Insert category and click it.

4. Just below the Feature Categories entry field, the Features box now displays all of the WordPerfect features accessible from the Insert menu. Use the mouse to move the scroll bar, or press Alt+F and use the arrow keys, to highlight the Date Text feature.

5. At this point, your screen should look like the one shown in figure 1.5. Notice that the **A**ssign Feature button has been activated (for example, it is no longer grayed out). A description of the highlighted feature (Date Text) also now appears in the dialog box.

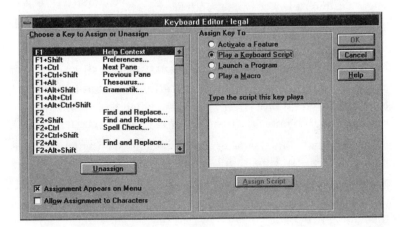

Fig. 1.5
Making a new
feature assignment.

6. Press the **A**ssign Feature button to complete the assignment. Notice that the newly assigned feature replaces the original assignment on the left side of the dialog box.

7. You can continue to make changes and reassignments from this screen. However, remember that to complete all new assignments and save them to your hard disk, you must exit this dialog box by choosing the OK button in the upper right hand corner. If you press Cancel, all of your changes will be lost.

Assigning Text to Special Keys

The Keyboard Editor also allows you to assign one or more characters or symbols to a key combination.

Let's say that you want to assign the paragraph marker ¶ to the keystroke combination Ctrl+P. Follow these steps:

1. With the Keyboard Editor dialog box on your screen and the name of your personalized keyboard showing in the title bar, choose the Play a **K**eyboard Script radio button. This is in the Assign Key To group in the right half of the dialog box.

   An editing window appears just below the listing of options, underneath the heading type the script this key plays.

2. Select key combination Ctrl+P in the left list box, as above.

   Depending on which keyboard you began with, you will find that this key has already been assigned to Print Document or Insert Page Number. If you do not want to overwrite the assignment that appears there, select a different key combination (perhaps Alt+P).

   The next few steps tell you how to assign the ¶ marker to that key combination.

3. Move the focus to the editing window on the right, either by clicking your mouse pointer in that window or pressing Alt+P.

4. Next, call up the WordPerfect Characters dialog box. While in the Keyboard Editor, the only way to do this is to press Ctrl+W.

5. Find the ¶ marker in Character Set 4, character 5, and highlight it with the mouse pointer. Choose **I**nsert or Insert **a**nd Close to place that symbol into the editing window.

6. Complete the assignment by pressing the **A**ssign Script button under the editing window.

Now, all you need to do to insert a ¶ marker anywhere in your document is to press Ctrl+P (or whatever combination you chose).

You can continue to assign other symbols to similar hot keys as you desire. Or, you can assign an entire string of characters to a hot key; for example, I might assign my entire name to the Ctrl+K key combination, or my firm name to Ctrl+A.

Be careful not to go wild with key reassignments, however, because you'll soon find that the more key assignments you make, the easier they are to forget. You then may find yourself pressing keys at random to find the right one, wasting time erasing the results of your erroneous guesses.

Table 1.2 lists suggested keyboard assignments. The suggested keystrokes are all combinations of the Ctrl+Shift keys plus a mnemonic letter. This combination, rather than the Alt key or the Ctrl key alone, is suggested because you frequently use the Alt keys to access menus or press buttons in dialog boxes, and you use Ctrl keys frequently in both the DOS and Windows standard keyboards for hot-key access to commonly used features. For the sake of consistency (and to make the keystrokes easier to remember) you should probably standardize on one basic formula for hot key assignments (for example, using all Ctrl key or Ctrl+Shift key combinations).

e **Legal Keyboard**

on

ht symbol

symbol

symbol

ph symbol

ed Trademark symbol

marker

ark symbol

A macro can be some-
to the keyboard scripts
mplex, programmed
it perform some special-
acros in Chapter 5).

WCM that inserts a for-
our document. You want
his, follow these steps (the
y make this assignment if
ent location (your default

On the Disk

your soft keyboard defini-
Macro radio button under
e dialog box. A new but-
tions.

those keys Again, de-
pending on which keyboard you began with, you will find that this key
has already been assigned to QuickMark Find or to Font. If you do not
want to overwrite the assignment which appears there, select a different
key combination (perhaps Alt+F).

3. Now press the **A**ssign Macrobutton. You will see the Select Macro dialog
   box shown in figure 1.6.

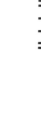

Fig. 1.6
Assigning a macro
to a hot key.

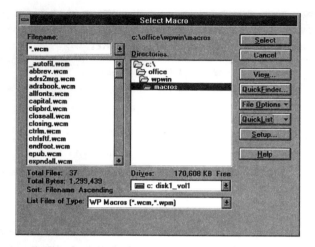

4. Locate the macro you want to assign in the Filename box. You can navigate to different directories if you need to in the Directories window.

5. After the Select Macro dialog box shows the complete path and filename for FOOTER.WCM, press the elect button.

   You will then see the dialog box shown in figure 1.7. This one requires a little explanation. If you answer Yes to the question, Save Macro with Full Path? the soft keyboard will remember the location of the macro on disk, and will always play the current version of that macro, even if you edit the macro after making this keyboard assignment. If you answer no, WordPerfect will copy the entire macro verbatim into the soft keyboard file, where it will not be modified by subsequent changes to the macro stored on your disk. Although there may be situations where you prefer to do this, in most cases you will probably want to answer Yes to this question.

Fig. 1.7
Saving a macro in
a soft keyboard.

6. Answer **Y**es or **N**o to the prompt.

Regardless of the option you choose in step 6, after you respond to that question your macro will be assigned to the designated key.

Using the Toolbar

Another powerful tool that WordPerfect provides to make life simple is the Toolbar. The Toolbar (called the Button Bar in version 6.0) is a row or group of specialized buttons that give you one-click access to virtually any WordPerfect feature, as well as keyboard scripts and any macro. You can display the toolbar anywhere at all on your screen—even in a cluster in the middle of the screen—and you can control most aspects of the appearance of the toolbar.

> **Note**
>
> Both versions 6.0 and 6.1 also include a separate bar called the "Power Bar," which appears immediately below the Toolbar/Button Bar. However, many of the feature icons that were on the default Power Bar in version 6.0 have been moved to the default toolbar in version 6.1, so if you're converting from 6.0 to 6.1 you may be confused at first as to which bar is which. The 6.1 toolbar buttons are also smaller than the 6.0 button bar buttons. To save space, the discussion and screen shots through this part of the chapter will include only the 6.1 toolbar. In most cases, if you substitute the word "button bar" for "toolbar" in the following discussion, the steps listed will work in version 6.0.

WordPerfect ships with a number of specialized toolbars, including a Legal Toolbar that groups together many WordPerfect features that law offices use frequently (see figure 1.8). You can modify any of the standard toolbars supplied with the program, or you can create your own.

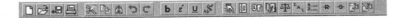

Fig. 1.8
WordPerfect's standard Legal Toolbar.

The only drawback to this feature is that it is not useful to mouseophobes. WordPerfect has taken great care to make the program usable by people who like to use only keystrokes, but the very nature of the toolbar feature lends itself to the use of a mouse. If you do not like to use the mouse, you will hate this feature. But if mousing around doesn't bother you, you may find the toolbar feature to be one of the quickest ways to greater efficiency.

Displaying the Toolbar

There are several ways to turn the Toolbar on and off. The most common is to choose **V**iew, **T**oolbar. If the toolbar is currently displayed, there will be a check mark next to the toolbar item on the list; clicking there will remove the check mark and hide the toolbar. If it is not displayed, clicking that item will display the toolbar and add a check mark next to the item on the list.

There is another way to hide a toolbar displayed on your screen. Simply move the mouse pointer to any position within the toolbar. It will change shape into an arrow. Pressing the right mouse button will bring up a QuickMenu with a list of the currently available toolbars, as well as a few options at the bottom of the list (see figure 1.9). The last option on the list is **H**ide Toolbar; click there or press **H** to remove the toolbar from your screen.

Fig. 1.9
The Toolbar
QuickMenu.

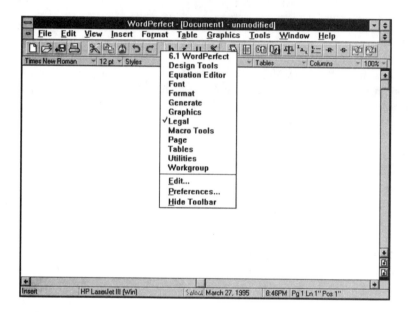

Choosing a Toolbar

There are two ways to display a toolbar, one easy and one hard.

The more involved process (and the only one you can do without a mouse) involves changing your Preferences. Follow these steps:

1. Choose **E**dit, Pr**e**ferences.

   Choose **F**ile, Pr**e**ferences.

2. Choose **T**oolbar. The Toolbar Preferences dialog box will appear (see fig. 1.10).

3. In the window marked Available **T**oolbars, use the mouse pointer or arrow keys to highlight the toolbar you want to display.

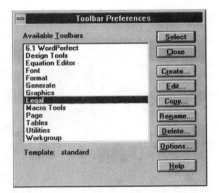

Fig. 1.10
Setting Toolbar
preferences.

4. Double-click the toolbar or press **S**elect. That toolbar is now selected. Choose Close in the Preferences dialog box to return to your document.

An easier way to do this once again involves the right mouse button. Simply move the mouse pointer into whichever toolbar is displayed and press the right mouse button. The QuickMenu that pops up shows all available toolbars, with a check mark next to the one that is currently displayed. Just click on the toolbar you want to select, and it will appear. (To cancel the QuickMenu, just click the mouse anywhere outside of the pop-up list, or press Esc.)

Changing the Appearance of the Toolbar

You can also change the appearance of all of your toolbars in several ways. You can display only icons in the buttons, or only text, or both. You can also move the toolbar to anywhere on your screen that you like.

To change the content of the buttons themselves, you must make adjustments to the Toolbar Options dialog box. There are two ways to open up that box:

1. Choose Pr**e**ferences from the **E**dit menu.

2. Choose **T**oolbar. The Toolbar Preferences dialog box will appear (refer to fig. 1.10).

   Or, if the toolbar is currently displayed, simply move the mouse pointer into the toolbar and click the right mouse button. Choose **P**references from the bottom of the QuickMenu (or just type **P**). The same dialog box will appear.

   Now press the **O**ptions button near the bottom right side of that dialog box. The Toolbar Options dialog box (see figure 1.11) will appear.

Fig. 1.11
Changing the
appearance of a
Toolbar.

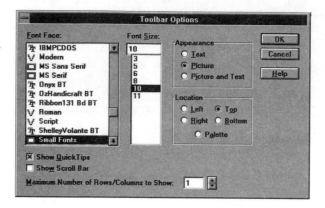

From this dialog box, you can change the appearance of your buttons in many interesting ways:

1. You can change the typeface for the text within the buttons by adjusting the **F**ont Face and Font **S**ize. (Adjusting the Font Size will also affect the width of the buttons.)

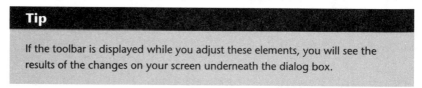

Tip

If the toolbar is displayed while you adjust these elements, you will see the results of the changes on your screen underneath the dialog box.

2. In the Appearance group, you can elect to display the button **T**ext only, the button icons (called **P**ictures) only, or both **P**icture and text.

   You can reduce the size of the buttons considerably by displaying text only, thereby freeing up screen space for your documents.

3. In the Location group, you can decide where you want the toolbar to be displayed. You can place it horizontally along the top or bottom of the document window, or vertically along either edge; or you can make it float in the middle of the document window by choosing P**a**lette.

   If you choose the palette option, you can drag the toolbar (it's really more of a button box in this configuration) around on your screen by left-clicking in the title bar and holding the mouse button down while you move it to the desired location.

> **Tip**
>
> Another way to change the location of the toolbar is to drag it with the mouse. Place the mouse pointer on any edge or on any gray space surrounding the buttons. The pointer will turn into a hand icon. While the mouse pointer has the shape of a hand, click the left mouse button and hold it down. Move the toolbar to whatever location you desire, and then release the mouse button.

4. Finally, depending upon the number, size, and configuration of buttons in a toolbar, you may find that not all of the buttons can be displayed at one time. You can, however, display up to three rows or columns of buttons; to do this, find the **M**aximum number of Rows/Columns to Show entry field at the bottom of the dialog box and adjust the number there.

Editing the Toolbar

Don't like the selection of buttons provided on any of the toolbars? You can change any of them. You can even create your own buttons, complete with custom images and text (something you might consider doing if you want to put one of your own macros on the toolbar).

To change the content of the toolbar, use the Toolbar Editor dialog box. Follow these steps:

1. First, be sure that the screen displays the toolbar you want to modify.

2. Next, open the Toolbar Editor dialog box by choosing **E**dit from either the Toolbar Preferences dialog box (refer to 1.10), or from the QuickMenu that appears when you click the right mouse button inside the displayed toolbar. The toolbar should still be visible above the Toolbar Editor, as shown in figure 1.12.

3. To delete a button from the displayed toolbar, just click your left mouse button on that button and drag it off the bar. When the button is pulled into the document window, the mouse pointer will turn into an icon of a button falling into a trash can; when you release the mouse button the toolbar button will be removed.

4. To add a button, select the type of object you want to place on the button. The possible objects you can add are listed in a group of radio buttons in the top half of the Toolbar Editor; they correspond to the types of actions you can assign to a soft keyboard, as described earlier in the chapter. Refer to that section of this chapter for more help on assigning features, scripts, and macros to buttons.

Fig. 1.12
Adding or
changing the
buttons on the
toolbar.

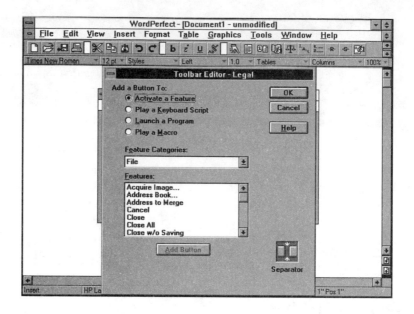

Fig. 1.12
Adding or
changing the
buttons on the
toolbar.

You can add buttons to activate features, play keyboard scripts, or play macros in the same manner as you selected those items to be assigned to hot keys in the Keyboard Editor. For example, to add a button to activate the Close All feature, double-click that feature in the Features box (refer to fig. 1.12). The button appears at the right edge of the active toolbar.

5. To move a button, just click your mouse on it and drag it to any other position on the toolbar. When you release the mouse button, it will be inserted at that location.

6. To add a visual gap between buttons (for example, to create logical groupings), click on the Separator icon in the lower right hand corner of the Toolbar Editor and drag the separator to the location in the toolbar where you want to insert it.

7. Finally, to customize the appearance of any individual button, just double-click that button. You will see the Customize Button dialog box shown in figure 1.13.

   To change the QuickTip text (the little yellow pop-up reminder that appears when the mouse pointer passes over the button), type in a new description in the QuickTip/Button text entry field.

   To change the Help Prompt (the message that appears in the title bar when the mouse pointer passes over the button), type in a new prompt in the Help prompt entry field.

To edit the button image, or create a new image, pixel-by-pixel, click Edit in the Image group box and edit or create the button's image.

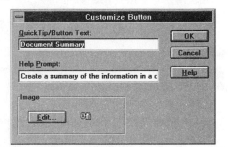

Fig. 1.13
Creating a custom button.

Creating Your Own Toolbars

Finally, if none of the standard toolbars that ship with the program suit your needs, you can create an entirely new toolbar. You might consider doing this, for example, to put your favorite macros on a special toolbar for easy one-click access. Your customized toolbars will also show up in the QuickMenu that appears when you click the right mouse button in the toolbar.

> **Note**
>
> If you create a "macros only" toolbar, you will need to use text instead of icons in your toolbar, because every macro icon will be identical to every other macro icon.

If you want to create your own toolbar for your most frequently used macros, follow these steps:

1. Open the Toolbar editor dialog box by choosing Edit from either the Toolbar Preferences dialog box, or from the QuickMenu that appears when you click the right mouse button inside the displayed toolbar. You will see the Create Toolbar dialog box (see fig.1.14).

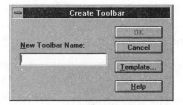

Fig. 1.14
Creating a new toolbar.

2. By default, the new toolbar you create is stored in the template used to create the document in the active document window. Unless you specified a template when you created the document, the document will be based on the STANDARD,WPT template, which contains most of the default settings for your preferences. To be sure that the template is going to be stored where you can find it later, press the **T**emplate button. You will see the Toolbar Location dialog box shown in figure 1.15. For more information about templates, see chapter 7.

Fig. 1.15
Specifying the template in which to store a new toolbar.

3. The **C**urrent Template: radio button will be marked, and the name of the template used to create the current document will be shown. In figure 1.15, this option shows that the current document is based on the chapter template rather than the default Standard Template. If you want your new toolbar to be available to all documents that are based on the Standard Template, you need to mark the **D**efault Template: radio button by clicking on it or by pressing **D**.

> **Note**
>
> Earlier documents that you created using different templates will not have access to your special toolbars unless you copy the toolbar from the template in which it was created to the template upon which your documents are based. To do this, use the Co**p**y button in the Toolbar Preferences dialog box (refer to figure 1.10).

4. After you have verified that the new toolbar will be stored in the correct template, enter a name for the new toolbar in the entry window. In this example, type **Favorite Macros**. (Note that you are not limited to a standard DOS filename here.)

5. Click OK or press Enter. The Toolbar Editor will now appear, with the name of your new toolbar displayed in the title bar.

6. You can add buttons to activate any WordPerfect feature, play a keyboard script, launch a program, or play a macro. In this example, since you're creating a toolbar to contain your favorite macros, mark the Play a Macro radio button by clicking on it or by pressing **M**. The appearance of the Toolbar Editor will change, as shown in figure 1.16.

7. Press the **A**dd Macro button. The Select Macro dialog box will appear.

Fig. 1.16
Adding a macro in the Toolbar Editor dialog box.

8. Insert the name of the macro you want to add to the toolbar in the entry window. If you cannot remember the name of the macro, or its location, press the file icon at the end of that entry window to view the contents of your default macros directory. You can navigate to other directories from the right side of the Select File dialog box if the macro you're looking for is not in your default macros directory. For the purposes of this example, type in the name **FOOTER.WCM** (the macro described earlier in this chapter) and press **S**elect.

9. You will be asked to verify whether you want to save the macro with the full path or not. In most cases you should answer **Y**es, since this will ensure that the toolbar will always play the most current version of the macro, as stored on disk, including any changes made to the macro since the time you added the macro to the button. If you answer **N**o, WordPerfect will copy the current version of the macro into the template you designated, where it will not be affected by subsequent changes to the macro on your disk.

10. You will be returned to the Toolbar Editor. Repeat the steps above to add as many macros to your new toolbar as you want; then choose OK to save the changes to your new toolbar.

Using Replace to Quickly Modify Documents

You might wonder why this chapter includes this topic. After all, search-and-replace operations are pretty basic word processing tasks. But there are some not-so-obvious tricks built in to this feature that deserve a closer look.

Basic Replace Operations

Searching for one string of characters and replacing them with a different set of characters is often referred to as *search and replace*. In WordPerfect for Windows, it is called the Find and Replace feature (version 6.0 referred to it simply as Replace). It is useful for many tasks in a law office. For example, you may have prepared a document for one client that you want to use as a form for another client. Rather than manually scrolling through the document and finding each occurrence of the first client's name, you can use Find and Replace to automatically find all occurrences of the first client's name and replace them with the new client's name. Here's how you can do just that:

1. Be sure your insertion point is at the very beginning of the document you want to change.

2. Choose **E**dit, **F**ind and Replace. The Find and Replace Text dialog box (shown in figure 1.17) will appear.

Fig. 1.17
The Find and Replace Text dialog box.

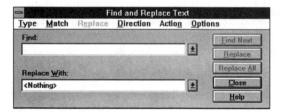

3. Enter the string of characters you want to eliminate from the document in the first entry field (labeled **F**ind).

4. Enter the new string of characters in the second entry field (labeled Replace **W**ith).

5. If you want to verify each replacement before making it, choose **F**ind Next. Replace will find the next occurrence of the string you entered in the first entry field, highlight it, and pause. If you want to replace it with the second string, just press the **R**eplace button.

6. If you want to simply replace all occurrences without having to manually check them, press the Replace **A**ll button. All occurrences will then automatically be changed, without further user intervention.

> **Tip**
>
> Either you can find and replace all occurrences which come *after* the current location of the insertion point, or you can do the same for occurrences which *precede* the insertion point. To change the direction of the search, select the option you want from the **D**irection menu of the Find and Replace Text dialog box.

Replacing Whole Words Only

The second option, Replace **A**ll, can be dangerous if the string you're looking for happens to be a common one. For example, suppose you are modifying a document that you prepared initially for one person to sign, but now needs to be signed by a husband and wife. You therefore want to replace the verb "is" with the plural form "are" wherever it appears. Let's also suppose that one of the paragraphs you are trying to change reads as follows:

> The undersigned is aware of the fact that this settlement will forever discharge and release all claims against the Defendants, their heirs and assigns, from all future liability for this injury.

If you do a straightforward Find and Replace to change the character string "is" to "are," you would get the following gibberish:

> The undersigned are aware of the fact that thare settlement will forever darecharge and release all claims against the Defendants, their heirs and assigns, from all future liability for thare injury.

There are two ways to avoid automatically changing the words "this" and "discharge" to "thare" and "darecharge." First, instead of searching for just the two letters "is" and replacing them with the three letters "are," you might search for the *four* characters " is " (note the spaces before and after the word "is") and replacing them with the five letters " are " (again, be sure to include the spaces).

That technique works so long as the word "is" is not the first or last word of a sentence, or is not preceded or followed by punctuation. A better way to do this is to use one of the hidden options found in the Find and Replace Text dialog box:

1. After entering the find and replace strings, choose the **M**atch option from the dialog box menu.

2. Choose the **W**hole Word option from that menu. (The box will disappear when you make your selection, but the next time you open that submenu you will see a check mark next to the option.)

3. Note that the designation Whole word now appears below the Find entry field, giving you visual verification that only the complete word "is" will be replaced.

Now when you perform the Replace function, WordPerfect will ignore words containing the two characters "is," and only the complete word "is" will be affected.

Case-Sensitive Replace

Another option in the **M**atch menu of the Find and Replace Text dialog box is **C**ase. This option allows you to limit replacements to strings that match the specified capitalization. For example, assume you had written the following sentence:

> The BOOKMARK macro helps you to place bookmarks in your document.

You later decide to change the name of the BOOKMARK macro to BKMRK. To be sure that you replace only the fully-capitalized word BOOKMARK, leaving all references to "Bookmarks" unchanged, choose the Case option from the Match menu.

Searching and Replacing Codes

You can also search and replace codes, such as [Bold>] or [Hd Left Ind]. You can also search for certain specific types of codes, such as all codes that activate a particular type of justification or set a specific line spacing option.

To include an attribute or other type of code in a text search, simply enter the code in the F**i**nd or Replace **W**ith entry fields along with the text (if any) you're searching for. To enter such a code, do the following:

1. Display the Find and Replace Text dialog box.

2. Be sure the focus of the dialog box is where you want it. For example, if you want to enter a code in the F**i**nd entry field, be sure that field has the focus either by clicking the mouse there or pressing **I**.

3. Now choose C**o**des from the **M**atch menu. The Codes dialog box will appear (see figure 1.18).

4. Select the code you want to search for from the list box, then press **I**nsert. That code will appear in either the F**i**nd field or the Replace **W**ith field, depending on where the focus is.

5. Complete the Replace operation in the usual way.

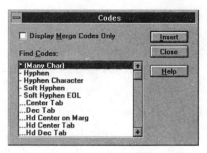

Fig. 1.18
Finding and replacing WordPerfect codes.

Here's another timesaving use of the Find and Replace Text feature. Suppose your document frequently changes fonts between Times New Roman and Humanst521. Suppose further that you want to replace all of the Times New Roman fonts with GeoSlab703. To do this, follow these steps.

1. From the Find and Replace Text dialog box menu bar, choose **T**ype.

2. Choose **S**pecific Codes. The Specific Codes dialog box will appear (see figure 1.19.)

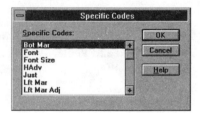

Fig. 1.19
Finding and replacing specific codes.

3. Select the type of code you want to replace from the list box in the Specific Codes dialog box; then press OK. In this example, highlight the Ln Spacing option using the mouse or the arrow keys.

4. The Find and Replace Text dialog box will have a different look. First, the title bar now will display the specific code you want to replace (in this example, it will read Find and Replace Fonts). Secondly, the text entry fields will be replaced with new controls that allow you to specify the value you want to look for. In this example, you can either type in the correct values or use the up and down arrow markers in the F**i**nd and Replace **W**ith controls to tell WordPerfect to find all Times New Roman font codes and replace them with Geo Slab703 font codes, as shown in figure 1.19.

5. Use the F**i**nd, **R**eplace or Replace **A**ll buttons as appropriate to complete the Find and Replace operation.

Replacing Word Forms

One of the slickest new features of version 6.1 is what WordPerfect calls its "PerfectSense" technology. This provides "intelligent" Find and Replace, which enables you to replace different forms of one word with the equivalent forms of another.

For example, say you are drafting a contract with the following language:

> The parties hereto agree to work together in the formation of a new business venture for the purposes set forth above. If the parties have worked in good faith but are unable to reach a mutually acceptable agreement, neither party shall be held liable to the other.

You want to change the word "work" to "cooperate" wherever it appears in the document, but a simple replacement of the word "work" with "cooperate" would result in the word "worked," in the example above, being turned into "cooperateed." PerfectSense technology can rescue you here.

All you need to do is set up your Find and Replace to find "work" and replace it with "cooperate" as you would normally. However, before choosing Replace **A**ll from the Find and Replace Text dialog box, do this:

1. Choose **T**ype, **W**ord Forms.

   The Find and Replace Text dialog box should now look like figure 1.20. Note that underneath the Find and Replace **W**ith dialog boxes there is a notation that the function will find and replace word forms of the specified words.

Fig. 1.20
Searching for word forms in Find and Replace.

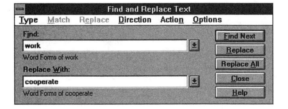

2. Now choose Replace **A**ll. All variations of the word "work" in your document will be replaced with the equivalent forms of the word "cooperate."

Replacing Within a Portion of the Document

One last trick may also prove useful. Suppose you have used a word or string of words frequently in a document, but want to change them only in a certain portion of your document.

You can limit the replacement to a selected part of the text. First, use the Select feature to highlight the area of your document that you want to limit the Replace operation to. Then, begin the Replace operation as you normally would. However, before you select one of the Replace buttons, open the **O**ptions menu of the Find and Replace Dialog Box, and then Choose the **L**imit Find Within Selection option.

A Trick with QuickCorrect

The QuickCorrect feature in WordPerfect 6.0 has been substantially revised in version 6.1. QuickCorrect works as an instantaneous spell checker, correcting common typographical errors as you type. The WordPerfect manual can give you guidance on the basics of using this feature; however, here is a trick you can use to make this tool even more powerful.

If you set up QuickCorrect to replace typographical errors as you type, you can define certain abbreviations as typographical errors. Then, if you intentionally type those abbreviations, QuickCorrect can automatically expand those abbreviations into the full words.

One common task that you can automate with this technique is to insert the names of attorneys in your firm using just their initials. Let us see how this works:

1. Choose **T**ools, **Q**uickCorrect. The QuickCorrect dialog box will appear.

2. In the **R**eplace edit box, type in the initial of the attorney (in this example, type **kdc**).

3. In the **W**ith edit box, type in the full name of the attorney (in this example, type **Kenneth D. Chestek**).

4. Make sure the R**e**place Words as You Type check box in the lower-left corner of the dialog box is selected (a little x will appear when you click on the box or press Alt+E).

   At this point, your dialog box should look like figure 1.21.

Fig. 1.21
Inserting an entry
in QuickCorrect.

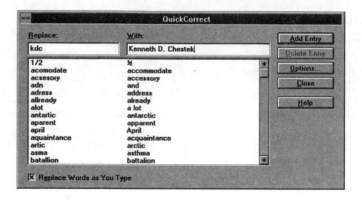

5. Choose **A**dd Entry to add this combination to the list of corrections that will be automatically made as you type.

6. Choose **C**lose.

Now, whenever you type "kdc" followed by a space, a hard return or a punctuation mark, the letters "kdc" will be replaced with the full name of the attorney.

You can use this trick to expand any number of commonly used phrases in your office (for example, "cpe" for "the Court of Common Pleas of Erie County").

Note

Be careful not to choose an abbreviation which is also part of a word by itself. For example, if your initials are "par" you will get your name rather than that word. Also note that the default settings of the QuickCorrect feature includes some "words" you may want to delete. For example, as shipped QuickCorrect defines the characters "(c)" as an abbreviation for the copyright symbol. You can delete that "correction" from the QuickCorrect dialog box to avoid this problem.

Beware of Undo

Another enhancement in version 6.1 is the Undo/Redo History feature. But beware: this feature is both a trick and a trap for the unwary. Lawyers in particular need to be careful about how their offices use this feature—and perhaps ought to change their computers from the default settings of this feature.

Undo allows a user to reverse the most recent editing of a document. The enhanced Undo/Redo History feature of version 6.1 allows for a variable number of recent changes to be selectively reversed. As shipped, WordPerfect remembers the last ten editing actions, or changes, in a document, and allows you to select which one or ones to reverse; but you can set the feature up to remember up to the last 300 editing actions. You can even save these editing actions with the document so that you can return to the document later and undo them.

What is an "editing action?" It can be anything from the deletion or insertion of a single character, to a font change, or even to a global Find and Replace action. It is important to understand this: if a Find and Replace action has changed 25 words in 25 different locations in the document, WordPerfect considers this one editing action; undoing that action will reverse all 25 replacements.

This section tells how the feature works and then examines a potential trap for the unwary lawyer:

1. Open any document.

2. Make some editing changes at random. Delete a few words, type a few words, move the cursor around, it doesn't matter for this exercise.

   Now look at the Undo/Redo History dialog box and see what options you have:

3. Choose **E**dit, Undo/Redo **H**istory.

   The Undo/Redo History dialog box will appear. It should look something like figure 1.22.

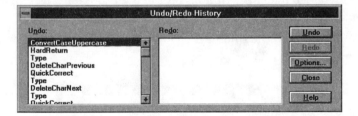

Fig. 1.22
The Undo/Redo History dialog box.

Notice that a series of editing actions appear in the U**n**do: list box on the left side of the dialog box. If the list is too long to display in full, a scroll bar appears in that window so you can examine items farther down the list.

4. To Undo any of the editing actions, select the action you want to undo by clicking it in the Undo group box. Then choose **U**ndo.

> **Note**
>
> Changes are listed in reverse order, with the most recent editing change listed first. If you select an item below the first item on the list, all actions you performed previous to it will be automatically selected as well.

Although the Undo/Redo History dialog box will remain visible, the appearance of your document behind the dialog box will change to reflect the items you undid. You can move the dialog box out of the way by clicking in its title bar and dragging it to a new location on your screen with your mouse if it obscures the undone items.

Notice also that the undone items now appear in the Redo group box.

5. If you want to undo the undo (that is, return to the previous condition of the document prior to the undo) select the action you want to redo by clicking it in the Redo group box and then choosing **R**edo.

> **Caution**
>
> WordPerfect will keep the Redo items only until you make further changes to the document. Once you close the Undo/Redo History dialog box and make any change to the document, the Redo items will be lost.

While this feature may be handy to assist in editing and revising documents, buried under the **O**ptions button is an additional feature that could prove to be embarrassing to the unwary lawyer.

6. Choose **O**ptions. The Undo/Redo Options dialog box will appear, as shown in figure 1.23.

Fig. 1.23
The Undo/Redo Options dialog box.

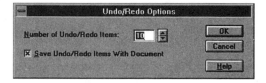

This dialog box allows you to do two things. First, it allows you to specify the number of Undo/Redo items that WordPerfect will keep track of. Although the default setting here is 10 items, you can specify up to 300 items if you like.

The second item is the catch. The **S**ave Undo/Redo items With Document check box gives you the option of saving Undo/Redo items with the document. This means that all of the editing actions (up to the number you specify) will be stored with the document on disk, so that you can close the document, even leave WordPerfect, then return to the document later and go back to undo any previous change to the document.

As shipped by WordPerfect, the program defaults to enable this saving feature. *You should probably disable it.* There are two reasons why. First, enabling this feature will consume disk space, especially if you set a high number of Undo/Redo items to remember. Since the changes must be saved on disk, they take up space. Even deleting many pages of material will not shrink the size of your document by one byte if those pages are stored on disk with the other Undo/Redo items.

But far more importantly, this feature can cause a serious breach of security or confidentiality. More and more law offices are starting to share documents on disk; even within law offices various co-workers share many confidential documents. Suppose you have a confidential document that you want to share with others, with the confidential portions redacted. You make the changes on disk, save it in the expectation that the portions you have removed are permanently gone, then pass the document on disk to the recipient. If you have the Save Undo/Redo Items With Document feature enabled, the recipient of the document will be able to go into Undo/Redo History, undo all of your changes, and view the confidential information you thought you had removed.

1. To disable this feature, click the **S**ave Undo/Redo Items With Document check box (so that no X appears there).
2. Choose OK to save this change and return to the Undo/Redo History dialog box.
3. Choose **C**lose to return to your document.

Using Bookmarks

Bookmarks are a handy feature that many users overlook. Since many of the form documents described in Part II of this book use bookmarks, it is useful to gain a basic understanding of this feature.

A bookmark is simply a code, inserted in the document, that marks a location you may want to find again. For example, if you're drafting a document and need to refer to another part of the document which may not be on your screen at the moment, you can set a bookmark at the area you're editing and then go elsewhere in the document. When you have found what you are looking for, you can return to the original location quickly by finding the bookmark you set there. Or, you may set a bookmark in a form document that enables you to quickly move to a specific location whenever you open it.

There are two types of bookmarks available: the WordPerfect QuickMark, and user-specified named bookmarks. You can have any number of bookmarks in any document.

Using QuickMarks

Setting and finding the QuickMark is easiest to do from the keyboard. If you're using the Windows keyboard, press Ctrl+Shift+Q to insert a QuickMark at the location of the insertion point. Press Ctrl+Q to find it quickly. If you're using the DOS-compatible keyboard, press Ctrl+Q to set the QuickMark and Ctrl+F to find it.

> **Tip**
>
> You can also direct WordPerfect to automatically set the QuickMark at the current location of the insertion point every time you save a document. Simply choose **E**dit, P**r**eferences, **E**nvironment, (Or **F**ile in version 6.0) and check the Save **Q**uickMark on Save option box. You can then use the Find QuickMark feature to immediately jump to the last location of your insertion point when you reopen the document, enabling you to start back to work right where you left off.

Using Named Bookmarks

There can be only one QuickMark in a document, and it will get moved around from time to time. You may, however, want to create a "permanent" bookmark that won't move every time the document is saved; to do this you need to create a *named bookmark*.

To create a named bookmark, you need to display the Bookmark dialog box (shown in fig. 1.24). Choose **I**nsert, **B**ookmark, then Cr**e**ate. Then just type in the name you want to give to the bookmark and choose OK; that bookmark will be placed at the insertion point.

To return to any named bookmark, display the Bookmark dialog box again. All of the named bookmarks will appear there, along with the QuickMark (if it has been previously set). Highlight the bookmark you want to move to and press the **G**o To button.

You can also move any bookmark by highlighting it in the Bookmark dialog box and pressing the **M**ove button. You can also rename or delete any bookmark using the other buttons in that dialog box.

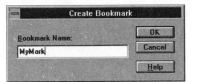

Fig. 1.24
Creating a new bookmark.

You can also move any preexisting bookmark using these steps:

1. Put the insertion point where you want to move the bookmark.

2. Choose **I**nsert, **B**ookmark to open the bookmark dialog box.

3. Highlight the bookmark you want to move and then press the Move button.

   The bookmark is automaticaly moved to the location of the insertion point. You can also rename or delete any bookmark using the other buttons in the dialog box.

From Here...

This chapter took a quick look at some of the more useful (and frequently overlooked) features of WordPerfect that can be of great use in most offices, but particularly in law offices. The next chapter examines some slightly more advanced features that are (or should be!) frequently used by lawyers.

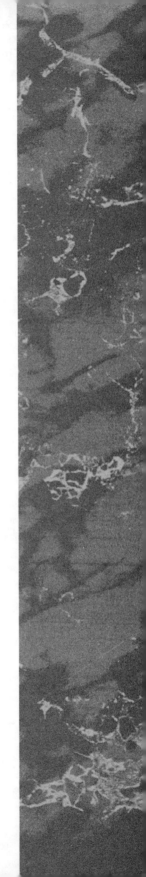

Outlines, Numbers, and More

Lawyers are accustomed to thinking in very structured ways. Solving a legal problem requires a very precise process of analyzing the issues, breaking them into smaller pieces, and applying the law to each piece. While this "head work" is easy for most lawyers, communicating the results is sometimes a different story. Even though a lawyer clearly understands the legal issue in her head, she may have difficulty putting it on paper in such a way that others can understand it too.

WordPerfect includes several features that not only help you express your thoughts in a structured way, but also can help your thought processes along. This chapter looks at the following:

- How to create various numbering schemes that automatically update themselves as you add or delete items
- How using outlines can help you organize and present your thoughts

An Overview of Paragraph Numbers

Lawyers have been numbering things ever since they learned how to count. There is a good reason for this, of course. Many legal documents, especially contracts and agreements, require precision. Numbers beside the paragraphs in such documents not only make them more understandable and easy to follow, they provide easy points of reference if disputes later turn up. How much more precise and easier it is to say, "Your client is in violation of ± 4.01 (c) of the contract" instead of "Your client has violated the third sub-paragraph that appears halfway down on page 6."

In the old days (i.e., before word processing), you had only one option: typing the paragraph numbers manually. It is surprising how many typists still do this today. Unfortunately, this can lead to problems when a document is edited. If a lawyer drafts a 75-paragraph complaint, then adds a new defendant and a new paragraph 2, paragraphs 3 through 75 must then be manually identified and changed. And then there are the cross-references to different paragraphs to worry about....

WordPerfect includes several systems for generating numbers automatically. As you add and delete paragraphs or sections from your document, it can automatically update all paragraph numbers for you. Three WordPerfect features create numbering schemes that automatically update themselves:

- Counters
- Paragraph Numbers
- Outlines

These three systems are similar to each other in many ways, and are even related to each other in ways that are not immediately obvious. This leads to a great deal of confusion as to how they work and which system is most appropriate for your specific needs. This chapter will give you some ideas as to how these features work and when to use them; but hang on, this will get complicated!

Using Counters

Of the three systems mentioned above, counters are the least automatic and therefore give the user the most manual control over the final results. They are also therefore the hardest to use, although for some common law office problems they are the only solution.

Counters allow the user to create numbered lists of various things within the document. You can define any number of lists, and each list will keep track of the proper numbering independently of every other list.

An examination of a common law office task will help illustrate how this feature works and how counters can solve it. Lawyers often need to create documents that keep track of several things independently. For example, in a complaint, most courts require sequential numbering of paragraphs, with Arabic numerals, beginning with one and continuing consecutively throughout the complaint. If a lawyer is drafting a complaint that pleads more than one cause of action, or alternative theories of recovery, he is likely (and may be required by court rule) to separate each cause of action or theory of recovery into separate counts, each of which may be numbered independently of the allegations of the complaint. A typical complaint might look something like figure 2.1.

IN THE COURT OF COMMON PLEAS OF
YOKNAPATAWPHA COUNTY, MISSISSIPPI

THE ESTATE OF WILLIAM
FAULKNER, a dead white male;

Plaintiff

v.   No. 234527 of 1995

KEN CHESTEK, an author of technical non-fiction;

Defendant

COMPLAINT

NOW COMES the Estate of William Faulkner, a dead white male, and brings this cause of action against the Defendant, Ken Chestek, setting forth as follows:

1.   The Plaintiff, the Estate of William Faulkner, is the personal representative of one Mr. William Faulker, a dead white male and author of many peculiar works of fiction.

2.   The Defendant, Ken Chestek, is a natural person and an author of several books of non-fiction of a technical nature.

COUNT I -- MISAPPROPRIATION

3.   The Defendant, in his writings, has shown a propensity for ripping off various names and locales commonly associated with the Plaintiff's deceased, including *inter alia* the fictional jurisdiction of Yoknapatawpha County, Mississippi.

4.   The Plaintiff did not seek permission to so appropriate the names invented by the Plaintiff's deceased, and nothing the deceased did in his lifetime would have led a reasonable person to assume that such use of the deceased's creative genius would have been approved by the deceased.

Fig. 2.1
An excerpt from a sample complaint, with different counts.

Notice that, while the introduction and the various counts shown in figure 2.1 use uppercase Roman numerals, which flow sequentially, they do not interrupt the sequencing of the numbered paragraphs that contain the allegations of the complaint. Thus, Count I of the complaint contains Paragraphs 3 through 6, while Count II continues with Paragraph 7. While these numbers appear to be part of an outline, the sequencing is not how an outline would work. Once the code is inserted for Count II, in an outline the next Arabic number would be reset to 1, rather than 7.

Creating Counters

You can solve this problem by creating independent counters for the two different items being tracked: (a) headings for each count of the complaint, and (b) total number of paragraphs in the complaint. Here's how to do it:

1. Choose **I**nsert, **O**ther, **C**ounter.

   The Counter Numbering dialog box, shown in figure 2.2, appears.

Fig. 2.2
The Counter
Numbering
dialog box.

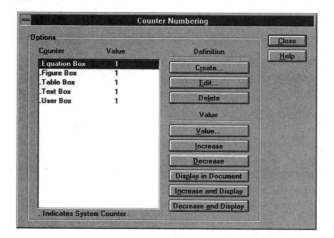

In the list box in the left half of the window, you will see a list of available counters for the current document. The first five entries (indicated by a period before each name) are system counters, which cannot be deleted but can be edited. If your document includes any text or graphics boxes (or any of the other boxes listed as one of the five system counters), you can change the style of the number for those boxes by editing the corresponding system counter in this window. The current value (that is, the next number that will be printed) of each counter in your document is also shown in the list box.

Because you need a specialized counter to keep track of the counts in your hypothetical complaint, you need to create a user-defined counter.

2. Choose **C**reate to display the Create Counter Definition dialog box shown in figure 2.3.

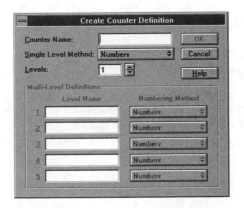

Fig. 2.3
Creating a new counter.

3. Enter the name of the new counter in the Counter Name entry field; for this example, type **Count Number**.

   You can specify counters with up to five levels. A multilevel counter allows you to create an outline effect in which lower-level counters are reset to their initial values (1 or a) when a higher-level counter is incremented. For the Count Number counter, you'll use just a single-level counter. But since you want to use Roman numerals to mark each new count in your complaint, you need to set the numbering method for this counter to Roman numerals.

4. Click on the pop-up button next to **S**ingle Level Method (the default value is Numbers). The pop-up list is shown in figure 2.4.

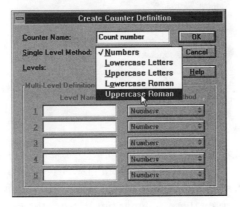

Fig. 2.4
Changing the numbering method for a counter.

5. Choose U**p**percase Roman from the pop-up list; it will appear on the button after you choose it.

6. Choose OK to save the new Count Number counter. You will be returned to the Counter Numbering dialog box.

Now you need to create a *separate* counter to keep track of paragraph numbers. (Notice that if you had used a two-level counter for Count Number, with the second level reserved for paragraph numbers, you would not be able to number the paragraphs consecutively, since increasing the Count Number level would reset the second level numbering system back to 1.)

7. Choose Create again.

8. Type **Para. Number** in the Counter Name window.

Because you may want to include subparagraphs in your complaint which *should* be reset for each paragraph, this time you will create a multilevel counter.

9. Click once on the up arrow or type **2** in the entry field designated **L**evels:.

Notice that the first two entry fields in the Multi-Level Definitions group box are now active, while the Single Level Method entry window has been grayed out, as shown in figure 2.5.

Fig. 2.5
Creating a multi-level counter definition.

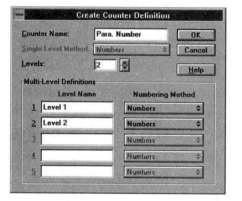

10. Although it is not necessary to do so, for the sake of clarity you may wish to change the Level Names from "Level 1" and "Level 2" to something more descriptive, such as "Paragraph" and "Subparagraph." You can do so by typing these designations in from the keyboard.

11. You do, however, need to change the Numbering Method for subparagraphs from Numbers to another option (probably Lowercase Letters). See Steps 5 and 6 above.

When you have completed these steps, your Create Counter Definition dialog box should look like figure 2.6.

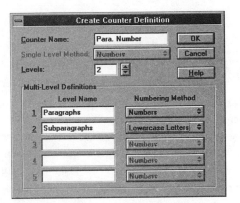

Fig. 2.6
Completing the Para. Number counter definition.

12. Choose OK to complete this operation.

13. Finally, choose **C**lose from the Counter Numbering dialog box to complete the creation of your two new counters.

Using Counters

Creating these two new counters is not the end of the job, however. Using counters in a document is not as easy as one might expect, either.

The trick to using counters is to recognize that *incrementing* (or increasing the number) of the counter is independent of *displaying* that counter. That is to say, to put in a counter that calls the second paragraph of your complaint number 2 requires two separate WordPerfect codes: one to increase the value of the counter by one, and a second code to display the counter at the beginning of your paragraph.

> **Note**
>
> Although the following two-step process may seem clumsy at first, you may soon find that this feature gives you some additional flexibility in how you use counters. For example, you may wish to refer to the current paragraph number within the text of that paragraph; you can accomplish this simply by including the proper code to display the current paragraph number without increasing its value.

When you first created the Count Number and Para. Number counters, their initial value was set at I or 1. This means the first time you want to display those counters, you need not increase their values. For example, the first time you want to display the Count Number counter in your document, do the following:

1. If you have not created a counter for the document in the active window, do so first following the instructions above.

On the Disk

> **Note**
>
> Counters are stored with individual documents, and therefore you must create them for each document that uses them. The Companion Disk includes a macro, PARANUM.WCM, which creates a five-level counter called Paranums and allows you to insert a counter at the current location of the insertion point. This macro is described in more detail later in the chapter.

2. Place your insertion point where you want to insert the counter.

3. Open the Counter Numbering dialog box by choosing **I**nsert, **O**ther, **C**ounter.

4. Highlight the Count Number entry in the list box in the left side of the dialog box (refer to fig. 2.2).

5. Choose Dis**p**lay in Document. The dialog box will be dismissed and that counter will appear in your document.

For the rest of the counts in your hypothetical complaint, you will need to explicitly increase the value of that counter before displaying it. Follow these steps:

1. Place your insertion point where you want to insert the counter.

2. Open the Counter Numbering dialog box by choosing **I**nsert, **O**ther, and **C**ounter.

3. Highlight the Count Number entry in the list box in the left side of the dialog box.

4. Choose **In**crease and Display. The dialog box will be dismissed and that counter will appear in your document, increased by one since the last time the counter was increased.

Note that WordPerfect has inserted two codes in your document at the location of your insertion point. You can see them in Reveal Codes (see fig. 2.7). The first code, [Count Inc], is the code that increases the value of the counter by one. The second code, [Count Disp], is the code that displays the current value of the designated counter.

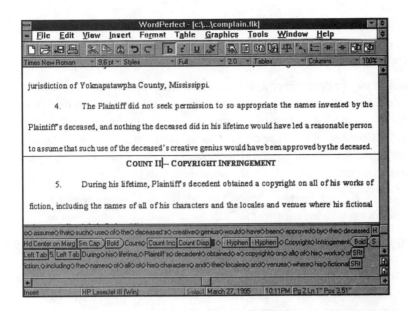

Fig. 2.7
The codes that
increase and
display a counter.

Note that whenever you display the Counter Numbering dialog box, the
value listed for the specified counter in the list box will be the current value,
at the location of the insertion point, for the specified counter.

Changing a Counter

It is important to recognize that both of the codes exist, because they may
trip you up if you later edit the document to delete one or more counters. If
you want to delete a counter, and have all subsequent counters adjust themselves, *you must delete both codes*. Deleting the [Count Disp] code will only delete the appearance of the reference at that point; if you do not delete the
corresponding [Count Inc] code the value will remain unchanged, and all
subsequent counters will be one number too high.

You can reset a counter's value at any point in your document by choosing
Value in the Counter Numbering dialog box. Doing so will insert a [Count
Set] code in your document, changing the value of the specified counter as
of that point in the document. You can also decrease the value of a counter
from the Counter Numbering dialog box if you so choose.

Automating Counters

While counters work perfectly well, by themselves they are somewhat limited. For example, in most cases you want a period to follow an Arabic numeral; and sometimes you want a lowercase letter enclosed in parentheses.

Counters, by themselves, don't do these things; all you get is the bare numeral or letter. Wouldn't it be nice if you could specify a few more adornments to these naked characters, instead of having to type them manually?

There is a way to dress up counters and make them more automatic and more flexible. The trick is to combine them with the Style feature. Instead of going through the lengthy process of creating and manually inserting the counters from the Counter Numbering dialog box as described above, you can insert counters into styles that contain the formatting you want. Then to insert a counter, you need only turn on the appropriate style.

Time out. What is a "style," anyway? Wouldn't using them be just substituting one dialog box for another?

Not quite. As you see in a minute, WordPerfect has already done most of the work of combining styles and counters for you; it puts this combination right onto the **I**nsert menu. However, before you get into this, you need to take a brief detour through the Styles feature. A minimal understanding of styles will help solve many of the mysteries of paragraph number creation.

This section does not deal comprehensively with styles, but focuses only on the basics that you need to make the Counter, Paragraph Numbers, and Outline features work the way you want them to.

What Is a Style?

A *style* is a set of formatting codes that you can turn on or off at any point in your document. Styles enable you to specify a format for different types of documents—or different parts of a single document—and turn those codes on and off with a single action.

The obvious advantage of this arrangement is that, rather than having to manually re-create the line spacing, appearance and font codes, and other items you may wish to specify, you can do it once and save the results in a style that you can access at any time later on. There is a hidden advantage as well. For example, if you use styles to format a discrete part of your document such as headings, and you later decide to change the appearance of the headings, you can make global changes throughout the document simply by changing the style definition, rather than having to locate every heading and change the formatting codes in each one.

There are three types of styles available:

- Character (paired)
- Paragraph (paired)
- Document (open)

The paired styles (character and paragraph) include a Style On and a Style Off code. Only the text which is enclosed between these two codes is affected by the codes within the style. You can apply a character style to any block of text; it can begin and end at any location you specify. A paragraph style affects the current paragraph only. If you turn on a paragraph style anywhere in the middle of a paragraph (defined as any text which appears between two hard return codes), WordPerfect will automatically place the Style On code at the beginning of the paragraph and the Style Off code at the end of the paragraph.

A document style, on the other hand, does not use a Style Off code. Once turned on at any point in the document, it remains in effect from that point forward for the remainder of the document. You cannot turn it off, although you can later delete the Style On code to delete the formatting instructions. If you want to use a type of style that you can turn on and off again, use a character or paragraph style.

For more help on creating and using styles, see the Reference Manual that comes with the WordPerfect software.

Where Are Styles Stored?

This is a surprisingly tricky question. For users of any prior version of WordPerfect, the answer is easy: Styles are stored with each document (in the "document prefix," for the technical purists). That is not necessarily true with WordPerfect *6.x* for Windows, however. Version 6.0 of WordPerfect for Windows introduced the concept of templates. Although Chapter 7 covers templates, you need to understand a little bit about them and how they affect styles.

A template is just what it sounds like: it is a basic format for a document. WordPerfect ships with numerous templates, including useful templates that quickly create memoranda, letters, and other standard documents. But it also includes a Standard Template, which is the default for all documents. That is, unless you explicitly tell WordPerfect to use a specialized template, every new document you create will start with the formatting codes found in the Standard Template.

Templates store a lot of information. For example, you can use a template to specify which keyboard definition, which toolbar, and which menu bar, among other objects, you want WordPerfect to use for a particular document. For your immediate purposes, it is important to know that you can store styles in the template as well.

For example, the Standard Template is shipped with six styles: an Initial Style and five heading styles. The Initial Style is a document style that contains basic formatting instructions for your entire file, such as hyphenation or typesetting codes, initial values for line numbering, initial margins, or just about anything you want to appear as standard initial values in your default documents.

If you want to create new style definitions to have available for all new documents, you must do so by editing the Standard Template and saving them there. For more information on doing this, see Chapter 7.

Now things get tricky. If you do not want your existing documents to be affected by changes you make to the styles in your Standard Template, you need to set up your system in a certain way. Here's how:

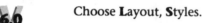

1. Choose For**m**at, **S**tyles.

Choose **L**ayout, **S**tyles.

The Style List dialog box, shown in figure 2.8, will appear.

Fig. 2.8
The Style List
dialog box.

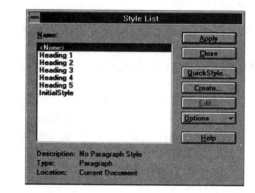

2. Choose **O**ptions.

3. From the drop-down list, choose the first option, **S**etup. The Style Setup option box appears, as shown in figure 2.9.

Fig. 2.9
Setting Style
options.

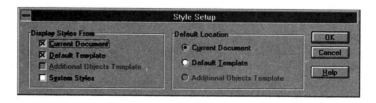

In the left-hand box, you can elect to display any combination of styles located in the current document, the default template (Standard unless you have specified a different template), and system styles. System styles affect things like footnotes, headers and footers, tables of authorities, and tables of contents. (Chapter 4 discusses some of those styles further.)

4. Click the boxes for the styles you wish to display; an X will appear in the check box.

   In the right-hand box you can specify where to store new styles. (You cannot delete any system style or change its location.) If you specify Current Document, WordPerfect will store all styles used in the document in the document itself, where subsequent changes to the styles in the default template will not affect them. If you specify Default Template, however, any styles you create or modify are stored in the default template (STANDARD.WPT unless you specified a different one) and may affect other documents that use those same styles. You will probably prefer to routinely store your styles in the Current Document.

5. Select the location where you want to store new styles.

6. Choose OK to save this setup.

7. Choose Close to return to your document window.

Using Styles to Create Counters

Now you're rounding the corner and closing in on the finish line. This discussion began by stating that you can automate the counter feature by using a style to turn it on and off; and that the style could not only display the counter and increment it, but also add any necessary punctuation, trailing spaces, and other formatting. In this way you could make the creation and use of counters to keep track of paragraphs much more automatic.

This sounds like a good idea, but it also sounds complicated. Counters are hard enough, but to have to deal with styles too? You might be tempted to take a pass on that one. Fortunately, the combination is built in to the program for you. You can easily activate it, not from the Style List, but from the Insert menu. Take a look:

1. Start in a new document window. Choose Insert, Bullets & Numbers.

   You see the Bullets & Numbers dialog box, as shown in figure 2.10.

Fig. 2.10
Inserting a
formatted counter
through the
Bullets & Numbers
dialog box.

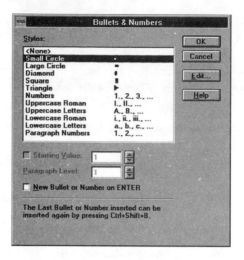

Beginning about midway down in the list box, you will see five styles of numbers that you can insert from this dialog box: Numbers, Uppercase Roman, Uppercase Letters, Lowercase Roman, and Lowercase Letters. (It is no coincidence that these are the same five options WordPerfect gives you when you create a type of counter, as discussed above.)

2. Just to see how this feature works, highlight the Numbers option, just about in the middle of the list box, and choose OK.

The dialog box disappears, and you should see an Arabic numeral 1, followed by an indent, appear just before the insertion point. At this point, you can type whatever text you need to.

3. For the purpose of this demonstration, just type the words **This is a test document** and press Enter.

4. If you want to insert another paragraph number, simply repeat steps 1 through 4. Each time you do this, the paragraph number will increase by one.

Now let's take a closer look at how this feature operates.

1. Place the insertion point near the first number you inserted above, then turn on Reveal Codes (**V**iew, Reveal **C**odes). Your screen should look something like figure 2.11.

2. In the Reveal Codes window, notice that the text you typed is enclosed between paired paragraph style codes. The name of the style that this pair of codes turns on and off is "1, 2, 3."

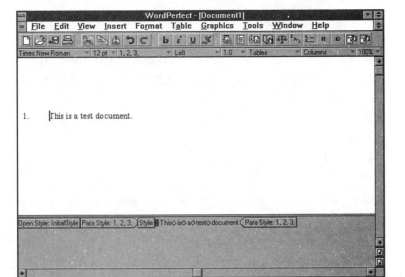

Fig. 2.11
A counter in a
paragraph style in
Reveal Codes.

3. Notice also that, immediately after the [Para Style: 1,2,3>] code you will
find another code, [Style]. Using the left and right arrow keys, move the
insertion point so that it is immediately in front of that code. It will
expand and show you its contents, as shown in figure 2.12.

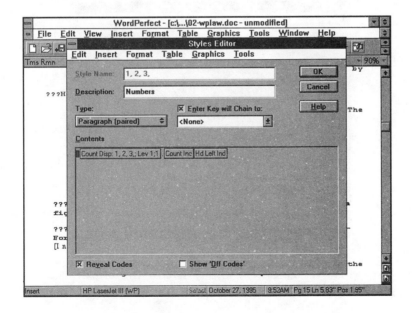

Fig. 2.12
The contents of
the style code in
the Reveal Codes
window.

4. In the example in figure 2.12, the style code contains the following codes:

- A [Count Disp] code to display the counter (an Arabic numeral)
- A period to insert a period immediately after the displayed number
- A [Count Inc] code to immediately increase the value of the counter by one; and
- A [Hd Left Ind] code to indent all text that follows the number.

As you can see, this style has been set up to create a numbered list with the list numbers made visible by isolating them to the left of the body of the list. This is probably not what you want to do, however. Fortunately, you can change this style, either for the current document or as a default for all future documents.

To change this style for just the current document, do the following:

1. Display the Bullets & Numbers dialog box by choosing **I**nsert, Bullets & **N**umbers.

2. Highlight the Numbers style; then choose **E**dit. The Style Editor (see fig. 2.13) will appear.

Fig. 2.13
The Styles Editor.

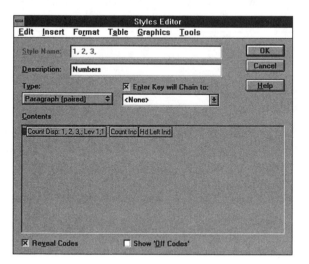

3. Make whatever changes you wish to make to the formatting codes in the **C**ontents entry window.

For example, if you wish to add a Left Tab before the [Count Disp] code, simply place the insertion point in the window immediately before that code and press Ctrl+Tab (the Ctrl key is required to prevent the Tab key from simply shifting the focus to another part of the dialog box). You may also wish to replace the [Hd Left Ind] code at the end with a couple of spaces or Left Tab.

4. Click OK when you have finished to return to the Bullets & Numbers dialog box. From there, you can either choose OK to insert a number, or Cancel to return to your document.

You can also make the same types of changes to the uppercase Roman, lowercase Roman, and other counter types shown in the Bullets & Numbers dialog box.

The default values for these counter styles are stored in the Standard Template. Thus, if you want to create new defaults for these styles, you will need to edit the styles found in that document. Here is the simplest and safest way to do that:

1. Choose **F**ile, **N**ew.

   Choose **F**ile, **T**emplate.

2. The New Document dialog box will appear with the default template Create a blank document already highlighted; note that the name of your default template, most likely STANDARD.WPT, will appear above the list box.

   Move the highlight bar to the Standard Template.

3. Choose Options, then Edit Template from the drop-down list. The Standard file will be opened into an editing window.

4. Choose Fo**r**mat, **S**tyles.

   Choose **L**ayout, **S**tyles.

   Notice that the Style List dialog box looks slightly different than it did earlier in this chapter (refer to fig. 2.8). There is a new entry for the style 1,2,3. This was automatically inserted into your Standard Template the first time you turned that style on from the Bullets & Numbers dialog box.

5. Move the highlight bar to the 1,2,3 style.

6. Choose Edit.

   The Styles Editor appears, with the current codes associated with this style appearing in the Contents editing window that consumes the bottom half of the dialog box.

7. Make whatever changes you desire in that window; then choose OK to exit and save the changes.

8. Close the Style List by choosing Close. This will return you to your Standard Tmplate.

9. Finally, choose the Exit Template button from the Template Feature Bar, remembering to answer Yes to the dialog box asking if you want to save the changes you just made.

A Macro to Insert Counters

If this seems more complicated than it needs to be, it is. Most lawyers just want a simple numbering scheme so that they can put a paragraph number anywhere in the document they want, without worrying about styles. And they don't want the numbers to change depending on how many tab stops there are in front of the code.

The Applications Disk includes a macro named PARANUM.WCM to do just this. It relies on the counter feature to create numbers (for up to five levels) at the location of your insertion point. You might consider assigning this macro to a button on your toolbar or to a hot key on your keyboard for quick access to it; see Chapter 1 for help on doing this.

The macro creates a five-level counter called Paranums; the five levels are shown in figure 2.14. This simple menu box will appear each time you play the macro PARANUM.WCM.

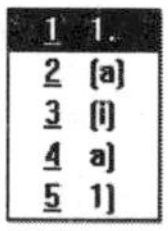

Fig. 2.14
The PARANUM.WCM menu with the available numbering levels.

To insert a paragraph number using PARANUM.WCM, follow these steps:

1. Play the macro. Choose **T**ools, **M**acro, **P**lay. Or if you have assigned this macro to a hot key, press the hot key. (See Chapter 1, "Making WordPerfect Work the Way You Do," for help on assigning macros to hot keys.)

2. Use the mouse or arrow keys to highlight the level of number that you want to insert; or just type the corresponding level number.

   The counter will be automatically created and inserted into your document at the insertion point.

3. If you want to cancel the macro, simply press Esc.

Note that the macro inserts punctuation and a [Left Tab] code after the counter has been displayed. If you later want to delete the counter you will have to also delete the associated punctuation and tab codes in addition to deleting both the [Count Disp] and the [Count Inc] codes.

Note

Be sure to delete all [Count Inc] codes whenever you delete a [Count Disp] code, so that all subsequent counters are correctly updated.

Paragraph Numbers

You may have noticed in the Bullets & Numbers dialog box (refer to fig. 2.10) an option not discussed in the previous section: Paragraph Numbers. This is because paragraph numbers are different from counters. If you insert a paragraph number in your document, it will not affect any counter that then exists or is later added to the document; nor will counters affect paragraph numbers. This can lead to confusion because both systems create identical-looking numbers that automatically update themselves. You should decide upon one method and stick to it throughout the document; if you use both systems in the same document, you may become frustrated in trying to get the numbers to adjust themselves properly.

Paragraph numbers are slippery little beasts. They sometimes behave in unexpected ways, if you are not careful in using them. For this reason, it is best when learning about them to turn on Reveal Codes (**V**iew, Reveal **C**odes) so you can keep an eye on what codes are being inserted into your document and how they affect its appearance.

Manually Inserting Paragraph Numbers

Let's first consider the simplest task: manually inserting a first-level paragraph number.

What is a "first-level" paragraph number? Paragraph numbers, like counters, are hierarchical. You can have subsidiary paragraph numbers, which are reset after any higher-level paragraph number is inserted, creating an outline effect. Table 2.1 shows the different levels of standard paragraph numbers.

Table 2.1	The Eight Levels of Standard Paragraph Numbers
Level	**Level Displays**
1.	Arabic numeral
a.	Lowercase letter
i.	Lowercase Roman numeral followed by a period
(1)	Arabic numeral in parentheses
(a)	Lowercase letter in parentheses
(i)	Lowercase Roman numeral in parentheses
1)	Arabic numeral followed by a single parenthesis
a)	Lowercase letter followed by a single parenthesis

To insert a first-level (Arabic numeral) paragraph number, follow these steps:

1. Begin with a blank document window, and turn on Reveal Codes so you can watch what is going on.

2. Choose **I**nsert, Bullets & **N**umbers. The Bullets and Numbers dialog box appears (it was shown as figure 2.10 earlier).

3. In the **S**tyles list box, highlight the last entry, Paragraph Numbers.

4. Choose OK. The dialog box will disappear and you will see a paragraph number in your editing window.

   Now take a look at the Reveal Codes window (shown in figure 2.15). Notice that *two* codes have been inserted: an [Outline] code and a [Para Num] code. Let's see what they are doing.

5. Press the left arrow key twice to move the insertion point in the Reveal Codes window to the left of the [Outline] code.

   That code will expand to show this: [Outline: Numbers] This shows you that the Paragraph Number feature is a part of the Outline feature of WordPerfect (which this chapter discusses later); specifically, it uses the numbers style of an outline in order to define how the number is going to appear in your document.

6. Now press the right arrow key once to move the insertion point between the [Outline] and [Para Num] codes.

   Note that the second code has expanded to show this: [Para Num: 1;[Para Num Disp].] This code, similar to the [Counter Disp] code discussed earlier in the chapter, is the code that actually displays the paragraph number. You can see that in this case the code will display a first-level paragraph number, which is an Arabic numeral.

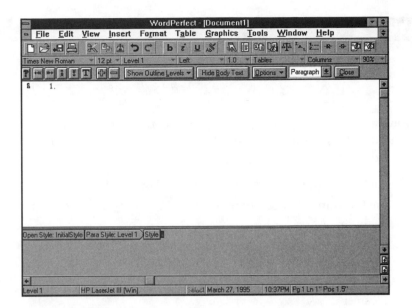

Fig. 2.15
A paragraph number code in Reveal Codes.

7. Press the right arrow key one more time to return the insertion point to the right of the [Para Num] code.

Now suppose you want to insert a tab before beginning to type the text of your paragraph.

8. Press the Tab key.

Surprise! Rather than moving the insertion point to the next tab stop, your Arabic numeral has just turned into the small letter a. What happened?

9. Press the left arrow key to move the insertion point immediately before the [Para Num] code.

The code now looks like this: [Para Num: 2;[Para Num Disp].] When you press the Tab key with the insertion point immediately to the right of a [Para Num] code, that key takes on a different function: it takes the level of the paragraph number down one increment (in this case, from first level to second level).

10. To change the paragraph number code back to the first level, move the insertion point back to the right of the [Para Num] code by pressing the right arrow key once.

11. Press Shift+Tab to return the paragraph number to a first-level (Arabic numeral) style.

12. Now press Ctrl+Tab.

Tip

Use Ctrl+Tab to force WordPerfect to insert a real tab immediately after a [Para Num] code, rather than simply change the level of the number.

If you want to insert a paragraph number other than a first-level number, all you need to do is specify the desired level in the Bullets & Numbers dialog box. Here's how to insert a second-level paragraph number:

1. Choose **I**nsert, Bullets & **N**umbers to display that dialog box.

2. The Paragraph Numbers option should be highlighted in the list box.

3. Use the counter control arrows following the Paragraph Level entry window to change the level up or down (or just type the number of the level you want).

4. Choose OK to insert that level of a paragraph number into your document.

Automatically Inserting the Next Paragraph Number

The Paragraph Number feature includes an option that allows you to automatically insert new paragraph numbers as soon as you press Enter. However, you should be careful if you decide to use this feature, because it may not operate in the way you expect it to. Let's examine how it does work by continuing the previous example.

1. Continue the preceding example by typing some text after the [Left Tab] code.

2. At the end of the paragraph, press Enter.

   If a new paragraph number does not appear, you need to set an option in the Bullets and Numbers dialog box to insert a new number when you press Enter.

3. Choose **I**nsert, Bullets & **N**umbers to display that dialog box.

4. Click in the check box marked **N**ew Bullet or Number on ENTER to select that option; an X will appear in the check box.

5. Choose OK. A new paragraph number now appears on the next line.

6. To see how this option works, press Enter again. In Reveal Codes, you will see that WordPerfect has inserted two codes: the [HRt] code you expected, followed by a new [Para Num] code.

If you want to continue numbering your paragraphs, you are all set. If you want to turn off the paragraph numbers, just use the Backspace key to delete the [Para Num] code.

A Few Words of Caution

The paragraph number feature includes a couple of "gotchas" that may drive you nuts. Before using this feature heavily, you should be aware of the following:

The Trouble With Automatic Insertion of Paragraph Numbers

An anomaly appears to exist in the way the Paragraph Number feature positions paragraph numbers if you have selected the option to automatically insert them when you press Enter. It is this: any paragraph number code you insert manually from the Bullets & Numbers dialog box will appear at the location of the insertion point, and will retain the level you specify for it, without reference to the nearest tab setting. Any paragraph number code that is inserted automatically will take the level of the previous code, and will be placed at the tab stop corresponding to that level. If you add or delete tabs or indents before the code, or even if you insert text before the code, this type of code will change its display to the level of the nearest tab stop.

What makes this anomaly maddening is that there is no way to tell, from examining a paragraph number code in Reveal Codes, whether it was inserted manually or automatically. Thus, you won't know if the paragraph number will stay put when you begin to edit text. Worse yet, if you combine both automatic codes with manual codes in the same document, existing codes in the document might not be correctly updated.

This difficulty may be cleared up in future releases of WordPerfect. However, for now it would appear that the best option is to avoid using the automatic paragraph number entry feature, unless you want your paragraph numbers to be automatically adjusted as they are moved during editing.

Don't Use Paragraph Numbers in an Outline

When you first insert a paragraph number from the Bullets & Numbers dialog box, WordPerfect will insert the [Outline] style code discussed above. This code will appear at the very top of the document, regardless of where you insert the paragraph number.

This presents a problem if you're using the Outline feature (which is discussed next). This code defines the type of numbering scheme your outline will use. If you're using the Outline feature, using Paragraph Numbers will change your outline style from whatever you were using to the numbers style.

You can always change your outline style back to whatever type you were using, but doing so will also change the paragraph numbers to that same style of numbering. Also, any manual paragraph number codes will change to automatic codes, and therefore will now be at the tab stop corresponding to the level of the number.

Outlines

Because the Paragraph Number feature used alone presents some difficulties, for many users a better solution to creating automatic numbering schemes may be the Outline feature. Moreover, using Outline may not only help you create easy-to-understand documents, it may even help you organize your thoughts while you are writing.

At one level, an outline is just paragraph numbers with styles. That is to say, just as you saw how combining counters with styles could lead to a more automated system for creating a numbering system, combining Paragraph Numbers with Styles can do the same thing: the result is the Outline feature. But that is an oversimplification. The Outline feature is greater than the sum of those parts.

The Outline Style

Outlines are defined by a style code placed at the very top of any document using an outline. The codes contained in that Document Style code are quite flexible.

> **Note**
>
> You may define more than one outline style in a document, but this can lead to some confusion. Avoid doing this if at all possible.

The outline style that you use for a document can specify:

- The appearance of the number or marker denoting each level of the outline
- The format of the text on any line beginning with an outline number or marker
- Any codes or other formatting that takes effect after the style is turned off (that is, at the end of the outline entry)

You can use the Outline feature to create not only a traditional outline, but also multilevel headings for briefs, contracts, agreements, or just about any other legal document. You can even embed Table of Contents codes into your outline style definitions to make the creation of a table of contents for your document virtually instantaneous.

WordPerfect comes with seven predefined outline styles. You can edit any of those styles to suit your needs, or you can create your own outline style according to your preferences.

Creating an Outline

A look at how to create an outline is in order. Like many WordPerfect features, Outline offers several ways to approach it. We'll first take a look at the long way, and then learn the shortcut keys that make this feature extremely easy to use. As with Paragraph Numbers, the easiest way to observe how the Outlines feature works is to turn Reveal Codes on and do the following:

1. Choose **T**ools, **O**utline.

    Several things will happen to your screen (see fig. 2.16). First, the Outline Feature Bar will appear immediately above the editing screen. (A discussion of its various buttons follows in a moment.)

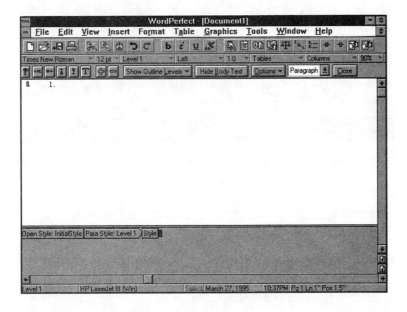

Fig. 2.16
A new outline, seen with Reveal Codes on.

Second, an Arabic numeral 1 appears on the first line of the document, and the insertion point has moved to the right one tab stop.

Third, two new codes have been inserted in the document and are visible in the Reveal Codes window: [Para Style: Level 1>] and [Style]. This section discusses the relationship between these two codes in a moment too.

Finally, a strange-looking "hollow" numeral 1 appears in the left margin. If you are accustomed to the famous "clean screen" of WordPerfect for DOS products, this visible code in the editing window may distract you at first; but you'll soon see how it can come in handy. This funky-looking character is called a Level Icon; it displays the level of the paragraph number WordPerfect will insert on this line. Let's study how that works first.

> **Tip**
>
> If you don't like the distraction of seeing Level Icons displayed in the left margin, you can turn them off by choosing the Options button from the Outline Feature Bar, then deselecting the Show Level Icon option on the drop-down list that appears.

2. Press Tab.

   The Arabic numeral 1 not only moves one tab stop to the right, but it also turns into a lowercase letter a. Note also that the Level Icon 1 in the left margin has now changed to a 2, indicating that a second-level character will appear on this line.

3. Press Shift+Tab to return the code to the left margin and change its level back to level 1.

> **Note**
>
> This feature works the same way as Paragraph Numbers, discussed above. If you want to force a tab to appear after the outline number, without changing the level of that number, use Ctrl+Tab.

4. Now type some text after the Outline number that is displayed on your screen and press Enter.

5. Note that a new first-level paragraph number will appear at the left margin (in this case the Arabic numeral 2).

   You can enter another string of text, or press Tab to move to the next level and keep typing. But suppose you want to put a blank line between these two level 1 entries; how do you do that?

Special Features

6. With the cursor immediately after the number 2 (that is, with no other text on that line), press Enter again.

Somewhat surprisingly, rather than simply entering another level 1 outline number, pressing Enter just moves the number down a line, leaving the blank space you wanted. But look at the left margin; next to that blank line you will see a character T as the Level Icon (see fig. 2.17).

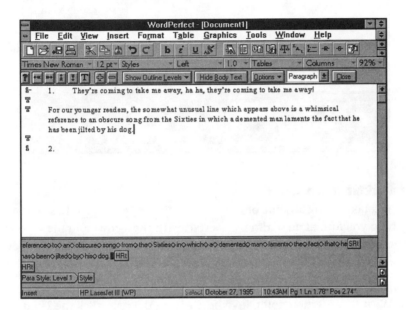

Fig. 2.17
The code for a blank text line in an outline.

The T Level Icon in the left margin tells you that you can enter text on that line, unaffected by any paragraph or outline numbers or styles or codes of any sort. Essentially, Outline has been turned off for any line that follows the T Level Icon.

This can have a great deal of utility for a lawyer.

7. Press Enter twice more, so that there are three blank lines between the two displayed numbers.

8. Now press the up arrow key twice to place the insertion point next to the middle of the three blank lines.

9. Type some additional text here, in this case more than one line long, to see what happens.

Your screen should now look something like figure 2.18. Notice that, as the words wrapped automatically, no additional T Level Icons appeared.

Fig. 2.18
Inserting
unformatted text
into an active
outline.

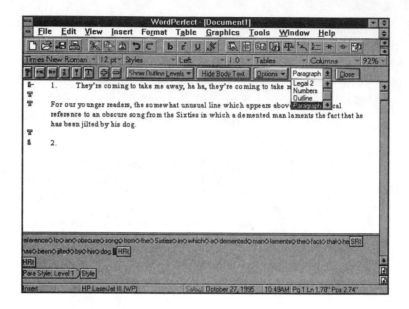

Formatting an Outline

Now let's take a look at some of the buttons on the Feature Bar to see how
they help you format an outline. Let's start with the arrows and the T button
on the left side of the Feature Bar. Suppose you wanted to take the text you
entered between the two outline numbers and convert it from unmarked text
to an entry in the outline.

1. With the insertion point anywhere within the text, click the T button
   on the Feature Bar.

   The text is indented and now becomes the second item at level 1 of the
   outline. Notice that the T Level Icon in the left margin has changed to
   a 1.

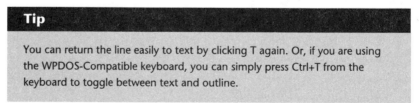

   Tip

   You can return the line easily to text by clicking T again. Or, if you are using
   the WPDOS-Compatible keyboard, you can simply press Ctrl+T from the
   keyboard to toggle between text and outline.

   Suppose you decide that this text should really be subsidiary to the line
   above, and should appear as a level 2 entry in your outline. You could
   move the insertion point to the spot immediately following the [Style]
   code and press Tab, but that would take a bit of tricky maneuvering.
   There is an easier way:

2. With the insertion point anywhere within the text, click the **right arrow** button in the Feature Bar.

WordPerfect will indent the text and make it a level 2 entry in the outline. Notice that it has updated the Level Icon in the left margin as well. You can click the right arrow again to move the entry to an even lower level, or click the left arrow to move it back up one level at a time.

Wait a minute. We've been referring to this document as an outline, but it doesn't look much like a traditional outline. A traditional outline is supposed to start with uppercase Roman numerals as level 1, uppercase letters as level 2, and so on, isn't it?

You can make your outline look like that, or like anything else you desire, simply by specifying a different outline definition. Do that next.

Near the right edge of the Outline Feature Bar, notice a little window with a drop-down menu indicator on the right side. In the example (refer to fig. 2.18), the entry in the window is Paragraph. This indicates that the active outline definition is Paragraph, one of the seven definitions supplied with the program.

3. To change the definition, simply click the drop-down menu indicator; your screen should look like figure 2.19.

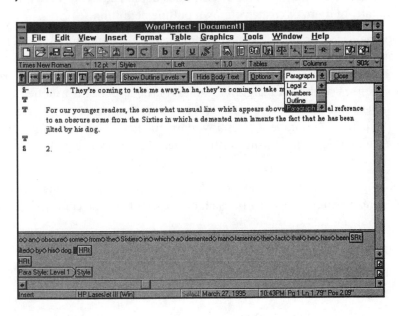

Fig. 2.19
Changing the outline definition from the drop-down menu.

4. Choose Outline from the drop-down menu.

The outline will now take on the look of a traditional outline, the kind you learned about in elementary school.

Table 2.2 shows the seven types of outline definitions supplied with the program.

Table 2.2 The Seven Standard Outline Definitions	
Definition	**Level Displays**
Bullets	-, *, +, •, x
Headings	No numbers displayed; text format changes
Legal	1, 1.1, 1.1.1, 1.1.1.1, etc.
Legal 2	1, 1.01, 1.01.01. 1.01.01.01, etc.
Numbers	1., a., i., (1), (a), (i), 1), a)
Outline	I., A., 1., a., (1), (a), i), a)
Paragraph	1., a., i., (1), (a), (i), 1), a).

Customizing an Outline Definition

If one of the seven built-in outline definitions doesn't suit your needs, you can edit any of them or create your own outline definition.

Suppose you want to use the Legal Outline Definition to produce contracts and other documents. However, there are certain aspects of the default definition that you may not like. For example, the default definition places all paragraph numbers at the left margin, regardless of the level of the number. It then indents the text of every paragraph and does not include any periods after the paragraph numbers. Thus, if you use the Legal Outline Definition as shipped with the program, your contract might look something like what is shown in figure 2.20.

Suppose further that you would like to use more traditional-looking paragraphs and a centered heading for each major section of the contract, as shown in figure 2.21.

To do this, you will need to edit the Legal Outline Definition, as follows:

1. Begin with a new document screen.

2. Display the Outline Feature Bar by choosing **T**ools, **O**utline.

3. Use the drop-down menu button to change the current outline definition to Legal.

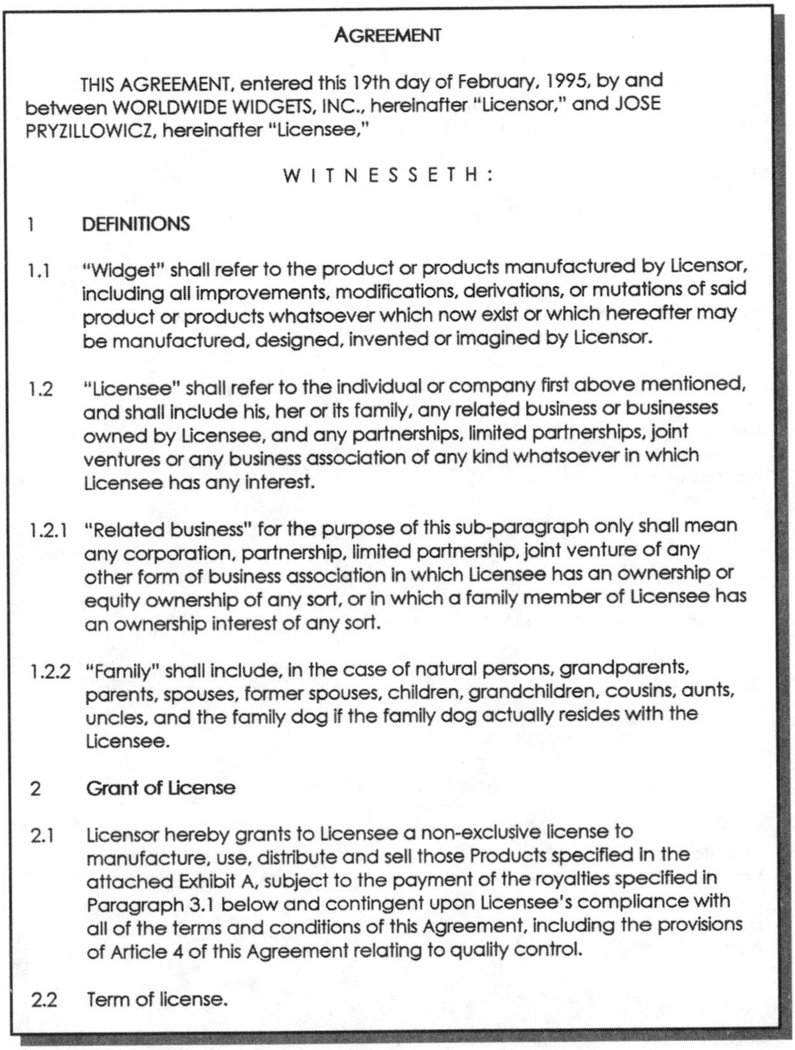

AGREEMENT

THIS AGREEMENT, entered this 19th day of February, 1995, by and between WORLDWIDE WIDGETS, INC., hereinafter "Licensor," and JOSE PRYZILLOWICZ, hereinafter "Licensee,"

W I T N E S S E T H :

1   DEFINITIONS

1.1   "Widget" shall refer to the product or products manufactured by Licensor, including all improvements, modifications, derivations, or mutations of said product or products whatsoever which now exist or which hereafter may be manufactured, designed, invented or imagined by Licensor.

1.2   "Licensee" shall refer to the individual or company first above mentioned, and shall include his, her or its family, any related business or businesses owned by Licensee, and any partnerships, limited partnerships, joint ventures or any business association of any kind whatsoever in which Licensee has any interest.

1.2.1   "Related business" for the purpose of this sub-paragraph only shall mean any corporation, partnership, limited partnership, joint venture of any other form of business association in which Licensee has an ownership or equity ownership of any sort, or in which a family member of Licensee has an ownership interest of any sort.

1.2.2   "Family" shall include, in the case of natural persons, grandparents, parents, spouses, former spouses, children, grandchildren, cousins, aunts, uncles, and the family dog if the family dog actually resides with the Licensee.

2   Grant of License

2.1   Licensor hereby grants to Licensee a non-exclusive license to manufacture, use, distribute and sell those Products specified in the attached Exhibit A, subject to the payment of the royalties specified in Paragraph 3.1 below and contingent upon Licensee's compliance with all of the terms and conditions of this Agreement, including the provisions of Article 4 of this Agreement relating to quality control.

2.2   Term of license.

Fig. 2.20
The first page of a sample contract that uses the default Legal Outline Definition.

Let's stop here for a moment and take a look at what codes have been inserted into the document and how they affect it. When you first turned on the outline in step 2, two new codes were inserted into the document: [Para Style: Level 1>] and [Style]. If you take a peek in Reveal Codes now, you'll see some changes.

4. If Reveal Codes is not already on, display it now.

As shown in figure 2.22, the [Para Style: Level 1>] code has turned into [Para Style: Legal 1>]; in addition, a third code, [Outline], has joined the two codes.

Fig. 2.21
The same contract,
with a revised
Legal Outline
Definition.

AGREEMENT

THIS AGREEMENT, entered this 19th day of February, 1995, by and between WORLDWIDE WIDGETS, INC., hereinafter "Licensor," and JOSE PRYZILLOWICZ, hereinafter "Licensee,"

W I T N E S S E T H :

Article 1. Definitions

1.1. "Widget" shall refer to the product or products manufactured by Licensor, including all improvements, modifications, derivations, or mutations of said product or products whatsoever which now exist or which hereafter may be manufactured, designed, invented or imagined by Licensor.

1.2. "Licensee" shall refer to the individual or company first above mentioned, and shall include his, her or its family, any related business or businesses owned by Licensee, and any partnerships, limited partnerships, joint ventures or any business association of any kind whatsoever in which Licensee has any interest.

1.2.1. "Related business" for the purpose of this sub-paragraph only shall mean any corporation, partnership, limited partnership, joint venture of any other form of business association in which Licensee has an ownership or equity ownership of any sort, or in which a family member of Licensee has an ownership interest of any sort.

1.2.2. "Family" shall include, in the case of natural persons, grandparents, parents, spouses, former spouses, children, grandchildren, cousins, aunts, uncles, and the family dog if the family dog actually resides with the Licensee.

Article 2. Grant of License

2.1. Licensor hereby grants to Licensee a non-exclusive license to manufacture, use, distribute and sell those Products specified in the attached Exhibit A, subject to the payment of the royalties specified in Paragraph 3.1 below and contingent upon Licensee's compliance with all of the terms and conditions of this Agreement, including the provisions of Article 4 of this Agreement relating to quality control.

2.2. Term of license.

The [Outline] code sets the Outline Definition for the remainder of the document. When you changed the definition to Legal in step 3, that code was inserted. If you change the definition at any time in the future, at any point in the document, WordPerfect will change that code to reflect the new definition, and the appearance of the entire document will be affected.

The [Para Style: Legal 1>] code specifies the level of the number displayed at that location. You can see this for yourself by doing the following:

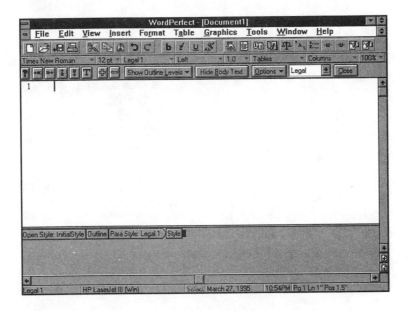

Fig. 2.22
The codes which
create the Legal
outline number,
shown in Reveal
Codes.

Special Features

5. With the insertion point immediately following the [Style] code, press
Tab to change the level.

You'll see the number in the document window change to 0.1, and the
level code in Reveal Codes will change to [Para Style: Legal 2>] to reflect
the new level of the number.

6. Press Shift+Tab to return the code to a level 1 display.

Now. to begin the process of editing the Legal Outline Definition to
create the document shown in figure 2.21.

7. Choose Options from the Outline Feature Bar. You will see a drop-down
list, as shown in figure 2.23.

8. Choose **D**efine Outline from the drop-down list.

The Outline Define dialog box will appear, as figure 2.24 shows. Because you have already set the outline definition for this document to
Legal, that option is already highlighted in the Outline Define dialog
box.

9. Choose **E**dit.

The Edit Outline Definition dialog box now appears, as shown in figure
2.25. This one requires a bit of explanation.

Fig. 2.23
Displaying the
Edit Outline
option from the
Outline Feature
Bar.

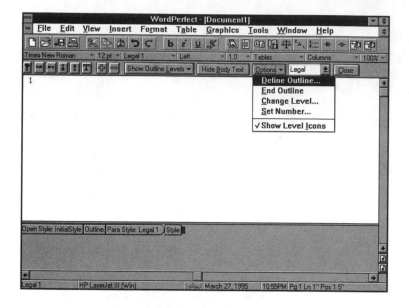

Fig. 2.24
Editing an outline
definition.

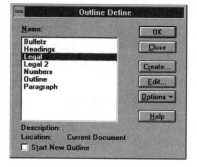

The key to understanding how Outlines work is to understand the way
the [Para Style: Level *x*>] and [Style] codes work together. An outline
definition is essentially a group of [Para Style: Level *x*>] codes that are
associated with different formatting codes contained in the [Style] code.
These associations are depicted in the Edit Outline Definition dialog
box, shown in figure 2.25.

In the left-hand list box, marked Levels, the eight levels of numbers for
the displayed outline definition are shown. The right-hand list box
shows a number of different styles that can be associated with any level
of numbering. You can change either the numbering method, or the
style associated with it, or create an entirely new set of either numbers
or styles.

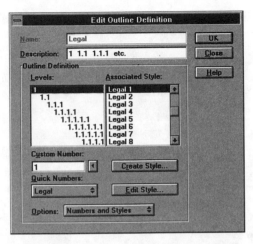

Fig. 2.25
Editing the Legal
Outline Definition.

Special Features

How can you tell which style is associated with each numbering level? Notice that one item is highlighted in each list box; the numbering level that is highlighted is associated with the style that is highlighted. To change an association, all you need to do is click on the style you want.

The problem with the example, however, is that none of the predefined styles fits the desired result. Thus, you will have to edit the existing styles to make them do what you want.

Look at figure 2.21 again. You want the first-level number to be centered and begin with the word "Article" in boldface type. You need to edit the style associated with level 1 to accomplish this:

10. With the first numbering level highlighted, the default Associated Style is Legal 1. To edit this style, choose the **E**dit Style button below the **A**ssociated Styles [/] list box.

Your screen will display the Styles Editor, with the current contents of the Legal 1 style in an editing window, as shown in figure 2.26.

There are two codes in the **C**ontents editing window: a [Para Num 1.Para Num Disp] code, which displays the first-level Legal number, and a [Hd Left Ind] code. This is what causes all the text in figure 2.20 to be indented. Here's how to change these codes to format the first level the way you want it.

11. Insert a [Hd Center on Marg] code as the first formatting code inside the **C**ontents editing window (from the menu inside the dialog box, choose Fo**r**mat, **L**ine, **C**enter).

Choose **L**ayout, **L**ine, **C**enter.

Fig. 2.26

The default values for the Legal 1 style in the Styles Editor.

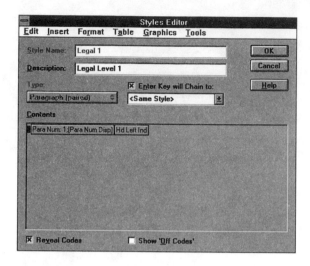

12. Next, press Ctrl+B to insert a [Bold>] code.

13. Type the word **Article**, followed by a space.

14. Press the right arrow key once to move the insertion point to the right of the [Para Num] code.

15. Type a period.

16. Type one or two spaces, depending on your preference.

17. Delete the [Hd Left Ind] code at the end of the style.

18. If you want a new paragraph number to appear on the next line every time you press Enter, leave the box marked Enter Key will Chain to: checked, with Same Style showing in the entry window (refer to fig. 2.26). If you don't want to insert a new paragraph number each time you press Enter, simply click that box to remove the check mark.

    The Styles Editor dialog box should now look like figure 2.27.

19. Choose OK, **C**lose, and **C**lose to exit all dialog boxes and return to your document, to see how the new style affects the document.

    As you can see, your first-level legal number is now in boldface type, centered, and followed by a period and two spaces. You can type the heading for Article 1 at this point, and it will remain on the same line, still centered and in boldface type.

    Now you'll finish by modifying the second and third levels to match figure 2.21.

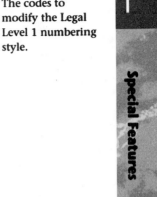

Fig. 2.27
The codes to
modify the Legal
Level 1 numbering
style.

Special Features

20. Return to the Edit Outline Definition dialog box by choosing the **Op**-tions button from the Outline Feature Bar; then choose **D**efine Outline, Edit.

21. Move the highlight bar in the **L**evels list box to the second level (shown as 1.1); the highlight bar in the **A**ssociated Style list box should move to Legal 2.

22. Choose **E**dit Style.

23. In the **C**ontents window of the Styles Editor, press Ctrl+Tab to insert a [Left Tab] code as the first code in that window.

> **Note**
>
> Because the Tab key by itself is used to move the focus within the dialog box from button to button, you cannot simply press Tab to insert this code.

24. Move the insertion point to the right of the [Para Num] code using the right arrow key.

25. Delete the [Hd Left Ind] code.

26. Type a period.

27. Type either several spaces, or press Ctrl+Tab again to insert another [Left Tab] code (to move the text that follows the paragraph number over to the next tab stop).

28. Choose OK.

29. Move the highlight bar in the **L**evels: list box down to the third level (depicted as 1.1.1). Again, verify that the Associated Style is Legal 3.

30. Choose **E**dit Style again.

31. Because you want to indent subparagraphs to distinguish them from the main paragraphs (refer to fig. 2.21), the first code inside the Contents window this time should be either a [Hd Left Ind] or a [Hd LeftRight Indent] code, depending on your preferences (choose Fo**r**mat, **P**aragraph and either **I**ndent or **D**ouble Indent).

32. Now repeat steps 22 through 27 to insert the remaining codes.

33. When you have finished, choose all of the OK and Close buttons you see to return to your document.

34. Before you lose all these changes, save the document to your hard disk. Remember the filename you give it, because you are going to return to this file in a few moments.

Now the Legal Outline Definition for this document will create the headings and paragraph number styles shown in figure 2.21. (You can continue to modify levels 4 through 8 in the same fashion if you choose to.)

Using the Legal Outline Definition

Using the style you just defined is simple; just type your text after each of the paragraph numbers as they appear in your document.

If you checked the box marked E**n**ter Key will Chain to: when creating the Legal Outline Definition earlier, every time you press Enter a new paragraph appears on the next line. This is because the outline definition you have created chains to itself every time you press Enter.

To change the Paragraph Number down a level, just press the Tab key; to move back up a level, press Shift+Tab.

What if you don't want a number on a particular paragraph? Just click the T button on the Feature Bar or press Ctrl+T to turn off the outline. Click or press Ctrl+T again to turn the outline back on again and get the next number when you are ready for it.

What if you want to rearrange paragraphs that are already numbered in an outline? You could do a cut-and-paste, or you could use the up and down arrows found on the Outline Feature Bar. With the insertion point at any location within the paragraph you want to move, clicking the up or down arrow will move the entire paragraph in that direction, automatically causing renumbering of the paragraphs as they pass each other by. Clicking the right arrow button moves the paragraph down one level, and clicking the left arrow button moves the paragraph up one level.

Saving the New Legal Outline Definition

As you can see, modifying an outline definition to get it just right takes some effort. You surely do not want to repeat all 34 steps you just went through for every contract you create.

The outline definition you just created was saved with the document, but it will not affect the default values for legal outlines defined in future documents unless you take further action. To save this outline definition for use in future documents, you need to save it in a template (either the Standard Template or a custom template that you create). For more information on doing this, see Chapter 7.

Or, you can put an outline definition stored in one document into a new document. Let's see how this is done.

1. Open a new document window.

2. Turn on the Outline Feature Bar by choosing **T**ools, **O**utline.

3. Choose **O**ptions, then **D**efine Outline.

4. Choose **O**ptions from the Outline Define dialog box.

5. Choose R**e**trieve from the drop-down list that is displayed.

   The Retrieve Outline Definitions From dialog box will appear, as shown in figure 2.28.

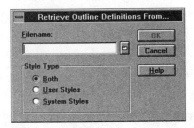

Fig. 2.28
Retrieving an outline definition from another document.

6. Type the path and filename of the document you saved earlier in this chapter (or use the File Insert icon at the end of the **F**ilename entry field to find the file).

7. Choose OK when the correct path and filename are displayed.

8. Answer **Y**es to the `Overwrite current styles?` message box that appears.

WordPerfect will insert the outline definition you created earlier into your new document, where you can save and retrieve it later.

> **Note**
>
> The program appears to have a bug that causes the level 1 style codes to be omitted from the imported outline definition in some cases. Generally, the program will copy all levels below level 1 correctly. To correct this problem, after you have retrieved the outline definition as shown above, retrieve all styles from the same source document by choosing Format, Styles, Options, Retrieve and following the same steps as above for retrieving outline definitions. This may overwrite some preexisting styles in your target document, however.

A Custom Outline Style for a Brief

Now let's take a look at one more example of how outlines can make life much easier for one common word-processing task: writing a brief.

You may not think that Outline is a very useful feature for writing a brief, since few of the paragraphs in a brief are numbered. But as mentioned earlier, Outline is useful in many ways, not only to create traditional outlines but also to help create highly structured documents that are easier to follow and understand. Plus, many courts, especially appellate courts, require tables of contents for briefs of any length; the Outline feature can fully automate this chore.

Take a look at the first page of the sample brief shown in figure 2.29. All the headings, including the subheading marked A near the bottom of the page, are parts of a customized outline definition. The text that falls between the headings is not part of the outline at all.

At this point it's not necessary to go through the steps necessary to create this type of an outline; it is included as the special outline style named Brief in a template of the same name included on the Applications Disk.

> **Tip**
>
>
> On the Disk
>
> The Brief outline style is contained in the BRIEF template so that you can easily retrieve and use that definition. For help on using templates, see Chapter 7, "Using Templates."

**IN THE THE COURT OF COMMON PLEAS
OF YOKNAPATAWPHA COUNTY,
MISSISSIPPI**

THE ESTATE OF WILLIAM
FAULKNER, a dead white male;

Plaintiff

v.   No. 513414 of 1994

KEN CHESTEK, an author of
technical non-fiction;

Defendant

**BRIEF IN SUPPORT OF MOTION FOR
INJUNCTIVE RELIEF**

I. FACTS

William Faulkner died a long time ago. He wrote a lot of books about people in a fictional county he called Yoknapatawpha County. Recently, an author of computer books started writing examples for his book and ripped off the name Yoknapatawpha County for his screen shots. Mr. Faulkner is probably rolling over in his grave even as the Court reads this Brief.

II. ISSUES

1. May a living author of computer books take advantage of the inventions of the creative genius of a literary giant, merely because that author is dead and can no longer defend himself?

2. Is the risk of rolling over in a grave a sufficient threat of irreparable harm to justify equitable relief?

III. DISCUSSION

A. **It is Unfair Competition for a Living Author to Rip Off the Inventions of a Deceased Author Who Can No Longer Defend His Creations**

It is beyond cavil that an author who is dead is in no position to protect his

Fig. 2.29
A sample brief, with headings derived from an outline.

To understand how the Brief outline style works, and to see what steps it is saving you, take a look at the codes used to create the headings shown in figure 2.29. Follow these steps:

1. Choose **F**ile, **N**ew.

    Choose **F**ile, **T**emplate.

2. Find the description of the BRIEF.WPT template in the list box.

    Highlight the BRIEF template in the list box.

> **Note**
>
> If that template does not appear in your listing, it is because the template was not installed in the correct location when you installed the files from the Applications Disk, or you have changed your preferences to reflect a different location for templates after you installed the Applications Disk files.

3. Choose **S**elect.

   Choose OK.

   The template supplied on the Applications Disk will automatically start two macros, the first of which writes or retrieves a case caption and the second of which helps you write a title for the brief. The operation of these macros is described in Chapter 10, "Litigation Documents." For now, just cancel them by choosing Cancel in the macro's dialog box. You will then see a new, apparently blank, document window. But this new document is based on the BRIEF template, which defines an outline style also called Brief. To view the codes in that outline definition:

4. Choose **T**ools, **O**utline.

   Notice that the outline definition now in the Outline Feature Bar is Brief, the new definition in this template.

5. Click the **O**ptions button; then choose **D**efine Outline.

6. Choose **E**dit.

   Before editing, first take a look at the codes used to create the main headings (that is, the major subdivisions of the brief, such as Facts, Discussion, etc.).

7. With the first level highlighted in the Edit Outline Definition dialog box, choose **E**dit Style.

   You should see the Styles Editor dialog box shown in figure 2.30.

   This is how all the codes in the **C**ontents editing window affect the appearance of the first level of this outline definition:

   ■ [Hd Center on Marg] centers the text appearing on that line.

   ■ [Large>] turns on the Large relative size attribute.

   ■ [SmCap>] turns on the Large & Small Caps appearance attribute.

   ■ [Bold>] turns on the Bold appearance attribute.

■ [Mrk Txt ToC>] marks the beginning of a first-level Table of Contents entry. By placing this marker after the appearance attributes, you can generate a table of contents which will display the entry in normal type. For more information on using Tables of Contents, see Chapter 4.

■ [Para Num] displays the first-level Paragraph Number for this style (in this case, an uppercase Roman numeral).

■ The two diamonds immediately after the [Para Num] code are just a visual representation of two spaces. They are here so that when you turn on this level of the outline, your text will be automatically offset by two spaces from the paragraph number.

■ You may not be able to see all of the next code, but that is not important; it simply marks the location at that WordPerfect will insert the user's text. All of the codes that affect that text appear to the left of that marker; all of the codes that take effect after the user's text is typed appear to the right of the marker (which in this case is on the second line of the editing window).

■ The [<Mrk Txt ToC] code marks the end of the item.

■ The [<Large], [<Bold], and [<Sm Cap] codes simply turn off the attributes that were turned on before the text.

■ Finally, because most briefs are required to be double-spaced, the final [Ln Spacing] code changes line spacing to double.

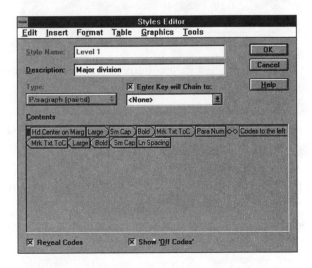

Fig. 2.30
The codes used to create the first-level style in the Brief outline definition, as shown in Reveal Codes.

You can edit any of these codes to suit your preferences. You can even delete the [Para Num] code (and its two trailing spaces) if you prefer not to number the major headings of your brief.

This outline definition has a few more wrinkles. They're in the second-level definition, so let's take a look at that one too:

8. Choose Cancel (or choose OK to save any changes you made).

9. In the Edit Outline Definition dialog box, move the highlight bar in the left window down to the second level.

10. Choose **E**dit Style again to display the Styles Editor for the second level of this definition (see fig. 2.31).

Fig. 2.31
The codes used to create the second-level style in the Brief outline definition.

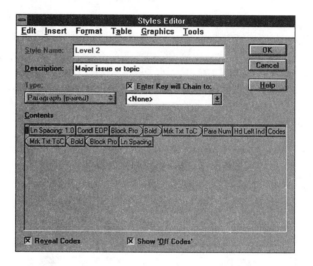

This level uses only one appearance attribute, [Bold>][<Bold]. But take a look at the other codes in the **C**ontents editing window:

■ The first code, [Ln Spacing], changes line spacing back to single spacing, in case the heading runs longer than one line (as it does in figure 2.29).

■ The [Condl EOP] is a Conditional End of Page code; it forces a soft page break if it falls within (in this case) three lines of the bottom of a page (so that the heading will appear with at least some text below it on the page on which it appears).

■ The [Block Pro>] code (coupled with its mate [<Block Pro] after the text) ensures that the heading will not be broken across a page.

■ The [Mrk Txt ToC>] code, in this case, marks the beginning of a *second-level* table of contents entry (again inside all formatting codes to ensure a normal appearance in the table of contents itself).

- Finally, the [Hd Left Ind] code, which appears after the [Para Num] code, indents the text of the heading, creating the hanging indent effect seen in figure 2.29.

Levels 3 and 4 of the Brief outline definition are very similar to level 2, although they use slightly different formatting and appearance attributes. Levels 5 and 6, however, are a bit different. Level 5 simply inserts a tab, an Arabic numeral followed by a period, and another tab, so that you can create a simple numbered paragraph (such as the two numbered paragraphs under the Issues heading in figure 2.29). Level 6 inserts an Indent code first, then a tab, a small letter enclosed in parentheses, and another tab, to create a simple indented subparagraph.

Figure 2.32 shows the six levels defined in the Brief outline definition.

> I. LEVEL ONE — MAJOR DIVISION
>
> A.   Level Two — Major Issue or Topic (Note that This Level is Indented and Single Spaced, in Boldface Type
>
>   1.   *Level Three — Sub-issues or topics, also indented and single-spaced, and in bold italic type*
>
>   a.   *Level Four — Sub-sub issues or topics, in italics only, also indented and single-spaced*
>
>   1.   Level Five. This level does not include any Table of Contents codes
>
> (all of the first four levels do). Use this level if you want to create a simple
>
> numbered paragraph with no special appearance attributes; since it is such a
>
> low level it will be reset to 1 each time you move to a new major issue, sub-issue
>
> or sub-sub-issue.
>
>   (a)   Level Six. This is similar to Level Five in that it does not appear
>
>   in the Table of Contents. Its only difference is that it is indented and uses a
>
>   different type of number at the beginning, to distinguish it from a regular
>
>   numbered paragraph. This level will be reset back to (a) when you insert a
>
>   new numbered paragraph at level 5.

Fig. 2.32
The six levels of the Brief outline definition.

I

Special Features

Collapsing an Outline

Another feature of Outlines may be quite useful for anybody who writes at the computer: collapsing. This feature helps you visualize the structure of the document you are creating, thus helping you organize your thoughts and your writing.

"Collapsing" an outline means hiding the text and showing only those outline levels that you choose to show. Here's an example that demonstrates how this works.

Consider the brief shown in figure 2.29. Because it was created with the Brief outline style described earlier, you can collapse the outline to get a "big picture" of the structure of the brief. To view only the major divisions of the brief, do the following:

1. With the document in the active window, display the Outline Feature Bar by choosing **T**ools, **O**utline.

2. From the Outline Feature Bar, choose Show Outline **L**evels.

 Skip this step.

3. From the drop-down list of the outline levels, choose 1.

 Click the button marked 1 immediately following the word Show: on the Outline Feature Bar.

All text, and all level headings lower than the first level, will vanish, leaving only the first-level headings on screen. The brief now looks like figure 2.33.

Fig. 2.33
The sample brief, showing only the first-level headings.

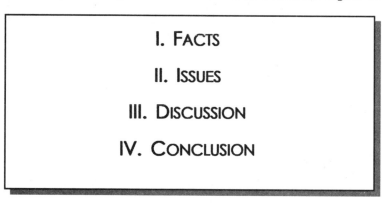

I. FACTS

II. ISSUES

III. DISCUSSION

IV. CONCLUSION

The disappearance of your text may alarm you at first, but don't worry; it is still safely tucked inside of your document, ready to be recalled whenever you want to see it. It is stored in some new codes, named [Hidden Txt], which have been inserted into your document; they are visible in Reveal Codes (see fig. 2.34).

Suppose you now want to take a little wider view of the brief, including all subheadings (down to level 4, the last level in the Brief outline style for subheadings). Simply choose level 4 from the drop-down list under Show Outline Levels on the Outline Feature Bar (or, in version 6.0, click the button marked 4 in the group of numbered buttons). Your view of the document will change to appear as shown in figure 2.35.

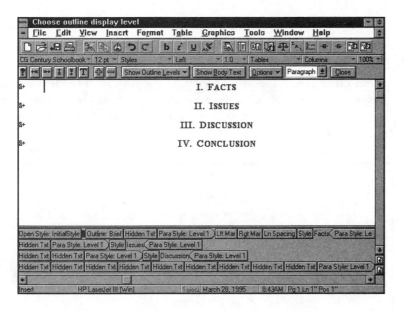

Fig. 2.34
The sample brief
showing only
Level 1 headings,
shown in Reveal
Codes.

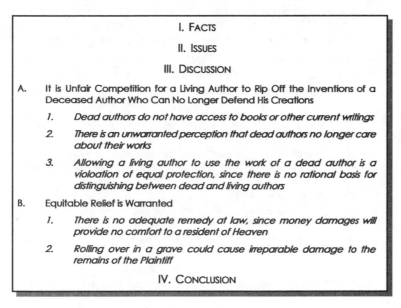

Fig. 2.35
The sample brief,
now showing all
subheadings down
to level 4.

If you want to include all of the numbered subparagraphs (including the issues which were placed in such paragraphs in the sample brief), display level 5 or 6 instead.

Notice that the captions and all text have been hidden, including the caption of the case. If you want to open up just one section of the text so you can work on it, while leaving the rest of the text hidden, do the following:

1. With the outline collapsed, place the insertion point on the heading for the level you want to reopen.

2. Click the + button on the Outline Feature Bar.

That section of the brief will open up, displaying all of the text in that section. You can then write or edit that section of the text. Figure 2.36 shows the sample brief, displaying the levels of headings and one section of text.

Fig. 2.36
The sample brief, with one section of text open to be edited.

> I. FACTS
>
> II. ISSUES
>
> 1.   May a living author of computer books take advantage of the inventions of the creative genius of a literary giant, merely because that author is dead and can no longer defend himself?
>
> 2.   Is the risk of rolling over in a grave a sufficient threat of irreparable harm to justify equitable relief?
>
> III. DISCUSSION
>
> A.   It is Unfair Competition for a Living Author to Rip Off the Inventions of a Deceased Author Who Can No Longer Defend His Creations
>
> It is beyond cavil that an author who is dead is in no position to protect his creative genius against its unauthorized use in silly ways by authors who have the advantage of still being alive. There are several reasons for this.
>
>   1.   *Dead authors do not have access to books or other current writings*
>
>   2.   *There is an unwarranted perception that dead authors no longer care about their works*
>
>   3.   *Allowing a living author to use the work of a dead author is a violation of equal protection, since there is no rational basis for distinguishing between dead and living authors*
>
> B.   Equitable Relief is Warranted
>
>   1.   *There is no adequate remedy at law, since money damages will provide no comfort to a resident of Heaven*
>
>   2.   *Rolling over in a grave could cause irreparable damage to the remains of the Plaintiff*
>
> IV. CONCLUSION

To rehide that section of text, with the insertion point anywhere within that section simply click the – button in the Outline Feature Bar.

To redisplay the entire text of a collapsed outline, click the All button that follows the numbered buttons in the Show section of the Feature Bar.

Moving Families of an Outline

Users of versions 5.1 or 5.2 of WordPerfect may be familiar with a feature of that program that allowed you to move a family of entries in an outline. For example, if you moved a second-level heading to a new position in the outline, in the process all third-level and lower entries subordinate to that heading went along with it.

You can still do this in versions 6.0 and 6.1, but the way to do it is not as obvious, because there is no longer a menu item marked Move Family. To see how to do it requires referring once again to the sample brief shown in collapsed form in figure 2.36.

Suppose you decide that your second argument, dealing with the propriety of equitable relief, is more important than the first argument, which deals with unfair competition. You wish to move the second argument ahead of the first, including all of the subarguments underneath it.

To move outline entries, you can use the up, down, left, and right arrows at the left side of the Outline Feature Bar. Simply place the insertion point in the heading you wish to move, and click the appropriate button to move it up or down in the outline (using the up and down arrow keys), or up or down a level (using the right and left arrow keys).

Here's the catch, however: the up and down arrow keys will only move the entry in which the insertion point is located. Thus, if you have the first four levels of the outline displayed, and you move one of the second-level headings, the entries subordinate to that heading *will not move with it*. This could scramble your brief in a hurry.

To ensure that subordinate headings and related text move with the higher-level headings, *collapse the outline down to the level you are moving*. Thus, if you want to move a second-level heading up, click the 2 button to collapse the outline down to the second level, hiding the third and lower levels. Now use the up or down arrow keys to move the second-level heading to where you want it. When you have it where you want it, show more levels and you will see that the subordinate entries have moved with the level 2 heading.

Cross-Referencing

Counters, automatic paragraph numbers, and outlines solve one common word-processing problem: the need for manually renumbering all paragraphs after one or more paragraphs are added or deleted in the revision process. But they create, or at least exacerbate, another common problem: the need to correct all of the cross-references within the document.

Lawyers use cross-references all the time. Rather than repeat all of the powers available to executors, trustees, or other fiduciaries under a will, for example, most lawyers draft wills that gather all of those powers into a separate article, and then refer to it at appropriate locations elsewhere in the will. However, when you add or delete a new article, you have to update all of those references by hand (or word the cross-reference in such a way as to delete all reference to the number of the article being referred to, rendering the reference less useful).

Happily, WordPerfect includes a solution to this problem too. It is called the Cross-Reference feature, and it allows you to build cross-references not only to paragraph numbers, but also to page numbers and footnote numbers, among other things.

An example of this feature occurs in the sample contract shown previously in figure 2.21. Note that in Paragraph 2.1 it contains two references to other parts of the contract. The Cross-Reference feature of WordPerfect generated these references. Here's how they are created:

Cross-reference codes work in groups. You need to insert (a) a single *target* code at the location of the item being referred to, and (b) a related *reference* code that displays the reference itself, at whichever locations refer to the target. In the case of the example contract, the numbers 3.1 and 4 in Paragraph 2.1 are the *references*; they refer to *target* codes located in, respectively, Paragraph 3.1 and Article 4 later in the document.

Each grouping of target and reference codes has a unique name, so that WordPerfect can insert references to the correct location. Since you may refer to the same paragraph or item more than once in any document, you may have any number of reference codes with the same name; but there can be only one target with that name.

Exactly how were the cross-references in figure 2.21 created?

Let us suppose that, when the contract was first typed, the cross-references were inserted manually; that is, Paragraph 2.1 included the typed characters 3.1 and 4 rather than any cross-reference codes. You now want to return to that document and replace those typed characters with Cross-Reference codes. Do the following:

1. Choose **T**ools, Cross-Re**f**erence.

   The Cross-Reference Feature Bar will appear. Because you want to tie your references to paragraph numbers, the first thing you need to do is set that option in the first button on that Feature bar.

2. Choose **R**eference on the Cross-Reference Feature Bar and select Paragraph/**O**utline from the drop-down list, as shown in figure 2.37.

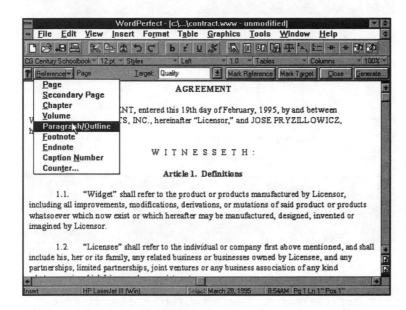

Fig. 2.37
Setting the type of reference to Paragraph/Outline on the Cross-Reference Tool Bar.

Note that the designation Paragraph/**O**utline now appears next to the **R**eference button in the Feature Bar, giving you a visual confirmation of the type of reference you're about to create.

The first cross-reference you want to insert will be to Paragraph 3.1 of the contract, dealing with the payment of royalties. You'll need to provide a name for this target so you can tie your references to the correct location.

3. Click in the **T**arget entry window in the Feature Bar; then type **Royalty**.

4. Move the insertion point to the location in the document where you want to insert this target code (in this example, just after the [Para Style: Legal 2>][Style] code pair that begins Paragraph 3.1.

5. Choose Mark T**a**rget from the Cross-Reference Feature Bar.

   The sample contract, shown in Reveal Codes, looks like figure 2.38 at this point.

   Next, you'll need to insert the reference code.

6. Move the insertion point to the location in the document where you need to refer to the paragraph dealing with royalties (in this example, near the end of the third line in Paragraph 2.1).

Fig. 2.38
The sample contract, with the Royalty target code inserted, shown in Reveal Codes.

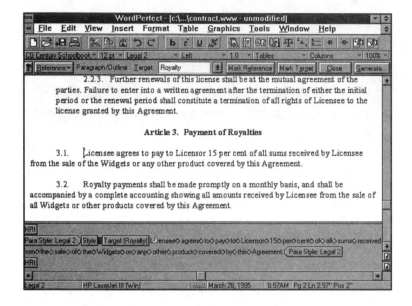

7. Delete any manual (or *hard-coded*) reference to Paragraph 3.1.

8. From the Cross-Reference Feature Bar, choose Mark Reference.

   The contract, shown in Reveal Codes, now looks like figure 2.39.

Fig. 2.39
The reference code tied to the Royalty target, shown in Reveal Codes.

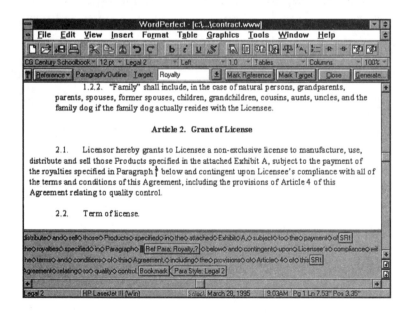

Notice that, in Reveal Codes, there is a [Ref Para] code, but in the document window there is only a question mark. This is because you need to perform one last step in order to allow the reference code to find the target code: you must *generate* the cross-reference. But, since the process of generating references will find all cross-references (as well as tables of contents and other items) at one time, you need to do this only once. Since you have other cross-references to create in this document, you'll wait until the end of this operation to generate the cross-reference.

9. Repeat steps 3 through 8 to create a cross-reference to Article 4, changing the name of the target from "Royalty" to "Quality."

10. Mark all other cross-references in a similar fashion.

11. From the Cross-Reference Feature Bar, choose **G**enerate; then choose OK.

The final document, with all cross-references generated, should look in Reveal Codes like figure 2.40.

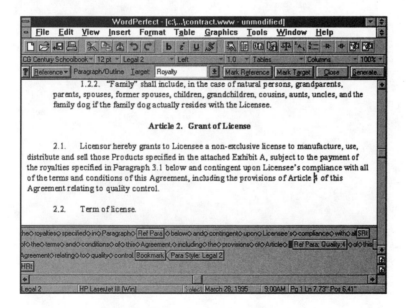

Fig. 2.40
The final contract, with all cross-references marked and generated, in Reveal Codes.

You can use Cross-Reference to create references to page numbers (for example, in a brief), footnotes or endnotes, counters, and other numbering schemes.

From Here...

As you can see, WordPerfect provides a dizzying array of options for creating headings, automatic numbers, and cross-references. It may take a little while to absorb the nuances of how these options work, but once you master the concepts, you will discover that they can make the creation of highly structured documents much easier.

The next chapter abandons substance for form as you look at the many ways WordPerfect can make you look good on paper. The chapters discuss the following:

- Using fonts
- Using codes to change the appearance of text
- Headers and footers
- Using boxes, graphic lines, and borders for visual effect

Tricks with Typography

We all know that substance is more important than form. That's why Chapter 2, "Outlines, Numbers, and More," precedes this chapter. Chapter 2 showed various ways in which you can make your documents more structured and therefore more substantively useful. But even though substance is more important than form, form does count! So, this chapter takes a look at how to make your documents more attractive, using some of the many tools WordPerfect provides.

Most of the topics covered in this chapter assume that you have a printer capable of printing graphics. Almost every printer on the market today has this capability, so the chances are excellent that your printer can do this. If you have a laser printer, you should be able to do everything this chapter describes.

In this chapter you learn how to:

- Use fonts
- Use codes to change the appearance of text
- Add headers and footers
- Use boxes, graphic lines, and borders for visual effect

Using Fonts

The ever-falling price and ever-increasing capabilities of laser printers have made most other printing technology obsolete. It is a rare office these days that still has an operational daisy-wheel or dot-matrix printer. The speed, quiet operation, and outstanding output of laser printers have made them a nearly universal standard even in the smallest offices.

It is therefore surprising to read so many legal documents still printed in the same old monospaced 10-character-per-inch Courier typeface. Why spend several thousand dollars on a computer and top-quality printer to produce documents that look like they were typed on your old IBM Selectric?

This section looks at some sources of livelier-looking fonts for your professional output.

Some Definitions

First of all, what is a font? The answer may seem obvious, but it isn't necessarily what you think it is. A *font* is a typeface or style of type. There are three components to most fonts: the shape of the characters (also known as the *font face*), the size of the characters (known as the *font size*), and in most cases, the style of the font (for example, boldface, italic, or the like).

Most people think that the characters in a font are letters, numbers, punctuation, and a few special symbols. However, this is not always true. Some fonts consist of nothing but symbols. For example, Windows ships with a TrueType font called Wingdings, which replaces every character on your keyboard with an oddball symbol. The word WordPerfect, typed in the Wingdings font, becomes ✳❏❏✿☆✳❏✿✳✳▼.

Fonts fall generally into two broad categories: *monospaced* and *proportional* fonts. In a monospaced font, such as Courier, every character is the same width, even the punctuation marks. This type of font originated with the typewriter, which could move the carriage only a certain amount of space for each character typed.

Most modern fonts are proportionally spaced; that is, each character has a different width. M's and W's, for example, are much wider than I's or punctuation marks. Because computers can keep track of how wide each character needs to be as it is typed, computers allow the user to freely choose proportional fonts, which are often easier to read and have a much more polished look.

Another way to distinguish between fonts is whether the letters contain *serifs*, or little tails at the end of each line of the character. Fonts with serifs are a bit dressier and more formal, whereas fonts without serifs (also known as *sans-serif* fonts) are considered more casual.

A typical example of a seriffed font is the TrueType font Times New Roman:

ABCDEFGHIJKLMNOPQRSTUVWXYZ

A typical example of a sans-serif font is Univers:

ABCDEFGHIJKLMNOPQRSTUVWXYZ

Another way of categorizing fonts is whether they are *scalable* or *fixed*. A fixed font prints in only one size; a scalable font can be increased or decreased to any size as the need arises. The calculations for increasing and decreasing the size are handled either in the computer or in the printer's memory. Almost all modern fonts are scalable.

The size of a font is measured in *points*. This is a printer's term that is coming into common parlance, thanks to word-processing programs. A point is 1/72 of an inch. The more points there are, the larger the typeface. A point size of 12 is considered typical for a typewritten sheet of paper (that is, it compares with the old 10 characters-per-inch standard Pica, or Courier, typewriter typeface).

Hardware Fonts

Font information can be stored in one of two places: in your printer or in your computer. Although there is little practical difference between the two, the fonts stored in your printer are usually called *hardware fonts*, and those stored in your computer are called *soft fonts*.

Virtually all laser printers come with several built-in fonts (another name for hardware fonts). They almost always include 10 characters-per-inch (cpi) and 12 characters-per-inch Courier (the standard monospaced typewriter typeface), something called line printer (a very small typeface that looks like an old-fashioned computer printout), and one or more proportional typefaces, generally some variation of a roman typeface. Some printers also have slots for one or more cartridges that can contain additional fonts; these are also classified as hardware fonts. To determine what fonts are built in to your printer, consult the printer manual (or the cartridge manual if you have a font cartridge).

The wonderful thing about WordPerfect is that it allows you to have access to all of your printer's built-in fonts, including those on cartridges, without leaving your desk to push buttons on the printer. It does this when you install WordPerfect by installing a file on your computer known as a printer driver. (If you buy a new printer, you can select a new printer driver file at any time.)

The printer driver actually has several jobs. Because many printers use different commands to perform the same tasks, the printer driver file acts as a translator between your computer and your printer, taking the printing instructions from WordPerfect and translating them into the commands that will perform the correct tasks on your printer. The printer driver file also contains information about what fonts and capabilities your printer has, so WordPerfect can allow you to select those fonts from your screen and even change them as necessary in the middle of any document.

WordPerfect is constantly updating printer drivers as new printers come onto the market. If you buy a new printer and cannot find the correct printer driver file on your WordPerfect disks, you can contact either WordPerfect or the printer manufacturer to obtain the correct printer driver file; one or the other should be able to supply you with the needed file.

Soft Fonts

Soft fonts are stored in files on your computer. Because most fonts are scalable, the font files simply contain outlines of the characters; other software determines the size and expands or reduces the outlines as necessary. This happens almost instantaneously.

The price wars that have raged throughout the computer industry in recent years have probably had the biggest impact in the area of soft font packages. When soft font technology appeared not too many years ago, a typical font outline could be between $100 and $200; you would then have to manually create the sizes and styles of the font face you wanted to use. Nowadays, fonts are virtually given away with many software packages. Both Windows and WordPerfect include a wide variety of good-looking scalable fonts, virtually eliminating the need to purchase any other typeface.

Soft fonts available on your computer are also installed in your printer driver files when you set up or update a printer. In the interest of space, and because the possible combinations of printers and soft fonts are virtually endless, this book does not go into detail about how to set up your printer; you can consult the WordPerfect manual or your printer manual for more help with this.

Printer Control

It's important to mention a few more things about controlling your printer from within WordPerfect. WordPerfect gives you two different ways to control your printer: you can use a WordPerfect printer driver, or you can use a Windows printer driver. Generally, the WordPerfect printer drivers are faster; but if you have a Windows printer driver that has already been set up for other applications, you may want to use that driver instead. Either driver gives you access to whatever fonts (hardware or software) have been installed in the driver.

You can tell whether a printer driver is a Windows or a WordPerfect driver by looking at the Printer dialog box, shown in figure 3.1. (To access this dialog box, choose **F**ile, **P**rint. The Current Printer group box at the top of the Print dialog box shows either WP or Win to designate whether the currently selected printer is a Windows or a WordPerfect printer driver.)

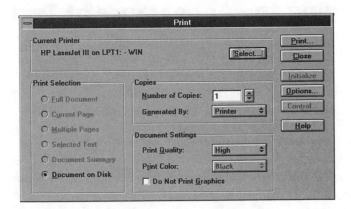

Fig. 3.1
The Print dialog box, showing the currently selected printer.

In version 6.1, you can display all currently available printer driver files by choosing **S**elect and displaying the drop-down list under Sp**e**cific Printer; Windows drivers are preceded by a Windows icon, and WordPerfect drivers are preceded by a WordPerfect icon.

You may be wondering what happens if you create a document on one machine and then put it on a disk and take it to another computer with a different printer. Or what if you get a new printer, or just select a different printer driver? Will all of the fonts you used in the document become garbled if the same fonts aren't on the new printer?

WordPerfect does its best to make documents portable from computer to computer and from printer to printer. When a document is saved, information about the printer it was created for is stored in the document itself. When the document is opened, WordPerfect immediately checks to see if the same printer is selected. If not, WordPerfect determines what the current printer is and automatically adjusts the fonts used in the document to the nearest matching fonts on the printer currently selected for the computer. These font changes are called *automatic font changes*.

For the most part, WordPerfect does a pretty good job in choosing new fonts to represent the original ones. There is an occasional hiccup, however; for example, early versions of WordPerfect 6.0 had some trouble converting documents created for WordPerfect 5.2, selecting a typeface with the Greek alphabet as the replacement font (thus giving new meaning to the phrase "Greeking a screen display"). If you experience problems like that, simply go to the Font dialog box (Format, Font) and select a font that uses the English alphabet.

Changing the Appearance of Text

With that introduction to fonts and printer control, you're ready for a discussion of how to use all the available fonts in your documents. There are two basic ways to do this: specific font changes and appearance attribute changes. Both techniques are useful for different purposes.

Specific Font Changes

A specific font change specifies precisely which font face, font style, and font size you want to use. Its advantage is that it gives you much more control over the precise font that appears in your document; its disadvantage is, if you use many of them in a document and later change your mind about the font you want to use, you may have to search through your document for all of them and change all of them.

The advantage of making specific font changes is that it gives you much more control over the precise font that appears in your document; its disadvantage is, if you change fonts frequently in a document and later change your mind about the "base" font you want to use, you may have to search through all of the font change codes and change all of them individually. If you are changing font families (for example, from Times New Roman to Univers), you have no choice but to use a specific font change because soft font changes cannot affect the font face. However, if all you want to do is change the size or style of the font for a particular section of text, you are better off changing the appearance attributes.

> **Note**
>
> Before discussing font changes, a word of caution may be in order. Just because WordPerfect makes it possible for you to use a variety of fonts in a document does not mean you should "show off" by using as many fonts as possible. Design professionals generally recommend that you use no more than two different fonts on a page. If more than two fonts are used the page may become too busy and hard to read.

To make a specific font change in the middle of a document, do the following:

1. Place the insertion point at the exact location where you want the font change to occur.

2. Choose Fo**r**mat, **F**ont.

   Choose **L**ayout, **F**ont.

   The Font dialog box appears, as shown in figure 3.2.

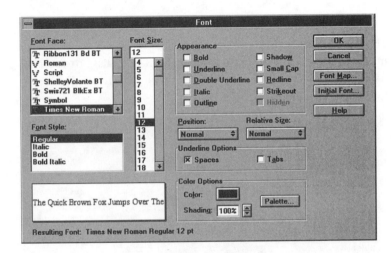

Fig. 3.2
The Font dialog box.

You use this dialog box to create both specific font and appearance attribute changes. The three controls that make specific font changes all appear on the left side of the dialog box: the **F**ont Face, the Font **S**ize, and the F**o**nt Style list boxes.

Suppose that you wanted to change from the current typeface of Times New Roman 12 point to Univers Bold 18 point.

3. Highlight the Univers entry in the **F**ont Face list box.

4. Change the F**o**nt Style to Bold (note that you may have to use the scroll bar to locate that style in the lower part of the list box).

Tip

There is a difference between specifying a bold font face and specifying a regular font face and applying the bold appearance attribute to it. Although the "resulting font" in both cases is the same, if you specify a bold font face, applying the bold appearance attribute will have no effect (that is, the type will not become double bold or toggle back to normal). The Bold checkbox in

(continues)

(continues)

the Appearance group on the right side of figure 3.2 allows you to control the bold appearance attribute; to specify a bold font face you must choose Bold in the Font Style box on the left side of the dialog box.

5. Change the Font Size to 18 point.

The Font dialog box should now look like figure 3.3. Note that the text in the window immediately below the Font Style list box has changed its appearance to give you a preview of what this font selection will look like in your document.

Fig. 3.3

Changing the font to Univers Bold 18 point.

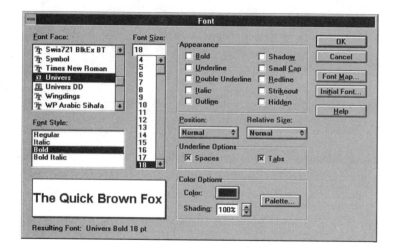

6. Choose OK to insert the new codes into your document.

To verify the insertion of the new font, turn on Reveal Codes. Notice that WordPerfect has inserted two codes into the document, as shown in figure 3.4: a [Font: Univers] code and a [Font Size: 18pt] code. The first code selects both the Font Face (Univers) and the Font Style (bold); the second code sets the point size. If you want to delete this specific font change, you must delete both of these codes.

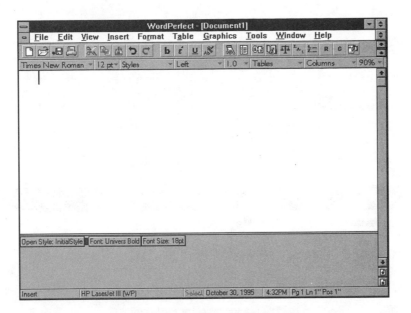

Special Features

Fig. 3.4
The two codes used to create a specific font change, shown in Reveal Codes.

> **Note**
>
> For users familiar with WordPerfect 5.1/5.2, this represents a change, because all three attributes of a specific font were combined into a single code in those versions of the program.

A specific font change can be permanent or temporary. A permanent specific font change remains in effect until the next specific font change code (if any) appears in a document. You can insert as many specific font changes in a document as you like. A temporary specific font change only affects a selected block of text; the font reverts to the original font face after that selected block of text. To create a temporary specific font change, select the text that you want to be affected by the font change. Follow steps 1 through 6 shown previously. Instead of a single font change code, WordPerfect inserts a pair of codes, before and after the selected text, to first change the font to the specified face and then return the document to the pre-existing font face.

Changing the Appearance Attributes

If you do not want to change the font face, but merely the style or size of the font, it is probably better to change the appearance attributes. That way, if you later decide to change the font face, you need only change it once; all other appearance attribute changes will follow along automatically.

An appearance attribute change relies on a pair of codes, which turn on (and then off) certain attributes, affecting only the text between them. They are quite similar to styles, which Chapter 2 discussed briefly. The attributes can affect either the appearance (or style) of the text, or they can affect its size.

Appearance Attributes

The appearance attributes that you can select are shown in a group box on the right side of the Font dialog box (refer to fig. 3.2). You can select any combination of nine different appearance attributes, shown in table 3.1.

Table 3.1   Available Appearance Attributes

Attribute	Sample
Bold	**This is a sample of the Bold attribute.**
Underline	<u>This is a sample of the Underline attribute.</u>
Double Underline	<u>This is a sample of the Double Underline attribute.</u>
Italic	*This is a sample of the Italic attribute.*
Outline	This is a sample of the Outline attribute.
Shadow	**This is a sample of the Shadow attribute.**
Small Cap	THIS IS A SAMPLE OF THE SMALL CAP ATTRIBUTE.
Strikeout	~~This is a sample of the Strikeout attribute.~~

Tip

You can use the Redline attribute (not shown above) to mark additions to a text and the strikeout attribute to indicate deletions when revising drafts of documents.

Suppose that you wanted to change from a standard Times New Roman typeface to Times New Roman Bold Italic. Follow these steps:

1. Choose Format, Font.

   Choose Layout, select Font.

2. In the Appearance group box, select the Bold and Italic check boxes. An X should appear in each one.

3. Choose OK.

Now look at your document in Reveal Codes (see fig. 3.5). Notice that the insertion point is between two pairs of codes: [Bold>][Italc>][<Italc][<Bold]. This means that any text typed at the insertion point (that is, between the two code pairs) will be both boldface and italic.

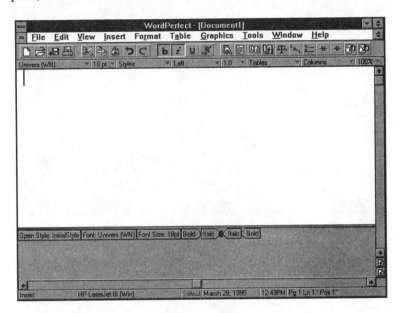

Fig. 3.5

The codes to create an appearance attribute change to bold italic.

To turn off any attribute, reverse the process (that is, deselect the item in the Font dialog box), or simply move the insertion point outside the applicable pair of codes.

Size Attributes

You can also change the size of type using a soft code known as a *relative size attribute*. Rather than specifying a precise point size, a relative size code enlarges or reduces the size of the type by a specified percentage, which you can change if you like. Thus, if you are using a 12-point typeface, using a [Large] relative size code increases the size to 120% of 12 points, or 14.4 points. If you later change the typeface to 14-point, text enclosed within the [Large] attributes automatically increases in size to 16.8 points.

Relative size codes are also entered from the Font dialog box. They work in on and off pairs just like the appearance attributes discussed in the preceding section. To enter a relative size code, do this:

1. Choose Format, Font.

Choose Layout, Font.

2. Click the pop-up list button under the heading Relative Size; it appears as shown in figure 3.6.

Fig. 3.6
Selecting a relative size attribute from the Font dialog box.

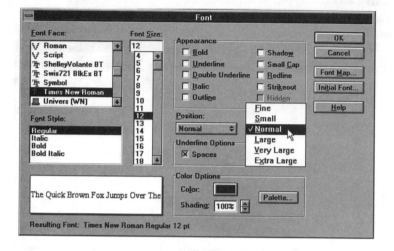

3. Select one of the relative size options from the pop-up list.

4. Choose OK to insert the codes for the selected size attribute into your document.

Table 3.2 lists the six different size attributes and the percentage change they make by default on the existing hard size code.

Table 3.2 Relative Size Codes and Their Default Values		
Attribute	**Default %**	**Sample Text**
Fine	60%	This is fine print.
Small	80%	This is small print.
Normal	100%	This is normal print.
Large	120%	This is large print.
Very Large	150%	This is very large print.
Extra Large	200%	This is extra large print.

If you want to change those percentages on your system, you can do so from the Preferences dialog box. Follow these steps:

1. Choose **E**dit, P**r**eferences.

   Choose **F**ile, P**r**eferences.

2. Choose the Print icon from the Preferences dialog box.

   The Print Preferences dialog box appears, as shown in figure 3.7. The group box at the left of the dialog box shows the current values of the relative size attributes.

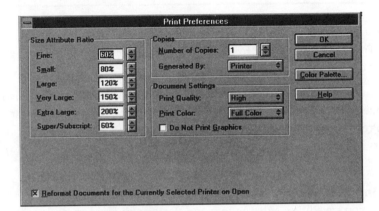

Fig. 3.7
The Print Preferences dialog box showing the default values for relative size attributes.

3. Change any of the attributes by using the arrow controls provided, or by typing the percentage you want to use.

4. Choose OK to accept your changes.

Note

WordPerfect saves the changes you make in your system files; thus they will affect all documents on your disk that use size attributes. Also note that, if you print your document on another computer, it will use the size percentages specified on that computer's setup. For this reason you should be very careful about changing these settings.

Just as with the appearance codes, to turn off a relative size code after typing text, either reverse the process listed previously or use the arrow keys to move the insertion point beyond the attribute off code.

Subscript and Superscript Text

Another type of appearance attribute change is referred to in the Font dialog box as **P**osition. This means that text can appear either above or below the baseline of the current line of text. Superscript text appears above the baseline (such as a footnote number in the text), whereas _{subscript} text appears below the baseline. For example, <small>this is superscript text</small> while <small>this is subscript text</small>.

> **Note**
>
> When using the Footnote feature, the note numbers automatically appear as super-script, so there is no need to specify that attribute manually.

You select Superscript and Subscript text attributes from the **P**osition button in the Font dialog box (refer to fig. 3.6) in exactly the same manner as you select relative size codes.

By default, both superscript and subscript text appear at 60% of the existing font size. You can also change this default value to anything else from the Print Preferences dialog box (refer to fig. 3.7). Simply change the value that appears in the last entry in the Size Attribute Ratio group box at the left side of the dialog box.

Applying Appearance and Size Attributes to Existing Text

What if you are editing existing text and decide you want to make an appearance attribute change to change either its size, appearance, or location? You can do this easily without deleting the text and retyping it. Follow these steps:

1. Select the text you want to change.
2. Display the Font dialog box (choose Fo**r**mat, **F**ont).
3. Select the attributes you want to add. You can select as many as you like.
4. Choose OK to clear the dialog box and insert the codes.

You will notice (in Reveal Codes) that the "attribute on" codes you selected have been placed at the beginning of the selected text, whereas the corresponding off codes now appear at the end of the selected text.

Combining Styles and Specific Font Changes

Specific font changes and appearance attribute changes are not the only methods of changing the appearance of your text. You can also combine a specific font change with the Style feature to create a temporary specific font change. This method gives you more power than a typical appearance attribute change, because with it you can affect not just the size and style of the font, but the basic face as well. You can change the size to anything you like; you are not limited to the six relative sizes available through the relative size codes.

Combining a specific font change with the Style feature also is more useful than a specific font change because, like an appearance attribute change, you can limit its application to only a portion of the text. This means you don't need to insert two specific font changes (one to change to the new style, another to return to the old style). And it's a snap to edit it if you change your mind later: rather than search the whole document for numerous specific font changes, you can just edit the Style once! This changes the appearance of all the text in the document that uses that Style.

Chapter 2 briefly discusses Styles. As in that chapter, it's not necessary here to go into depth about the Style feature; all you really need to know is the few steps for creating a Style that makes a temporary specific font change.

Suppose that you want to create a style that uses the TrueType font face Blackletter 686 BT to create the fancy headings for the deed form shown in figure 3.8. (Save the style in a template called OLDENGLS for future use.) Follow these steps:

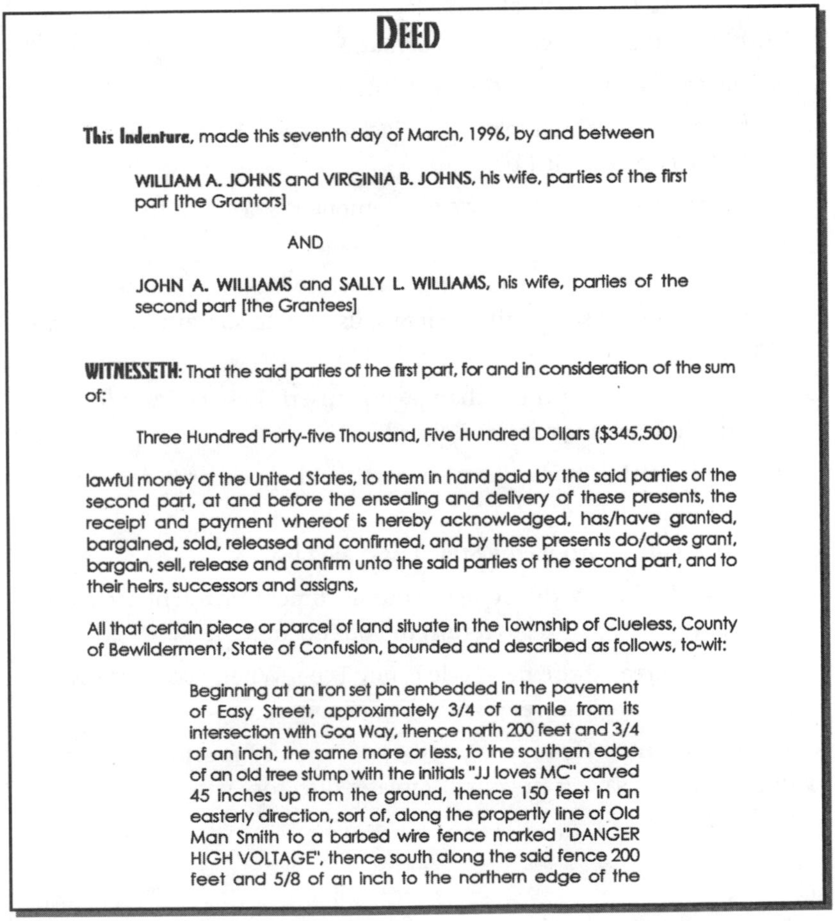

Fig. 3.8
A sample deed form using the Blackletter 686 BT typeface.

Special Features

1. Open a new document window.
2. Choose Format, **S**tyles.

   Choose Layout, **S**tyles.
3. Choose Create.
4. In the Styles Editor, type a descriptive style name in the first entry window. For this example, type **Fancy Type**.
5. In the **D**escription entry window, type a description of what the font does. In this example, type **Set up Old English lettering**.
6. Click the button marked **T**ype and select Character (paired) from the pop-up list.

   This creates a Character type of style that you can turn on and off at any point in the document.
7. From the E**n**ter Key Will Chain To pop-up list control, select None.
8. Now move the insertion point to the **C**ontents editing window by clicking there or pressing Alt+C.
9. Within the dialog box, choose Fo**r**mat, **F**ont.

   Within the dialog box, choose **L**ayout, **F**ont.
10. In the Font dialog box, select the Blackletter 686 BT font from the listing in the Font Face list box.

    If this font is not installed on your computer, select another font just to see how this works.
11. Because the 12-point version of this typeface is almost too small to read, increase the size in the Font Size list box to something larger, such as 16-point.
12. Choose OK to accept these changes and insert these codes into the editing window of the Styles Editor.

    At this point, the Styles Editor screen should appear as it does in figure 3.9.
13. Choose OK to return to the Style List dialog box.
14. If you want to apply this style to your document now, choose **A**pply; otherwise, choose **C**lose to return to your document.

    You've just created the new style Fancy Type. When you save this document, WordPerfect stores it with the document.
15. To preserve this style for use in other documents, for now, exit the document and save it in your Templates directory with the filename OLDENGLS.WPT.

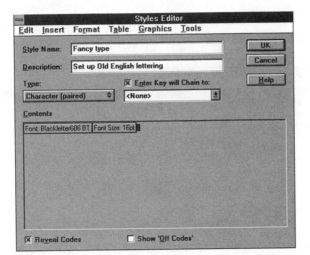

Fig. 3.9
The codes to create
a temporary font
change style.

Chapter 7, "Using Templates," explains more about how to use the Template
feature. For now, if you'd like to experiment a bit with this style to see how it
works, do the following:

1. Choose **F**ile, **N**ew.

2. Select OLDENGLS from the list box; then choose OK.

> **Note**
>
> If that template does not appear in the listing, then you did not save it to the
> correct directory for your templates in the previous exercise. See Chapter 7,
> "Using Templates," for a discussion of where templates are stored.

A new, blank document window appears. However, because this document is based on the OLDENGLS template, the Fancy Type style you
created in the previous exercise is available.

3. Choose Fo**r**mat, **S**tyles.

   Choose **L**ayout, **S**tyles.

4. Select Fancy Type from the list box showing the names of available
   styles, and then choose **A**pply.

5. Now type some text. Notice that it now appears in the Blackletter 686
   BT typeface (or whatever typeface you chose when you created the
   style).

If you turn on Reveal Codes, you'll see a pair of Style on and off codes that surround your text, as shown in figure 3.10.

Fig. 3.10
The codes that
turn on and off
the temporary
specific font
change.

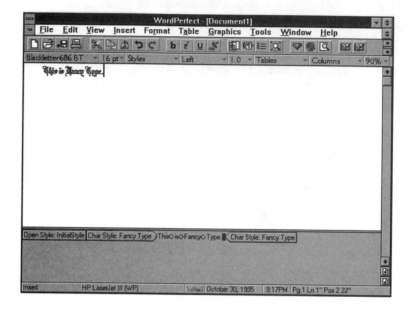

6. Move the insertion point to the right of the style off code (in this case, [<Char Style: Fancy Type]).

7. Type some additional text. You will notice that this text appears in the default font face for the document, unaffected by the temporary specific font change.

   Now to apply this new style to existing text. Skip a line or two and type some additional text in the default font, something like you see in figure 3.11.

8. Select some text you want to change to the Fancy Type style. (In the example shown in figure 3.11, select the words to the new Fancy Type style.)

9. Repeat steps 3 and 4.

   WordPerfect inserts the style on and off codes for Fancy Style at the beginning and end of the selected text, leaving the rest of the text unaffected, as figure 3.12 shows.

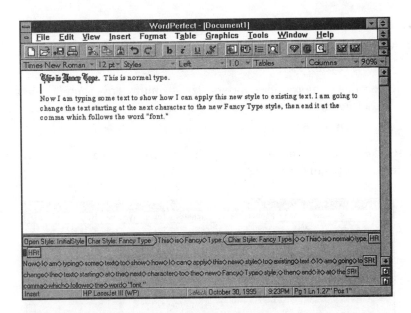

Fig. 3.11
A sample document showing how the style off code works.

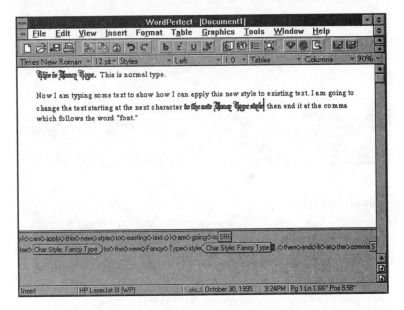

Fig. 3.12
The Fancy Type style on and off codes, inserted around the selected text.

For even more flexibility, you can combine a temporary specific font change with an appearance attribute change so that, if you decide later to change the specific font change in the Fancy Type style, it will retain the same size and appearance attributes wherever the style is used in the document. Let's see how this works by continuing the example.

1. Reselect the same text you selected in step 8.

2. Choose Format, Font.

   Choose Layout, Font.

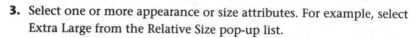

3. Select one or more appearance or size attributes. For example, select Extra Large from the Relative Size pop-up list.

4. Choose OK to insert the new attributes around the selected text.

The selected text now takes on the appearance attribute change attributes you selected, as shown in figure 3.13.

Fig. 3.13
The new appearance attribute changes that affect the Fancy Type style.

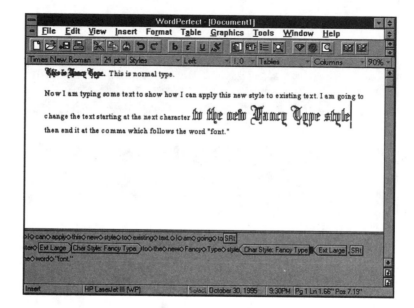

Line Justification

Another way you can dress up your documents and give them a little more polish is to use full justification. No, this does not mean coming up with a really good excuse for a mistake you made; justification refers to the alignment of characters relative to the left and right margins of your document.

Old-style typewriters aligned everything with the left margin, because that's all they could do. Each line ended at a different place as it neared the right margin, depending on when the typist threw the carriage back. (Remember typing with a manual carriage return?) The result was that the right edge of the paper had a ragged look to it.

Special Features

Thanks to technology, computers can now figure out how wide each line of type is and insert enough extra space between the letters and words to make each line the same length. The computer can distribute this space evenly throughout the line so that, in most cases, the extra space is not even noticeable.

This capability gives you the option of creating several types of *justification*, or margin alignment. You can stay with the old-fashioned left-alignment, or left justification; or you can align text on the right margin, leaving the left edge ragged. You can also center every line of the document. Or you can align text on both margins, for what is known as *full justification*.

A special code controls justification. To turn on a specific type of justification, do this:

1. Choose **Fo**r**mat, J**ustification.

   Choose **L**ayout, **J**ustification.

2. Choose the style of justification you want.

Tip

The All option is a variation of Full justification. Full justification aligns all lines with both margins, except lines that end in a [HRt] (such as the last line of a paragraph). All justification aligns every line, including those ending with a [HRt], with both margins. In most cases, you will prefer to use Full justification.

The new justification code affects both the current paragraph and all subsequent text. If you want to apply this style of justification only to a portion of your existing text, simply select the text you want to change and repeat steps 1 and 2; by doing this you insert two codes, one to turn on the new justification before the selected text and another to turn it off after the selected text.

Tip

The justification you use is a matter of personal preference. You may decide to use different types of justification for different types of documents. If you are using proportional type, Full justification is considered more "typeset quality" and more formal, and therefore might be appropriate for an appellate brief, for example. On the other hand, left justification, which creates a ragged right margin, is more informal and modern, and might be a better choice for correspondence.

Headers and Footers

This may seem like a fairly simple topic for a book like this, but you might be surprised to learn how many experienced WordPerfect users have never discovered the basic features of headers and footers. Many users still manually format each page of a document, inserting headers or page numbers by hand; others rely on the Page Numbering feature to insert unadorned page numbers.

If you have already discovered the Headers and Footers feature, go ahead and skip this section. Otherwise, read on to learn how you can use these features to add an additional touch to your professional-looking documents.

What Are Headers and Footers?

Although headers and footers sound like terms you would use on a soccer field, in a word-processing context they relate to similar things: repeating text that appears either at the top (a header) or the bottom (a footer) of every page of a document. The text might be the title of the document, or the file number, or a page number, or the current revision date of the document, or any of a wealth of other things you might want to show on every page. You can even define two separate headers and two separate footers for every document, and alternate them on even and odd pages. For example, if you're preparing a brief for the Supreme Court of the United States that will be bound in booklet form, you might want a footer that displays the page number in the left corner for the even pages and the page number in the right corner for the odd pages.

You can even change headers or footers in the middle of a document. For example, you may want to have one footer in your Table of Contents and Table of Authorities for a brief, and a different footer for the body of the brief.

Creating a Header for a Letter

Suppose that you want to create a simple header that inserts the following at the top of the second and every subsequent page of a letter: the name of the recipient of the letter, the date of the letter, and the current page number. To accomplish this, follow these steps:

1. Move the insertion point to the very top of the document.

2. Choose Format, choose Header/Footer.

    Choose Layout, Header/Footer.

   The Headers/Footers dialog box appears, as shown in figure 3.14.

Caution

It is a good idea to get in the habit of placing all headers at the very top of the document, even if you don't want them to print on the first page. You can prevent the header from printing on the first page with a single code, which you'll see in a moment. Placing the header at the top of the document makes it easy to find it later if you need to edit it. Also, if you placed the header at the top of page 2, you might accidentally delay its display by a page or more if you later add text to page one, pushing the header code farther into the document than you wanted it.

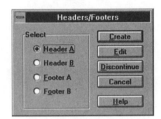

Fig. 3.14
The Headers/
Footers dialog box.

3. Leave the Header A radio button selected and choose Create.

   An odd thing happens. You see what appears to be a new document window, with a few things that look different (see fig. 3.15). This window appears to be a new document window because, in fact, it is! It is only a temporary document, however, because once you close this editing window, the text you entered is inserted into a Header code in the document from which you started. (You may notice that some functions of WordPerfect, such as Save and Save As, have been greyed out from some of the menus because those functions are not compatible with the limited purposes of this temporary document.) You will also notice that the title bar of the document reveals that you are in Header A, and that the Header/Footer feature bar has appeared underneath your Menu, Button, and Power Bars.

4. Because you want the first line of the header to be the name of the recipient, type that name on the first line of the editing window and press Enter to move to the next line.

Fig. 3.15
The editing
window for a
Header, showing
the Header/Footer
feature bar.

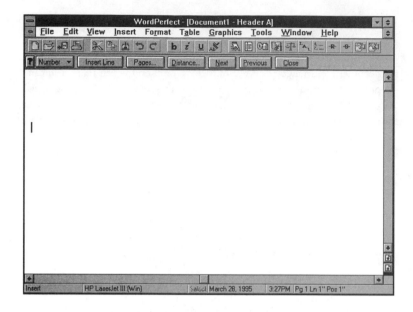

Tip

Here's where the advantage of the temporary document trick comes in. If you forget the correct spelling of the name, you can use the Window menu to switch back to the body of the letter for which you are creating the header, copy the name of the recipient to the capture buffer, and then switch back to the Header window and paste it in.

---

5. You want line two of the header to be the current date. The easiest way to insert this is to insert it from the computer's clock. Choose **I**nsert, **D**ate.

6. Choose either Date **T**ext to type the current date as text in your letter, or Date **C**ode to insert a special code that displays and prints the current date whenever the document is opened.

Tip

Use Date **T**ext whenever you want to set the date in the document so it will not change if the document is opened or printed at a later date, and use Date **C**ode if you want the date to be automatically updated as you open and edit the document on later dates.

7. Press Enter.

8. You would like for the third line of the header to contain the page number. Type the word **Page** followed by a space.

9. To display the current page number, click the **N**umber button on the Header/Footer feature bar; then choose **P**age Number.

   The number 1 is displayed in the editing window. If you turn on Reveal Codes (see fig. 3.16), you can see that this is really a [Pg Num Disp] code, which displays the current page number for each page on which the header appears.

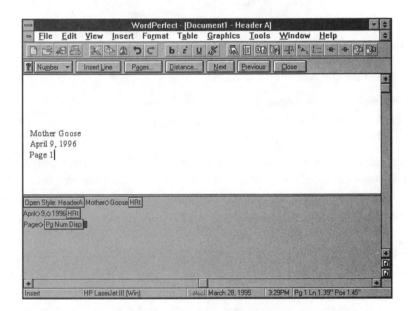

Fig. 3.16
The codes used to create the header for a standard letter.

10. Choose Close from the Header/Footer feature bar to complete your header.

    The screen returns to the document for which the header was being created. If you turn on Reveal Codes, you will notice that a [Header A] code now appears just before the insertion point. If you move the insertion point to the left of that code, it expands to show you the contents of the header you just created.

    Because you placed this Header at the very top of your document, it is now set to print at the top of page 1. This is usually unnecessary, and in the case of a letter downright silly. Although you've just created the header, you need to immediately *suppress* it so that it does not appear on page 1 of the document.

11. Choose Fo**r**mat, **P**age.

Choose **L**ayout, **P**age.

12. Choose S**u**ppress.

The Suppress dialog box appears, as shown in figure 3.17.

Fig. 3.17
The Suppress
dialog box.

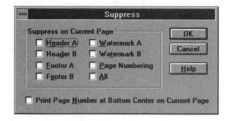

13. Select H**e**ader A; then choose OK.

A [Suppress] code now appears after the [Header] code in your document. Header A does not appear on any page with this [Suppress] code, but appears on all other pages.

To automate this process even further, you can use a macro. The Companion Disk includes a macro, HEADER.WCM, which tries to find the recipient of the letter, copies that name into a header, and places the header and a [Suppress] code at the very top of your document. All you need to do to create the type of header described in this exercise is play this macro once in your letter.

HEADER.WCM assumes that the name of the recipient is the very first line after the date in your letter. Whether you use the Date Text or Date Code feature to insert that date, HEADER.WCM should be able to find the date, and then will skip to the next line to find the name of the addressee. If the macro finds no date in your document, it pauses and allows you to manually place the insertion point on the name of the addressee.

Note

If you use the Date Text method for inserting a date in your letter, or if you simply typed the date manually, HEADER.WCM looks for the string , 199 and assumes that it has found the date. If you use a different date format, or if you run this macro in the next century, HEADER.WCM will not find the date.

Creating a Footer to Display the Document File Name

Many offices have a problem locating a document on a hard disk after it has been saved. Perhaps it is being revised several months after it was first created; or perhaps the original typist is on vacation and another typist is having trouble figuring out the organizational logic (or lack of it!) of the original typist's directory structure. For whatever reason, you don't know or can't figure out the filename or path where the document is stored.

Many people have solved this problem by creating a footer on the last page of the document that prints the file name in fine print, saving you the headache of trying to remember it. Here's how you can create one:

1. Position the insertion point at the very end of the document.

2. Choose Format, **H**eader/Footer.

   Choose **L**ayout, **H**eader/Footer.

3. Select **F**ooter B; then choose Create.

   You can use either Footer A or Footer B for this. It may be a good idea to use Footer B for this purpose, however, because you may already have a Footer A in your document, which inserts a page number or performs some other task. Whichever one you decide to use, however, you should get in the habit of consistently placing this type of footer in the same place in each document.

4. Choose Format, **F**ont.

   Choose **L**ayout, **F**ont.

5. Select the **F**ine Relative Size attribute in the Font dialog box, and then choose OK.

6. Choose **I**nsert, **O**ther.

7. Choose **P**ath and Filename from the fly-out menu.

   If you look in Reveal Codes, you will see that WordPerfect has inserted a [Filename:] code between two codes which turn on, then off, the Fine size attribute. This code inserts the path and file name for the document into the footer, in fine print.

8. Choose Close from the Header/Footer feature bar to complete your footer.

Note that this footer prints only on the last page so long as it remains the last code in the document. If you later decide to add some text to the end of your document, be sure to insert the text before the [Footer B] code at the very end of the document.

On the Disk

The Companion Disk contains the macro NAMEFOOT.WCM, which creates the filename footer just described. Simply play the macro once in any document where you want to display the path and filename of the document at the end in this fashion.

Borders and Lines

Sometimes you want to add an extra touch to a document, to make it look professionally typeset and just that much more credible. There is something about a well-presented brief, or settlement brochure, or offering circular, that says, "This is a very serious document that deserves your careful consideration."

Using a tasteful selection of proportional fonts in various sizes and styles goes a long way towards achieving that look. But sometimes you want a little more. Consider adding some lines or boxes to create visual interest in your document.

There are several ways to do this, each of which has its own set of advantages and disadvantages.

Page Borders

One of the easiest ways to add a bit of polish to a document is to use a page border. You can customize this border, which appears in the margins of your document, in many different ways. You can easily turn it off at any point; for example, you may want the border to appear only on the title page but not on the remainder of the document.

Figure 3.18 shows a rather ho-hum title page of a brief. Suppose that you wanted to add a border and make other changes to spice it up and give it more punch. Figure 3.19 shows one possible result of such a make-over. Here's how it was done.

The most obvious change is the new base font. Rather than the boring monospaced Courier font, the typeface is a proportional font with serifs (in this case a Century Schoolbook font). Any variant of the roman typeface would produce similar results.

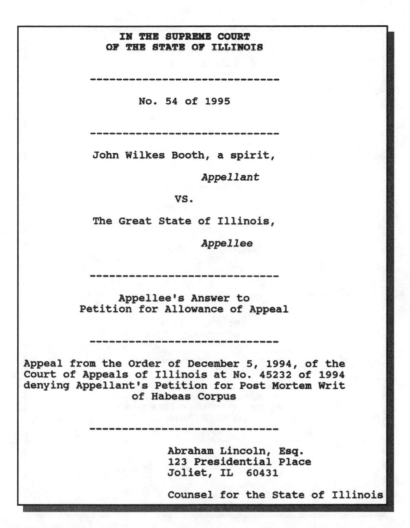

Fig. 3.18
The sample title
page of a brief.

Next, various size and appearance attributes emphasize different elements of
the title page. For example, the name of the court at the very top of the document is in Very Large type, with Small Caps and Bold effects also. The names
of the litigants and the title of the pleading also use the Small Caps attribute,
and bold and italics occur throughout.

Fig. 3.19
The same brief,
with page borders
and other features
to dress it up.

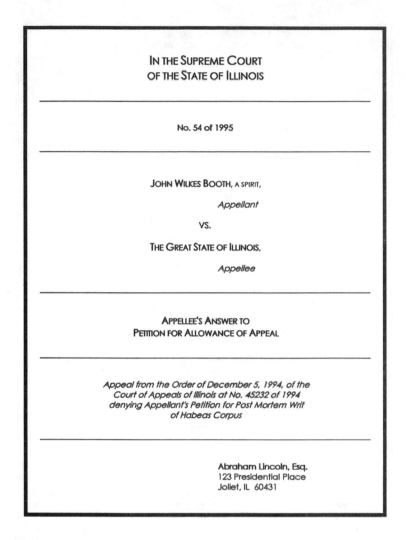

Many typists still use the underscore key or (in the case of fig. 3.18) the hyphen key to create horizontal lines. There is an easier way, as demonstrated in figure 3.19:

1. Make sure that the Underline Tabs option is selected in the Font dialog box (choose Fo**r**mat, **L**ayout, Font, and select **Ta**bs in the Underline Options group box).

2. With the insertion point at the left margin, turn on the Underline attribute (choose Fo**r**mat, **L**ayout, **F**ont, **U**nderline, or use a shortcut key or button from the Power Bar).

3. Insert a [Hd Flush Right] code (choose For**m**at, **L**ayout, **L**ine, **F**lush Right or use a shortcut key).

This inserts a single line spanning the page from the left to the right margin, as shown in several places in figure 3.19.

Finally, the entire product is wrapped in a page border consisting of a single thick line. To insert such a page border, do the following:

1. Position the insertion point at the top of the document.

2. Choose For**m**at, **P**age.

Choose **L**ayout, **P**age.

3. Choose **B**order/Fill.

The Page Border dialog box appears, as shown in figure 3.20.

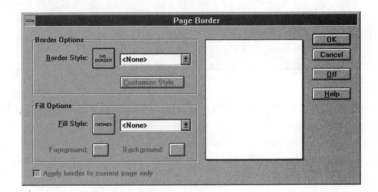

Fig. 3.20
The Page Border dialog box.

4. Choose a Border Style from the drop-down list. You can specify various thicknesses and styles of lines from the list. The brief shown in figure 3.19 uses a single Thick line.

An approximation of what the line will look like appears in the empty box on the right side of the Page Border dialog box. You can keep an eye on that box as you change styles and customize the border to get an idea of what your border will eventually look like.

5. Choose OK to insert the border into your document.

In figure 3.19, the title page is the only page of the document that uses a border. In the full brief, the title page ends with a [HPg] code; to ensure that the border does not continue past the title page, continue as follows:

6. Place the insertion point at the top of the second page (in this example, immediately after the [HPg] code).

7. From the Page Border dialog box (refer to fig. 3.20), choose **Off**.

You can customize the appearance of a page border in a variety of ways. After selecting a border style in the Page Border dialog box, choose Customize Style. You'll see the Customize Border dialog box shown in figure 3.21.

Fig. 3.21
Customizing your page border.

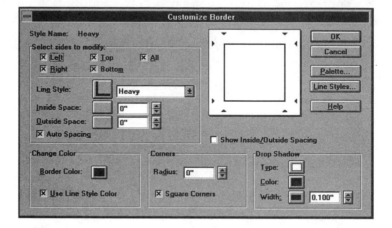

You can experiment with all the options in this dialog box, again watching the edit window in the upper-right portion of the dialog box to get an idea of what the box will look like. The possible combination of options, including line styles, shadows, rounded corners, and even color printing, is virtually endless.

> **Caution**
>
> If your printer is low on memory, you may have difficulty printing pages with borders that include too many options. In particular, using rounded corners on a page border requires a lot of printer memory.

You can even fill the box with gray shading of various densities, if you like. This option is in the Page Border dialog box, in the group box just below the Border Options controls.

Paragraph Borders

You can also create a similar type of border or fill around any paragraph in your document. This option is found under Format, Paragraph, Border/Fill and works in almost exactly the same way as the Page Border feature described in the previous section. As you edit or delete text in a paragraph that's inside a Paragraph Border, the border expands or contracts is necessary.

> You can use this feature to highlight or emphasize certain paragraphs of your text, like this paragraph.

Unlike the Page Border feature, which uses a single [Pg Border] code to turn on the border until explicitly turned off by another [Pg Border] code, paragraph borders are controlled by a paired code: [Para Border>][<Para Border]. You can therefore include more than one paragraph within the border if you choose.

To turn off the paragraph border, you can choose Off from the Paragraph Border menu, or you can simply move the insertion point beyond the [<Para Border] code.

Graphic Lines

Another way to create lines on your page is with a Graphic Line. Graphic Lines are actually graphic images created by WordPerfect, you can place them anywhere on the page. Graphic Lines overwrite any text or other image that appears in the document. They can be horizontal or vertical, in any width or length you specify, and can be displayed in combinations (for example, a thick and a thin line side-by-side). You can also edit an existing line to change its appearance if you like.

You access this feature from the **G**raphics menu, which figure 3.22 shows. Choosing **H**orizontal Line creates a default horizontal line that runs from the left to the right margin; the **V**ertical Line option creates a vertical line from the top to the bottom margin. You can edit either type of line (for example, to change its width, length, or location) after you create it. You do this by placing the insertion point immediately after the [Graph Line] code in your document and choosing Edit Line. Or, you can create a line with features you specify simply by choosing **G**raphics, Custom **L**ine.

Fig. 3.22

The options for creating Graphic Lines under the Graphics menu.

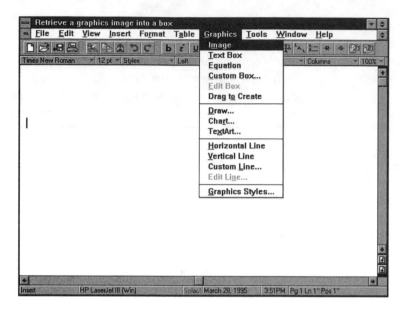

Text Boxes

WordPerfect includes a variety of other graphics options under the Graphics menu. You can include clip-art images by creating an Image box. If you have installed the proper files, you can use TextArt to squish your words into all sorts of odd shapes. You can use Draw to create new images, and you can create graphs using the Chart feature.

> **Note**
>
> If you are using WordPerfect as part of the PerfectOffice suite, you may have Presentations installed rather than Draw.

Although these features can be fun, they are not terribly useful for most law office applications, so this book does not cover them. But the Graphics menu does contain a hidden treasure that you may want to use from time to time—the Text Box feature. This gives you a handy way to create counterfeit letterhead, that is, a letterhead for your firm that is printed by your laser printer each time you write a letter, freeing you from the necessity of leaving your desk to be sure that a preprinted letterhead form is inserted in the computer at just the right moment. (This also allows you to fax documents directly from your computer that appear to have been typed on your preprinted letterhead.) If the font selection on your computer is a close enough match to the preprinted form, even a very careful reader may never notice that the letterhead was printed by the laser printer.

For example, figure 3.23 is a letterhead form that WordPerfect creates on a laser printer, every time a letter is printed, with four text boxes.

Fig. 3.23
A sample letterhead, printed by a laser printer.

Here are the steps for creating the Text Box that contains the firm name.

1. Open a new document window.

2. Choose **G**raphics, **T**ext Box.

    You see a new editing window, shown in figure 3.24, much like the Header/Footer editing window discussed earlier. This window is one of the nine available WordPerfect document windows.

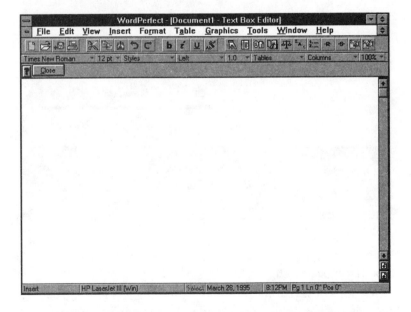

Fig. 3.24
The Text Box Editor window for creating a new text box.

3. Select a font and font size for the text in this window. This example uses the TrueType font Caslon OpenFace BT, in a 24-point size.

    If that font is not available on your printer, select any other font.

> **Note**
>
> Because you have inserted this specific font change in a text box, it affects only the text within that box; it has no effect on the remainder of the document.

4. To air out the names vertically for a more pleasing effect, this example has Line Spacing set at 1.3.

5. Type the four names of the partners in the firm, one per line, as shown in figure 3.23.

6. Choose **C**lose from the Text Box feature bar.

You return to your main document screen, which should now look something like figure 3.25 (shown in Reveal Codes).

Fig. 3.25

The text box shown in reveal codes format.

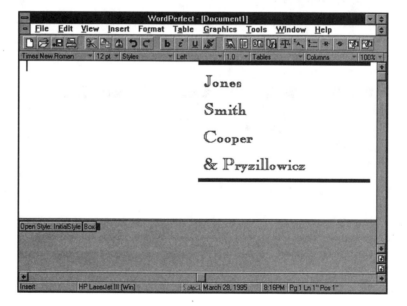

Now you need to edit the line options for the box to conform to the box that appears in figure 3.23.

7. Move the mouse pointer anywhere within the text box and click the right mouse button to display the QuickMenu shown in figure 3.26.

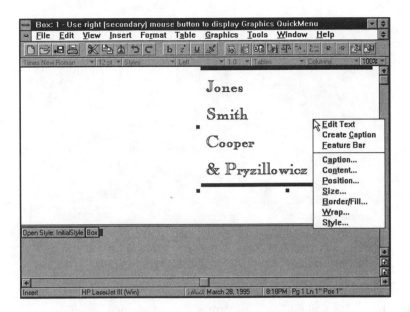

Fig. 3.26
The QuickMenu to
edit a text box.

8. Choose **B**order/Fill from the QuickMenu.

9. In the Box Border/Fill Styles dialog box, from the drop-down list
   marked **B**order Style, choose the Thick Right/Left style.

10. Then choose **C**ustomize Style.

11. In the Customize Border dialog box, deselect the Le**f**t check box in the
    Select Sides to Modify group box.

    This step ensures that the left line is *not* affected by the next change
    you make. At this point, the Customize Border dialog box should look
    like figure 3.27. Notice that there is no X in the Le**f**t check box, and
    two small arrows appear above and below the line at the right side of
    the preview window, indicating that that line is affected by any
    changes you now make to the line style.

Fig. 3.27
Preparing to make
a change to the
right line of the
text box.

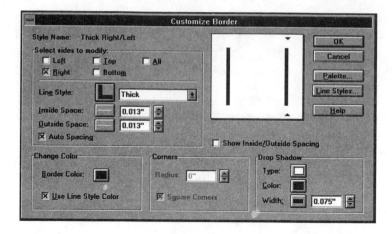

12. Now display the drop-down list marked Line Style and choose None. The right line in the preview window disappears.

13. Choose OK and OK again to return to the document.

    Notice that the text box is still much wider than it needs to be. The easiest way to size this box is by using the mouse to drag the sides of the box to the correct size.

14. Notice that the text box is still much wider than it needs to be. The easiest way to size this box is by using the mouse to drag the sides of the box to the correct size. The text box should still be surrounded by little black squares, indicating that you are still in the text box edit mode. Position the mouse over one of the two black squares that appear in the middle of either the right or left vertical edge of the text box. When the shape of the pointer turns into a two-sided horizontal arrow, click the mouse and drag the edge of the box towards the opposite side, making the box narrower (see fig. 3.28).

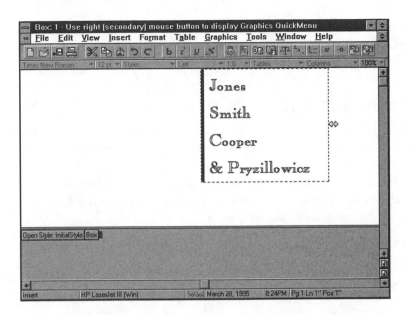

Fig. 3.28
Reducing the
width of the box
by dragging one
edge.

Finally, drag the entire box into the correct location at the upper-right
corner of the page.

15. Position the mouse anywhere within the text box. When its shape
changes to a four-directional arrow, click the mouse and drag the entire
box to the desired location, as shown in figure 3.29.

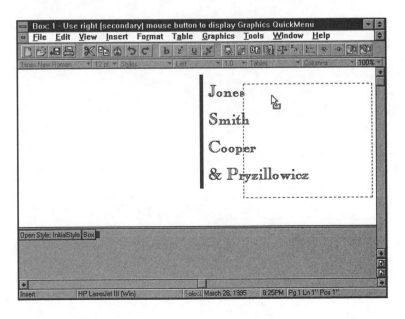

Fig. 3.29
Dragging the
completed text
box to its final
destination.

You can create the remaining text boxes in the same manner and then push them around on your screen with the mouse until the finished document looks just as you would like it to look.

From Here...

This chapter, hopefully, gave you a quick look at some of the not-so-obvious features of WordPerfect that can help you dress up your documents. The best way to learn how to use these features is to experiment with them. Be creative! A document that gets noticed because it is presented in an interesting and attractive way has an instant advantage over a competing document that relies on "the way we've always done it."

The next chapter focuses on some features of WordPerfect that were designed specifically for lawyers.

4

Footnotes, Tables, and Compare

Up to this point, this book has discussed various features of WordPerfect that, while they are very useful in the law office setting, they are useful in just about any kind of office. The program also includes a number of features that look like they were designed specifically with lawyers in mind. Who else, for example, would need to build a table of authorities?

This chapter takes an in-depth look at four features that are either designed exclusively for lawyers or are used more heavily by lawyers than by any other profession.

These features are:

- Footnotes
- Tables of Contents
- Tables of Authorities
- Compare Document

Footnotes

Lawyers love footnotes. Well, okay, maybe academic lawyers love footnotes more than other lawyers, but footnotes are still pretty heavily used by lawyers, especially those in litigation and appellate advocacy. WordPerfect has a very robust footnote feature that allows you a great deal of flexibility in creating and displaying footnotes.

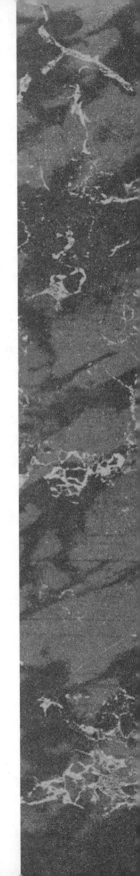

Creating Footnotes

As you've done elsewhere in this book, you learn about this feature by examining a sample document. In this case (with apologies to our academic brethren and sisteren), we use a law review article as a sample document because such writings are frequently laced with footnotes. You can follow along by trying out footnotes in any document on your computer.

The first page of the sample law review article is shown in figure 4.1.

Fig. 4.1

The first page of a sample law review article.

THE CONSTITUTIONAL IMPLICATIONS OF HOCKEY'S TWO-LINE PASS RULE: VIOLATION OF SUBSTANTIVE DUE PROCESS?

by Kenneth D. H. Chestek IV, Esq.

The[1] two-line pass rule in ice hockey is one of the most difficult rules in all of sports to conceptualize, rationalize and implement. Long overlooked in the days when hockey was not considered a "major" sport, the growth and popularity of the sport during the past decade, coupled with the enormous economic benefit which may accrue to teams (and the players who populate them) which persevere and attain the rank of champion in their sport,[2] have caused renewed interest in all aspects of the game, including the underpinnings of the more obscure rules of puck advancement (RPA's). And, of all of the RPA's in the game, the two-line pass rule is almost certainly the most difficult to understand and enforce, and is therefore probably the second most frequent source of conflict among players, coaches and referees.

This Article examines the history of the two-line pass rule, beginning from the

---

[1] Webster's New World Dictionary of the American Language defines the word "the" as giving reference to a particular person or thing. Oddly, the pronounciation of the word "the" varies depending upon whether it is followed by a consonant sound or a vowel sound; if it precedes a vowel sound, the proper pronounciation is with a long "e": "thee". The word is sometimes used as an adverb, as in "*the* better to eat you with, my dear" (*cf. Little Red Riding Hood*), but in this article we will generally employ the word in its more customary usage as a definite article.

[2] In hockey, teams compete for a large silver bowl commonly referred to as the "Stanley Cup", although it resembles a large trophy more than a tea cup.

Because most law review articles require detailed citation of authority for most assertions, as well as footnotes cross-referencing other parts of the article, you need to insert these footnotes into the sample document. There are some minor variations in the process depending on whether you are using WordPerfect in Draft or Page mode; this section discusses both screens.

To insert a footnote in Draft mode, follow these steps:

1. First, be sure that WordPerfect is set to Draft mode (choose **V**iew, **D**raft).

2. Position the insertion point at the precise location in the text where you want the footnote to appear.

3. Choose **I**nsert, **F**ootnote.

4. Choose Create from the fly-out menu that appears.

   You see a new Footnote editing window, which is one of the nine document windows that can be open at one time in WordPerfect. (This works much like the Header/Footer Create feature discussed in Chapter 3, "Tricks with Typography.") If you need to refer back to the document to create the text of your footnote, you can switch between the document and the Footnote editing window using the Window menu, or by tiling the document windows and clicking in the window you need to move to. The Footnote feature bar appears immediately above the editing window, as shown in figure 4.2.

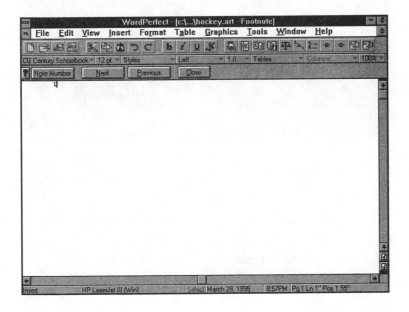

Fig. 4.2
A new Footnote editing window.

5. Type the text of your footnote.

Because you are in an ordinary editing window, a full range of formatting features are available to you, including size and appearance attributes, indentation, and so on. You can even copy and paste information between the body of any open document and the footnote if you need to.

6. When you have finished entering the text of your footnote, choose **C**lose from the Footnote feature bar.

Your document returns to the screen, as shown in figure 4.3. In this example, a footnote has been inserted immediately after the word "the" in the first line of the article; you can see the numeric representation of the footnote in the editing window and the [Footnote] code that creates it in the Reveal Codes window.

Fig. 4.3

The document with the new footnote (shown in Reveal Codes).

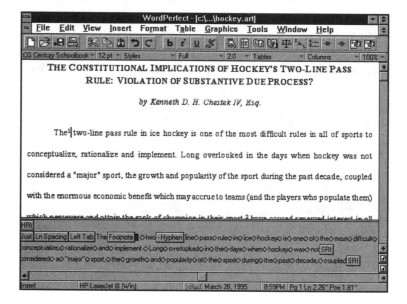

In contrast, here's how to create a second footnote in Page mode:

1. Switch the view mode to Page (choose **V**iew, **P**age).

2. Move the insertion point to the location in the text where you want the next footnote to appear.

3. Choose **I**nsert, choose **F**ootnote.

4. Choose **C**reate from the fly-out menu.

This time, you remain in the current document, but the insertion point appears at the bottom of the page, where the footnote actually appears. Previous footnotes appear as well, and the body of the text is visible above the footnotes already on the page, as shown in figure 4.4. The Footnote feature bar appears. Also, notice that the document title bar has the word "Footnote" appended to it, giving you another visual indication that the insertion point is now within a footnote.

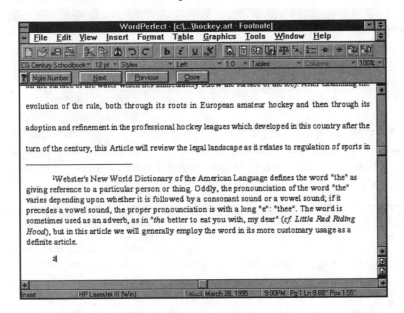

Fig. 4.4
Entering a new footnote in page mode.

5. Type the text of the second footnote, and then choose Close from the Footnote feature bar.

You once again return to the text location in the editing window that is immediately after the new footnote number. Notice, however, that because you are using WordPerfect in Page mode, you now can see the text of your footnotes at the bottom of the page; in Draft mode they were not visible on the main editing screen.

Editing Footnotes

To edit an existing footnote, once again the process varies slightly depending on whether you are using WordPerfect in Draft or Page mode.

If you are using Draft mode, the only way to return to a footnote to edit it is this:

1. Choose Insert, Footnote.

2. Because there are now footnotes in the document, the Edit option in the fly-out menu is activated; choose it.

3. Type the number of the footnote you want to enter in the dialog box that appears; then choose OK.

You see an editing window containing only the text of the footnote you specified.

> **Tip**
>
> If you want to edit other footnotes without returning to the main document window, you can use the Next and Previous buttons on the Footnote feature bar to move forward or backward through the existing footnotes in the document.

If you are using Page mode, there is an easier solution. All you need to do is click in the footnote you want to edit, and you go immediately to that footnote. When you want to return to the main document window, just click in the document.

> **Note**
>
> You cannot use the arrow keys to move the insertion point from the document to a footnote or vice versa; nor can you use them to move between footnotes.

You can also use the **I**nsert, **F**ootnote, **E**dit route to specify a footnote number to edit in Page mode.

Changing the Display of Footnotes

There are a few more important concepts about formatting footnotes. To illustrate them I've added some footnotes. Figure 4.5 shows the first two pages of the article at this point.

The format in which the footnotes appear is the default format (the format that WordPerfect first sets up). Chances are you may not like this appearance for one reason or another. Although you can enter new formatting codes in each footnote, there is a much easier way to alter their appearance.

THE CONSTITUTIONAL IMPLICATIONS OF HOCKEY'S TWO-LINE PASS
RULE: VIOLATION OF SUBSTANTIVE DUE PROCESS?

by Kenneth D. H. Chestek IV, Esq.

The[1] two-line pass rule in ice hockey is one of the most difficult rules in all of sports to conceptualize, rationalize and implement. Long overlooked in the days when hockey was not considered a "major" sport, the growth and popularity of the sport during the past decade, coupled with the enormous economic benefit which may accrue to teams (and the players who populate them) which persevere and attain the rank of champion in their sport,[2] have caused renewed interest in all aspects of the game, including the underpinnings of the more obscure rules of puck advancement (RPA's). And, of all of the RPA's in the game, the two-line pass rule is almost certainly the most difficult to understand and enforce, and is therefore probably the second most frequent source of conflict

---

[1] Webster's New World Dictionary of the American Language defines the word "the" as giving reference to a particular person or thing. Oddly, the pronounciation of the word "the" varies depending upon whether it is followed by a consonant sound or a vowel sound: if it precedes a vowel sound, the proper pronounciation is with a long "e": "thee". The word is sometimes used as an adverb, as in "*the* better to eat you with, my dear" (*cf. Little Red Riding Hood*), but in this article we will generally employ the word in its more customary usage as a definite article.

[2] In hockey, teams compete for a large silver bowl commonly referred to as the "Stanley Cup", although it resembles a large trophy more than a tea cup.

---

among players, coaches and referees.[3]

This Article examines the history of the two-line pass rule, beginning from the days when hockey was played on frozen ponds without lines of any sort (because it is impossible to paint lines on the surface of the water which lies immediately below the surface of the ice). After examining the evolution of the rule, both through its roots in European amateur hockey and then through its adoption and refinement in the professional hockey leagues which developed in this country after the turn of the century, this Article will review the legal landscape as it relates to regulation of sports in general and hockey in particular. In Part II,[4] this Article will test the modern-day validity of the rule against commonplace legal concepts such as the Equal Protection Clause, the First Amendment, and the Rule

---

[3] The most frequent source of conflict among players, coaches and referees is, of course, the use of excessive physical force in personal contacts during a contest, or at least the perception of such excessive physical force. It is quite common for one player, believing that another player has engaged in the use of excessive physical force or violence, to retaliate with physical force that would, in another setting (for example, Aunt Mabel's sitting room), be considered inappropriate or even criminal. For a complete discussion of the potentialities of criminal sanctions being imposed as a remedy for excessive force during a sporting contest, *see* Chestek, *Excessive Force During Sporting Contests: An Argument for Application of Criminal Sanctions in Order to Prevent the Giving of Bad Examples to Impressionable Children and Thereby Save Society From its Ultimate Destruction,* 40 University of Pittsburgh Law Review 1004 (1979).

[4] *See infra*, pp. 458-521.

-2-

Fig. 4.5
The first two pages of the article, with footnotes inserted.

Special Features

The Footnote Style

If you examine one of your footnotes with Reveal Codes on (see fig. 4.6), you will notice that the first code in the footnote is [Open Style: Footnote]. By changing that style, you can change all the footnotes in the document at once.

Fig. 4.6

The [Open Style: Footnote] code in a footnote.

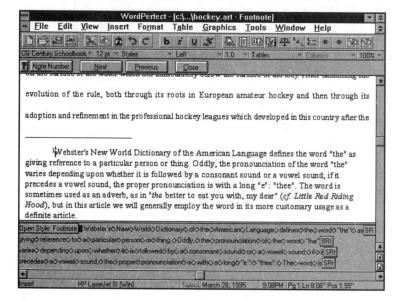

Suppose that you want to make the following changes to the appearance of all the footnotes in your document:

- You want the footnote number to be in the left margin, and the remainder of the footnote text to be indented to the first tab stop.

- You want the footnote text to appear in a smaller font size.

- You want the footnote text to be fully justified (rather than having the default left justification).

- You want to print a message in each footnote spanning two pages that indicates that the footnote continues from one page to another.

You do not edit the Footnote style in the way you might expect (that is, from the Styles dialog box under Format). Instead, here's how you make those changes:

1. If your insertion point is in a footnote, exit from the footnote by choosing **C**lose from the Footnote feature bar and return to the main body of the document.

2. Choose **I**nsert, **F**ootnote, **O**ptions.

The Footnote Options dialog box appears, as shown in figure 4.7.

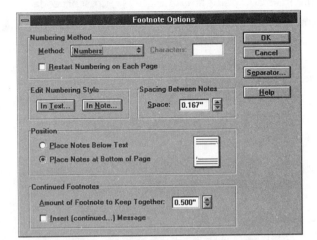

Fig. 4.7
The Footnote
Options dialog
box.

3. In the Edit Numbering Style group box, choose In **N**ote.

The Styles Editor dialog box appears; it resembles the Styles Editor you would see if editing any other type of style. The Contents editing window shows the default values for the format of the footnotes: an [Open Style: Initial Style] code (containing the same codes as the Initial Style code for the main document), a [Hd Left Tab] to indent the footnote one tab stop, and a [Footnote Num Disp] code, enclosed between a pair of [Suprscpt] codes to display the current footnote number.

You may want to delete the [Open Style: Initial Style] code from the editing window. If you leave that code there, subsequent changes to the [Open Style] code to the main document also are reflected in the footnotes. If this is what you want, leave the code there. But if you want to leave your footnote format unaffected by later changes to the initial code of your document, delete that code from the editing window.

4. If you choose to delete the [Open Style: Initial Style] code, simply place your insertion point to the right of that code using the arrow keys, then press Backspace.

5. Delete the [Hd Left Tab] code as well, to display the footnote number at the left margin.

Here's how to enter the codes necessary to display the footnote in the style set out above.

6. To have the footnotes appear fully justified, choose Format, Justification, Full from the Styles Editor dialog box.

7. Move the insertion point after the final [<Suprscpt] code.

8. To indent the body of the footnote at the next tab stop, choose Format, Paragraph, Indent (or press the hot key for the keyboard you are using to insert a [Hd Left Ind] code).

9. To make the text of the footnote appear in a smaller typeface, choose Format, Font, and the desired size from the Font Size control.

   The Styles Editor dialog box should look something like the box shown in figure 4.8.

Fig. 4.8
The codes to change the footnote style to the format described in text.

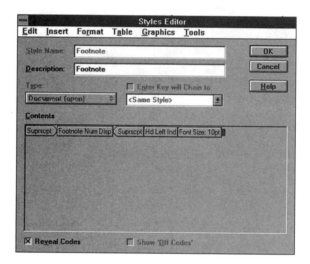

10. Choose OK to return to the Footnote Options dialog box.

11. To print a "continued . . ." message in the middle of footnotes that break from one page to another, select the Insert (continued...) Message control in the Continued Footnotes group box at the bottom of the dialog box.

Tip

You can adjust the Amount of Footnote to Keep Together control to prevent "widows" and "orphans" (that is, only one line of the footnote on either page).

12. If you want to change the appearance of the line that separates your footnote from the body of your text, choose Separator at the top right of the Footnote Options dialog box.

    The Line Separator dialog box appears, as shown in figure 4.9.

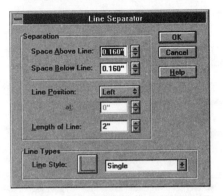

Fig. 4.9
The Line Separator dialog box.

13. Make whatever adjustments you prefer to the appearance of the separator line; then choose OK.

14. Choose OK from the Footnote Options dialog box to accept these changes and insert the new footnote options into your document.

The footnotes, with this new format, now appear as shown in figure 4.10.

Storing a Footnote Style for Future Use

The footnote style is stored within each document, so that changing the style in one document won't affect any other document. You can have only one footnote style in a given document; changing the style in a document affects all footnotes in the document. There is no way to copy or retrieve a footnote style from one document to another. Does this mean you have to create the footnote style from scratch for each document?

Well, not exactly. You can use the Template feature to save a footnote style for future use. If you want all of your documents to default to a particular footnote style, you need to edit the Standard Template so it will insert the footnote style you prefer as the default. If you simply want to create a footnote style for particular types of documents, you can do so by changing the footnote style in the templates for those documents. For example, the Brief template described in Chapter 3 includes a special footnote style similar to the one described in this chapter.

For help on editing and using templates, see Chapter 7, "Using Templates."

Fig. 4.10
The new appearance of the footnotes.

THE CONSTITUTIONAL IMPLICATIONS OF HOCKEY'S TWO-LINE PASS
RULE: VIOLATION OF SUBSTANTIVE DUE PROCESS?

by Kenneth D. H. Chestek IV, Esq.

The[1] two-line pass rule in ice hockey is one of the most difficult rules in all of sports to conceptualize, rationalize and implement. Long overlooked in the days when hockey was not considered a "major" sport, the growth and popularity of the sport during the past decade, coupled with the enormous economic benefit which may accrue to teams (and the players who populate them) which persevere and attain the rank of champion in their sport,[2] have caused renewed interest in all aspects of the game, including the underpinnings of the more obscure rules of puck advancement (RPA's). And, of all of the RPA's in the game, the two-line pass rule is almost certainly the most difficult to understand and enforce, and is therefore probably the second most

---

[1]   Webster's New World Dictionary of the American Language defines the word "the" as giving reference to a particular person or thing. Oddly, the pronounciation of the word "the" varies depending upon whether it is followed by a consonant sound or a vowel sound; if it precedes a vowel sound, the proper pronounciation is with a long "e": "thee". The word is sometimes used as an adverb, as in "*the* better to eat you with, my dear" (*cf. Little Red Riding Hood*), but in this article we will generally employ the word in its more customary usage as a definite article.

[2]   In hockey, teams compete for a large silver bowl commonly referred to as the "Stanley Cup", although it resembles a large trophy more than a tea cup.

---

frequent source of conflict among players, coaches and referees.[3]

This Article examines the history of the two-line pass rule, beginning from the days when hockey was played on frozen ponds without lines of any sort (because it is impossible to paint lines on the surface of the water which lies immediately below the surface of the ice). After examining the evolution of the rule, both through its roots in European amateur hockey and then through its adoption and refinement in the professional hockey leagues which developed in this country after the turn of the century, this Article will review the legal landscape as it relates to regulation of sports in general and hockey in particular. In Part II,[4] this Article will test the modern-day validity of the rule against commonplace legal concepts such as the Equal Protection Clause, the First Amendment, and the Rule in Shelley's Case. With that background, the

---

[3]   The most frequent source of conflict among players, coaches and referees is, of course, the use of excessive physical force in personal contacts during a contest, or at least the perception of such excessive physical force. It is quite common for one player, believing that another player has engaged in the use of excessive physical force or violence, to retaliate with physical force that would, in another setting (for example, Aunt Mabel's sitting room), be considered inappropriate or even criminal. For a complete discussion of the potentialities of criminal sanctions being imposed as a remedy for excessive force during a sporting contest, *see* Chestek, *Excessive Force During Sporting Contests: An Argument for Application of Criminal Sanctions in Order to Prevent the Giving of Bad Examples to Impressionable Children and Thereby Save Society From its Ultimate Destruction*, 40 University of Pittsburgh Law Review 1004 (1979).

[4]   *See infra*, pp. 458-521.

-2-

Tables of Contents

Tables of contents are, of course, not unique to legal documents. But they are frequently used by lawyers in more complex documents, such as appellate briefs, lengthy contracts, and so on. It is important therefore to learn how they operate.

Creating a table of contents for any document is a three-step process:

- Mark the location in your document where you want the table of contents to appear and specify headings and other characteristics of the table (this process is called "defining a table of contents").

- Mark the items in the body of your document that you want to display in the table of contents.

- Insert the items marked, together with their current page numbers, into the table of contents (this is the process of generating a table of contents).

Now to take a closer look at each of these three steps.

Defining the Table of Contents

The first thing you need to decide about a table of contents is whether you want to place it on a page by itself. WordPerfect gives you the option of placing it on a separate page or blending it in with the remainder of your document; either way, the page numbers generated will be accurate (regardless of the length of the table of contents generated).

Chapter 2, "Outlines, Numbers, and More," used a sample brief to demonstrate the Outline feature. This chapter shows how to add a table of contents to that brief. You can follow along with this exercise using a brief or other document of your own.

To define a table of contents, do the following:

1. Place the insertion point at the location in your document where you want the table of contents to appear.

> **Tip**
>
> If you want the table to appear on a separate page, place [HPg] codes before and after the page, as needed, to separate the table from the remainder of the document.

In this example, you do want to place the table of contents on a separate page, as shown in figure 4.11.

Fig. 4.11

Placing a table of contents on a separate page between two [HPg] codes (shown in Reveal Codes).

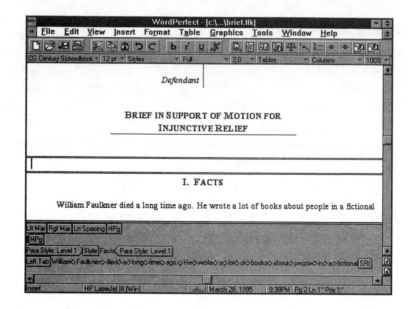

2. Type the title of the table of contents, formatted as you want it to appear on that page.

In this example, you want the title "Table of Contents" to appear at the top of the page, centered, boldface, in Large print with the Small Caps appearance attribute. You can, of course, use any title, formatted any way you choose.

3. Press Enter to skip a line or two to place the insertion point at the location where you want the first entry to appear.

4. Choose **T**ools, Table of **C**ontents. Or, simply choose the ToC button from the Legal Toolbar.

The Table of Contents feature bar appears immediately above the document window, as shown in figure 4.12.

5. From the Table of Contents feature bar, choose **D**efine.

The Define Table of Contents dialog box appears, as shown in figure 4.13.

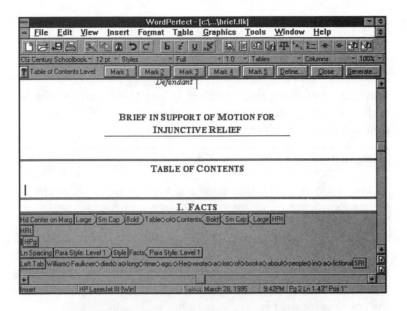

Special Features

Fig. 4.12
The Table of
Contents feature
bar.

Fig. 4.13
Defining a Table
of Contents.

In this dialog box, you need to specify how many levels you want to
display in your table of contents. These work much the same way that
Outline levels work; in fact a multilevel table of contents resembles an
outline in format. You can specify as many as five different levels. The
sample brief used three levels of headings, so this ToC displays that
many also.

6. In the **N**umber of Levels (1-5) control, set the number of levels you want to display (in this example, 3).

Notice that the number of levels you specify becomes active in the Numbering Format group box in the middle of the dialog box. Before dismissing this dialog box, you must specify the format for the entry of each level in the table of contents. You can specify the location and the style of the page number as well as the style of the entry.

Note

There is no way to edit a table of contents definition after it is inserted into your document; if you dismiss this dialog box and insert your definition into your document, the only way to change it is to delete it and redo these steps.

---

7. For each level, define the position for the page number by choosing the Position button for each level you want to change and then selecting the position for the page number from the pop-up list shown.

The available options are shown right in the pop-up list, as shown in figure 4.14. The default is shown as Text . . . . . #, which means that the page number appears flush right, with a dot leader, after each entry. You can skip this step if the default is how you want the numbers to appear.

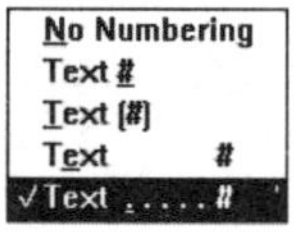

Fig. 4.14
The available page number options for a table of contents.

8. If you want to change the format of the entries in the table of contents, from the Define Table of Contents dialog box choose **S**tyles.

The Table of Contents Styles dialog box appears, as shown in figure 4.15. This process is very similar to editing the style of an outline, as described in Chapter 2. The style definition for each level of the table of contents controls the display of each level in the table itself; it does not affect the appearance of the entries in the body of the document.

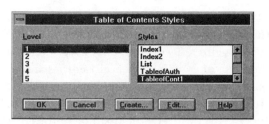

Fig. 4.15
Editing the format
of table of
contents entries.

You can associate any of the predefined styles (shown in the list box on the right side of the dialog box) with any of the levels of the table of contents.

9. To associate a style with a table of contents level, simply highlight the level in the left box and the style you want to associate with it in the right box; WordPerfect will save the association when you choose OK.

If you don't like any of the predefined styles, you can edit any of them, or use the Create button to make your own style. The steps for editing one of the predefined styles follow:

1. Highlight Level 1 in the list box on the right; then choose Edit.

   The Styles Editor appears (see fig. 4.16), showing the current contents of the selected table of contents style.

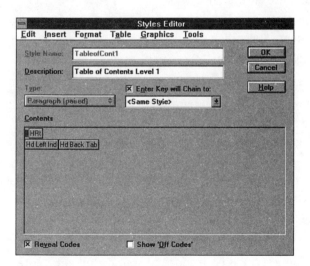

Fig. 4.16
Editing the Table
of Contents Level
1 style.

Take a look at the contents of the style. The first code is a [HRt] code, which ensures that every Level 1 entry will have a blank line between it and the previous entry. (By default, only Level 1 entries have this code, creating the effect of grouping all Level 1 entries and subentries together; you can of course change this if you don't like this look.) Next, you see a [Hd Left Ind] followed by a [Hd Back Tab]. This creates a hanging indent effect whereby the first line of the entry appears at the left margin, but any further lines of a multiline entry appear indented to the first tab stop.

You can change these codes to anything you want.

2. In this case, you want to delete the [Hd Left Ind] code and replace it with a [Hd LeftRight Ind] code (choose Format, Paragraph, Double Indent).

   Why do this? By using a simple left indent, the right margin of the text is unaffected. This means that, if you have a table of contents entry that spans more than one line, the text of the first line may run all the way to the right margin, appearing directly over the page number on the next line down. This makes it more difficult to spot the page numbers quickly in a table of contents. By indenting both the right and left margins, you can insure that the page numbers on the right margins stand out from the entries.

3. After making any changes you want, choose OK to return to the Table of Contents Styles dialog box.

4. Repeat steps 1 through 3 for any other style you want to change.

5. Choose OK to return to the Define Table of Contents dialog box.

6. If you want to change the appearance of the page number itself, choose Page Numbering.

   The Page Number Format dialog box appears, as shown in figure 4.17.

7. Make any changes you want to the appearance of the page number, which appears in the entry field near the bottom of the dialog box. Then choose OK.

8. Choose OK to insert the table of contents definition into your document.

Notice that some text has been added to your document: `Table of Contents will generate here`, as shown in figure 4.18. This is just a visual marker to show you where your table of contents will go when you generate it; WordPerfect deletes this marker when you generate the table of contents later.

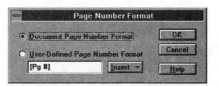

Fig. 4.17
Changing the
appearance of a
page number in a
table of contents.

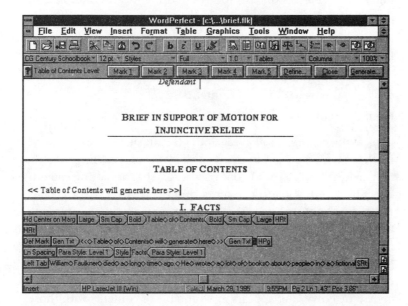

Fig. 4.18
The marker
showing where the
table of contents
will go.

If you look carefully in Reveal Codes, you see that WordPerfect has inserted
several other codes before and after the marker. The first code is a [Def Mark]
code. This designates where the table of contents appears. It also contains information about the format of the table of contents, which this chapter discusses later. The other codes are a pair of [Gen Txt] codes, surrounding the
marker. These codes mark the beginning and end of the text of the table of
contents. Because you have not generated the table yet, the only contents are
the marker inserted by WordPerfect. Each time you generate a table of contents, everything between the two [Gen Txt] codes is erased and replaced
with the new table of contents.

Marking Items to Include in the Table of Contents

Typically the hardest part of creating a table of contents is marking the items
it will include. If you use Outline Styles to create your headings, you can automate this process completely. But before learning about that, it's best to see
how to insert table of contents marks manually.

Manually Inserting Table of Contents Marks

Suppose that you want the first entry in your table of contents to be the table of contents heading itself. Using the sample brief as an example, here's how to do it:

1. If the Table of Contents feature bar is not displayed, display it by choosing **T**ools, Table of **C**ontents (or by choosing the ToC button from the Legal button bar).

2. Position the insertion point on the first letter (or code) that you want to include in the table of contents entry.

3. Select the text you want to include in the table of contents (in this example, the words Table of Contents).

4. From the Table of Contents feature bar, choose Mark **1**.

Look at the example, in Reveal Codes (see fig. 4.19). Two new codes mark the text you want to insert in the table of contents. Note that the first code, [Mrk Txt ToC>] appears after all the formatting codes that affect the words Table of Contents, and the [<Mrk Txt ToC] code appears in front of the codes that turn those attributes off. This is so that the words "Table of Contents" appear in the table of contents without those formatting codes, because the only thing found between the two [Mrk Txt ToC] codes are the letters of the words themselves. If you include attribute appearance and size codes between the [Mrk Txt ToC] codes, the entry later appears in your table of contents with those attributes.

Fig. 4.19
The Table of Contents marks for an entry, shown in Reveal Codes.

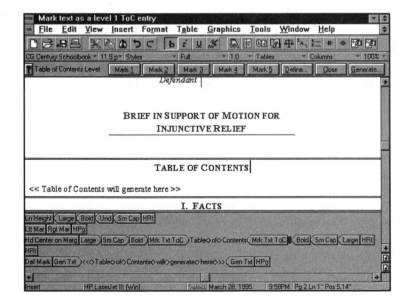

5. Repeat this process for every entry you want to include in the table of contents, selecting the proper level for each entry from the Table of Contents feature bar.

Automating the Marking Process Using Outlines

If you don't want to bother with manually searching through your document to find each entry for the table of contents, then squinting at the little red dot in Reveal Codes to make sure that you place the [Mrk Txt ToC] code in *exactly* the right place every time, there is good news. Automating the creation of a table of contents has become much easier with the advent of version 6.0 of WordPerfect. By placing table of contents codes in an outline style, and then using Outline to create the various headings and subheadings you need, you can automatically insert all of the target table of contents codes as you create the document.

For a complete description of how to accomplish this, see the discussion of the Brief outline style in Chapter 2.

Generating the Table of Contents

The last step in creating a table of contents is the easiest. From the Table of Contents feature bar, choose **G**enerate, and then choose OK.

That's it! Your table of contents appears in your document. The finished table of contents for the sample brief is shown in figure 4.20.

TABLE OF CONTENTS

Table of Contents 2

I. Facts 3

II. Issues 3

III. Discussion 3
- A. It is Unfair Competition for a Living Author to Rip Off the Inventions of a Deceased Author Who Can No Longer Defend His Creations 3
  - 1. Dead authors do not have access to books or other current writings 3
  - 2. There is an unwarranted perception that dead authors no longer care about their works 5
  - 3. Allowing a living author to use the work of a dead author is a violation of equal protection, since there is no rational basis for distinguishing between dead and living authors . . . 9
- B. Equitable Relief is Warranted 10
  - 1. There is no adequate remedy at law, since money damages will provide no comfort to a resident of Heaven 10
  - 2. Rolling over in a grave could cause irreparable damage to the remains of the Plaintiff 15

IV. Conclusion 17

Fig. 4.20
The finished table of contents.

Tables of Authorities

The Table of Authorities feature is, obviously, designed for lawyers. It helps take the drudgery out of manually creating the table of authorities that is required by most appellate courts.

Tables of authorities are similar to tables of contents in that they require the same three-step process to create:

- Define the table of authorities
- Mark items for the table of authorities
- Generate the table of authorities

Unfortunately, because citations to cases and statutes and other legal authorities come in so many different shapes and styles, it is impossible to completely automate the process of marking items for the table of authorities in the same way you can automate the marking of table of contents entries. However, you can automate most of the process by using a set of macros provided on the Applications Disk, as you see later in the chapter.

The last step, generating, is shared with the Table of Contents feature discussed earlier in this chapter and the Cross-Reference feature discussed in Chapter 2; when you generate a document, you can generate all tables and cross-references at one time.

This chapter discusses the macros later. For now, looking at the process of creating a table of authorities manually will help you understand how the macros operate.

Defining a Table of Authorities

This discussion continues using the sample brief from earlier in this chapter, now adding a table of authorities to it. The text of the discussion section of the brief, containing some of the citations you need to include in this table, is shown in figure 4.21. Notice that it includes citations to Constitutional provisions, cases, statutes, and a law review article. You can gather and display each of these categories (and any others you care to create) separately in the final table of authorities.

To create a table of authorities, do the following:

1. Place the insertion point at the exact location where you want to create the table of authorities.

   As with the table of contents, if you want to place the table of authorities on a separate page, put it between two [HPg] codes. In this example, put the table of authorities immediately after the [HPg] code ending the table of contents, and before another [HPg] code marking the beginning of the body of the brief.

---

1. FACTS

William Faulkner died a long time ago. He wrote a lot of books about people in a fictional county he called Yoknapatawpha County. Recently, an author of computer books started writing examples for his book and ripped off the name Yoknapatawpha County for his screen shots. Mr. Faulkner is probably rolling over in his grave even as the Court reads this Brief.

2. ISSUES

(a)   May a living author of computer books take advantage of the inventions of the creative genius of a literary giant, merely because that author is dead and can no longer defend himself?

(b)   Is the risk of rolling over in a grave a sufficient threat of irreparable harm to justify equitable relief?

3. DISCUSSION

a.   It is Unfair Competition for a Living Author to Rip Off the Inventions of a Deceased Author Who Can No Longer Defend His Creations

It is beyond cavil that an author who is dead is in no position to protect his creative genius against its unauthorized use in silly ways by authors who have the advantage of still being alive. There are several reasons for this.

i.   Dead authors do not have access to books or other current writings

One of the fundamental precepts of our system of justice is that all persons have equal access to the court system to protect their interests. *Happy Horse Farms vs. T. Feasor,* 189 Miss. 358, 87 So. 123 (1897); Mississippi Constitution, Article IX, § 4. Any rule of law which tends to deprive a person of that equality of access is therefore suspect and subject to challenge. *Society of Left-Handed Bird Watchers vs. the National Rifle Association,* 487 Miss. 16, 490 So.2d. 985 (1978).

While the Plaintiff in this action is legally no longer a person, since he is

---

Fig. 4.21
The text of the sample brief, containing citations of authority.

2. Type the title of the table of authorities, in whatever format you prefer.

3. Leave a few blank lines under the title, to separate it from the text of the table that will follow.

4. Display the Table of Authorities feature bar by choosing **T**ools, Table of Authorities.

The sample brief at this point looks like figure 4.22, shown in Reveal Codes.

Fig. 4.22
The title for the table of authorities, shown in Reveal Codes.

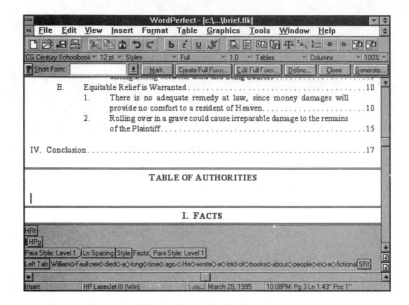

5. Choose **D**efine from the Table of Authorities feature bar.

The Define Table of Authorities dialog box appears, as shown in figure 4.23.

Fig. 4.23
The Define Table of Authorities dialog box.

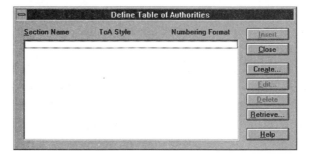

You need to create a section name for each of the groupings of authorities you want to list. This example will create groupings for cases, statutes, and other authorities.

6. Choose Cre**a**te.

The Create Table of Authorities dialog box appears, as shown in figure 4.24.

Fig. 4.24
Creating a new section for a table of authorities.

7. Type the word **Cases** in the Name window near the top of the dialog box.

   You can change the style or the position of the number that will follow each entry by making adjustments in the Numbering Format group box shown in figure 4.24. These controls work the same way as they do for tables of contents; see the preceding discussion of that feature for help on how to use them.

   You can also change the style of the text of each entry in a similar fashion.

8. Choose **C**hange in the Current Style group box at the bottom of the dialog box.

   The Table of Authorities Style dialog box appears, as shown in figure 4.25. Because the levels of a table of authorities are defined differently from the levels in a table of contents (they are called *sections* rather than *levels*), you do not need to associate a style with a level in this dialog box. You simply need to select from this listing which of the styles you want to use for the cases section of the table of authorities.

   If none of the listed styles contains the formatting you want, you can either edit one of the default styles or you can create your own style. This example assumes that you edit the default style, TableofAuth.

9. Move the highlight bar to the TableofAuth entry (if it's not already there) and choose Edit.

Fig. 4.25

Selecting a style for the entries in the cases section of a table of authorities.

The Styles Editor appears. In this case, the only code that appears in the Contents box is a [HRt] code, which will appear after each entry, putting one line of blank space between each case listed. But suppose you wanted to create a hanging indent, where the first line of the case is flush with the left margin but subsequent lines are indented on both sides, to make it even easier to spot the first word of each case (on the left margin) and the page number (on the right margin).

10. Move the insertion point inside the Contents editing window, just before the [Codes to the left are ON - Codes to the right are OFF] code.

11. Place a [Hd LeftRight Ind] code as the first code in the Contents window (choose Format, Paragraph, Double Indent) to indent both sides of the entry to the next tab stop.

12. Insert a [Hd Back Tab] code to move the first line of text back to the left margin (Ctrl+Shift+Tab).

    The Styles Editor should now look like figure 4.26. Note that WordPerfect has left the [HRt] in place to make sure that a blank line appears between each entry in the Table.

13. Choose OK, Close, OK to return to the Define Table of Authorities dialog box.

    Notice that under Section Name, the new Cases section appears. In the column marked ToA Style, the default TableofAuth style is marked, and the numbering format you chose is shown in the last column.

14. Repeat steps 6 and 7 to create sections for Constitutional provisions, statutes, and other authorities.

You can select different styles for each section of the table of authorities if you like, or you can use the same style for all sections.

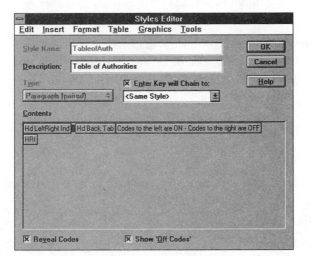

Fig. 4.26
The codes to create a hanging indent to display cases in the table of authorities.

Special Features

Note

If you decide to use a different style for different sections, be sure you that do so by specifying different default styles, or by creating new styles of your own. If you edit the TableofAuth style several times while creating different sections and then use that style for all sections, all the sections will look like the final version of the style.

When you are finished creating all three sections, the Define Table of Authorities dialog box should look like figure 4.27.

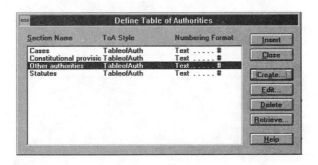

Fig. 4.27
The four sections of the table of authorities for the sample brief.

15. Choose **C**lose to save this definition in your document.

You're not done yet, however.

In contrast to a table of contents, when you define a table of authorities you must explicitly put the headings into the table and specify where each section will be built. This gives you a great deal of control over how the final result looks, but it takes a few extra steps at the beginning.

Say that you want the case authorities displayed first, followed by the Constitutional provisions, statutes, and then the other authorities, in your final table of authorities. Continue as follows:

1. At the location where you want the cases to be listed, type in a heading (for example **Case Authorities**) formatted in any fashion you prefer.

2. Press Enter twice to put a blank line between the heading and the first case citation.

3. From the Table of Authorities feature bar, select Define to redisplay the Define Table of Authorities dialog box.

4. With the section name Cases highlighted, choose **I**nsert.

   You then return to your document. WordPerfect has inserted a new marker, <<Table of Authorities will generate here>>, in your document, as shown in figure 4.28. There is also a new [Def Mark: ToA: Cases] code inserted, as well as the same pair of [Gen Txt] codes you saw when you created the table of contents earlier. These codes place the cases section of the table of authorities at this spot.

Fig. 4.28

The codes to create the case authorities section of the table of authorities.

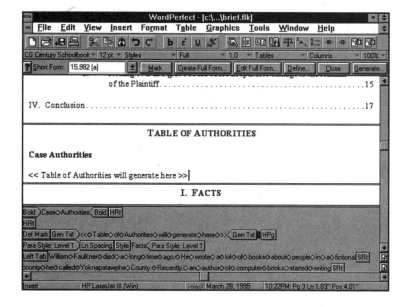

But because the [Def Mark] code relates only to the cases section, you must go back and put in similar marks for the Constitutional provisions, statutes, and other authorities sections.

5. Repeat steps 16 through 19 for the remaining sections of your table of authorities.

When you have finished, the table of authorities page in your document should look something like figure 4.29. You are now ready to begin marking items to place in the table.

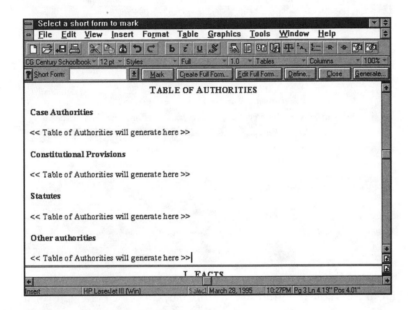

Fig. 4.29
The completed table of authorities, shown in Reveal Codes.

Marking Items for the Table of Authorities

Marking an item for a table of authorities is also somewhat more complicated than marking something for a table of contents. That is because, while a table of contents entry by definition appears only in one location in the body of your document, the argument in a brief may rely on a case citation or other authority many times in a brief. So, rather than repeat the same case 15 times in the table of authorities, WordPerfect allows you to mark the complete citation only once, and then add additional page references to that entry in the table of authorities for each time the authority is referred to later in the brief.

In WordPerfect parlance, the first reference is called the *full form* Table of Authorities mark, whereas subsequent references are known as the *short form* Table of Authorities marks. Each authority cited can have only one full form mark, but it can have as many short form marks as there are references to that authority.

Marking a Full Form Table of Authorities Item. To mark an item for the table of authorities, follow these steps:

1. Find the first reference to an item that you want to include in your table of authorities.

2. Select the complete text of the reference you want to mark, as shown in figure 4.30.

Fig. 4.30
Selecting the text of the citation to include in a table of authorities.

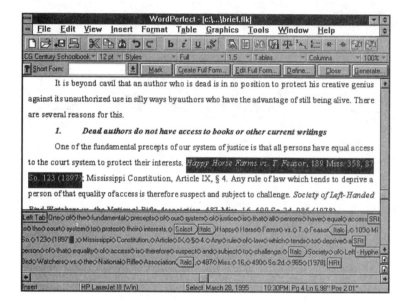

3. From the Table of Authorities feature bar, choose Create Full Form.

   The Create Full Form dialog box appears, as shown in figure 4.31. You need to specify two pieces of information for this dialog box: the section in which the citation is listed and a short form name to identify later references (if any) to the same authority.

4. If you want to place the citation into any section of the table of authorities other than the one that appears in the Section Name field, click the drop-down list arrow at the end of that field and select one of the defined section names from the list that appears.

5. For the sake of simplicity, you may also want to change the short form name that appears in the Short Form entry window to something, well, shorter.

6. When you have entered the information in this dialog box the way you want it, choose OK.

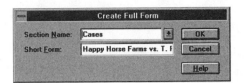

Fig. 4.31
Specifying a
section and a short
form for a citation.

You see what looks like an ordinary WordPerfect editing window, but is actually a little different. Like the Footnote editing screen and several others discussed in earlier chapters, this is a subsidiary window to your main document. You can switch in and out of it using the Window menu if you like. It also has a feature bar that is used only in editing a Full Form Table of Authorities reference, as you can see in figure 4.32.

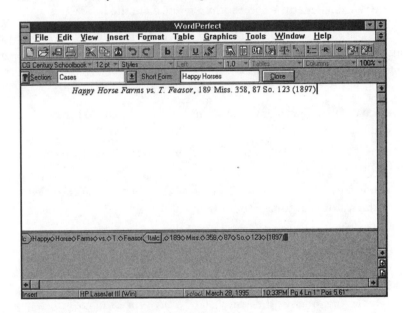

Fig. 4.32
Editing a full form
Table of Authorities reference.

The Full Form Table of Authorities feature bar gives you a second crack at changing the section or the short form name for the item if you like. More important, it gives you a chance to edit the text of the full form citation. Often, a reference to a published case may include a pinpoint citation to the exact page in the book where the quotation is found. In all likelihood you do not want to include this pinpoint citation in the table of authorities, since you may refer to other pages in the opinion at other places in your brief. This screen gives you the ability to add or delete anything in the citation, or to change its appearance attributes or other formatting.

7. After you have completed editing the citation, choose Close from the feature bar.

   Your document returns to the screen. Notice that a [ToA] code now appears before your citation. If you place the insertion point immediately to the left of the citation, it expands to reveal the section and short form of the reference, as well as a designation that this is the full form reference.

8. Repeat steps 2 through 7 for every case, statute, or other authority you want to list in your table of authorities.

Marking the Short Form References. Marking the short form references to citations is the easy part. Finding the references you want to mark and deciding if the reference merits a short form reference are the headaches.

Although you can use the Search feature of WordPerfect to help you spot the secondary references in your brief to each item in the table of authorities, you have to read each reference to see if it merits including a page number in the table of authorities. If you decide it does, follow these steps.

1. Place the insertion point in or immediately adjacent to the reference you want to mark.

2. From the Table of Authorities feature bar, select the short form name you want to insert.

   You can use the drop-down list of available short forms at the left edge of the feature bar to pick the correct short form easily.

3. When the correct short form is listed there, choose **M**ark.

   WordPerfect inserts a short form reference at that location.

Generating the Table of Authorities

As with tables of contents, the easiest step in the process of creating a table of authorities is generating it. After you have defined the table of authorities and marked all full form and short form references in your document, just choose **G**enerate from the feature bar, and WordPerfect automatically creates it. (If you choose **G**enerate from any feature bar, this table is updated). It is automatically alphabetized within each section, and all full and short form references are marked by page number.

A copy of the completed table of authorities for the sample brief is shown as figure 4.33.

Special Features

TABLE OF AUTHORITIES

Case Authorities

Happy Horse Farms vs. T. Feasor, 189 Miss. 358, 87 So. 123 (1897) 4, 6, 9

In re: Estate of Ichabod Crane, 261 Miss.Super. 192 (1950) 15

Rooty-Toot-Toot Engine Company vs. WorldWide Widgets, 87 F.2d 678 (Seventh Cir. 1990) 7

Smith vs. Smith. 452 Miss. 422, 685 So.2d 114 (1989) 10

Society of Left-Handed Bird Watchers vs. the National Rifle Association, 487 Miss. 16, 490 So.2d. 985 (1978) 4, 6

Constitutional Provisions

Mississippi Const., Art. I, § 4.62 12

Statutes

56 Miss.Stat.Ann. § 15.982 (a) 4

56 Miss.Stat.Ann. § 15.989 . . . . 5, 9

Other Authorities

Nelson, *A Modest Proposal: Allowing Corporations to Marry*, 98 Utah L.Rev. 523 (1990) 4

Fig. 4.33
The completed Table of Authorities.

Automating Tables of Authorities with Macros

As mentioned earlier, it is possible to automate most of the process of creating a table of authorities with macros. The Applications Disk includes macros to help you define the table, and to enter long form references to various authorities.

Defining a Table of Authorities with MAKETOA.WCM

Defining the four-section table of authorities described in this chapter is completely automated by the macro MAKETOA.WCM, included on the Applications Disk. Simply place the insertion point where you want the table of authorities to appear and play the macro; MAKETOA places the table of authorities definition at the insertion point. It includes a hard page break before and after the table of authorities to ensure that the table appears on a separate page.

If you do not want the table on a separate page, or if you want to delete or change the heading of any section created by MAKETOA.WCM, after playing the macro you can simply edit the resulting Table of Authorities page to conform to your own needs.

On the Disk

Marking Full Form References

The Applications Disk also includes four macros to automate the insertion of full form references to cases, statutes, Constitutional provisions, and other authorities. They are CASECITE.WCM, CONSTCIT.WCM, STATCITE.WCM, and OTHERCIT.WCM.

On the Disk

The trick to each of these macros is to use them to enter the citation initially into the body of the document. They do not go looking for citations that you have already typed in; they will insert the citations in the text for you, and insert a full form reference simultaneously, saving you the trouble of doing it manually.

All four macros work in similar ways. Because the CASECITE.WCM macro is a little more complicated (to allow for different tastes in how a case citation is formatted), it's worthwhile to take a look at how that macro works.

When you come to a spot in your brief where you need to type a case citation, follow these steps:

1. Instead of typing the name of the case and its citation, play the macro CASECITE.WCM.

   The first time you play it, you see a screen asking you to select your preferences for case citations, as shown in figure 4.34; WordPerfect stores these for future use, although you can change them at any time.

Fig. 4.34
Selecting the options for the format of a case citation.

2. Select any combination of appearance attributes.

   The attributes you select apply to the case name only.

3. Choose OK to save your preferences.

   The Insert Case Citation dialog box appears, as shown in figure 4.35. Note that, after you have played this macro once, this is the only dialog box you see when you play the macro.

> **Note**
>
> The appearance preferences you set will be stored in a special file named MACROS.BIF in your default macros directory. If you delete that file, or if you change your default macros directory, the CASECITE.WCM macro will not be able to locate your preferences, and you will be asked again to specify them.

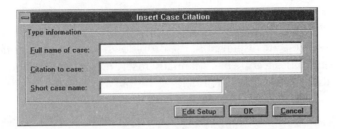

Fig. 4.35
Entering the case name and citation in CASECITE.WCM.

4. Type the full name of the case in the first entry field; this case name appears with the attributes you selected in step 2.

5. Type in the full citation to the case in the second entry field; this appears in normal type.

6. Type an easily recognized shorthand reference to the case in the last entry field; this becomes the short form reference for the table of authorities.

7. Choose OK when you have finished.

The macro types in the case name and citation and immediately inserts a table of authorities full form reference at that spot.

Use CONSTCIT.WCM, STATCITE.WCM, and OTHERCIT.WCM in a similar fashion to put other types of authorities into your brief. Because these all appear in normal typeface, you need not select any special appearance attributes when you play these macros. If you want to format part of the resulting citation in anything other than normal type, you can apply any appearance attributes you want manually after playing the macros.

The Brief Button Bar

To make using these macros even easier, the Brief template on the Applications Disk includes a special button bar. If you use this template to begin your brief, you can display this button bar to give yourself one-click access to all five of the macros described earlier, along with the Outline, Table of Contents, and Table of Authorities feature bars. The button bar also includes a button to instantly insert the section symbol: **§**.

Automating Short Form References

If you refer to a case or other authority more than once in your brief, you will probably want to include short form references for later references to each authority. Unfortunately, finding each individual reference and deciding whether to include it in the table of authorities requires some decision-pmaking that you cannot delegate to a silicon chip. Thus, there is really no way to automate the insertion of short form references.

The job is not difficult to do, however. In the process of creating the full form reference, the table of authorities generates a convenient list of available short forms. These are displayed in the drop-down list on the left side of the Table of Authorities feature bar. Manually inserting any short form reference from this list is a simple task. For help with this, see the preceding discussion.

Document Compare

The final feature covered in this chapter is another one that, while it may not be used exclusively by lawyers, is used most frequently by lawyers. How many times have you exchanged drafts of documents with somebody and then wondered what words have been changed from draft to draft? In a complicated negotiation this can become very important.

Commercial products are available on the market that compare different versions of the same document, adding notations to show additions and deletions. Probably as a result of the popularity of these standalone programs, WordPerfect has incorporated a feature called Compare Document. Although it is not yet as powerful as some of the standalone systems, it is pretty good and still getting better.

To see how this feature works, refer back to the sample contract in Chapter 2. Suppose that you represent Worldwide Widgets, Inc., and you are responding to the licensee's proposed contract language with a few additions or language changes. As a courtesy to counsel for the licensee, you want to highlight those changes for his quick reference. By using the Compare Document feature, you can produce a marked up copy of the contract that looks something like figure 4.36.

In figure 4.36, text that appears with a line through it (using the Strikeout appearance attribute) is text you have deleted. Text that appears in the shaded areas (using the Redline appearance attribute) is text you've added to the document. (It appears in red on your color monitor, but prints in red only if you have a color printer.)

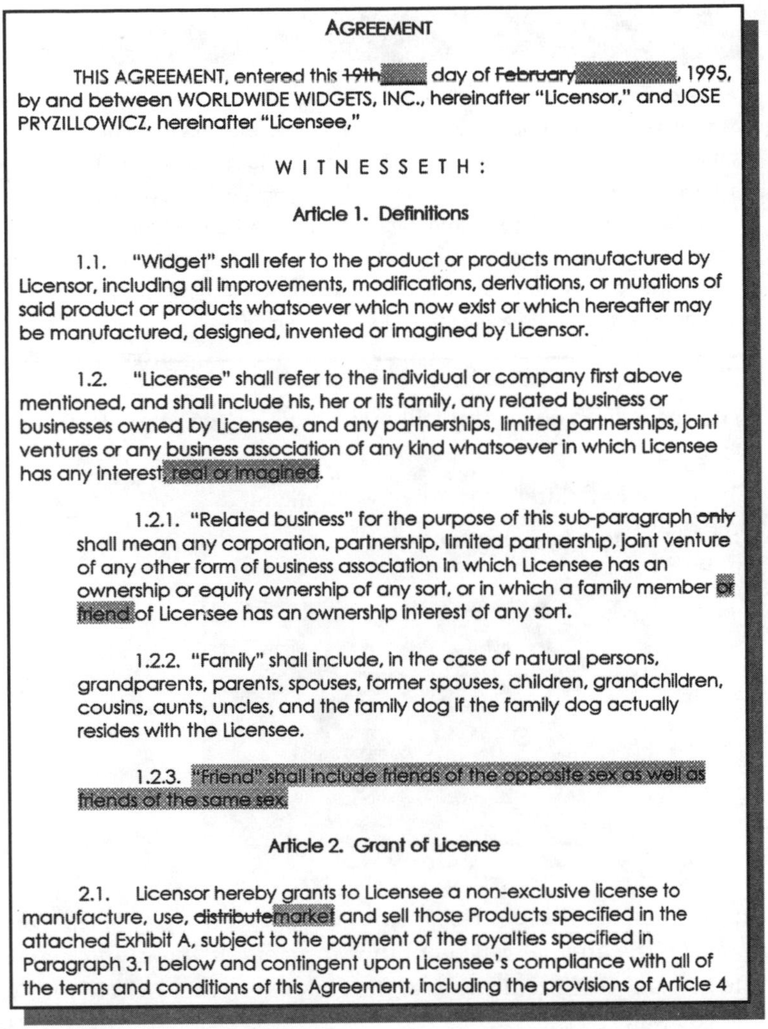

AGREEMENT

THIS AGREEMENT, entered this ~~19th~~ day of ~~February~~, 1995, by and between WORLDWIDE WIDGETS, INC., hereinafter "Licensor," and JOSE PRYZILLOWICZ, hereinafter "Licensee,"

WITNESSETH:

Article 1. Definitions

1.1.   "Widget" shall refer to the product or products manufactured by Licensor, including all improvements, modifications, derivations, or mutations of said product or products whatsoever which now exist or which hereafter may be manufactured, designed, invented or imagined by Licensor.

1.2.   "Licensee" shall refer to the individual or company first above mentioned, and shall include his, her or its family, any related business or businesses owned by Licensee, and any partnerships, limited partnerships, joint ventures or any business association of any kind whatsoever in which Licensee has any interest, real or imagined.

1.2.1.   "Related business" for the purpose of this sub-paragraph ~~only~~ shall mean any corporation, partnership, limited partnership, joint venture of any other form of business association in which Licensee has an ownership or equity ownership of any sort, or in which a family member or friend of Licensee has an ownership interest of any sort.

1.2.2.   "Family" shall include, in the case of natural persons, grandparents, parents, spouses, former spouses, children, grandchildren, cousins, aunts, uncles, and the family dog if the family dog actually resides with the Licensee.

1.2.3.   "Friend" shall include friends of the opposite sex as well as friends of the same sex.

Article 2. Grant of License

2.1.   Licensor hereby grants to Licensee a non-exclusive license to manufacture, use, ~~distribute~~ market and sell those Products specified in the attached Exhibit A, subject to the payment of the royalties specified in Paragraph 3.1 below and contingent upon Licensee's compliance with all of the terms and conditions of this Agreement, including the provisions of Article 4

Fig. 4.36
The first page of a revised contract, marked to show additions and deletions.

Here is how to add these markings to your document:

1. First, be sure you have the original version of the document stored on disk.

2. Make a copy of the document; then save it to a different filename.

3. Now make the revisions you want to make to the new copy of the original document.

> **Caution**
>
> You can compare a document on your screen with the original version of the document, stored under the same filename; however this is dangerous. One of the first things you learned when you began using computers (or have learned the hard way later on!) was to frequently save your work as you go along. If you have developed good computer habits, you will periodically click the Save icon on the Power Bar to ensure that your work is safely stored on disk. If you simply modify the original file and click that Save icon, you will overwrite the original version and make it impossible to compare.

4. With the revised document still on your screen, choose **F**ile, Compa**r**e Document.

5. Choose **A**dd Markings from the fly-out menu.

   The Add Markings dialog box appears, as shown in figure 4.37.

Fig. 4.37
The Add Markings dialog box.

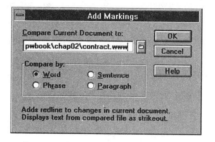

6. In the **C**ompare Current Document To entry window, type the file-name for the original version of the document. If you cannot remember the filename, use the file icon at the end of the entry field to locate the file you want.

   WordPerfect allows you to specify how closely you want to compare the two documents. Notice that in the Compare By: group box you are given the option of comparing by word, phrase, sentence, or paragraph. For most work, you will want to leave this at the default value, word, to minimize the amount of text that is marked for minor changes. For example, if you choose to compare by paragraph and you had a para-graph in your document where you merely changed the location of a comma, the entire paragraph would be marked as deleted, and retyped with the new comma location as a complete new paragraph being added to the document.

7. Select the level of detail to examine in the Compare By: group box.

8. Choose OK.

Depending on how long your document is, the Document Compare Status dialog box displays on your screen momentarily to give you a visual update on the progress being made. For a short document this may flash on your screen so fast you can hardly read it; for longer documents it will stick around longer. You need do nothing in this box because it disappears as soon as WordPerfect completes the comparison.

Notice that the redline and strikeout appearance codes now are in the new version of the document on your screen. If you want to save the marked-up version of this document, you should use Save As to save it to a third file name. If you merely use Save, the marked-up version overwrites your new version.

This is not nearly the disaster that overwriting the original version of the document would have been because you can easily recover from this. You can quickly remove all redline and strikeout markings and delete all stricken text simply by choosing File, Compare Document, Remove Markings.

From Here...

This chapter explained several features that seem to be designed expressly for lawyers, including Footnotes, Tables of Contents and Authorities, and Compare Document.

Each of the first four chapters has dealt with groups of related WordPerfect features that are useful in law offices. All those features had something in common: they helped add content and style to your documents.

The next three chapters change the focus a little bit. Each chapter takes a single WordPerfect feature and shows how it can make you more productive at the computer. These chapters are not so much about how to add information to your document as they are about how to expedite the process of preparing documents. Think of the next three chapters as the technical reference section of this book; they help you learn how the forms and documents described in Part II work and help you create your own forms and documents that work in the same way.

Automating With Macros

Well, you've made it this far. Until now you've been learning more about things you've heard of before. You know what an outline is supposed to look like, and where footnotes go on a page, and what a table of authorities is.

Now you're going to learn about a feature that even *sounds* different: macros. What is a macro, anyway? Something big, right? (As in "the opposite of micro"?)

WordPerfect macros are big only in the sense that they are very powerful and very useful. Indeed, the official Macros Manual supplied by WordPerfect Corporation (for Version 6.0) is over 1,000 pages long, nearly 100 pages larger than the Reference manual that covers the rest of the WordPerfect program.

Obviously, the subject of macros could consume an entire book by itself. It is not the purpose in this book to teach you how to write complex programmed macros; you are a lawyer or a legal assistant, not a computer programmer. This chapter covers the following:

- Recording and using simple macros
- Editing simple macros after you've recorded them
- A quick overview of complex or programmed macros

Part II of this book is jammed with complex macros; this chapter is intended to give you a few screwdrivers and wrenches that you can use to tinker with them when necessary.

Recording and Using Simple Macros

WordPerfect offers two kinds of macros—*simple macros* and *programmed macros*—and they're very different from each other. A simple macro is a series of keystrokes, recorded and replayed extremely quickly by your computer. WordPerfect even uses the analogy of a tape or video recorder; you "record" the keystrokes and then "play" them back whenever you want to repeat them.

A programmed macro, however, is really a miniature computer program. It takes control of WordPerfect and makes it do different things depending on the state of affairs it finds. It may stop and ask you for some information, or to make a decision. It may not type anything at all, depending on what its function is. A programmed macro uses commands that have no keystroke equivalents, and therefore cannot be recorded in the same way that a simple macro can.

This section deals only with simple macros you record from the keyboard. The next two sections, "Playing Macros" and "Editing Macros," apply to both recorded and programmed macros. The final section of this chapter deals exclusively with programmed macros.

Analyzing the Function of a Macro

First, you must learn to record a simple macro. But before you record anything, pause for a moment and think about exactly what you want your macro to do and the different contexts in which the macro is to be used. You want to record a macro that works correctly in all the situations in which it is likely to be played.

For example, suppose that you want to create a macro that types a signature block for the end of a pleading. This sounds simple enough, but consider these points:

- Where do you want the insertion point to be when the macro is played?

  If you expect to play the macro with the insertion point just after the last character of the last paragraph of the pleading, you need to record the hard returns necessary to place the insertion point at the proper line below the last paragraph; but if you expect to have placed those hard returns manually before you play the macro, you do not want to record any more hard returns.

- Will all the documents in which you play the macro use the same tab settings?

If you use different tab settings for different types of pleadings, you cannot reliably use the Tab key to position the signature block on your page; you have to use an Advance code instead.

■ What will the line spacing for the document be when you play the macro?

Many pleadings are double-spaced, whereas the signature blocks are usually single-spaced; you may therefore have to record a line spacing change in addition to the text of the signature block.

■ Will the macro be more useful if it pauses or ends at some point to allow the user to type in a special word or phrase?

The wonderful thing about simple unprogrammed macros is that they always type the very same text, exactly the same way, every time you play them. The limitation of simple, unprogrammed macros is also that they always type the very same text, exactly the same way, every time you play them. Look for opportunities to make your macro useful in more situations by incorporating pauses, using more general words, or by ending the macro at a point where the next words may vary depending on the situation in which the macro is played.

Take all these considerations into account when planning what you are going to record in your macro. This leads to another point: You need to develop some consistency in how you create the documents in which you play your macros. It is okay to sometimes insert the hard returns at the end of the document and sometimes leave them out, if you don't mind going back after playing your macro and taking out the hard returns it inserted; but the more manual editing you have to do after a macro has been played, the more you are defeating the only reason for having a macro in the first place: saving keystrokes.

Storing Macros

One more thing deserves mention before the explanation of how to record simple macros. Version 6.1 introduced the capability to record a macro that is stored in a template file rather than as a separate disk file. This has certain advantages if you want to store a group of macros in a single file and distribute them as part of a template; it also has some advantages if you want a macro with one name to perform different actions depending on which template you are using at the time. However, for the most part you do want to store your macros as separate files on your disk, because they will be easier to locate and do not depend upon which template was used to create the active document. For that reason, the remainder of this chapter discusses macros stored as a disk file.

Recording a Simple Macro

Suppose that you want to create a macro to close a pleading. Follow these steps:

1. Place the insertion point at the end of your pleading, at the location where you want to insert the signature block.

   You can record a macro from a blank document screen, of course, but it is usually easier to record a macro while editing a typical document, so you can get a better feel for how the finished result will look. The actual format of a live document also reminds you of some of the considerations discussed earlier and forces you to record a more complete macro the first time around.

2. Choose **T**ools, **M**acro.

3. Choose **R**ecord.

   The Record Macro dialog box appears, as shown in figure 5.1.

Fig. 5.1

The Record Macro dialog box.

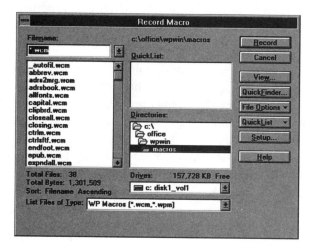

4. Type a name in the File**n**ame entry field. In this example, type **PLCLOSNG**.

   Because WordPerfect stores macros as separate files on your disk, you can use no more than eight characters that are legal characters for a DOS file (that is, no asterisks, spaces, slashes, or similar characters). You can add a three-character extension if you like, but it is better if you don't; if you specify no extension, WordPerfect automatically adds the extension WCM, which makes it easy to identify a file as a macro and locate it from the Play Macro dialog box. You can also specify a path, but again it is not usually a good idea to do so; if you specify no path

WordPerfect stores the file in your default macros directory, which is where you probably want to put it anyway.

5. Choose **R**ecord.

   You then return to your document, but notice that the mouse pointer now looks something like a Ghostbuster icon (see fig. 5.2). This is to remind you that you cannot use the mouse to move the insertion point, select text, or make other changes to the text on your screen while recording a macro. If you move the mouse to a button, menu, or scroll bar, however, it resumes its standard arrow shape and you can use it to access menus and buttons.

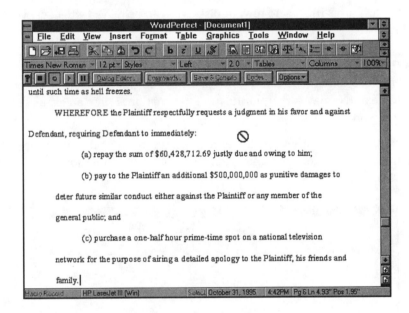

Fig. 5.2
The shape of the mouse pointer in the editing screen while recording a macro.

6. Type the signature block as you normally would.

In the example shown in figure 5.2, the insertion point was left immediately after the period in the last sentence of the document. If this is where you expect to leave the insertion point when creating pleadings, you would therefore need to do these steps:

1. Insert a hard return to move to the next line of the document.

2. Change the line spacing to single spacing, because the body of the pleading was double-spaced.

3. Type the name of the firm and the remainder of the signature block, formatted as you prefer.

You can even go one step farther if you like. Many attorneys prefer to designate the party they represent in the pleading at the end of the signature block. You can add the words "Attorney for" and quit there, leaving the insertion point in the proper location to allow the user to finish the signature block by typing the appropriate name or entity for this case.

When you have finished typing the standard signature block text, end recording by choosing **T**ools, **M**acro, **R**ecord. Note that when you see the Macro fly-out menu, the **R**ecord option appears with a check mark, indicating the Record Macro is currently active. Choosing **R**ecord removes the check mark and turns off the recording function; the Macro feature bar also disappears.

WordPerfect saves the macro to your disk, ready to be played whenever you need it.

Recording a Pause to Allow User Input

As mentioned earlier, you can record a *pause* in your macro to allow the user to enter text that may vary from situation to situation. Here's an example of how this works.

Suppose that you want several different attorneys in your firm to use the signature block macro. The signature block for your pleadings looks like figure 5.3.

Fig. 5.3
The sample
signature block.

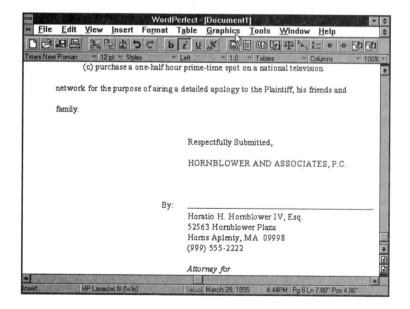

You can make the macro pause immediately before it types the attorney name, so that the user can type that name manually. The macro then resumes as soon as the user presses Enter. Here's how to do that:

1. Begin recording the macro, as described earlier.

   To distinguish this macro from the earlier macro, which does not pause, give this macro a different file name, such as PCLOSE2.

2. When you get to the line where you would ordinarily type in the name of the attorney signing the pleading, choose **T**ools, **M**acro.

   Notice that the Record choice on the fly-out menu has a check mark next to it, indicating that a macro is currently being recorded. The Pause option, which had been grayed out when you started recording, is now active as well.

3. From the fly-out menu, choose Pause.

   This does several things. First, it temporarily turns off the recording function, much like pressing the Pause button on a VCR. Secondly, it places a command into the macro so that, when you play it, the macro also pauses at exactly the same location.

4. Type the name of the attorney signing the pleading, but do not press Enter yet.

   Because the name was typed while the macro recording was paused, the name you typed is not saved with the macro.

5. Resume recording the macro by once again choosing **T**ools, **M**acro, **P**ause.

6. Now press Enter to move to the line below the attorney's name and continue typing the rest of the signature block.

7. Turn off the record function as you did in the previous example when you have finished.

As you see in a moment, when you play this macro, it pauses and waits for you to type something. It resumes playing as soon as you press Enter.

Ideas for Simple Recorded Macros

Once you get the hang of recording macros, you might be tempted to record lots of simple macros. Here are some ideas for using simple macros:

- Inserting signature blocks for letters and pleadings.
- Inserting the formatting codes for a special type of document (although creating a template, as discussed in Chapter 7, "Using Templates," might be a better way of doing this).

- Inserting standard allegations or denials for a pleading.

- Inserting standard paragraphs of a contract or an agreement.

- Inserting a time stamp into a header or footer.

- Creating an inter-office memo (although again the Template feature might do a better job here).

In general, look for large blocks of text that you type frequently. It does not make much sense to record a macro that will only be used once or twice, because this only fills up disk space and makes it harder to find the truly useful macros. It also does not make much sense to record a macro that only types a few words because you can probably type them just as fast by hand as you can play the macro. The point of macros is to save keystrokes and therefore time; used selectively, macros are wonderful tools for doing just that.

Playing Macros

Now you're ready to play the two macros you wrote earlier. Like many other features of WordPerfect, you have a number of options for playing macros. You start with the standard way and then learn a couple of shortcuts.

Using the Play Macro Dialog Box

The most common way to play any macro is to select it from the Play Macro dialog box:

1. Choose **T**ools, **M**acro.

2. Choose **P**lay. The Play Macro dialog box, shown in figure 5.4, appears.

Fig. 5.4

The Play Macro dialog box.

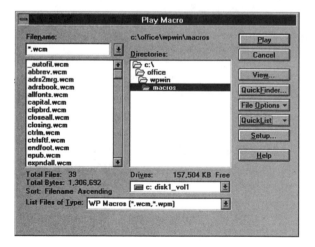

3. Type the name of the macro to play in the File**n**ame entry window. In this example, type **PLCLOSNG** to play the first version of the signature block macro that you recorded earlier.

   If you cannot remember the name of the macro, you can select any file in the list box, or navigate to any other directory and select any macro found anywhere on any disk; the macro you select appears in the File**n**ame entry field in the Play Macro dialog box.

4. Choose **P**lay.

   The PLCLOSNG.WCM macro you recorded earlier plays, retyping the signature block exactly as you typed it.

Now test the second macro that you recorded earlier. Follow steps 1 through 4, but type **PCLOSE2** for the macro name this time. The macro types up to the point where the attorney's name goes and then stops. Type in the name of the attorney who will sign the pleading; then press Enter. The macro then resumes and types the rest of the signature block.

Tip

While a macro is paused, you can operate most of WordPerfect's features normally. You can tell that a macro is paused, however, because the status bar shows the status *Play Paused* grayed out. Also, both the **P**lay and Pa**u**se options in the fly-out menu (**T**ools, **M**acro) will have check marks next to them. You can cancel the macro by clicking **P**lay from that fly-out menu, or you can resume the macro without pressing Enter simply by clicking Pa**u**se.

You can play any macro on your disk, or on any floppy disk, including both simple and programmed macros, in this way.

For macros that you only play once in a while, the Play Macro dialog box is the best way to go. But you may soon find that there are a number of macros that you use frequently that you would like to have quicker access to. WordPerfect offers four different ways of quickly starting macros and thus bypassing the Play Macro dialog box:

■ The Macro menu

■ Using hot key names for the macro

■ Assigning macros to buttons on the button bar

■ Assigning macros to keys on a soft keyboard.

Using the Macro Menu

In Version 6.0, WordPerfect gave you the option of specifying up to nine macros that were always displayed with the Macro menu. This capability changed somewhat in Version 6.1. You can no longer specify any macros for permanent display on the Macro menu. WordPerfect does, however, keep track of the four most recently played macros and displays them in reverse chronological order (that is, the most recently played macro appears at the top of the list), as shown in figure 5.5.

Fig. 5.5

The Macro menu showing the four most recently played macros.

This feature is useful when you're writing and testing new macros, or when you're writing a macro to perform a series of tasks on multiple files. It saves you the trouble of having to find your macro from the Play Macro dialog box.

Using Hot Key Macros

Another way to gain quick access to your macros is to give them special names that allow you to access them directly from the keyboard. These special names describe the hot keys that activate the macro.

For example, a macro with the file name of CTRLO.WCM plays as soon as you press Ctrl+O on the keyboard. Likewise, a macro called CTRLSFTO.WCM plays when you press the keys Ctrl+Shift+O.

Table 5.1 lists the only keystroke combinations that WordPerfect recognizes and the corresponding file names.

Table 5.1 Possible Key Combinations for Hot Key Macro Names	
Key Combinations	**File Name Convention**
Ctrl+*letter*	CTRL*X*.WCM
Ctrtl+Shift+*letter* where *X* is an alphabetic or numeric character on the keyboard.	CTRLSFT*X*.WCM

In WordPerfect 5.1 for DOS, the program would also accept ALT*x*.WPM as a valid macro file name that could be executed simply by pressing Alt and the designated letter (*x*). This has changed in WordPerfect 6.1 for Windows. You cannot use the Alt key as a macro file name because Windows reserves that key to access menus, buttons, and other controls.

Assigning Macros to the Button Bar and Keyboard

However, you can use the Alt key to have access to hot key macros by assigning a macro to an Alt+*x* key combination on a soft keyboard. You can assign any macro on your disk to any key or combination of keys using the soft keyboard feature. For more information on how to do this, see Chapter 1, "Making WordPerfect Work the Way You Do."

Caution

You should be careful about assigning macros to any Alt+*x* key combination for the same reason that WordPerfect does not allow you to name a macro ALT*x*.WCM: WordPerfect uses Alt+*letter* combinations to access various menus and submenus. If you create a soft keyboard that redefines Alt+F, for example, you may not be able to access the **F**ile menu from the keyboard.

You can also assign macros to buttons on any button bar, or even to the menu bar. Chapter 1 describes these methods also.

Editing Macros

Suppose that you want to change something in a macro you have recorded; for example, your office moves to a new address or changes the phone number. Do you have to re-record all your macros?

You can re-record them if that would be easiest. However, in most cases, the easiest way to make simple changes in a recorded macro is simply to edit the existing macro. This is easy to do, because a WordPerfect for Windows macro is an ordinary WordPerfect document. You can open it, modify it, print it, and save it just as you would any other document.

You may be intimidated by this at first, however, because a macro *looks* different on the screen. For example, if you expect the macro PLCLOSNG.WCM that you recorded earlier in the chapter to resemble the signature block for your pleading, you'll be disappointed. That macro actually looks like figure 5.6.

Fig. 5.6

The content of the PLCLOSNG.WCM macro file.

```
1    Application (A1; "WordPerfect"; Default; "US")
2    HardReturn ()
3    LineSpacing (Spacing: 1.0)
4    HardReturn ()
5    Tab ()
6    Tab ()
7    Tab ()
8    Tab ()
9    Tab ()
10   Tab ()
11   Type (Text: "Respectfully Submitted,")
12   HardReturn ()
13   HardReturn ()
14   Tab ()
15   Tab ()
16   Tab ()
17   Tab ()
18   Tab ()
19   Tab ()
20   Type (Text: "HORNBLOWER AND ASSOCIATES, P.C.")
21   HardReturn ()
22   HardReturn ()
23   HardReturn ()
24   HardReturn ()
25   Tab ()
26   Tab ()
27   Tab ()
28   Tab ()
29   Tab ()
30   Type (Text: "By:")
31   Tab ()
32   AttributeAppearanceToggle (Attrib: Underline!)
33   FlushRight ()
34   AttributeAppearanceToggle (Attrib: Underline!)
35   HardReturn ()
36   Tab ()
37   Tab ()
38   Tab ()
39   Tab ()
40   Tab ()
41   Tab ()
42   Type (Text: "Horatio H. Hornblower IV, Esq.")
43   HardReturn ()
44   Tab ()
45   Tab ()
```

```
46     Tab ()
47     Tab ()
48     Tab ()
49     Tab ()
50     Type (Text: "52563 Hornblower Plaza")
51     HardReturn ()
52     Tab ()
53     Tab ()
54     Tab ()
55     Tab ()
56     Tab ()
57     Tab ()
58     Type (Text: "Horns Aplenty, MA  09998")
59     HardReturn ()
60     Tab ()
61     Tab ()
62     Tab ()
63     Tab ()
64     Tab ()
65     Tab ()
66     Type (Text: "(999) 555-2222")
67     HardReturn ()
68     HardReturn ()
69     Tab ()
70     Tab ()
71     Tab ()
72     Tab ()
73     Tab ()
74     Tab ()
75     AttributeAppearanceToggle (Attrib: Italics!)
76     Type (Text: "Attorney for")
```

It would be a good idea to examine this file for a moment before changing anything.

First, your macro does not show the numbers in the left margin of figure 5.6; but don't worry—it shouldn't. I have put them in this example so that I can draw your attention to particular lines without your having to count the line numbers down from the top each time. (In case you're wondering, the line numbers were generated by the Line Numbering feature, which I turned on at the top of the document. To enable this feature, choose Format, **L**ine, **N**umbering.)

> **Note**
>
> All discussion of macro code uses Line Numbering to facilitate discussion. If you want to add line numbers to your macros, do so by using the Line Number feature; if you type the line numbers or use an automatic numbering system to put numbers directly into the document, the macro will not function.

Line 1 of figure 5.6 contains a command (the standard Application command) that tells WordPerfect where to find certain information it needs to play the macro. You need not concern yourself with this command; just don't change it!

Each line after the first line of the macro represents a separate keystroke or some completed action that has been recorded. For example, if you recall, the first thing you did when recording the PLCLOSNG.WCM macro was to insert a hard return after the end of the text to move the insertion point to the next blank line; line 2 records that action as HardReturn (). Likewise, the next thing you did in recording the macro was to change the line spacing to single; that shows up on line 3 as LineSpacing(Spacing: 1.0).

These words are referred to as *commands* or *macro commands*. In each case, the command is a single word (sometimes a combination of words) that describes the action to be performed. In some cases, there is a pair of empty parentheses following the command; in other cases, there is additional information inside the parentheses.

The information inside the parentheses is called the *parameters*. Parameters are used to specify or clarify an action to be performed by the command. Some commands require no parameters, such as the HardReturn() and Tab() codes you see in figure 5.6 (these actions are so simple they need no further explanation). Others do require more information before they can be executed, like the LineSpacing command on line 3. You can't just tell WordPerfect to change the line spacing; you have to tell it what setting to change it to. Thus, the new line space setting (shown as Spacing: 1.0) is a required parameter to tell the command what the new setting should be.

WordPerfect automatically writes all of these commands when you record the macro. However, you can change them at any time to change how the macro operates. For example, if you change the spacing parameter on line 3 to read Spacing: 1.5, the next time you play the macro it changes the line spacing to 1.5 instead of 1.0.

Most of what this macro does is type text. The commands to do this are shown on lines 11, 20, 30, 42, 50, 58, 66, and 75. The command on each line is Type; the required parameter (inside the parentheses) is Text:.

The use of quotation marks and punctuation in a macro command is critical to its operation. Parameter names are always followed by a colon and are never enclosed in quotation marks. Characters that are to be typed (for example, on line 11) are always enclosed in quotation marks. Numeric values needed to specify a setting are not enclosed in quotation marks (for example, on line 3). And you occasionally see an exclamation point after some parameter (such as on lines 32 and 34). These are specific values for parameters that recognize only certain values.

Now that you understand the macro file in figure 5.6 a bit better, you're ready to edit it. Assume that the proprietor of the law firm for whom the macro was written takes on a partner and needs to change the name of his firm. To edit this macro, do the following:

1. Open the macro file using the Open File dialog box (choose File, Open). Or, choose **T**ools, **M**acro, **E**dit, and then select the macro you want to edit in the Edit Macro dialog box and choose **E**dit.

   Whichever route you choose, the macro appears in an open document window. The Macros feature bar appears immediately above the text of the macro, as shown in figure 5.7.

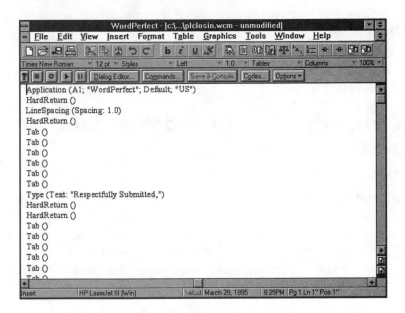

Fig. 5.7
The Macros feature bar just above the text of a macro.

2. Move the insertion point to the line which reads Type(Text: "HORNBLOWER AND ASSOCIATES, P.C.").

3. Change the words inside the quotation marks to the new name of the firm.

   Be sure to change only the text between the quotation marks, because this is the text that appears when the macro is played. Leave the rest of the command alone.

   Notice that when you make a change to the macro, the Play button on the Macro feature bar is grayed out and the Save & Compile button is

activated. This is because WordPerfect must translate the words you
type on the screen into code that your computer can execute. This
translation process is called *compiling*. A macro is automatically com-
piled when you record it. However, if you modify it in any way,
WordPerfect must reexamine the macro and retranslate the new version
back into machine code. WordPerfect saves and compiles the macro
automatically when you close the macro. Alternatively, you can cause
WordPerfect to compile the macro without closing the file (for example, if you want to test the macro by playing it while the macro file
is still open); just choose Save & **C**ompile from the Macro feature bar.

4. Choose Save & **C**ompile from the Macro feature bar.

If you want to test the macro immediately, you can choose **P**lay from
the Macro feature bar right now; but this would insert the pleading
signature block into the middle of your macro, so in this case don't play
the macro.

5. To close the macro, either choose **F**ile, Close, from the WordPerfect
menu bar, or choose Options from the Macro feature bar and choose
Close Macro.

An Introduction to Programmed Macros

Now comes the hard stuff: programmed macros.

Actually, programmed macros are only hard when you write them. If properly written, they are very easy to use. In fact, their principal purpose is to
take some task that you do frequently and make it as automatic and as simple
as possible for the user. A good programmed macro dramatically reduces the
time it takes you to create or edit a document, or perform some other function, making you far more efficient in your daily work.

The *really* complex programmed macros may take hours and hours of work
to get just right; there are plenty of examples of those in Part II of this book.
The purpose of this chapter is not to touch the subject of how to write such
things, but to explain a few concepts and teach you some fairly simple programming commands that you can grasp easily and put to good use with
only minimal effort. Hopefully, this chapter will give you some ideas on how
you can use these commands to win friends and influence people, or at least
to write some pretty slick macros.

Some Basic Concepts

Before learning the commands themselves, it will help you to become
familiar with some basic concepts. To some extent this discussion is an

oversimplification, because there are many nuances and details within each of these concepts that are not really essential to understanding the commands discussed later. The purpose of this section is to provide a very general background on how programmed macros work, not to go into the finer details of this feature.

If you want to learn more about the intricacies of writing programmed macros, consult the WordPerfect Macros Manual, available separately from WordPerfect Corporation.

Commands and Syntax

To a degree, learning to write programmed WordPerfect macros is like learning a foreign language. To tell WordPerfect what you want it to do, you have to speak to it in its own language (sometimes referred to as the WordPerfect Macro Language). This new language has words (called *commands*) and grammar (called *syntax*).

There are two basic types of WordPerfect macro commands: *product* or WordPerfect commands and *programming commands*. Each WordPerfect product command activates some feature available in the program. There are more than 1,600 WordPerfect product commands, but you need not learn how to write them. Almost all these commands can be recorded from the keyboard; if you want to find out what the command name is and what its syntax is, all you need to do is record a macro that activates the function you want; then open the resulting macro and study what was recorded.

All WordPerfect product commands conform to this structure:

```
MacroCommand (Parameter 1: value; Parameter 2: value)
```

Most product commands require parameters that define specifically what the command is supposed to do; some require more than one parameter. All parameters are enclosed within parentheses and each is separated from the others by a semicolon. The parameter name is always followed by a colon, and the value may be enclosed in quotation marks, or followed by an exclamation point, or may have no punctuation at all, depending on the type of value required by the parameter. You need not be too concerned about when to use each type of punctuation, however, because the proper punctuation is always included when you record the macro.

The programming commands, however, cannot be recorded from the keyboard. You must insert them by typing them in from the keyboard. The programming commands provide the logic through which a macro decides what to do next. They ask the user for input and then evaluate the input and perform different tasks depending on the input.

For example, one programming command is IF. This command tells the macro what to do "if" a certain condition exists. It works just like you do. Suppose that you go to the store to purchase a gallon of milk. You "program" yourself so that when you arrive at the store, you will make the purchase IF the store has milk; but IF it does not, you will go to another store. The IF command can "program" a WordPerfect macro to act in different ways if different conditions exist.

The syntax of most macro programming commands is very similar to that of the product commands, with the exception that you do not need to use parameter names. It is critically important, however, that if a programming command requires more than one parameter, you put the parameters into the command in the correct order, or the macro will not work.

Variables

Shades of high school algebra class! What is a *variable* and what does it have to do with word processing?

A WordPerfect macro variable is actually quite similar to a variable in an algebraic equation. Just like the variable x in the equation $2x = 4$ stands for something (in that case the number 2), a WordPerfect variable named *author* can stand for the string of characters which spell your name. You can put different strings of characters (or numbers or other types of information) into a WordPerfect variable. Hence, the name variable: the contents may vary.

There are many different types of variables in WordPerfect, but this chapter deals with only two of them: character variables and system variables. Character variables contain strings of characters, assigned by a WordPerfect programming command. You can use these to store information typed by the user in response to a programming command, and then type that information into your document at appropriate places. For example, in the command:

```
Assign(myvar;"Kenneth D. Chestek")
```

The 18 characters (including spaces and the period in the string "Kenneth D. Chestek" will be stored in a character variable named "myvar."

Most character variables are erased from your computer's memory as soon as the macro has finished playing.

When looking at a macro file, you can distinguish a character variable from a string of characters by punctuation. A string of characters, to be used literally by WordPerfect, is always enclosed in quotation marks. A character variable is *never* enclosed in quotation marks.

> **Note**
>
> In writing macro commands you must use the standard straight quotation marks, not the curly quotation marks inserted by the SmartQuotes feature. If you are writing or editing macros, be sure to disable the SmartQuotes feature before typing any quotation marks. In version 6.1, SmartQuotes is automatically disabled whenever the Macro feature bar is displayed.

System variables contain information about the current state of affairs within WordPerfect, for example, whether the Italic attribute is on or off at the insertion point, and what the number of the active document window is.

You cannot change the value of any system variable through a macro, but you can use information contained in system variables to make different decisions, as this chapter shows later. For example, if you want to make sure that the active document window is blank before you play a macro, you can include commands within your macro to check the system variable that keeps track of whether the active document is blank or not. You can write the macro so that if the screen is blank, the macro plays in that window; but if the screen is not blank, WordPerfect opens a new window before playing the macro.

Expressions and Operators

To go back to that high school algebra class for just a second: Some WordPerfect commands use *expressions* and *operators* to make comparisons or evaluations. These things look, and work, a lot like simple equations.

The best way to learn about expressions and operators is to look at an example. The programming command IF, discussed below, is one command that requires an expression as its parameter. The expression must make some kind of comparison so that IF can decide when to do one thing and when to do something else.

For example, in the command:

```
IF (name=Ken Chestek)
```

the macro compares the current contents of the variable *name* with the string of characters Ken Chestek. If it finds a perfect match, the expression (name=Ken Chestek) is evaluated as *true*, and some action takes place. If there is no match, the expression is evaluated as *false*, and either a different action, or no action, takes place.

The equation inside the parentheses in this example is called a *relational expression*, because it examines the relationship between two values. The equals sign in the expression is a *relational operator*, because it returns a value based on the relationship between two values. In this case, it returns a value of true if the items on either side of the operator match exactly.

Table 5.2 lists available relational operators.

Table 5.2 Relational Operators	
Expression	**Evaluation**
Value 1 > Value 2	Value 1 is greater than value 2.
Value 1 >= Value 2	Value 1 is greater than or equal to value 2.
Value 1 < Value 2	Value 1 is less than value 2.
Value 1 <= Value 2	Value 1 is less than or equal to value 2.
Value 1 = Value 2	Value 1 and value 2 match exactly.
Value 1 <> Value 2	Value 1 and value 2 are different.

Using GETSTRING

Now to get specific and take a look at just a few of the WordPerfect macro programming commands that you can use without much effort.

One of the simplest and most useful programming commands is GETSTRING. Its function is to pause the macro and ask the user to supply certain information. It then stores the user's response in a variable, which can be used at any location in the macro.

The syntax of the GETSTRING macro command is as follows:

```
GetString(VariableName;"Prompt";"Title";[Length])
```

As you can see, this command has four parameters, although the last one (Length) is optional. They perform these functions:

- *VariableName*. This is the name of the variable that stores the user's response. Most any word will work so long as it's not the name of another WordPerfect command (for example, you cannot use the word Return as a variable name because it is the name of a programming command). Do not enclose the name of the variable in quotation marks.

> **Note**
>
> If you inadvertently use a reserved word (that is, one of the words that does not work as a variable name), you get a compilation error when you next play the macro. All you need to do is to edit the macro and change the variable name to something else and try again.

- *Prompt*. This is the message that WordPerfect shows to the user. You can use this to give the user instructions on what kind of information she should enter into the data window. You should enclose the complete message in quotation marks.

- *Title*. This is a very brief message that appears in the title bar of the GETSTRING dialog box. Again, you should enclose any title you place here within quotation marks.

- *[Length]*. This is an optional parameter. If you want to limit the user's input to a specified number of characters, just type that number, not in quotation marks, in this location.

Here are a couple of examples of how this command works. First, you'll create a simple macro that uses the GETSTRING command.

1. Open a new document window.

2. On the first line of the new window, type the following macro command:

    `GetString(username;"Type the user's name";"Test GETSTRING command")`

3. Press Enter.

4. On the next line, type the following macro command:

    `Type(username)`

    Note that there are *no* quotation marks around the variable name *username*. If you put quotation marks here, WordPerfect assumes that you want to type the word *username* and not the contents of that variable.

5. Save the document with any file name. Because this is a test macro, you might want to name this document TEST.WCM.

> **Note**
>
> To make it easier to play this macro, it is best to save it in your default macros directory.

6. Close the document or switch to another blank document window.

7. Now play the macro (choose **T**ools, **M**acro, **P**lay, and specify the path and file name for the test macro you just saved).

   You see a dialog box that looks like figure 5.8. This is the dialog box that is created by the GETSTRING command you entered in step 2.

Fig. 5.8
The dialog box
created by the
sample
GETSTRING
command.

8. Enter your name, or some other string of characters.

9. Choose OK.

The characters you entered in step 8 are typed into your document. This is because the Type command you inserted in step 4 recognizes *username* as a character variable and types the contents of that variable, instead of the variable name itself.

Suppose that you want to limit the user's response to only a few characters, such as when you are prompting for information to insert in an address. You can do this by using the Length parameter, as in this example:

```
GETSTRING(zipcode;Enter the zip code;Address Macro;10)
```

This command would allow the user to type in ten characters (the five-digit main ZIP Code, a hyphen, and the four-digit extended ZIP code). If the user tried to enter more than ten characters, subsequent characters would be rejected with a beep to alert the user that the full allotment of characters has been used.

A sample of a simple address-gathering macro is shown in figure 5.9. You add to this macro later in the chapter to demonstrate a few other programming commands.

Note that this simple macro combines the programming command GetString (the first six lines) with the WordPerfect product commands Type and HardReturn (lines 7 through 19), which insert and format the address.

Using IF Structures

Another useful and relatively simple programming command is the IF/ENDIF structure. This command allows the macro to evaluate some condition and take alternative actions depending on what it finds. You'll see how this works in the sample macro in just a moment.

```
1          GetString(addressee;"Name of addressee";"Address Macro")
2          GetString(address1;"First line of address";"Address Macro")
3          GetString(address2;"Second line of address (if any)";"Address Macro")
4          GetString(city;"Enter the City";"Address Macro")
5          GetString(state;"Enter the State (two-letter abbreviation)";"Address Macro";2)
6          GetString(zipcode;"Enter the Zip Code";"Address Macro";10)
7          Type(addressee)
8          HardReturn
9          Type(address1)
10         HardReturn
11         Type(address2)
12         HardReturn
13         Type(city)
14         Type(", ")
15         Type(state)
16         Type(" ")
17         Type(zipcode)
18         HardReturn
19         HardReturn
```

Fig. 5.9
A sample macro
using GETSTRING
to write an
address.

The syntax of the IF/ENDIF structure is as follows:

```
IF (test)
   [commands to perform if test is true]
ELSE
   [commands to perform if test is false]
ENDIF
```

The ELSE command is optional; you may have a situation where the macro should do nothing if the test condition is not true. In fact, that's the situation in the sample macro.

In the sample, what happens if there is no second line of the address? Line 11 tries to type the contents of the variable *address2*, and it is followed by a hard return. If the user enters nothing in response to the GetString prompt on line 3, however, that causes the macro to type an unnecessary blank line.

You can avoid this blank line by adding an IF structure at line 11, as shown in figure 5.10.

On line 11 is the command IF (address2"<>"). In this expression, the <> means "is not equal to" and the pair of quotation marks just inside the right parenthesis indicates that you are testing for a variable that contains no characters. This can be paraphrased in English like this: If the variable address 2 is not equal to nothing, then do the next commands. Sure, this is a double negative, but macros aren't bothered by this; they use different rules of grammar than humans do.

Fig. 5.10

Modifying the
macro to skip the
second address
line if the user has
skipped it.

```
1       GetString(addressee;"Name of addressee";"Address Macro")
2       GetString(address1;"First line of address";"Address Macro")
3       GetString(address2;"Second line of address (if any)";"Address Macro")
4       GetString(city;"Enter the City";"Address Macro")
5       GetString(state;"Enter the State (two-letter abbreviation)";"Address Macro";2)
6       GetString(zipcode;"Enter the Zip Code";"Address Macro";10)
7       Type(addressee)
8       HardReturn
9       Type(address1)
10      HardReturn
11      IF(address2<>"")
12          Type(address2)
13          HardReturn
14      ENDIF
15      Type(city)
16      Type(", ")
17      Type(state)
18      Type(" ")
19      Type(zipcode)
20      HardReturn
21      HardReturn
```

Lines 12 and 13 contain the commands which are supposed to be performed
if the expression is evaluated as *true* (that is, there is something, or more
precisely not nothing, in the variable *address2*): type the contents of that variable and then enter a hard return. Line 14 marks the end of the commands
that are performed only if there is something in the variable.

If the user enters nothing in response to the command on line 3 of the
macro, the variable *address2* contains nothing. In that situation, the IF statement on line 11 evaluates as *false*: since there is nothing in the variable, the
macro skips the commands on lines 12 and 13 (since the IF command is looking for "not nothing"). The macro thus skips to line 15 and continues from
there.

Suppose that you want the macro to do something different instead of just
skipping a step, depending on the outcome of the IF test. The macro shown
in figure 5.11 is an example of how you can use an ELSE command in the
middle of an IF/ENDIF structure to accomplish this.

This macro asks for the name of the author of a letter, then types a signature
block for that person. The IF structure beginning on line 30 looks to see if the
user entered the string of characters **Kenneth D. Chestek**; if she did, then
the expression is evaluated as *true* and the command on line 31 is played. If
the user enters anything else, the macro skips to the ELSE command on line
32 and executes lines 33 and 34. After either alternative is executed, the
macro continues with line 36.

```
 1      GetString(author;"Name of the person signing letter";"Signature Macro")
 2      HardReturn
 3      HardReturn
 4      Tab
 5      Tab
 6      Tab
 7      Tab
 8      Tab
 9      Tab
10      Type ("Very truly yours")
11      HardReturn
12      HardReturn
13      Tab
14      Tab
15      Tab
16      Tab
17      Tab
18      Tab
19      Type("_____")
20      HardReturn
21      Tab
22      Tab
23      Tab
24      Tab
25      Tab
26      Tab
27      Type(author)
28      HardReturn
29      HardReturn
30      IF(author="Kenneth D. Chestek")
31          Type("KDC")
32      ELSE
33          GetString(initials;"Type initials of author";"Signature Macro")
34          Type(initials)
35      ENDIF
36      Type(":kdc")
```

Fig. 5.11
An alternative IF
structure.

Special Features

Using System Variables

The address macro introduced above illustrates one way in which you can use a system variable as part of an expression in an IF command.

Suppose that you are writing the macro to help you write an address for an envelope, and therefore you wanted to be sure that the address always appears in a new document window. You could, of course, try to remember to open a new document before playing the macro, but human nature being what it is, you want to automate that step, too. It's easy with a system variable.

Many system variables are available to use. They are all documented in the online Macros help file, under the System Variable Index.

This example uses a system variable to check to see if the current document window is blank. If so, it plays the macro in this window; otherwise, it has to open a new window. Here's the command to perform this test:

```
IF(?DocBlank=TRUE)
ELSE
    FileNew()
ENDIF
```

Look at this command for a moment. First, examine the expression in the IF command. The word ?DocBlank is the name of the system variable which keeps track of whether the active document is blank or not. All system variables begin with question marks.

The possible values for this system variable (as reported to you by the on-line Macro help) are TRUE (the document is blank) and FALSE (the document is not blank). These values are *not* character values; they are something called Boolean values (*i.e.*, either true or false). Thus, they are *not* enclosed in parentheses, but are used by themselves.

Thus, the English translation of the IF command is this: If the document is blank....

Now notice that the very next command is an ELSE command. This means that there are no commands to be performed if the document is blank; you can go ahead and start with the rest of the macro immediately.

If, however, the document is not blank, the expression is evaluated as FALSE and the macro performs the commands immediately following the ELSE command; in this example, it opens a new document window.

The address macro example, modified to include this test at the beginning, is shown in figure 5.12.

There are nearly 300 different system variables that you can use in different expressions. You can test for current settings of WordPerfect, the location of the insertion point in the active document, and many other things that space simply won't allow discussing in this book.

Creating Menu Controls

This section switches gears and discusses another simple programming command that can add a lot of functionality with very little effort. The command MENU allows you to generate a quick on-screen menu from which the user makes a selection; the macro then evaluates the choice made by the user and branches accordingly.

```
1     IF(?DocBlank=TRUE)
2     ELSE
3         FileNew()
4     ENDIF
5     GetString(addressee;"Name of addressee";"Address Macro")
6     GetString(address1;"First line of address";"Address Macro")
7     GetString(address2;"Second line of address (if any)";"Address Macro")
8     GetString(city;"Enter the City";"Address Macro")
9     GetString(state;"Enter the State (two-letter abbreviation)";"Address Macro";2)
10    GetString(zipcode;"Enter the Zip Code";"Address Macro";10)
11    Type(addressee)
12    HardReturn
13    Type(address1)
14    HardReturn
15    IF(address2<>"")
16        Type(address2)
17        HardReturn
18    ENDIF
19    Type(city)
20    Type(", ")
21    Type(state)
22    Type(" ")
23    Type(zipcode)
24    HardReturn
25    HardReturn
```

Fig. 5.12

Testing to see if the current document window is blank.

Special Features

The syntax for the MENU command is as follows:

```
Menu(VariableName;MnemonicType;horizontal position;vertical
position;{"menu choice 1";"menu choice 2"; . . . "menu choice n"})
```

To examine each of those parameters:

- The *VariableName* parameter is similar to the variable name parameter of GETSTRING; you can use any legal variable name here. This variable contains the number of the menu item selected by the user.

- *MnemonicType* specifies whether letters or numbers are to be displayed with each item. The two legal values for this parameter are Digit! and Letter!

- The horizontal position parameter is optional. If you use this parameter, you can specify the number of pixels between the left side of the document window and the left side of the menu. If you omit this parameter, WordPerfect centers the menu horizontally; but you must remember to include a semicolon, with nothing in front of it, as a place marker when you omit this parameter.

- The vertical position parameter works in the same way as the horizontal position parameter.

■ The last parameter is the list of items to be displayed in the menu. You can have up to nine items if you use Digit! and 26 items if you use Letter! in the MnemonicType parameter. All items are enclosed within curly braces, and each item is included in quotation marks; use a semi-colon to separate items from each other.

Once again, the easiest way to see how this command works is by looking at an example. Chapter 4, "Footnotes, Tables, and Compare," describes five macros that help you insert citations into a table of authorities for a brief. If you are like this author, you sometimes have a hard time remembering the names of macros. The Applications Disk includes a macro called BRFMENU.WCM which uses the MENU command to create a pop-up menu for these macros and then plays the selected macro.

On the Disk

The MENU command in that macro looks like this:

```
MENU(choice;Digit!;;;{"Define ToA";"Mark constitutional
reference";"Mark case authority";"Mark statutory authority";"Mark
other authority"})
```

This command displays the menu box shown in figure 5.13. Here's how it works.

Fig. 5.13
The menu box
created by the
MENU command.

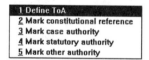

The first parameter, choice, is the name of the variable that contains the number of the user's selection. The second parameter, Digit!, forces the menu to place numbers before each of the five menu options shown in figure 5.13.

Notice that after the semicolon which marks the end of the MnemonicType parameter, there are two more semicolons with nothing in front of them. These are the place markers for the horizontal position and vertical position parameters. Since the example did not specify any values for those parameters, this menu box is centered on your screen, which is what you want most of the time anyway.

The last parameter shows the five options available (in this example the five macros which assist in the creation of a table of authorities). Notice that they are all enclosed in quotation marks and separated by semicolons; the entire parameter is wrapped inside of curly braces.

The SWITCH Command

Okay, so how do you tell the macro what to do after the user has made a choice from the menu? You know that the user's choice is stored in the variable you created, but what do you do with that?

You could, of course, write a series of IF statements, something like this:

```
IF (level=1)
   [command for level 1 number]
ENDIF
IF (level=2)
   [command for level 2 number]
ENDIF
. . .
```

and so on. But this involves a lot of unnecessary typing and is hard to read. A simpler solution is to use the SWITCH/ENDSWITCH macro commands to set up a list of options. The syntax for this command is as follows:

```
Switch(variable)
   CaseOf(1):      [command]
   CaseOf(2):      [command]
   . . .
   CaseOf(n):      [command]
   Default:        [command]
EndSwitch
```

In English, this command says, Take a look at the contents of this variable. If it is a 1, do this. If it is a 2, do something else. . . . If it is none of these things, take this action by default.

Now to look at how this command works in the BRFMENU.WCM macro mentioned above. The full text of the SWITCH/ENDSWITCH structure from that macro is as follows:

```
SWITCH(choice)
   CASEOF(1):      macroname=MAKETOA.WCM
   CASEOF(2):      macroname=CONSTCIT.WCM
   CASEOF(3):      macroname=CASECITE.WCM
   CASEOF(4):      macroname=STATCITE.WCM
   CASEOF(5):      macroname=OTHERCIT.WCM
   DEFAULT:        QUIT
ENDSWITCH
```

In this command, depending upon which of the five options the user selects, the SWITCH command assigns the name of the corresponding macro to a variable named *macroname*. The commands which follow the ENDSWITCH command simply play the macro stored in the variable *macroname*.

What is the DEFAULT: command doing? You may wonder how it is possible for the user to put anything other than a 1, 2, 3, 4, or a 5 into the variable *choice*, since the MENU command has no other options. Actually, it has one other option. If you press Esc or click the mouse anywhere outside of the menu box, you cancel the macro, and the variable *choice* does not contain any of the options listed. You then get a cancellation message on your screen, which is unnecessary. To avoid that message, the DEFAULT: command simply tells the macro to immediately quit if it is canceled.

From Here...

This chapter has tried to compress a major subject into just a few pages. You've learned how to record, play and edit simple macros, and have had a very brief introduction into the subject of programmed macros. Hopefully, this brief discussion, coupled with the macros described in Part II of this book, will pique your interest in the subject of macros, since a good collection of programmed macros is probably the fastest way to increased productivity that WordPerfect has to offer.

The next chapter takes up the somewhat related subject of Merge. You learn about the following:

- How to perform a simple merge
- Using the Quick Data Entry dialog box to create data files
- How to pause a merge so the user can add input from the keyboard
- How to perform a conditional or programmed merge

6

A Merge Primer

The preceding chapter dealt with macros and touched on programmable macros; that is, macros that can change directions depending upon user input or other conditions. WordPerfect for Windows contains a second programming language as well, in the Merge feature. Although the Merge feature exists and operates independently from the macro programming language, it bears some similarities to the complex macro commands and can work with macros. You can use merges to accomplish many of the tasks you can perform with macros; and in some cases, merges are better tools.

This chapter covers the following:

- Running a simple merge
- Pausing a merge to obtain user input
- Performing complex, or "programmed" merges

An Introduction to Merge

Many users familiar with basic word processing are familiar with the concept of merging documents (sometimes known as *mail merge*). In its simplest form, merging consists of taking a *form document* (such as a letter with blanks left in for the address and the salutation) and combining it with a list of information (such as the addresses and salutations for all persons who will receive the letter) to produce many copies of the same basic document. Each is customized slightly with specific information inserted in the blanks.

Many word processors allowed for minor variations in each copy. For example, you can instruct most programs to skip a field if it contains no information. But several years ago, WordPerfect for DOS introduced the concept of the *conditional merge,* which took the merge feature far beyond the simple "Skip this field if blank" types of special instructions. The conditional merge feature of WordPerfect (also referred to as a *programmed merge*) shares most of the commands and features of WordPerfect programmed macros.

Now for a closer look at how Merge operates.

Performing a Simple Merge

A merge is a process in which information from two or more sources is combined into a single document. It is as simple, and as complicated, as that.

Combining a form letter with a mailing list is an example of a merge process involving only two sources of information: the form letter and the mailing list. But the process may also involve more than two sources. You may need to create a merge that combines several forms into one, or that combines several lists of specific information (for example, if you have several different mailing lists that need to receive the same letter). Another merge may need to pause and prompt the user to type in specific information, such as a salutation for a letter. A merge may also need to retrieve another document into the resulting document, verbatim. Thus, the possible sources of information that can be combined during a merge are as follows:

- The form file (the basic form letter, for example)
- The data file (the mailing list, for example)
- Complete document files
- The keyboard

Any merge process may make use of any or all possible sources of information.

Figure 6.1 graphically depicts the merge process.

The components that are combined are sometimes referred to collectively as *source documents*. The finished product (after the merge has been performed) is referred to as the *merged document* or the *resulting document*.

Suppose that you want to maintain a list of clients using the WordPerfect merge feature so that you can quickly send invoices, reminder notices, announcements, or other information to them. You want to store your clients' names, addresses, and other pertinent information in such a way as to be able to automatically send these various items either to selected persons or to everybody on the list.

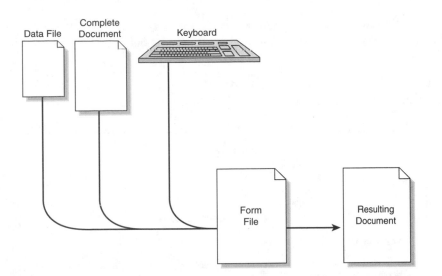

Fig. 6.1
The merge process.

The exercise this portion of the chapter uses is creating a cover letter to send with monthly bills to active clients in this database. In the process, you see how a relatively simple merge might use all four of the possible sources of information discussed earlier. You'll create the documents necessary to run a conditional merge and along the way learn some of the things you can do with this technique.

Note

This database forms the basis for an accounts receivable tracking system for lawyers described in Chapter 14, "Client/Case Management." That chapter describes how to use macros to create and maintain such a system; this chapter uses the system as an example of how the Merge feature operates.

Planning a Merge

To create "form" letters using Merge, you need to do the following:

1. Create a form file.
2. Create a data file.
3. Perform the merge.
4. Print the resulting document containing your form letters.

Before you begin this process, however, you need to analyze the kinds of information you need to insert into each document during the merge process.

This gives you the list of *fields*, or kinds of information, to be inserted into the form document. Once you have determined the fields, you can create the data file.

For the billing cover letter to clients, the straight text (without any merge commands inserted) might look like that shown in figure 6.2.

Fig. 6.2
A sample firm announcement.

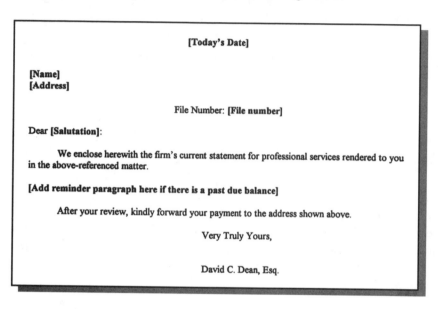

> [Today's Date]
>
> [Name]
> [Address]
>
> File Number: [File number]
>
> Dear [Salutation]:
>
>   We enclose herewith the firm's current statement for professional services rendered to you in the above-referenced matter.
>
> [Add reminder paragraph here if there is a past due balance]
>
>   After your review, kindly forward your payment to the address shown above.
>
>   Very Truly Yours,
>
>   David C. Dean, Esq.

As you can see, each letter requires five specific pieces of information, unique to each client:

- The client's name
- The client's address
- The file number or billing identification number
- A salutation for the client
- A field to contain the past due balance, if any

Each piece of information is called a *field*. WordPerfect form files are simpler to read and understand if you use named, rather than numbered, fields. So for the remainder of this example, the five fields will be called Name, Address, File number, Salutation, and Balance due.

The Form File

Next, you need to create the form file to use in the merge. Every merge requires a form file, regardless of what other sources of data it may use.

The form file is the traffic cop that controls the entire merge process. It can be as simple as a form letter that calls for certain types of information (names, addresses, and so on) to be inserted in the correct places; or it can be as complicated as a programmed macro. The form file can even turn over control of the computer to macros or other form files, either temporarily or permanently.

WordPerfect stores a form file on your computer just like an ordinary document file. What distinguishes it as a form file are the various merge commands stored in it. These commands do nothing at all until the merge process begins. Once the merge process reads the form file, the computer executes the merge commands in it, in the order in which they appear.

The specific types of client information required (the name, address, file number, salutation, and balance due) are referred to as *fields*. You specify where information of each type is to be inserted in a form document by placing a FIELD code at the proper location.

To insert the proper merge codes for the cover letter, follow these steps:

1. If the form document you want to use already exists, and just needs the proper merge codes, open the file in a new window; otherwise, open a new blank document window.

2. To identify a file as a WordPerfect merge form file, choose **T**ools, **M**erge.

3. In the Merge dialog box (see fig. 6.8), choose **F**orm.

4. If you are starting with an existing document, you see the Create Merge File dialog box shown in figure 6.3. To use the document in the active window, leave that radio button selected and choose OK.

Fig. 6.3
The Create Merge
File dialog box.

Note

If you started from a blank document, WordPerfect assumes that you want to create a new form document in that window, and you do not see this box.

Next, the dialog box shown in figure 6.4 gives you the option of associating the form file with a data file.

Fig. 6.4

The Create Form File dialog box.

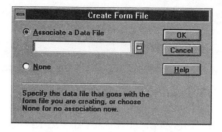

5. Because this example does use a data file, enter the path and file name of the data file you created earlier in this chapter (SAMPLE.DAT) in the **A**ssociate a Data File entry field; then choose OK.

If you started with an existing document (such as figure 6.2 earlier), your screen should now look something like figure 6.5.

Fig. 6.5

Creating a form file.

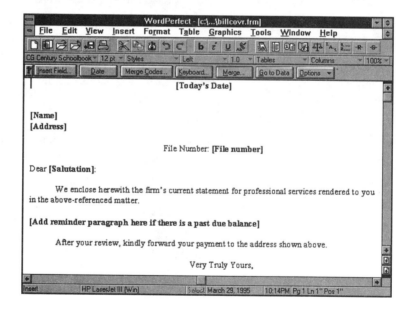

Here's how to automatically insert the current date (taken from your computer's internal clock) by using the DATE merge command:

6. Place the insertion point where you want the date to appear (deleting any markers or words you may have inserted in an existing document to mark the location of where the date should go).

7. Choose **D**ate from the Merge feature bar (just above the document).

Special Features

Tip

You can also accomplish this auto-date feature by placing a WordPerfect [Date Code] into the document at this location. However, the disadvantage of this option is that the [Date Code] changes every time the file is opened, while performing a merge with a DATE merge code permanently affixes the date of the merge into the document.

Next, you need to insert FIELD commands to tell the form file where to insert information. Here's how:

8. At the location on your screen where you want the client's name to appear, delete any markers or prompts you may have left in the document, and then choose **I**nsert Field from the Merge feature bar.

The Insert Field Name or Number dialog box appears. Because you have associated this form file with the data file containing the five fields you need to fill in for each client, those field names appear in the dialog box.

9. Select Name from the pick list in the Insert Field Name or Number dialog box; then choose **I**nsert.

The FIELD(Name) command then appears in your document where you want the name to appear in the letter, as shown in figure 6.6.

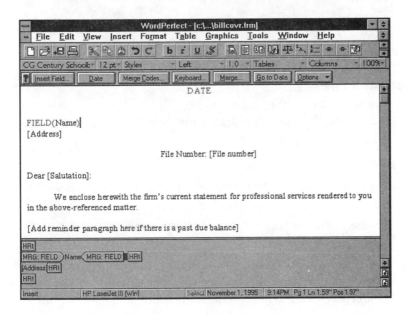

Fig. 6.6
The form document with the first field code inserted (shown in Reveal Codes).

10. Continue by inserting the address, salutation, and file number fields. (Leave the Balance due reminder alone for the moment.)

When you are done, your form document should look like the one shown in figure 6.7.

When you have completed typing the letter, with the merge codes inserted as described earlier, save it to disk. For the purposes of this exercise call the file BILLCOVR.FRM.

Fig. 6.7
The partially completed form file.

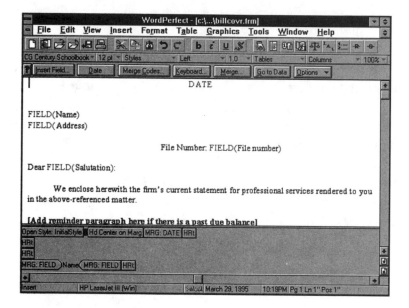

The Data File

Next, you need to create the data file to hold the records that will be merged with the form file. To create the data file for the example letter, follow these steps:

1. Open a new document window.

2. Choose **T**ools, **M**erge. The Merge dialog box appears, as shown in figure 6.8.

3. Because you're creating the data file first, choose **D**ata. The Create Data File dialog box appears.

4. Now create the list of fields you need for your form. For example, type in the word Name in the **N**ame a Field text box; then choose **A**dd. WordPerfect adds the field name to the list of field names in the list box below the name entry field.

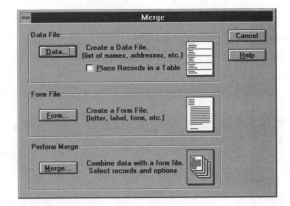

Fig. 6.8
The Merge dialog
box.

Special Features

5. Repeat the process for all of the fields you need for your form. When
   you are finished, the Create Data File dialog box should look like
   figure 6.9.

Fig. 6.9
The Create Data
File dialog box.

WordPerfect inserts the names of the fields you just entered into a
FIELD NAMES command in your data file; they are separated by semicolons. The FIELD NAMES command is followed by another merge code,
END RECORD, and a hard page break. WordPerfect uses this code, and
the hard page break, to mark the end of records.

A *record* is a set of pieces of information that relates to the same document. In this example, the five pieces of information (name, address,
file number, salutation, and balance due) constitute the record for each
client.

You do not see these codes immediately, however, because WordPerfect
takes you immediately to the Quick Data Entry dialog box, where you
can begin adding records for each of your clients to the data file.

6. From the Create Data File dialog box, choose OK.

You immediately see the Quick Data Entry dialog box, shown in figure 6.10.

7. Add the name, complete address, file number, salutation, and balance due information for your first client.

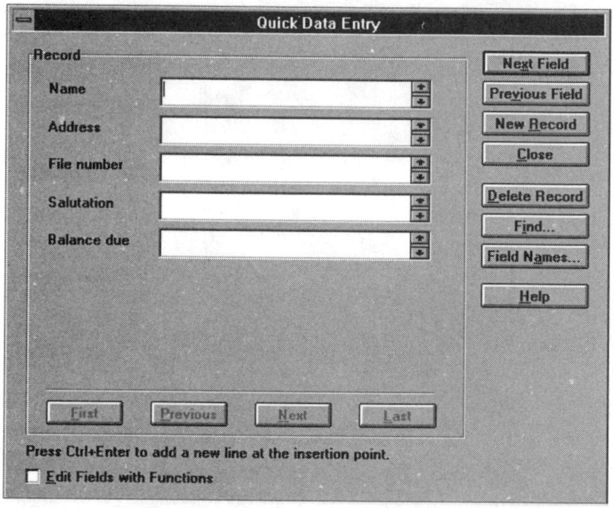

Fig. 6.10

The Quick Data Entry dialog box.

Tip

You are not limited to one line per field. A field can contain as much information as you require, and can include formatting or other special WordPerfect codes. However, you cannot add such codes during Quick Data Entry; you must add them directly to the file in the regular document screen.

Note

If you need to enter more than one line of data in a field (for example, in the Address field), press Ctrl+Enter instead of Enter at the end of a line. You can use the up and down arrows at the right of each field to move through the text you have entered in the field.

You can continue to add clients from this screen simply by choosing New **R**ecord. But for now, exit from the Quick Data Entry dialog box and take a look at what the data file looks like thus far.

8. Choose **C**lose.

9. The screen prompts you at this point to provide a file name in order to save the data file to disk; do so and choose OK.

Your data file, with the first record added, should look something like figure 6.11.

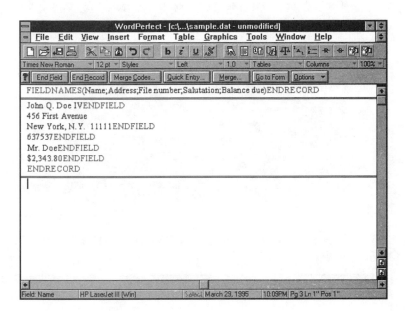

Special Features

Fig. 6.11
The sample data file showing the first record.

Notice that the Merge feature bar appears above your document. You can use this bar to edit the document. For example, if you want to return to Quick Data Entry to create records for additional clients, you can simply choose **Q**uick Entry from the feature bar and return to the Quick Data Entry screen to enter more records.

> **Note**
>
> Although you can insert records manually from the document shown in figure 6.11, you'll probably find that using the Quick Data Entry dialog box is faster and more accurate because it eliminates the possibility of inadvertently omitting a field.

When you have finished adding client records, save the data file to disk and exit it. For the purpose of this example, save the file as SAMPLE.DAT in whatever directory you prefer.

Performing the Merge

Before you go on to complete the form file by handling the problem of when and how to insert a reminder paragraph for a past due balance, it might be a good idea to pause and test out the form and data files to see how the merge process works.

1. Choose **T**ools, **M**erge. The Merge dialog box (refer to fig. 6.8) appears.

2. Choose **M**erge in the Perform Merge group box. The Perform Merge dialog box appears, as shown in figure 6.12.

Fig. 6.12

The Perform
Merge dialog box.

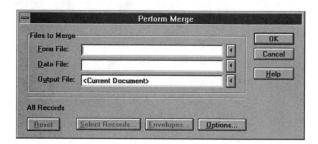

3. Insert the name of the form file (BILLCOVR.FRM in the example) in the **F**orm File text box.

Note

If you cannot remember the name of your file, you can click your mouse on the left arrow button just to the right of the entry window. From there you can specify whether to use the document currently on-screen as the data file, or you can display a listing of files on your computer to select from.

---

4. Insert the name of the data file (SAMPLE.DAT) in the **D**ata File window. (You have the option of choosing the left arrow button to specify that no data file be used, or selecting a data file from a directory listing.)

5. You can direct the output (the resulting file) to one of four destinations: a new blank document window, the current document window, the printer, or a disk file. You do this by choosing the left arrow button in the O**u**tput File window. For now, direct the output to a new document window.

6. Finally, perform the merge by choosing OK.

When you have finished, you have a single document containing as many copies of the form file as you had records in the data file. Each copy is separated from every other copy by a hard page break, and each copy is unique in that it is separately addressed to each of your clients.

Obtaining User Input During a Merge

As noted earlier, the keyboard is the third possible source of information for a merge. This chapter shows you one of the many merge commands that cause the merge to pause and ask for further information or instructions from the user.

As figure 6.2 shows, the billing cover letter includes the signature of an attorney. But suppose that more than one attorney in your firm will be sending these cover letters. One way to solve the problem would be to make a separate copy of this file for each attorney. Each file would be saved under a different name and contain the applicable name at the signature location.

Another way would be to use the same file and make the merge pause each time it gets to the end of the form document and ask the user to supply the name of the attorney who will sign the letter.

To insert a pause in the merge to allow input from the keyboard:

1. Open the form file BILLCOVR.FRM.

2. Delete the name of the attorney on the last line of the form file, but leave the insertion point where you want the user to type the new name.

3. Select **K**eyboard from the Merge feature bar. The Insert Merge Code dialog box for the KEYBOARD command appears, as shown in figure 6.13.

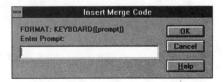

Fig. 6.13
Inserting a KEYBOARD command.

4. Type in a message prompting the user to type the name of the attorney at the location of this code. For example, type **Name of Attorney**. WordPerfect displays this message during the merge for each letter being created.

> **Note**
>
> If you use the QuickCorrect feature of WordPerfect to define an attorney's initials as a typographical error for his or her full name, you can expedite the process of typing in the attorney names during the merge process. For example, if you have defined David C. Dean, Esq. as the correct spelling for dcd, when the merge pauses at the end of a letter from Mr. Dean, the user need only type **dcd** and a space and the full name is inserted automatically. (Make sure the Replace Words as You Type check box is selected in your QuickCorrect dialog box before you do this.) For more information on QuickCorrect, see Chapter 1.

5. Choose OK. The revised form file now looks like figure 6.14.

Fig. 6.14
The revised cover letter form document (in Reveal Codes).

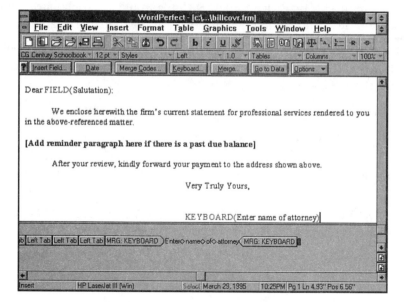

Performing a Conditional Merge

This example is, of course, quite simple. It is a straight, unconditional merge. A more complex conditional or programmed merge can accomplish many other things. This section expands the example to illustrate just some of the additional things you can do with conditional merges.

As mentioned earlier, four possible sources of information can be combined in a merge. You've learned something about three of them already: the form and data files, and the keyboard. The fourth possible source of information for a merge is a document file. That is, the merge may pick up a complete document and insert it verbatim into the resulting document created by a merge process.

The sample cover letter can use this technique effectively. Recall that you left room in the form file to include an optional reminder paragraph in cases where the client has a past due balance. Now you'll learn how to modify the form file in the cover letter example so that WordPerfect automatically inserts such a paragraph into the cover letter.

WordPerfect contains the merge command DOCUMENT, which retrieves a designated document, intact, into the resulting document during a merge. The entire document is placed at the location of the DOCUMENT command. You can even "selectively" include the new document in some letters and not others if you put into the data file information that tells WordPerfect whether to include the special document file in the letter.

1. First, in a new blank document window, create the special reminder paragraph you want the merge to insert.

   A sample of such a paragraph is shown in figure 6.15, in Reveal Codes format.

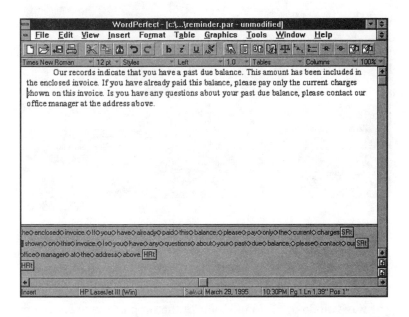

Fig. 6.15
A sample reminder paragraph, shown in Reveal Codes.

2. Save the reminder paragraph to disk (this example uses the file name of REMINDER.PAR).

Note that the sample paragraph concludes with two hard returns (shown in Reveal Codes as [HRt] codes). The two ending hard returns are to ensure that this paragraph is inserted as a discrete paragraph, separated from the following paragraph by a blank line.

3. Next, you must modify the BILLCOVR.FRM form file (refer to fig. 6.5) to provide instructions on when to include this special paragraph. Open that file in a new document window.

4. Delete the bracketed prompt about the reminder paragraph in the middle of the document.

5. Be sure to delete the two hard returns following that prompt, so that an extra space is not in the middle of the letter for clients who have no past due balance.

At this point, your screen should look like figure 6.16.

Fig. 6.16
Editing the
BILLCOVR.FRM
file.

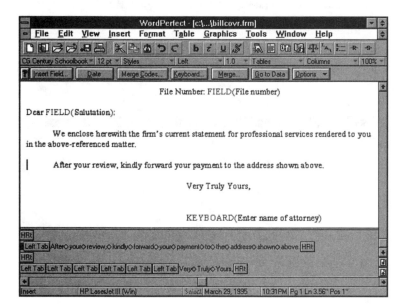

So that WordPerfect can determine whether to include the special reminder paragraph in a particular record, you're going to instruct the merge to test the content of the FIELD(Balance due). If that field contains information, the merge includes the paragraph.

The way you do this is to use some of the simpler merge programming commands, IF and ENDIF. These commands test for certain conditions, and if the conditions are found to be true, change the merge process in some fashion (hence the term "conditional" merge). The best way to understand how these commands work is to continue with the example.

6. Leaving the insertion point just before the final paragraph (refer to fig. 6.16), choose Merge **C**odes from the Merge feature bar. The Insert Merge Codes dialog box appears, as shown in figure 6.17.

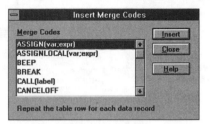

Fig. 6.17
The Insert Merge Codes dialog box.

7. Highlight the IF merge command by using the scroll bar and clicking on that command, or simply type **I** to invoke the mnemonic search feature.

8. Choose **I**nsert. The Insert Merge Code dialog box for the IF command appears, as shown in figure 6.18.

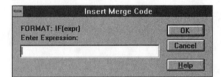

Fig. 6.18
The Insert Merge Code dialog box for the IF command.

The Insert Merge Code dialog box for the IF command is asking you to specify an *expression*. The expression is better thought of as a test condition. It is here that you tell the IF command what to look for to decide what to do next. In this example, you want to tell IF to check and see if there is any information stored in the FIELD(Balance due) in this record. Because you cannot enter another merge code in this text box, you'll have to go back and do that manually.

9. Choose OK. The IF command, without any test condition, has appeared in your document at the insertion point; your screen should now look like figure 6.19.

Notice that the insertion point in the main document window appears between the open and close parentheses immediately following the IF command. In Reveal Codes you can see that the IF is a paired code, and the insertion point is between the IF on and IF off codes. Do not move the insertion point yet! You need to insert the test condition in that exact spot.

Fig. 6.19
Inserting the IF merge command.

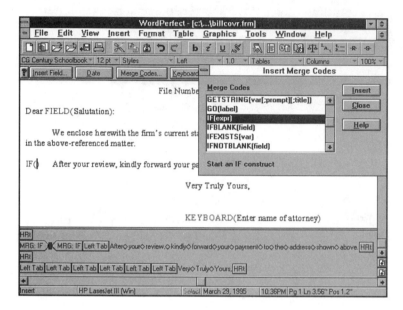

10. From the Merge feature bar, choose **I**nsert Field. The Insert Field Name or Number dialog box appears, showing the available fields in the associated data file (refer to fig. 6.6).

11. Select Balance due from the pick list and choose **I**nsert. A FIELD (Balance due) code now appears inside the parentheses of the IF command.

12. Choose **C**lose to dismiss the Insert Field Name or Number dialog box.

    Right now, the IF command makes no sense. It simply says, "If the balance due field." If the balance due field what? You need to complete the clause to read, "If the balance due field *is not blank,*" so the merge knows what it is looking for.

    In mergespeak, the expression that means is not is <> (literally, is either greater than or lesser than, and therefore not equal to). The expression that means blank is simply a pair of quotation marks, enclosing nothing (not even a space): "".

13. Immediately after the FIELD(Balance due) command but inside the second parenthesis (which marks the end of the IF command), type the characters <>"".

When you are finished the completed IF command should look like this:

```
IF(FIELD(Balance due)<>"")
```

14. Because you're now finished with the test condition, press the right arrow key once to move the insertion point outside of the IF off code.

Now you need to tell the merge what to do if the test condition is true; that is, what to do if the FIELD(Name) is not blank (and therefore there is a balance due owing). This is when you want WordPerfect to insert the special reminder paragraph. To do this, you can simply have the merge plunk the entire REMINDER.PAR document into the resulting document at this location, using the DOCUMENT merge command.

The DOCUMENT command, like many of the merge programming commands, requires a parameter, or more information, to properly execute. In this case, the command needs to know what document file to insert. The correct syntax for this merge command is:

```
DOCUMENT(filename)
```

15. In the Insert Merge Code dialog box, highlight the DOCUMENT merge command using the scroll bar or by typing **DO** to initiate a mnemonic search.

16. Choose **I**nsert. The Insert Merge Code dialog box for the DOCUMENT command appears.

17. Type in the complete path and file name for your REMINDER.PAR document, then choose OK. The DOCUMENT command is inserted into your file.

All that's left now is to tell the merge that it has no other special instructions if the name field is blank; in other words, it should return to the main merge and process the rest of the file in every case, whether or not that field is blank. The ENDIF command tells WordPerfect that the special handling is complete.

18. From the Insert Merge Codes dialog box, highlight the ENDIF command and choose **I**nsert.

19. Because you're now done inserting merge commands, dismiss the Insert Merge Codes dialog box by choosing **C**lose.

At this point, your document should look like figure 6.20.

Now, when the merge process encounters this string of commands for each record in the data file, WordPerfect looks to see if there is anything stored in the Balance due field of each record. If it is blank, the test condition fails and none of the commands between the IF and the ENDIF commands are executed. If, however, the field is not blank (that is, there is a balance due), the test condition is true, and the commands are executed, inserting the special paragraph into the resulting document for that record.

Fig. 6.20
The completed form file.

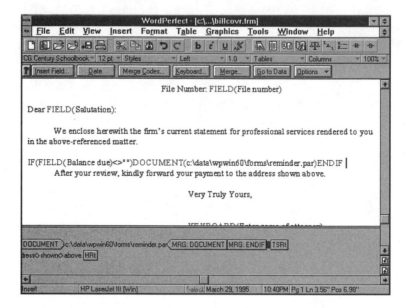

Combining More Than One Form File

The Merge feature has many capabilities beyond the simple IF/ENDIF analysis shown earlier. However, the more sophisticated programming features of the Merge language would take a book unto themselves to describe in detail. Now you look at just a few of the advanced capabilities of the Merge feature, so that you can use them to enhance your resulting document even further.

Because the data file you created above contains the exact dollar amount of the past due balance, it is possible to insert that figure into the resulting document. There are several ways to accomplish this. You'll choose one that makes use of another capability of Merge: the capability to use more than one form file in a single merge.

To do this, you need to set up the reminder paragraph as a form file. Follow these steps:

1. Open the REMINDER.PAR file created above (refer to fig. 6.15).

2. Choose **T**ools, **M**erge.

3. In the Merge dialog box (refer to fig. 6.8), choose **F**orm. The Create Merge File dialog box appears, as shown in figure 6.21.

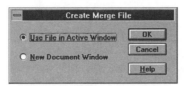

4. Because you want to convert the document REMINDER.PAR into a form
    file, leave the **U**se File in Active Window option selected and choose
    OK.

5. The Create Form File dialog box appears (refer to fig. 6.4). Because you
    want to associate this form file to the same data file as the main form
    file, type in the path and file name **SAMPLE.DAT** (or use the file icon
    at the end of the entry window to look through your directories to find
    the correct path and file name).

6. Choose OK; the Merge feature bar appears over your document.

    All you need to do is insert the word "of" and the amount of the
    arrearage immediately after the words "past due balance."

7. Place the insertion point immediately between the "e" in balance and
    the following period, and type a space, the word **of**, and another space.

8. From the Merge feature bar, choose **I**nsert Field.

9. From the pick list in the Insert Field Name or Number dialog box, high-
    light the field `Balance due` and choose **I**nsert.

    Your document screen should now look like figure 6.22.

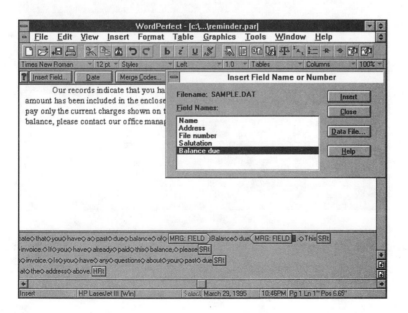

Fig. 6.22
Inserting a field
name code into
REMINDER.PAR.

10. Choose **C**lose in the Insert Field Name or Number dialog box.

11. Save the modifications to REMINDER.PAR to your disk.

    Next, you have to tell the BILLCOVR.FRM file that it should not simply insert the REMINDER.PAR document (with a raw FIELD code in it) directly into the resulting document where there is a balance due. Rather, it should transfer control of the merge temporarily to the new form file REMINDER.PAR so that it can process that code and extract the dollar amount out of the data file. You do this by nesting REMINDER.PAR as an additional data file to be processed during the merge.

12. Open the file BILLCOVR.FRM.

13. Delete the command DOCUMENT([path]\REMINDER.PAR) that you inserted in the preceding list of steps.

14. Leaving the insertion point where the DOCUMENT command had been, from the Merge feature bar choose Merge **C**odes. The Insert Merge Codes dialog box reappears (see fig. 6.17).

15. From the pick list, select the NESTFORM(filename) command and choose **I**nsert.

    Your document screen should now look like figure 6.23.

Fig. 6.23

Nesting a form file within another form file.

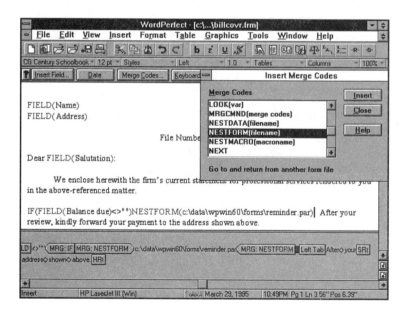

16. Choose **C**lose from the Insert Merge Codes dialog box to return to your document.

Your document is now ready for you to save and use it. When you use this version of REMINDER.FRM, for each record in the data file the following takes place:

- The merge inserts the date, name, address, and salutation.

- The merge looks for a balance due.

- If a balance due is found, the merge passes control of the merge to the REMINDER.PAR file.

- That file obtains the exact balance due and inserts it, with the rest of the reminder paragraph, into the resulting document.

- WordPerfect returns control of the merge to REMINDER.FRM

- REMINDER.FRM completes the merge for that record and then moves on to the next record and starts over.

Selecting Individual Records

Suppose that you don't want to send a cover letter to every client in your database. Although you could theoretically run a merge through the entire data file, producing letters for every client in the file, and discard those you don't need, this is wasteful. Merge has the capability to select specified records out of a large data file and use only those that meet specified criteria (in this example, all records where the balance due exceeds $100).

In prior versions of WordPerfect, this chore was possible only if you wrote a complex form file with many advanced programming commands. Fortunately, WordPerfect 6 has built this task in to the Merge feature; it is called Select Records. The cover letter example shows how this works.

1. From a blank document screen, choose **T**ools, **M**erge.

2. In the Merge dialog box (refer to fig. 6.8), choose **M**erge.

3. In the Perform Merge dialog box (refer to fig. 6.12), type in the path and file name of the form and data files in the respective fields (in the example, **BILLCOVR.FRM** and **SAMPLE.DAT**).

   At this point, the Perform Merge dialog box should look like figure 6.24. Notice that, between the Files to Merge group box and the row of buttons at the bottom of the Perform Merge dialog box, the phrase "All Records" appears. This is an indication to you that the resulting document includes all records in the specified data file.

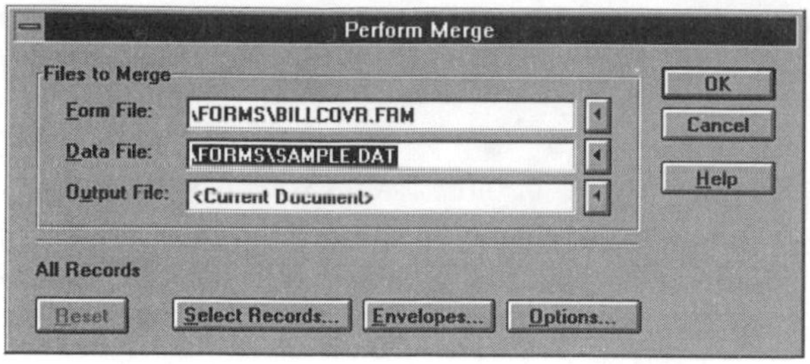

Fig. 6.24
Starting a merge
with the sample
database.

However, suppose that you want to select only one, or a few, records to include in the resulting document. Here's what do to:

4. From the row of buttons at the bottom of the Perform Merge dialog box, choose **S**elect Records. The Select Records dialog box appears, as shown in figure 6.25.

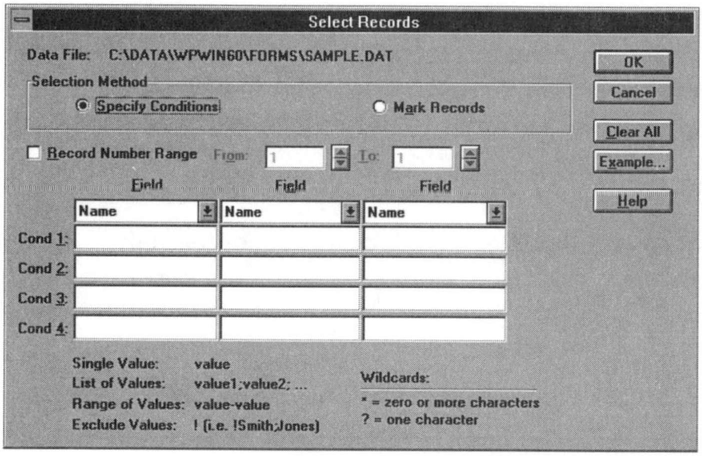

Fig. 6.25
The Select Records
dialog box.

This screen allows you to specify which records to include in the merge. You have two options, as noted in the Selection Method group box near the top of the dialog box: you can specify conditions, or you can specifically mark individual records to include.

Specifying conditions is useful if, for example, you want to include all file numbers between 40,000 and 45,000. This example does that.

5. In the first column, marked **F**ield, click the down arrow after the entry window containing the field Name; this displays a drop-down list of all available fields in your SAMPLE.DAT data file.

6. Select File Number from the drop-down list.

7. Move the insertion point to the Cond **1**: row in that column and type in **40000-45000** to specify the range of file numbers to include in the merge.

8. Choose OK to return to the Perform Merge dialog box.

Notice that this box has changed, as shown in figure 6.26. Instead of the designation that the merge includes all records, the box now notes that you have set Conditions. This is a visual reminder to you that your merge includes only those records you have specified.

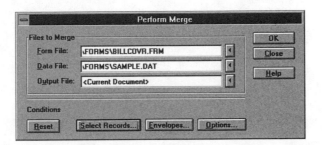

Fig. 6.26
The Perform Merge dialog box, with conditions set.

Note

The next time you perform a merge in the same session of WordPerfect, the Perform Merge dialog box remembers the prior form files and data files and all conditions previously specified. If you want to perform a general merge without conditions, remember to choose **R**eset in the Perform Merge dialog box to return to an all-records general merge.

Now, when you choose OK from the Perform Merge dialog box, the merge proceeds but includes only those records where the file number is greater than or equal to 40,000 and less than or equal to 45,000.

Suppose instead of specifying a range of numbers, you prefer to select individual records. The second option in the Select Records box, M**a**rk Records, makes this task easy. Return to that dialog box (preceding step 4) and do this:

1. Select M**a**rk Records in the Selection Method group box.

Notice that the appearance of the Select Records dialog box now changes; it appears as in figure 6.27.

By default, the Record **L**ist list box shows all records in your data file beginning with the first field in each record. In the example this is the Name field, as shown in the **F**irst Field to Display text box just above the record list. If you can identify the records you want to select from that list, just click on the check box next to each record you want to include in the merge.

Fig. 6.27
Specifying individual records in the Select Records dialog box.

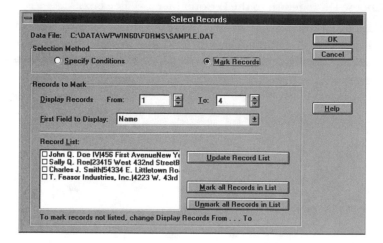

In this example, however, you want to select records by file number, and these aren't visible in the list box. You can find them easily, however, as follows:

2. Choose the drop-down arrow at the end of the **F**irst Field to Display text box; you see a drop-down list of the available fields in your data file.

3. Select File number from the drop-down list.

4. Select **U**pdate Record List.

The record list now changes and displays the records beginning with the File number field and continuing with the fields which follow File number in the data file, as shown in figure 6.28.

5. Mark the records you want to include by clicking in the check box next to each one.

6. Choose OK to return to the Perform Merge dialog box.

Now, when you perform the merge, it includes only those records that you have selected.

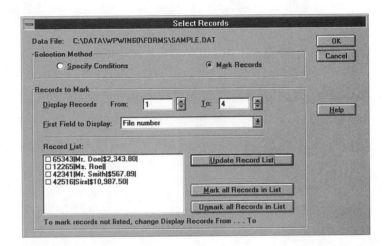

Fig. 6.28
Selecting records
by file number.

From Here...

In this chapter, you learned the basics of performing merges. You also touched on a few advanced merge commands, and learned how to perform a selective merge using the Select Records feature of Merge. This discussion only scratches the surface of what this powerful feature can accomplish.

The next chapter explains another powerful tool for quickly preparing documents: the Template feature. The next chapter covers the following:

- An overview of the Template feature and how templates work
- Creating new templates
- Automatically launching macros when a template is opened

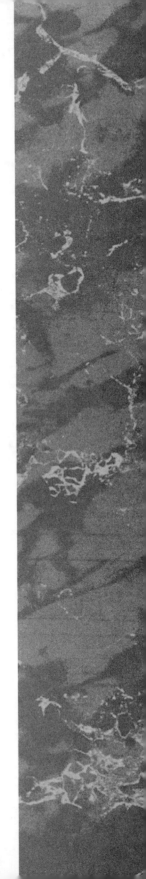

7

Using Templates

One of the most powerful new features of WordPerfect for Windows 6 is the Template feature. It is therefore odd that it is also one of the most poorly documented features in the program manual.

Some users of prior versions of WordPerfect may think of a template as a form document with blanks left in it for the user to fill in by hand. This is only partly true of a WordPerfect for Windows 6 template. Although WordPerfect for Windows 6 templates can contain blanks for the user to fill in, the feature takes this idea to the next logical step: the template can contain macros or macro-like features that prompt the user for information and fill in the form automatically.

Templates do more than just fill in the blanks, however. You can program them to perform tasks automatically on all sorts of different events (for example, every time a document is printed, a template could make a log entry to help monitor use of printer resources). They can also contain items such as special keyboards, toolbars or button bars, menu layouts, and so on, such that whenever a user opens a particular type of document, WordPerfect automatically displays or makes available the special tools he or she may need to work with that document.

A well-constructed template makes a user's life wonderfully simple. Imagine a notice of deposition template which, as soon as you open it, prompts you to either write a case caption or retrieve an existing one; then displays a list of the information it needs (name of deponent, time of deposition, and so on); and finally asks you which attorney in your firm will sign the notice (even showing you a list of the attorneys to save you having to type the name in yourself). By the time the template document is open you have a finished document, ready to print! Not only does WordPerfect for Windows offer you the possibility of creating such a template; the Companion Disk includes one, which Chapter 10, "Litigation Documents," describes.

This chapter takes an in-depth look at the Template feature of WordPerfect. It shows you:

- An overview of the Template feature
- How to copy macros, toolbars, and other "objects" from one template to another
- How to use *triggers* to launch macros at different times
- How to create prompts that gather information to insert in specified places in every new document

Introduction to Templates

You may be thinking at this point, "This sounds too complicated for me, so I don't want to use templates." Or you may be saying to yourself, "I don't want to know how these things work; just give me the finished templates so I can use them." Before you skip to the next chapter, wait just a moment! You really do need to know what is in this section of the chapter because you cannot use WordPerfect without using templates.

What? You may think you have created many documents already and never had to bother with templates before. What you may not realize is that every single document created in WordPerfect is based upon a template of some sort. There are no exceptions. So, because you are using templates without even knowing it, it would probably be a good idea to learn about what these things are doing for you and how they work.

What Is a Template?

It is sometimes easier to define what a template is *not* rather than what it *is*. A template is not a document; nor is a document a template. Nor is a template a macro, or a style, or anything else you may be accustomed to.

A template is kind of a cross between a document and a macro. It is probably easiest to think of a template as a "container" document. That is, it is a WordPerfect file that contains a variety of pieces of information, or "objects," including the following:

- Simple text
- WordPerfect formatting codes
- Customized menu bars
- Complete macros

- Simple macros that start other macros stored on your hard disk
- Customized button bars or toolbars
- Abbreviations
- Special styles for a particular type of document
- Customized (or "soft") keyboards

Not every template needs to contain all these items, however. But you might want to create a template for a particular type of document (a lease, for example), in which you'd like to include special macros that help you to assemble standard lease paragraphs from other sources, or that type certain standard phrases or terms. If so, you can accomplish this by embedding these things into a template document called LEASE.WPT and including either a custom menu bar, a button bar/toolbar, or a special keyboard to give the user quick access to those special macros. When the user creates a document based upon this template, the WordPerfect screen and/or keyboard may change to reflect the items contained in the template.

If you think of a template as a container, think of the macros, toolbars, keyboards, and other objects as the contents of the container. And, to carry the analogy to its logical conclusion, consider the process of using the template as the act of pouring the contents of this container into your new document. Once the contents have been poured into your new document, they can be saved (dried?) and become a permanent part of your new document.

The Default Template

As pointed out a moment ago, every single document you create is based upon a template, regardless of whether you specify a template. This is because if you specify no template, WordPerfect bases your new document on the default template. When WordPerfect ships a U.S. language version of the program, the default template is STANDARD.WPT. You can change this to anything else you like after installing the program, however.

Looking at the default template helps you better understand what templates are and how they work. Assume you have just installed WordPerfect (or at least that nobody has changed the default settings for templates since the program was installed). What follows is an explanation of what the default template is and where it is stored.

1. Choose **E**dit, Preferences.

   Choose **F**ile, Preferences.

2. In the Preferences dialog box, choose File.

3. In the File Preferences dialog box, select the **T**emplates radio button. The File Preferences dialog box should now look like figure 7.1.

Fig. 7.1
The File Preferences dialog box for templates.

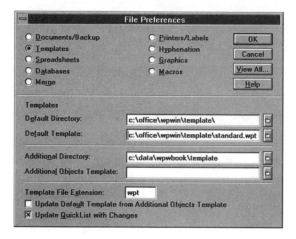

In the center of the dialog box, notice that the default directory and the default template are specified. The default template is usually defined as STANDARD.WPT, but you can change this by typing in a different file name or by searching for a different file name using the file icon at the end of that entry field. If you do not specify a path in the Default Template entry window, WordPerfect automatically stores the default template in the default directory.

You have the option of specifying an additional directory besides the default directory for templates. For example, you may want to designate the directory C:\WPWINLAW\TEMPLATE (where the installation program on the enclosed Companion Disk will store the templates for this book) as your Additional Directory; if you do so, templates in that directory automatically appear in your New Document dialog box.

> **Tip**
>
> The Default Directory is important, even if you store your default template in a different directory. When you invoke the Template feature of WordPerfect, it displays a list of templates. Whatever template files are found in the Default Directory and the Additional Directory appears in that dialog box automatically. Any template files located in subdirectories under either the Default Directory or the Additional Directory appear in the listing of available groups

in the New Document dialog box. You must store your templates in one of these two directories, or a subdirectory under them, to use them from the New Document dialog box.

In version 6.0, templates are accessed via the Template dialog box.

4. After specifying your default template and the directories, choose OK to return to the Preferences dialog box.

5. Choose **C**lose to return to your document.

What Is an Object?

As previously mentioned, a template is a container. To use the vernacular, the template contains things called *objects*.

An object is a feature or tool that can change from template to template. A custom toolbar is an object; so is a soft keyboard. Macros are objects. Next you'll look at a list of the types of objects that your STANDARD.WPT template contains.

To inspect the list of objects contained within any template, you need to edit it. Follow these steps:

1. Choose **F**ile, **N**ew.

Choose **F**ile, **T**emplate.

In version 6.1, you see the New Document dialog box, with the template Create a blank document selected. This is the STANDARD.WPT file, as noted, just above the list box containing the descriptions of the available templates. In version 6.0, you see the Templates dialog box with STANDARD.WPT selected.

2. Choose **O**ptions, **E**dit Template.

The STANDARD.WPT template opens into an editing window (see fig. 7.2), where you can edit it like an ordinary document. Notice that a special row of buttons, called the Template feature bar, has appeared just above the editing window.

3. To see a list of the objects contained in the STANDARD.WPT file, choose **C**opy/Remove Object from the Template feature bar. The Copy/Remove Template Objects dialog box appears, as shown in figure 7.3.

4. In the center left side of the dialog box, choose the pop-up button marked O**b**ject Type:. You see a list of the types of objects contained within any given template, as shown in figure 7.4.

Fig. 7.2

Editing the STANDARD.WPT template.

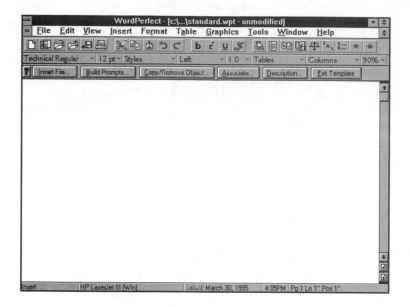

Fig. 7.3

The Copy/Remove Template Objects dialog box.

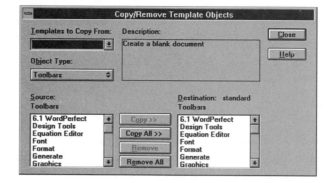

Fig. 7.4

The types of objects contained in a WordPerfect template.

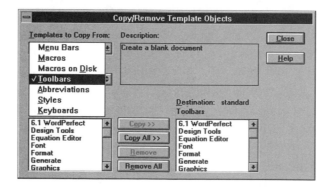

5. Later on, this chapter examines some of these types of objects; for now, simply choose **C**lose to dismiss the dialog box and return to the STANDARD.WPT editing screen.

What Is a Trigger?

WordPerfect templates also have a unique capability to change the appearance of your screen and to set features and processes in motion automatically upon the occurrence of certain events. For example, you can make a template automatically play a macro as soon as the template is used or opened, or when a document is printed, or when some other event takes place. The events that start the action are called *triggers*. The connection between the trigger and the action to be performed is called an *association*. For example, if a template associates a certain macro with the PostNew trigger, the macro plays as soon as you create a new document based upon that template.

If you want to see a list of available triggers and associations, perform the following steps:

6. Choose **A**ssociate from the Template feature bar. The Associate dialog box appears, as shown in figure 7.5.

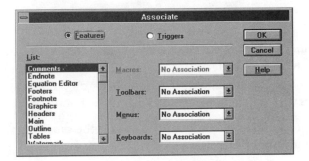

Fig. 7.5
The Associate dialog box.

This dialog box gives you the chance to associate different toolbars, menus, or keyboards with certain features, or to associate different macros with various triggers or events. To see how the first of these options works, associate the Legal toolbar with the Footnote feature (this causes the Legal toolbar to appear on-screen only while you are editing a footnote, but not while you are in the main part of the document).

7. In the **L**ist box at the left of the Associate dialog box, select Footnote.

8. Choose the down arrow next to the **T**oolbars entry window to display a list of available toolbars.

Choose Button Bars.

> **Note**
>
> This list includes all the toolbars contained within the template you are editing. If a particular toolbar is not available, you must copy that toolbar into this Template using the Copy/Remove Template Objects dialog box discussed above.

9. Select Legal from the list of available toolbars and release the mouse button.

The Associate dialog box should now look like figure 7.6.

Fig. 7.6

Associating a toolbar with the Footnote feature.

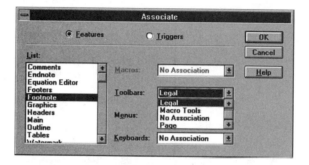

Now, after you return to WordPerfect, in any document created with the STANDARD.WPT template, when you invoke the Footnote feature your toolbar changes into the Legal toolbar. You can make other associations with different menus and keyboards as you want.

The more useful feature in this dialog box is the capability to associate macros to various triggers. Do that next:

10. Select the **T**riggers radio button near the top of the Associate dialog box. Notice that the appearance of the box changes, as shown in figure 7.7.

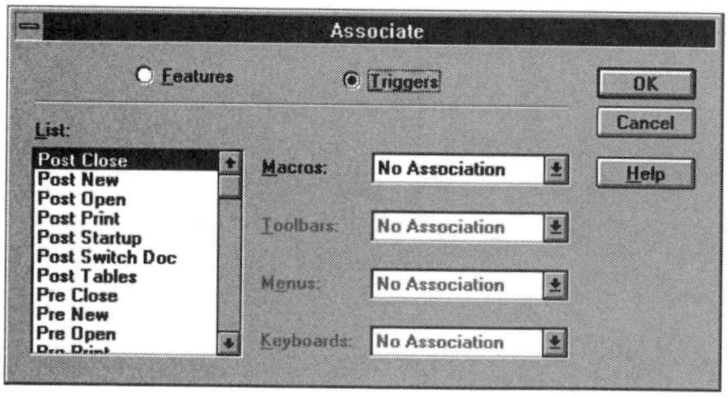

Fig. 7.7

Associating macros to triggers.

The box on the left now contains a list of events, or triggers, which can start a macro playing. The available triggers are listed in table 7.1.

Table 7.1 Available Triggers and Their Related Events	
Trigger	**Event**
Post Close	Macro runs after document is closed.
Post New	Macro runs after you select template from New menu.
Post Open	Macro runs after you open document originally created with this template.
Post Print	Macro runs after printing the document.
Post Startup	Macro in default template runs after you start WordPerfect for Windows.
Post SwitchDoc	Macro runs after you switch document windows.
Post Tables	Macro runs after table grid is drawn but before data is entered.
Pre Close	Macro runs before document is closed.
Pre New	Macro runs before you select template from New menu.
Pre Open	Macro runs before you open document originally created with this template.
Pre Print	Macro runs before printing the document.
Pre SwitchDoc	Macro runs before you switch document windows.
Pre Tables	Macro runs before table grid is drawn but before data is entered.

You learn how to associate different macros with these triggers later in the chapter; for now, return to a blank document screen as follows:

11. Choose Cancel from the Associate dialog box.

12. Choose **E**xit Template from the Template feature bar.

Copying Objects

Now to get into a bit more detail and explain how you can put these tools to use in a law office setting. This section of the chapter shows you how to create a template to begin a brief. You'll incorporate some of the toolbars and keyboards you created in Chapter 1 and some of the macros you wrote in Chapter 5.

First, you need to create a new template:

1. Choose **F**ile, **N**ew.

Choose **F**ile, **T**emplate.

2. From the **O**ptions drop-down menu, choose **N**ew Template.

From the Options drop-down menu, choose **C**reate Template, specify a file name and description in the Create Document Template dialog box, and choose OK.

You see a new template editing screen, as shown in figure 7.8. Note that the name of the open file in the title bar is [Template1], indicating that you are creating a new, as-yet-unnamed template file.

Fig. 7.8
Creating a new template.

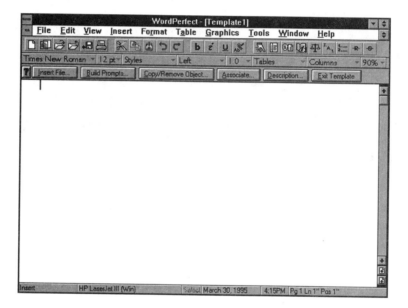

First, copy the customized Legal toolbar into the new template file.

3. From the Template feature bar, choose **C**opy/Remove Object. The Copy/Remove Template Objects dialog box appears, as shown in figure 7.9.

Note that on the left side of the dialog box, the "source" objects are listed. You can select the template from which to copy objects from the **T**emplates to Copy From entry window in the upper-left corner; because you stored the modified Legal toolbar in STANDARD.WPT, leave that window alone for now. You can also select the type of object to copy from the O**b**ject Type pop-up button. Because the default object is Toolbars, which is what you want at the moment, again leave that alone.

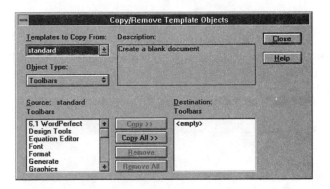

Fig. 7.9
Copying objects
into a new
template.

Above the list box in the bottom left corner of the dialog box, you see the message Source: standard, which verifies that you are currently viewing available toolbars in the STANDARD.WPT file.

Now look at the list box on the right side of the dialog box. It is described as the **D**estination template, and again the word Toolbars appears to remind you that you are copying Toolbars from the source template to the destination template (in this case the new, unnamed template in the active window).

4. In the Source list box showing available toolbars in the STANDARD.WPT file, use the scroll bar or click your mouse in that list box and type **L** to highlight the Legal toolbar. Note that the C**o**py button, which had been grayed out, now becomes active.

5. Choose C**o**py to copy the Legal toolbar from the STANDARD.WPT file to the new template file. (This does not affect that toolbar in the default template).

You see the word Legal appear in the **D**estination: Toolbars list box on the right side of the screen, as shown in figure 7.10.

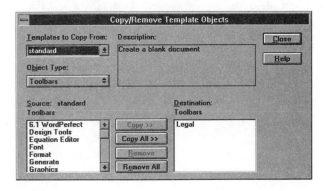

Fig. 7.10
Copying the Legal
toolbar into the
new template.

Special Features

Next, copy the special Legal keyboard you created in Chapter 1, "Making WordPerfect Work the Way You Do," into the new template.

6. Choose the O**b**ject Type: pop-up button. You see a list of available object types in the top left corner of the dialog box, as shown in figure 7.11.

Fig. 7.11
Choosing an object type to copy.

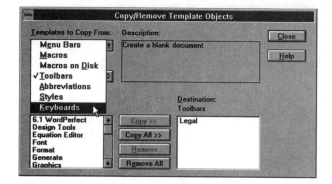

7. Select **K**eyboards from the pop-up list. A list of the keyboards stored in STANDARD.WPT now appears in the list box in the lower-right corner of the dialog box.

8. Select Legal from the list box.

9. Choose C**o**py to copy the Legal keyboard from the STANDARD.WPT to the new template file.

Before you move on, associate these objects with your new template, so that when you use the new template, the Legal toolbar and Legal keyboard are the default settings.

10. From the Copy/Remove Template Objects dialog box, choose **C**lose to return to the Template editing window.

11. From the Template feature bar, choose **A**ssociate. The Associate dialog box appears.

12. In the **L**ist window, highlight the Main item. (This ensures that the toolbar you specify appears in the main editing screen.)

13. Click the down arrow at the end of the Toolbars: entry window to see a list of the available toolbars in the template. The Legal toolbar you just copied is listed, as shown in figure 7.12.

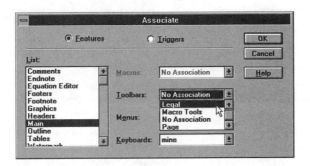

Fig. 7.12
Associating the
Legal toolbar with
the new template.

Special Features

14. Select the Legal toolbar with the mouse and release the button. The Legal selection now appears in the text box, indicating that it is now the default toolbar for this template.

15. Click the down arrow at the end of the Keyboards: entry window to see a list of the available keyboards in the template.

16. Select the legal keyboard in the same manner as above.

When you have finished making these associations, the Associate dialog box should look like figure 7.13.

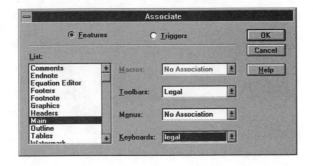

Fig. 7.13
Associating
features in the new
template.

Save the new template file to disk.

17. From the Associate dialog box, choose OK.

18. From the Template feature bar, choose **E**xit Template.

19. Choose **Y**es to the prompt box to indicate you want to save the new template.

20. In the Save Template dialog box, type a brief description of the template in the **D**escription edit box.

This step is unnecessary in version 6.0, because the file name and description are provided prior to opening the Template editing window.

> **Note**
>
> Remember that, in version 6.1, when the New dialog box is displayed, it lists your templates alphabetically by their descriptions, so remember to make the first word of your description something logical so you can later find the template quickly. In this case, a good description of the template might be "Brief, Create New."

21. Type a DOS file name in the Template **N**ame edit box. You can specify only the first eight characters, because WordPerfect automatically adds the default template extension of WPT to the template file name. The Companion Disk already includes a file called BRIEF.WPT; call this template MYBRIEF, to avoid accidentally overwriting that file.

22. If you have established template groups, the Template **G**roup list box displays them. Select the group you want to store the new template in.

    When you have made all of your selections, the Save Template dialog box should look like figure 7.14.

Fig. 7.14
Saving the new template.

23. Choose OK to save the new template and close the Template editing window.

Now, when you base a new document on the MYBRIEF.WPT template, WordPerfect automatically selects the custom Legal toolbar and Legal keyboard for you.

Using Triggers

The most useful feature of a WordPerfect template is its capability to start macros when certain events occur. For example, you may write a macro which determines the number of pages in a document and then makes a notation in a log document as to how many pages of the document were sent to the printer. If you set this macro up so that it automatically runs as soon as a document is sent to the printer, you can generate a log of printer usage automatically.

Many of the templates described in Part II of this book rely heavily on macros *triggered* by different events, usually the creation of a new document based on a specified template. In the following section, you'll further modify the MYBRIEF.WPT template to learn how this technique works.

The Companion Disk includes a macro called WRITECAP.WCM, which Chapter 10 describes in much more detail. This macro automates the process of creating, saving, and retrieving case captions for legal pleadings. Because you want every brief created using the MYBRIEF.WPT template to begin with a caption, you'll want to associate that macro with the template in such a way that it plays automatically as soon as the template is used. To accomplish this task:

1. Choose **F**ile, **N**ew.

   Choose **F**ile, **T**emplate.

2. Locate Mybrief in the list box (note that, in version 6.1, WordPerfect lists the file by the description you gave it above, although it displays the file name above the list box when you highlight the correct description).

3. From the Options drop-down menu, choose **E**dit Template. MYBRIEF.WPT now appears in an editing window with the Template feature bar displayed above it.

Before you can associate the WRITECAP.WCM macro to a trigger, you must copy an object into the template that you can associate to the trigger. WordPerfect offers two ways to incorporate macro objects into a template: you can either copy the entire macro code into the template, or you can simply incorporate a "pointer" that tells the template to play a macro on the disk. Each method has advantages and disadvantages.

If you copy the entire macro into a template, that template will be "portable"; that is, you can move it from computer to computer and it carries with it the macro code it needs to perform. The disadvantage is that it greatly increases the size of your template file.

If, however, you incorporate only a pointer, the size of the template does not expand very much. (This can result in a great savings of disk space, which is important if you have a lot of templates that incorporate the same macro). Plus, if you do use the same macro in many templates, using the pointer method allows you to modify all of the templates at once simply by modifying the central macro on disk. The disadvantage, of course, of using this method is that you must make sure that the macro is properly installed on all computers where the template will be used, or the template will not work.

Because you're going to create a number of templates that rely on WRITECAP.WCM and because the macro is a very large one, you use the pointer method in this exercise. But the way to do this is far from obvious; in fact, the obvious solution here is incorrect. Follow along for just a second:

4. From the Template feature bar, choose Copy/Remove Object.

5. Click the Object Type: pop-up button to see what object types are available to copy into the MYBRIEF.WPT. Your screen looks like figure 7.15.

Fig. 7.15

Copying a macro into a template.

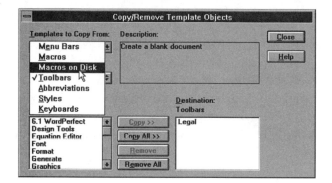

It would appear that, since you want to play a macro on the disk in this example, you should use the Macros on **D**isk option on the pop-up button. But this is wrong! Oddly enough, this option copies the entire macro on disk into the template, which is the opposite of what you are trying to do here. (This is, however, the option you should use if you want to copy the entire macro into the template.)

The other logical selection on the pop-up list is **M**acros. Guess what? This is wrong too! This option allows you to copy a template macro from another template into this template. However, there does not currently exist in any template a macro that plays the WRITECAP.WCM macro, so you cannot use this option.

What you need to do is to record a template macro that in turn plays the WRITECAP.WCM macro from the disk:

6. Release the pop-up list and choose **C**lose, without making any changes to the template.

7. From the WordPerfect main menu, choose **T**ools, Tem**p**late Macro.

   Choose **T**ools, **M**acro.

8. Choose **R**ecord.

   Choose **R**ecord; then choose **L**ocation. In the Macro Location dialog
   box, specify the template in which to record the macro.

9. In the Record Template Macro dialog box, provide a name for the
   macro to be recorded, and choose Record. In this case, because the
   macro you're recording will be stored in the MYBRIEF.WPT file, you
   can use the name WRITECAP without conflicting with the
   WRITECAP.WCM macro file stored in your macro directory.

You return to your Template editing window, in Macro Record mode. Notice
that the mouse pointer turns into a circle with a diagonal line through it, just
as it did when you recorded a disk macro in Chapter 5, "Automating with
Macros," indicating that you cannot use the mouse to move the insertion
point in the document.

Next, you need to record the commands to play the disk macro
WRITECAP.WCM.

10. Choose **T**ools, **M**acro.

11. In the Play Macro dialog box, type **WRITECAP** or use the scroll bar
    and mouse to locate the macro in whatever directory you placed it.

12. Choose OK to start the WRITECAP.WCM macro.

    For the present purposes, it is not important that the WRITECAP.WCM
    macro be played through to conclusion; the purpose of this template
    macro is just to set the disk macro in motion. Since you have now done
    this, cancel the WRITECAP.WCM macro.

13. In the initial WRITECAP.WCM dialog box, choose Cancel or press Esc.

14. Choose **T**ools, Tem**p**late Macro.

    Choose **T**ools, **M**acro.

    Note that the **R**ecord option has a check mark next to it, indicating
    that the program is currently recording a template macro.

15. Choose **R**ecord again to end recording of the template macro.

    Stop here for just a second and inspect the template macro you just
    recorded, to see how it's going to work.

16. Choose **T**ools, Tem**p**late Macro again.

    Choose **T**ools, **M**acro.

17. Choose **E**dit.

Choose **E**dit; then choose **L**ocation and specify the template you want to edit from.

The Edit Template Macro dialog box appears. Note that the template macro WRITECAP that you just recorded appears in the list box Macros in Template, as shown in figure 7.16.

Fig. 7.16

The Edit Template Macro dialog box.

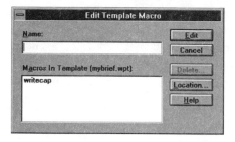

18. Select the WRITECAP macro in the list box and choose **E**dit.

You see a new editing window with the text of the WRITECAP template macro displayed beneath the Macro feature bar, as shown in figure 7.17. Note in the title bar that the name of the file is displayed as writecap, with no extension; this is an indication that you're dealing with a template macro rather than a disk macro.

Fig. 7.17

The text of the WRITECAP template macro.

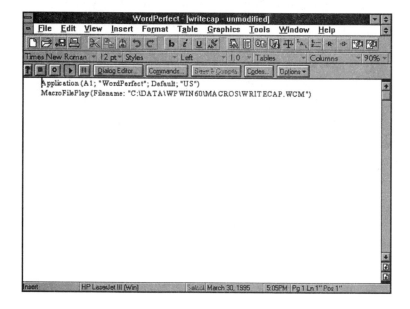

Take a moment to study the text of this brief macro. The first line is the standard Application command, mentioned in Chapter 5; you need not concern yourself with this command. The only other command in the macro is a MacroFilePlay command, and the parameter in that command is the specific path and file name for the WRITECAP.WCM macro on your disk.

This means that this template macro works only as long as the WRITECAP.WCM macro is located in the directory specified in the parameter of the MacroFilePlay command. If you move this template to another computer with a different directory structure, or where the file macro has not been installed, the template macro halts and displays an error.

If in the future you want to move WRITECAP.WCM to a different directory, or want to use this template on a different machine with a different directory structure, you'll need to edit the path in the MacroFilePlay command in this macro and save it. Because you don't need to do that for this example, just close the macro without saving it.

19. Choose File, Close.

You should once again return to the MYBRIEF.WPT editing screen. The final thing you need to do is to associate the new template macro WRITECAP with a trigger so that WordPerfect plays it automatically when the template is used.

20. From the Template feature bar, choose Associate. The Associate dialog box appears.

21. Select Triggers.

You want the WRITECAP macro to begin playing as soon as the user creates a new document with this template; this means you need to associate the macro with the Post New trigger (refer to table 7.1).

22. In the List box, select Post New.

23. Click the down arrow at the end of the Macros edit window to see a list of the available macro objects in this template.

In this case, you've created only a single macro object, the template macro WRITECAP, which the drop-down box displays, as figure 7.18 shows.

24. Select WRITECAP from the drop-down list and release the mouse button; the name of the template macro then appears in the Macros edit window.

25. Choose OK to return to the MYBRIEF.WPT editing window.

You are done editing this template, so now close it up and save it.

Fig. 7.18
Associating the
template macro to
the Post New
trigger.

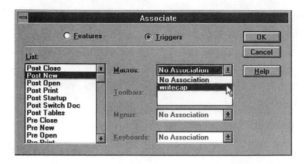

26. From the Template feature bar, choose **E**xit Template.

27. Choose **Y**es indicating that you want to save the changes.

Your template is ready to use. When you select it from the template listings, the template macro WRITECAP should in turn start the WRITECAP.WCM disk macro, enabling you to write or retrieve a case caption as the first part of your new brief.

Placing Standard Text in a Template

You may have noticed when you closed and saved MYBRIEF.WPT just now, the template window itself looked blank—that is, the screen contained no text and no special formatting codes. What was saved when you answered Yes was the toolbar, keyboard, template macro, and the association you described above.

This need not always be the case, however. You can also include ordinary text or WordPerfect formatting codes as part of any template, so that as soon as you use the template, it automatically types the text into your new document. For example, if you want all of your briefs to have a 1.5" top margin, to allow for stapling at the top, you can simply include a margin change code as the first code in the template from the MYBRIEF.WPT template editing screen.

Another example of including standard text in a template is printing your letterhead from WordPerfect. You can include all the font codes, names, addresses, and standard text of your letterhead, formatted as you want to have it printed, in a letterhead template. You can even include a WordPerfect [Date Code] where you want the current date to automatically appear.

Now for a look at a specific example of including text in a template. You'll also discover another feature of templates that can automate the preparation of customized documents.

Suppose that you have a standard form affidavit for parties to a lawsuit to sign. Figure 7.19 shows a sample of such an affidavit.

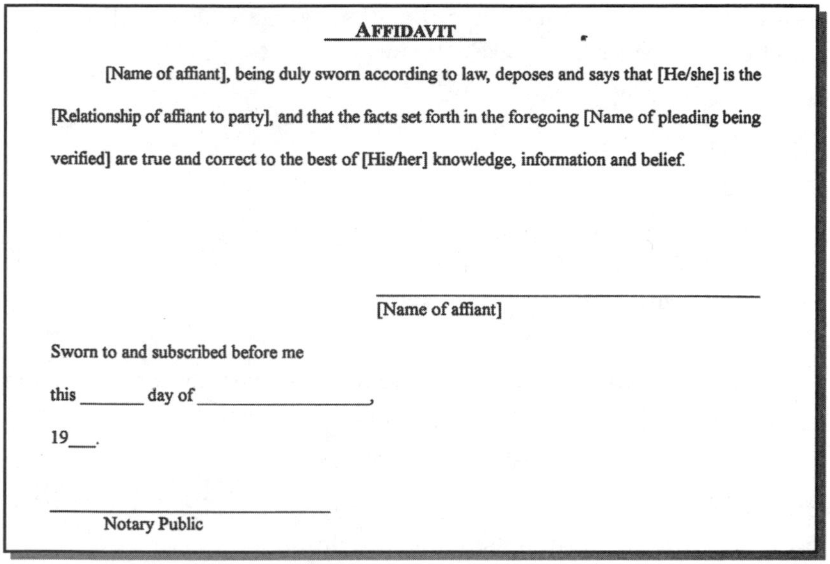

AFFIDAVIT

[Name of affiant], being duly sworn according to law, deposes and says that [He/she] is the [Relationship of affiant to party], and that the facts set forth in the foregoing [Name of pleading being verified] are true and correct to the best of [His/her] knowledge, information and belief.

____
[Name of affiant]

Sworn to and subscribed before me

this _______ day of ________________,

19___.

____
Notary Public

Fig. 7.19
A sample affidavit document.

Notice that this affidavit form contains bracketed "prompts" indicating that the user needs to fill in specific information in certain locations. These prompts are used in a moment to create automatic prompts; but first, you need to create a template.

There are two ways to do this. First, you could create a new template from the New dialog box (Template in version 6.0) and type in the form of the affidavit by hand. Or, if the document already exists, simply save it to a new file name with an extension of WPT and then move it to your default template directory.

For the purposes of this exercise, type the affidavit shown in figure 7.19 and save it to the file name AFFIDAVI.WPT in your default template directory.

Without doing anything else to this document, you already have a simple template document. When you use the template you have just created, it pours the text of the affidavit into a new document window, where you can edit it and save it in the usual way.

Using Prompts

But the real beauty of templates is their capability to start some action immediately upon using them. For example, WordPerfect templates have the ability to display a dialog box listing the kinds of information needed to fill in the blanks in the document. The user can type in the needed information, click OK, and by the time the template has finished, the document is ready to print, with all of the requested information correctly filled in. Here's how to modify AFFIDAVI.WPT to take advantage of this feature:

1. Choose **F**ile, **N**ew.

Choose **F**ile, **T**emplate.

2. Locate Affidavit in the list box.

3. From the Options drop-down menu, choose **E**dit Template. WordPerfect loads AFFIDAVI.WPT into an editing window with the Template feature bar displayed above it.

If you are using version 6.1, the first thing you'll probably want to do is to specify a descriptive file name, so that the template can be listed in the New dialog box by a descriptive name rather than its file name.

4. From the Template feature bar, choose **D**escription.

5. Type a descriptive file name, such as **Affidavit for legal pleading**.

6. Choose OK to return to the Template editing window.

7. From the Template feature bar, choose **B**uild Prompts.

Choose **T**ools, **M**acro. Then Play the macro PROMPTS.WCM.

The Prompt Builder dialog box appears, as shown in figure 7.20.

Fig. 7.20
The Prompt
Builder dialog box.

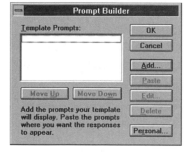

Note

In version 6.0, the Prompt Builder was contained in a macro; in version 6.1, it is a built-in feature. The Prompt Builder dialog box from the PROMPTS.WCM macro in version 6.0 is slightly different from the dialog box shown in figure 7.20, but the concept and operation of the macro is the same.

Next, you need to add the prompts for user input into the Template Prompts: list box:

8. Choose **A**dd. The Add Template Prompt dialog box appears, as figure 7.21 shows.

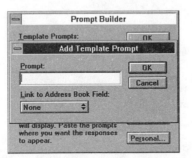

Fig. 7.21
The Add Template
Prompt dialog box.

9. Type in the first prompt (in this example, type Name of affiant); then choose OK.

> **Caution**
>
> Do not include the brackets that appear in the text of the AFFIDAVI.WPT document.

Note that Name of affiant now appears as the first prompt in the **Tem**plate Prompts list box.

10. Repeat step 9 for all of the remaining prompts.

Note that, in the AFFIDAVI.WPT template, the [Name of affiant] prompt appears twice. You need to place this prompt in the Prompt Builder only once, since the same name goes in both locations. The template automatically places the information in both locations.

> **Note**
>
> The Prompt Builder of the Template feature is limited to 12 prompts. If you have a form that requires more than 12 pieces of information, you'll need to write a custom macro to gather that information and insert it in the proper locations in the document. Several of the templates discussed in Part II of the book use special macros in just this way.

When you're finished, your Prompt Builder dialog box should look like figure 7.22.

Fig. 7.22
Inserting prompts into AFFIDAVI.WPT.

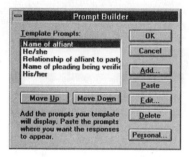

11. Choose OK to dismiss the Prompt Builder dialog box and continue preparation of the template.

You see a message box informing you that WordPerfect is preparing the template; that message box disappears in a moment and you return to the template editing screen.

The template is now ready to use. Before you close and save it, however, look at what the Prompt Builder did to your template.

12. From the Template feature bar choose **A**ssociate.

13. In the Associate dialog box, select **T**riggers.

14. In the **L**ist box, select Post New.

Notice that the Macros: field now shows that something called <dofiller> is now associated with the Post New trigger (see fig. 7.23). <dofiller> is not (quite) a macro; it is technically just an object that acts like a macro. The distinction is this: you cannot edit or change <dofiller>. Its job is to look for template prompts, show them to the user, and then fill in the blanks where noted.

Fig. 7.23
The <dofiller> object associated with Post New.

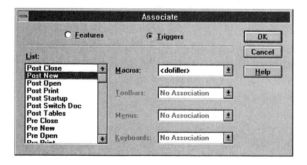

If you're wondering how <dofiller> knows where to put information, perform the following steps:

15. Dismiss the Associate dialog box using either OK or Cancel.

16. Turn on Reveal Codes (Choose **V**iew, **R**eveal Codes).

Your screen should look like figure 7.24. Notice that, before and after each bracketed prompt in your template, there is a [Bookmark>][<Bookmark] pair. Each pair of bookmarks is numbered to correspond with the prompts you defined in Prompt Builder. When <dofiller> fills in the document, it searches for these bookmarks and replaces everything between them with the information supplied by the user when the template is used.

The bookmarks placed in your document were put there when Prompt Builder searched for the prompts you specified in the preceding steps 9 and 10. For this to work, however, the document you are setting up with prompts must have the prompts already typed in, in brackets, before you run Prompt Builder. You might also be sure that the prompts are spelled exactly the same in the document and when you enter them in step 9.

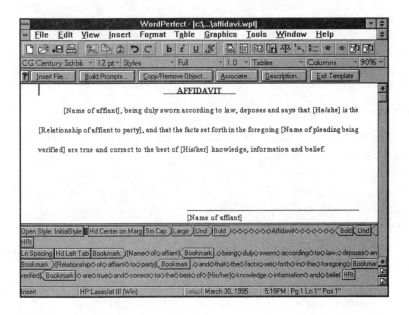

Fig. 7.24
The completed Affidavit template, shown in Reveal Codes.

17. Choose **E**xit Template, and respond Yes to the prompt that asks if you want to save the changes.

Now verify that the template performs as intended. Here's how:

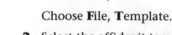

1. Choose **F**ile, **N**ew.

   Choose **F**ile, **T**emplate.

2. Select the affidavit template from the listing and choose OK. You see the Template Information dialog box shown in figure 7.25.

Fig. 7.25
The Template
Information
dialog box.

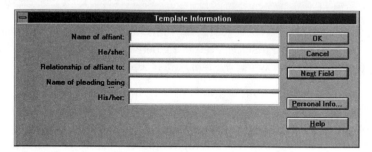

3. Type in some information responding to the prompts and choose OK.

The Template Information dialog box disappears, and WordPerfect automatically inserts the information you typed, in the proper places. Note that the name of the affiant appears in two places, since that prompt appeared in two locations in the template.

From Here...

This chapter has introduced you to the powerful Template feature. You've seen how you can use templates to store button bars and toolbars, keyboards, macros, and other information. You also saw how to make a template automatically play a macro immediately upon the occurrence of some event. And you learned how to make a simple fill-in-the-blanks template to speed creation of any type of document you can think of.

This also concludes Part I of the book. Part II builds on many of the features explained in Part I and use them in the various macros, form documents, and templates it presents and discusses. Part II moves away from the discussion of how individual features work, and moves into a practical discussion of how you can use these tools to produce specific types of documents for your law office.

Part II discusses the following:

- Some basic concepts behind document assembly systems
- Creating correspondence
- Creating documents for litigation
- Creating deeds, mortgages, and other real estate documents
- A menu-driven system for handling commercial cases
- Creating wills and other estate-planning documents
- A client and case management system

Part II

Assembling Documents

Document Assembly

It doesn't matter what kind of law you practice: as a lawyer you create documents. Lots of them. And for the most part, you don't create them from scratch every time. Lawyers frequently base their documents on pieces of other documents they have previously written: standard contract clauses, standard allegations or denials in a pleading, standard provisions of a will or trust document. While the documents certainly are edited and modified for content after the pieces are put together, there is no denying that the quickest way to prepare most any document is to start with an existing document and modify it to suit your needs.

Commercial packages are now available that help lawyers create new documents from old ones. They are called *document assembly packages*, and they do a nice job. They are also an extra expense and another barrier to productivity in the sense that they require you to become familiar with one more program in addition to your word processor.

WordPerfect has built into it the basic tools you need to perform document assembly. (In fact many of the commercial packages use these same tools in performing the assembly task.) If you know how to use these tools properly, you can save yourself the expense and the learning curve associated with a commercial package.

In this chapter, you:

- Get an overview of document assembly methods
- Learn how to break form documents into component building blocks, or *segments*
- Learn the operation of two macros that assist the user in quickly building new documents from the segments

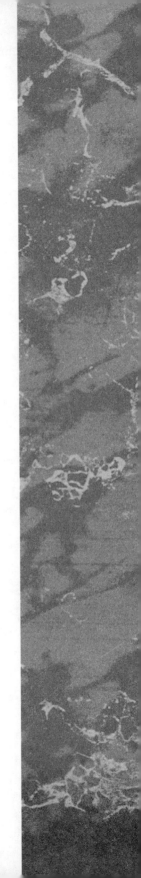

Document Assembly Methods and Tools

This chapter begins by examining the various ways in which you can build documents in WordPerfect. It starts with the simplest methods and then works up to more automated methods.

Manual Assembly

Of course the easiest, and therefore most widely used, method of document assembly is the old copy-and-paste routine. You open the *donor* document (that is, the one with the standard language) in one window, copy parts of it into the Clipboard, and paste it into a new document in a different document window. You probably have done this hundreds of times and never thought of it as document assembly, but that's what it is.

One annoying feature about using the WordPerfect Paste feature is that text copied from one source retains its attributes in the destination document. For example, if you are copying text from a document that used a Courier font, and pasting it into a document using a Times Roman font, the inserted text retains the Courier font, which may not be what you want. You may wonder why this happens, and how you can avoid it.

To help you understand why this occurs, create a test document:

1. In a blank document window, type some standard text in the document's default font.

2. Change the font to something else and type some additional text.

3. Change the font back to the original font and type some more.

4. Now return to the first part of the sample document, in the default font. Select a sentence or word.

5. Choose **E**dit, **C**opy. This copies the selected text into the Windows Clipboard.

> **Note**
>
> Here's an often-overlooked shortcut to performing a copy-and-paste opera-
> tion: After you select the text you want to copy, instead of choosing **E**dit,
> **C**opy, simply press Ctrl+C (for **C**opy). This pastes the selection into your Clip-
> board, overwriting anything that was already there. Then, when you place the
> insertion point where the text is to be inserted, again skip the mouse and just
> press Ctrl+V (for Mo**v**e; think of the V as resembling the editor's inverted carat,
> telling WordPerfect to set the Clipboard contents down at this spot).

6. Now move the insertion point to a spot within the text with a different font face.

7. Retrieve the selected text from the Windows clipboard by choosing **E**dit, **P**aste (or by pressing Ctrl+V).

Your document looks something like the one shown in figure 8.1.

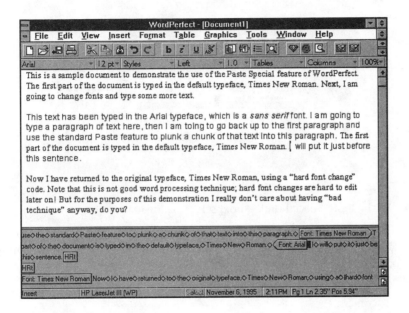

Fig. 8.1
A sample document showing copied text with formatting attached, in Reveal Codes.

Look carefully in the Reveal Codes window. Note that the sentence which has been copied from paragraph 1 (in a Times New Roman font) appears in that same font in paragraph 2, which was typed in an Arial font. The transplanted sentence is surrounded by two codes: [Font: Times New Roman>] and [<Font: Arial]. These codes, which are generated automatically by the Paste feature, turn on the Times New Roman font at the beginning of the selected text and return the font to Arial after the text.

8. To make the text of the inserted sentence match that of the remainder of the paragraph, simply delete one of the paired [Font] codes (be sure you have Reveal Codes on when you do this). The other half of the paired code disappears too, and the text takes on the appearance of the rest of the surrounding text.

There is an easier way to insert text without the original formatting. It is to use another little-known WordPerfect feature called Paste Special:

9. Leaving the insertion point within the text formatted with the new font, choose **E**dit, Paste **S**pecial.

The Paste Special dialog box appears, as shown in figure 8.2.

Fig. 8.2
The Paste Special dialog box.

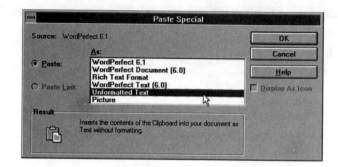

10. In the Paste Special dialog box, select Unformatted Text.

This tells WordPerfect to insert the contents of the Windows Clipboard into the document without any formatting codes (font changes, appearance attributes, etc.).

11. Choose OK to insert the unformatted text from the Clipboard into your document.

> **Note**
>
> If you find that you prefer to use Paste Special more often than the default Paste (which keeps the formatting), you may want to record a simple macro that performs the Paste Special function and then assign that macro to the Ctrl+V key or some other key on your keyboard. For help with recording macros, see Chapter 5, "Automating with Macros." For help on assigning macros to the keyboard, see Chapter 1, "Making WordPerfect Work the Way You Do."

Standard-Text Macros

Another common document assembly technique is the standard-text macro. Again, while this feature is not often thought of as document assembly, what else is it, really? A simple macro that types a signature block or a standard phrase, or even a paragraph, is helping to assemble your document by inserting that block of information wherever you need it.

This technique is certainly more automated than the manual copy-and-paste, but it obviously has its limitations too. Although it is theoretically possible to record hundreds of standard-text macros that type specific information and then write your new document by sequentially playing the desired macros, this method is obviously going to present a problem. You will have a hard time remembering and finding all of those macros, and in the end you may not save much time at all.

It is best to save this technique for the half dozen or fewer truly obvious and common bits of information you need routinely, such as signature blocks and letter closings.

Inserting Files

Another method of document assembly is to retrieve an entire file, or a series of files, into the document you are creating. And, by saving each standard paragraph or block of information for your document on disk as a separate file, again you can use this feature to assemble an entire document. But again, the disadvantage is similar to the disadvantage of using a large number of macros to assemble documents: hunting for just the right file to insert may slow you down considerably.

Nonetheless, this method is worth learning. To insert a complete file into the document in your active window, do the following:

1. Place the insertion point at the exact location where you want the first character of the inserted file to appear.

2. Choose **I**nsert, **Fi**le.

   The Insert File dialog box (which looks and functions just like the Open dialog box) appears.

3. Select the file you want to insert, then choose **I**nsert.

4. If you began with a document on your screen, you get a confirmation message asking if you want to insert the selected file into the document in the current window. Respond **Y**es.

WordPerfect inserts the document into your active document at the current location of the insertion point. Any font changes and formatting in the inserted file transfers over into the destination document, just as if you had used the Paste feature discussed above.

If you plan on using this technique extensively, you have to give some thought to how you format each of your form documents, including the inclusion of extra hard returns at the end of paragraphs so they appear as paragraphs in the finished document. Again, it is recommended that you use this

II

Assembling Documents

method sparingly, and only for easily remembered, frequently used standard blocks of text.

Automating with Templates and Macros

You have probably guessed where all of this is heading—toward automation of document assembly.

After you have decided on which technique to use in document assembly, you can automate the process with a template or a macro. For example, if you have a group of paragraphs or provisions stored as separate files on disk, you could write a macro that helps you identify the correct files and performs the insertion for you; or you could write a menu macro that controls the operation of all your standard text macros.

The Companion Disk contains several examples of document assembly macros, including the two principal ones discussed later in this chapter: DOCSETUP.WCM and DOCBILDR.WCM. But before learning how those macros work, it would be a good idea to think a little bit about how to set up the documents you're going to use with the system.

Preparing to Automate Document Assembly

The Document Builder system described later in this chapter is flexible and designed to work with any document on your computer. It allows you to organize your documents into segments and use those segments to create entirely new documents.

What Is a Segment?

Segments are the building blocks out of which your new document is constructed. They can be small blocks, as in a phrase or a sentence; or larger blocks such as paragraphs; or even multiple pages. The key is to think carefully about how the segments will be combined to make a final document.

How you define a segment depends entirely on the documents you are trying to create. In general, you need to think about which pieces of particular language must always appear together in a document, and which pieces of language are optional or may vary from document to document. If, for example, paragraph B must always follow paragraph A, the two paragraphs together should probably be a single segment.

Suppose instead that you have a paragraph in which one sentence, or even one word, may be in either of two forms depending on who the document is being prepared for. One way to handle this would be to break the paragraph into three segments:

- The first, unchanging part
- The variable sentence
- The remaining unchanged part

But a more efficient way to handle this might be to simply create two nearly identical paragraphs, one with sentence A and the other with the alternative sentence B. You can then simply include either alternative paragraph into your final document. This saves time and disk space in requiring fewer segments to be identified up front and allowing you to build a document by choosing one segment (that is, one of the alternative paragraphs) rather than three segments.

The principles used in determining the size of segments reflect two competing interests. First, you want segments small enough that you can customize a document relatively thoroughly on the "first cut"; that is, you want a selection that is wide enough to get you fairly close to a finished document on the first draft. Second, you want segments large enough that you don't need to select every single sentence when you go to assemble; the more selections you are required to make, the longer it will take you to build a new document, and the less benefit you are getting from setting up the document assembly system.

The user of the system is the only person who can determine the happy medium between these two competing goals. You'll probably find that one size does not fit all problems; depending on the type of document, your segments probably vary in size—from single sentences for a small document to major sections of a document covering several pages.

You need to consider how the document will be assembled before you attempt to answer the question of how large to make your segments. To use a will as an example, suppose that you have a standard form will, which includes provisions for marital deduction trusts, options to use inter vivos trusts to make distributions to heirs, options to appoint guardians for minor children when necessary, and so forth. Obviously, not all of your clients need all the various options in their wills. You want to create a single form document, however, which includes all of the options, and which allows you to pick and choose from those options as the client requires.

A standard will form may include these major divisions:

1. Introductory paragraph (identification of testator)
2. Identification of next of kin
3. Authorization to pay bills and last expenses
4. Specific bequests
5. Residuary bequest
6. Identification of personal representative
7. Identification of guardian of minor children
8. Administrative powers and liabilities of personal representative
9. Presumption of survivorship in simultaneous deaths
10. Miscellaneous provisions
11. Signature page for testator and witnesses

Is each of these divisions a segment unto itself? Or should you break down some of these divisions further? Or should you even combine some?

It's important to keep your eye on the ball here. What you're trying to accomplish is to give the lawyer a list of standard provisions, and then allow her to specify which items on the list to include in the finished will. Because it is easiest for the secretary preparing the will to run through the list and pick off the items in the order they will appear in the finished document, the list the lawyer is working from should be in the same order. And the document ought to store the segments in that same order, to make the segments easiest to find.

So, now to work through the list of major sections of the will and see how to define segments.

First, every testator will want to identify next of kin and authorize the payment of final expenses, so you may want to include items 1, 2, and 3 from above as a single segment. Since these items always appear first in the will, this should be the first segment.

Not every testator will want to make specific bequests, so item 4 needs to be a separate segment. Because the specific bequests vary in every case, the segment needs only to provide the heading and the introductory language indicating the purpose of the section; the specific bequests must be typed in later.

Item 5 probably needs to be broken down into many segments, so the lawyer can pick and choose from many options. If the testator is married, you will want a segment that provides for a marital deduction trust. If the testator has an inter vivos trust and wants to use it to distribute the residue of his estate, you need a segment to provide that option. If the testator wants to create testamentary trusts, you need segments with those options. Look over your own forms and include as many different options as you are likely to need in your practice.

Items 6 and 7 need to be separate segments as well; not every testator will need to provide for minor children. You may also want to include several options for different types of personal representatives. Item 8 is another section that you may want to break into separate segments depending on whether you'll want to provide different powers to different personal representatives.

Likewise, your office may use several different options for item 9 on the list; each one needs to be a separate segment, available for the lawyer to choose from. And item 10 may also need to be broken into several segments.

Your final list of segments to give to the attorney to choose from might therefore look something like this:

1. Testator name, identification of kin, and authorization to pay bills
2. Specific bequests
3. Residuary clause—introduction
4. Residuary clause—simple (no estate tax due)
5. Residuary clause—standard marital deduction trust
6. Residuary clause—A/B marital deduction trust option
7. Residuary clause—pour-over to inter vivos trust
8. Residuary clause—standard testamentary trust
9. Residuary clause—spendthrift testamentary trust
10. Personal representative—spouse or family member
11. Personal representative—corporate trustee
12. Appointment of guardian
13. Administrative powers—standard
14. Administrative powers—limited
15. Administrative powers—corporate trustee
16. Presumption of survivorship—simultaneous deaths
17. Presumption of survivorship—30-day survival
18. Miscellaneous provisions—heading
19. Miscellaneous provisions—standard definitions
20. Miscellaneous provisions—retention of counsel

21. Miscellaneous provisions—governing law

22. Miscellaneous provisions—revocability of will

23. Miscellaneous provisions—irrevocable (contracted) will

24. Miscellaneous provisions—number and gender

25. Signature page for testator and witnesses

The list could go on, of course, but it should give you an idea of how you can break down a standard will into discrete segments so as to allow a lawyer to pick and choose options and come up with a customized first draft. Notice that some of the segments contain multiple paragraphs, even pages, and others may be only a single paragraph.

Formatting Segments

Deciding what constitutes a segment is only part of the battle. The other part is deciding how to separate the segments in your standard form will so the user can quickly identify them as separate segments. There are several concerns here.

The first concern is obvious: what markers to use to separate the segments? You'll see some options in just a moment. The more difficult question is, how should the segments be formatted? Thinking these problems through when you set up your form documents can save you a lot of time later when you use the document assembly system.

Now to return to the example of the will discussed earlier. Because the objective is to allow the typist to simply grab the segments identified by the lawyer and plunk them into the new will, it is important to format the segments so that, when one segment is copied and pasted it will be properly separated from the preceding and following segments. Thus, if your basic building blocks are paragraphs, or even groups of paragraphs, you should adopt the practice of including two hard returns at the end of each segment. WordPerfect copies these hard returns later with the segment, providing the necessary blank line between paragraphs in the finished document. If every segment includes these hard returns, you can easily mix and match segments and not have to worry about adding lines and spaces later.

What about numbering the paragraphs? Recall the discussion in Chapter 2 of the various automatic numbering schemes available in WordPerfect. Be sure to use one of them in your form document! This way, if, for example, a testator elects to make no specific bequests (thereby skipping what would have been Article III in the will), the counter or paragraph numbering code in Article IV (residuary bequests) automatically updates itself to become Article III, and so on throughout the remainder of the will.

What about cross-references? In Article VI (identification of personal representative) you may want to refer to his or her administrative powers in Article VIII (powers and liabilities of personal representative). If, by deleting Article III (specific bequests), Article VI becomes Article V and VIII becomes VII, you want to use the cross-reference feature described in Chapter 2 to allow the automatic updating of these numbers in the finished document.

Of course, there are "blanks" to be filled in (for example, the names of the testator, his or her family, the personal representative, etc.). How do you identify these? The simplest way, of course, would be to use some sort of visual marker, such as a blank underscored line. Better yet would be a bracketed prompt to tell the typist what sort of information gets filled in that spot. If you want to get really fancy, you could include some FIELD() merge codes and set up the finished document as a merge form file; then you could fill in the blanks by merging the resulting document with a data file created for this client. (Later chapters give some examples of this technique.) For more information on inserting merge codes into your documents, refer to Chapter 6, "A Merge Primer."

Separating Segments from Each Other

The last thing you need to consider is how to physically identify where one segment begins and another one ends within your standard form will. You can either store segments as separate files on your disk or mark them as separate segments in one file; the method you choose depends primarily on how you want to retrieve segments later on.

Using Separate Files

One of the simplest ways to identify separate segments is to save them as separate files. This makes it easy to retrieve segments into the final document by choosing Insert, File. The difficulty is that the standard "eight-dot-three" limitation of DOS file names makes it difficult to save segments with meaningful file names. Using the Descriptive Filename option of WordPerfect is something of a help here if you don't mind the performance penalty of enabling that feature.

> **Note**
>
> If you decide to store segments in separate files, remember that the Open dialog box will sort the files by file name, date, or however you specify it. This will not likely be the same order in which the segments would naturally appear in any document unless you give each segment a file name that suggests its logical place in the finished document.

Separating Segments Within a Single File

It is probably better to store all segments in a single file and separate them internally within that file. This keeps the segments in the correct order (as they will appear on the list from which the attorney is working). Also it is easier for the typist to see what segment to retrieve because he or she is looking at the text of the segment rather than only a short or descriptive file name.

The markers that you use to separate segments within a single file should be something that can be easily searched and found; that is, an uncommon character or code or string of characters or codes. Another simple method that works well is to use a hard page ([HPg]) code between segments. Not only does this provide a good visual separation on the screen (by placing each segment on a separate page of the document), but also you can use the PageUp and PageDown keys to quickly move to the top or bottom of any segment, and it is easy to search for the [HPg] codes. Other options are to use oddball characters like tildes (~) or carats (^) between segments, because those characters are not likely to occur in the body of your text and therefore will not confuse a Find operation.

Another good option is to use paired bookmarks. Chapter 1 discussed bookmarks briefly; here is how to use that feature to great advantage in document assembly:

1. Open any document into an editing window; for the purpose of this exercise it doesn't matter what document you use.
2. Select some text.
3. Choose **I**nsert, **B**ookmark.
4. In the Bookmark dialog box, choose Cr**e**ate.
5. In the Create Bookmark dialog box, clear whatever text may appear already in the **B**ookmark Name entry window and type in a bookmark name (for this example type Segment 1).

You then return to your document. However, if you look in Reveal Codes, you'll see that the text you had earlier selected is now surrounded by a pair of bookmark codes, like this: [Bookmark>][<Bookmark]. If you put your insertion point to the left of either bookmark, the code expands to look like this: [Bookmark: Segment 1].

These codes work like any other paired codes; deleting one also deletes the related code. The advantage to using these paired bookmarks is that they make it extremely easy to reselect the text enclosed within the bookmark codes:

6. Move the insertion point to any other location in the document (for example, move to the very top of the document).

7. Choose **I**nsert, **B**ookmark again.

Notice that the appearance of the Bookmark dialog box has changed to include the Segment 1 bookmark you just created. Notice also that the screen identifies this bookmark as a Selected type of bookmark; this means that it is a paired bookmark enclosing a selection of text. When you highlight the Segment 1 bookmark by clicking on it, notice that the Go To & **S**elect button becomes active, as shown in figure 8.3.

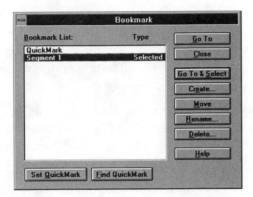

Fig. 8.3
Going to text preselected by paired bookmarks.

8. Choose Go To & **S**elect.

The text enclosed within the paired Segment 1 bookmarks is now reselected, available for you to copy into the Clipboard and move to a new document.

The advantage of using paired bookmarks to identify segments, in addition to this trick, is just the opposite of the using visual marks as discussed above: bookmarks do *not* affect the appearance of your document. If you want to be able to print your form documents and not have the visual markings or hard page codes interfere with your document, paired bookmarks do the job nicely.

The Document Builder Macros

Finally, it's time to learn about the Document Builder system mentioned earlier. Document Builder is actually two macros that work together. The way to use it is to use DOCSETUP.WCM to help you to insert paired bookmarks to identify segments of your form documents, and then use DOCBILDR.WCM to display a list of available form documents and the segments contained within each form. The typist can then select the segments he or she wants from a single screen, and DOCBILDR.WCM hunts them down and inserts them, in order, into a finished document, automatically.

An Overview of the Document Builder System

Document Builder works only with existing documents; you must have a completed form file stored on your hard disk before using DOCSETUP.WCM to convert it into Document Builder format. But it will work with any form document you create, so you can completely customize the system to your individual documents.

Document Builder stores all prepared documents in a single directory. Although you can use any existing directory on your computer, it is recommended that you create a separate directory for finished Document Builder forms. This allows you to quickly find all form files that you have created for the system.

The macros allow you to specify the directory to use. The first time you play either DOCSETUP.WCM or DOCBILDR.WCM WordPerfect asks you to specify the directory where you want to store your Document Builder files.

Document Builder stores information about the prepared forms in a file called DOCBILDR.BIF. This file is located in your default macros directory; if you change the designation of your default directory, or if you delete or move that file, you lose critical information about your Document Builder documents. If you do decide to change your computer settings to specify a different default macros directory, be sure to move the DOCBILDR.BIF file to the new default macros directory.

Setting Up Documents for Document Builder

Before you can use the Document Builder system, you must mark your documents as Document Builder documents, and identify the segments you want to list. The Companion Disk includes a macro called DOCSETUP.WCM, which makes this task much easier.

On the Disk

The following section shows how this macro works; in it you'll set up the hypothetical will form for use in the Document Builder system. After having identified the segments as noted above and included them all in one document (which this example calls WILL.FRM), save the file to disk, and then do the following:

1. Open the file you want to set up in the active document window (in this example, the file WILL.FRM).

2. Turn on Reveal Codes.

This step is not technically necessary, but it is a very good idea to do this routinely. You should be careful to include formatting codes and other special codes with the proper segments (Document Builder identifies the segments with special bookmarks, as you'll see later in this chapter). You can do this task most accurately with Reveal Codes on. Your document looks something like figure 8.4.

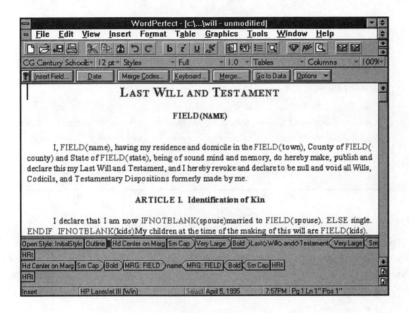

Fig. 8.4
Setting up the WILL.FRM file as a Document Builder file.

(Note that this form file uses various merge codes to indicate where information needs to be filled in. Chapter 13, "Wills and Estate Planning," describes a system to automate the filling in of the will using the Merge feature.)

Now that you have the form document on screen, use the DOCSETUP.WCM macro to mark the segments you identified earlier.

3. Choose **T**ools, **M**acro.

4. Choose **P**lay.

   Skip this step.

5. Select DOCSETUP.WCM from the listing of macros in the Play Macro dialog box and choose **P**lay.

   Type DOCSETUP in the Play Macro dialog box and choose OK.

You see the initial Document Setup Menu, as shown in figure 8.5. This menu gives you the option to add documents to the Document Builder system (by

II

Assembling Documents

choosing the **S**et Up Document option) or to delete documents from the system.

Fig. 8.5
The initial
Document Setup
Menu.

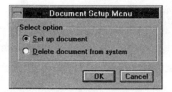

<table>
<tr><td>**Note**</td></tr>
<tr><td>

If this is the first time you have played either DOCSETUP.WCM or DOCBILDR.WCM, the macro detects that and asks you to specify a directory for your Document Builder files prior to showing you the initial menu screen. You may want to specify a separate directory for Document Builder files to keep them separate from other types of files; you can do so from the Select Directory dialog box while the macro is running by choosing File **O**ptions.

</td></tr>
</table>

6. Leave the **S**et Up Document option selected and choose OK.

Because you started with a document in the active window, the screen asks you to confirm that this is the document you want to set up for Document Builder (see fig. 8.6). If you started from a blank window, or if you select **N**o from this dialog box, WordPerfect asks you for the name of a file on disk that you want to set up.

Fig. 8.6
Confirming that
you want to set
up the current
document.

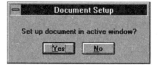

7. Choose **Y**es.

Once you have confirmed that the active window contains the document you want to set up (or if you specified a file name and the macro has opened the correct file), you see the Document Setup dialog box shown in figure 8.7. You need to specify two pieces of information in this window: a file name for the document (it is stored in the default directory under the file name you specify here), and a "descriptive name" for the file. This is the name that appears later in the Document Builder menu, so you should choose a name that helps you distinguish this file from other similar files that you may set up.

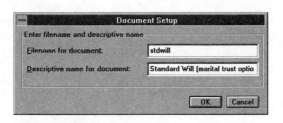

Fig. 8.7
Specifying a
file name
and descriptive
name for your
document.

8. Type in a file name and descriptive name in the appropriate entry windows and choose OK.

> **Note**
>
> Because WordPerfect stores the document under the file name you specify, you are limited to the standard eight characters, a period, and a three-digit extension. Be careful to use only legal characters for a DOS file name; that is, do not use any spaces, slashes, asterisks, question marks or other punctuation, or other characters that would not be accepted in a DOS file name.

You are now ready to begin marking segments; the Setup Document dialog box shown in figure 8.8 confirms this.

Fig. 8.8
Preparing to mark
segments.

9. From the Setup Document dialog box, choose OK.

10. Place the insertion point carefully to the left of the first character or code that you want to include in the first segment of your form document.

11. Activate the Select feature from your keyboard (F12 on the DOS-compatible keyboard; F8 on the CUA keyboard).

12. Use the arrow keys to select the entire first segment for your document.

In the example of the will, the first segment was a large one because it included the introductory paragraph, Article I (identification of kin), and Article II (authorization to pay final bills). At this point in the process, your document screen might look something like figure 8.9.

Notice that the example has extended the selection to include the two Hard Return codes which mark the end of Article II. This ensures that, whatever

II

Assembling Documents

Article is selected next by the lawyer, it will appear one line down from the end of Article II. Note also that the Article numbers have been marked by paragraph number codes, so that if one or more articles are deleted from the finished will, the remaining ones are still numbered properly. Finally, notice that the status bar carries a reminder that you need to press Enter when you have completed your selection.

Fig. 8.9
Selecting the text for the first segment.

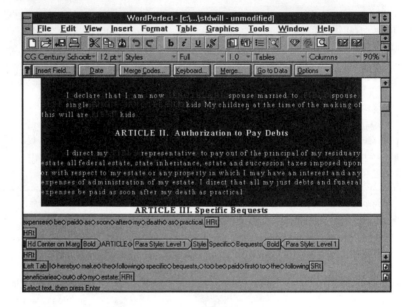

13. When you have selected the proper text, simply press Enter.

You see the Setup Document dialog box shown in figure 8.10.

Fig. 8.10
Naming the segment.

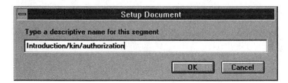

14. Type in a brief name for the segment you have just selected and choose OK.

> **Note**
>
> To squeeze as many descriptive names onto the Document Builder screen as possible, the macro limits you to 30 characters for descriptive names of segments. Be sure to choose names that suggest the content of each segment.

Next you'll see the Document Setup dialog box shown in figure 8.11.

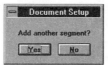

Fig. 8.11
The option to add
more segments to
the listing.

15. Choose **Y**es to continue to add the next segment.

DOCSETUP.WCM then adds a paired bookmark named DocBuild/*n*/ around
the selected text; DOCBILDR.WCM later uses those bookmarks to identify
which text goes with the descriptive name you specified in step 13. Each
DocBuild/*n*/ bookmark pair will be sequentially numbered as the marks are
added by the macro. You can see the closing bookmark for the first segment
of the sample will in Reveal Codes in figure 8.12.

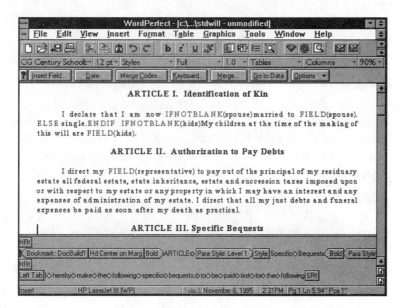

Fig. 8.12
The DocBuild
closing bookmark,
shown in Reveal
Codes.

For every segment you add to the listing for this document, repeat Steps 8
through 14. When you have added the last segment, choose **N**o from the
dialog box shown in figure 8.11 to break out of the loop. DOCSETUP.WCM
then saves the completed document in the directory you specified at setup
and then closes it.

> **Note**
>
> You can define up to 60 segments in a single document in the Document Builder system.

You can set up any number of documents for the Document Builder system in just this manner.

Assembling the Final Document

The last step in assembling documents with Document Builder is the easiest: just run the DOCBILDR.WCM macro (included on the Companion Disk) and choose the file and the segments within that file that you want to use.

1. Choose **T**ools, **M**acro.

2. Choose **P**lay.

 Skip this step.

3. Type **DOCBILDR** in the File**n**ame text box, or select DOCBILDR.WCM from the listing of macros in the Play Macro dialog box; choose **P**lay.

   Type **DOCBILDR** in the Play Macro dialog box and choose OK.

   A very useful feature of DOCBILDR.WCM is that it allows you to place segments from any file in the system into the active document at the location of the insertion point. If you have invoked DOCBILDR.WCM from an active document window, you see the dialog box shown in figure 8.13.

Fig. 8.13
Selecting the location for output of Document Builder segments.

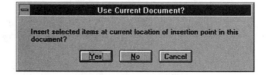

4. Choose the appropriate option from the Use Current Document? dialog box.

If you answer **Y**es, WordPerfect inserts the items you select into the current document. If you answer **N**o, DOCBILDR.WCM opens a new blank document to receive the selected items. Choosing Cancel ends the macro. After you have made your choice, you see the Available Documents dialog box shown in figure 8.14.

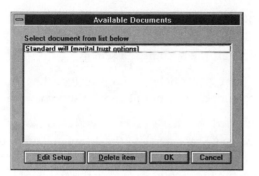

Fig. 8.14
The list of
available
documents.

The Available Documents dialog box is the main menu of DOCBILDR.WCM.
It provides several editing options in the row of pushbuttons at the bottom
of the box. If you want to change the directory designated for Document
Builder documents, you can choose **E**dit Setup and specify a new location. If
you want to delete a document from the list, simply click that document in
the list box and choose **D**elete item. You see a confirmation message asking if
you really want to delete the item from the list. Confirming the deletion does
not delete the document from your disk, but strips out a key bookmark so
that Document Builder no longer recognizes the file as having been set up.

As you can see in figure 8.14, you have set up only one document so far.

5. Highlight the document you want to load as the source document and
   choose OK.

   You see a list of the segments you defined in the document when you
   used DOCSETUP.WCM. The segments you defined for your sample Will
   document are shown in figure 8.15.

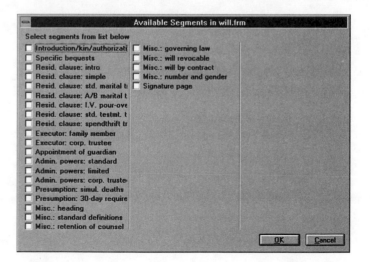

Fig. 8.15
Selecting segments
to assemble a will.

6. Select the segments you want to include in the finished document by clicking in the check box next to each segment name.

7. Choose OK to start the document assembly.

DOCBILDR.WCM then sequentially retrieves each of the items you checked, inserting them into your document in the order shown on the screen.

When you have finished, you have a good first draft of your finished document. You will have to go back and edit the document (or in the case of the will, perform a merge to insert correct information in the various fields), but the macro has done the hard work of copying the standard language into your document in a matter of seconds.

From Here...

The Document Builder system described in this chapter is useful in just about any type of law practice. You can use it to assemble litigation pleadings, leases, contracts, wills, and marital dissolution agreements—just about any kind of document that you may need to create routinely.

Several upcoming chapters show how Document Builder can fit into a variety of law practices. But the next chapter deals with other common word-processing problems that occur in all law offices—how to expedite the creation of the following:

- Interoffice memos
- Phone messages
- Letters (including maintenance of address lists)
- Fax cover sheets

Correspondence Systems

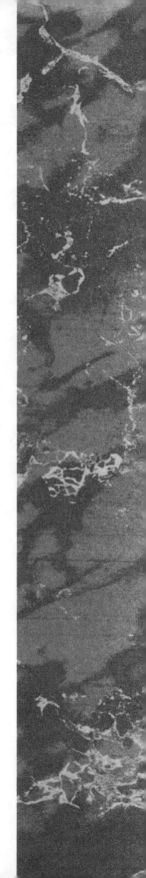

This chapter looks at one of the most common—and vexing—problems in just about any office:

- Creating phone messages and interoffice memos
- Managing address lists
- Creating correspondence
- Creating fax cover sheets

Interoffice Communications

Okay, I admit it; I tend to over-use my computer. It's just that, when it comes time to jot a note to my secretary, or to myself, it is usually easier for me to find my computer than it is to find a blank piece of paper, a pen (with ink), or a flat surface to write on (not that my desk is *always* cluttered, mind you). So I do tend to use my computer to make notes more than most people; at least my laser printer has better handwriting than I do!

This chapter begins by describing a few macros on the Companion Disk that accompanies this book that will help you with communicating with your co-workers.

Interoffice Memos

I tend to scribble lots of notes to my coworkers during the day. Unfortunately, my handwriting tends to be illegible at times. So I've gotten into the habit of doing quickie notes on my computer.

On the Disk

A simple macro called MEMO.WCM speeds up this process. There is nothing fancy about this macro; it just creates a standard memorandum like the one shown in figure 9.1.

Fig. 9.1

A sample memorandum created by MEMO.WCM.

> **MEMORANDUM**
>
> **TO:**   Bonnie F.
> **FROM:**   KDC
> **DATE:**   November 22, 1995
> **RE:**   Travel arrangements
>
>   I will be arriving in Harrisburg on Thursday evening, so any time you want to meet to discuss our project on Friday morning would be fine with me.

When you play this macro, it will automatically insert the current date (from your computer's system) and your initials. You will have to edit this macro in one place to change the initials from mine to yours; the line in the macro looks like this:

```
Type ("KDC")              //Put in your initials here; leave the
                            quotation marks!
```

This line is about halfway through the macro. Simply open the macro file, delete my initials and replace them with your own.

After you play the macro, it will leave you in the correct position to begin typing the name of the recipient. You can complete and print the memo just like you would any document.

Phone Messages

I hate those little pink "While You Were Away" slips. Not just because they sometimes pile up too fast; they are also easy to lose. Many of them get thrown away after I've returned the call, but some get put into the file because I want to record the fact that the phone call took place, or I want to keep the phone number, or because I made some notes on the slip about the conversation I had when I returned the call.

Unfortunately, for all of those purposes the little pink slip is not well designed. Because it is so small, it tends to get lost in the file, or fall out of the file. It is hard to photocopy if you want to share its contents with somebody else. And, if you are taking notes about your conversation, there just isn't that much room on the slip to do that.

On the Disk

The Companion Disk includes the macro PHONEMSG.WCM, which creates the Phone Message form shown in figure 9.2.

While You Were Away

TO:	KDC
FROM:	Bonnie
DATE:	November 15, 1995, 11:54 am
PHONE:	(717) 555-3421
MESSAGE:	Wants to get together with you on your next visit to Harrisburg to discuss computer project

Fig. 9.2
A sample phone message created by PHONEMSG.WCM.

To use this macro, simply play it and fill in the information in the dialog box shown in figure. 9.3.

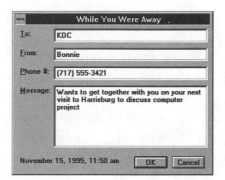

Fig. 9.3
The PHONEMSG.WCM dialog box.

Note that the macro automatically reads and inserts the current time and date from your computer's clock. If your computer's clock is inaccurate, be sure to correct it so that the time on your phone messages will be correct. See your computer manual for help on setting the time and date on your computer clock.

After you have filled in whatever information you want to include in the message, select OK. The message will appear on-screen, underneath a message box asking if you want to print the message now (see fig. 9.4). If you choose Yes, the Print dialog box will appear. Note that whether you choose Print or Close from that dialog box, the message you just wrote will be erased as soon as the dialog box is closed. If you want to edit or add to the message slip, choose No and the message slip will remain on your screen, ready for you to edit, print, or save as desired.

Fig. 9.4
The option to print the phone message immediately from PHONEMSG.WCM.

Creating Correspondence

How many times have you, or your secretary, retyped the same address?

WordPerfect for Windows comes with an "address book" feature that works with its letterhead templates. The feature helps you create and maintain address lists; you can even copy addresses that you have created into the Clipboard and retrieve them into your document using Paste. But the Address Book has some limitations:

- It does not provide you with a reference field to identify what the letter is about.

- It cannot handle multiple addressees automatically.

- It alphabetizes entries by first name, and if you use the feature extensively you may end up with a long list of names that is hard to search.

- Address information is stored in such a way that it is not easily accessible to the Envelope feature.

- On network installations it may be difficult or impossible to share Address Book information.

- It is limited to 100 names.

- Worst of all, the information is stored in a template file which is susceptible to corruption, putting all your address listings at significant risk of loss.

This portion of the chapter discusses the built-in Address Book and Envelope features, and provides a few tools to make them a bit safer and more convenient to use. A macro which provides an alternative Address Book-like function and which avoids many of the limitations and dangers of the built-in system is presented later in the chapter.

Using WordPerfect's Built-in Address Books

The trick to understanding how WordPerfect stores addresses is to realize one thing: there are really *two separate* address lists in the program. And guess what? They don't talk to each other.

The first list, called the Address Book, is used for storing and retrieving addresses for letters; it is integrated nicely with the various Letter templates which ship with the program, and can be accessed by any custom letter template you write. The second address list is used by the Envelope feature; addresses are stored in a different location and in a different format from the Address Book. The Envelope feature cannot access Address Book addresses, nor can Address Book read Envelope addresses.

This is generally not a problem for the main envelope; once you have retrieved an address and written your letter, the Envelope feature can read the letter and pick the address off of it rather quickly. But what about the recipients of carbon copies? Or when you want to print an envelope without having the letter on-screen first? The Envelope feature cannot refer to pre-existing addresses in the Address Book; you must re-create those addresses manually and store them in the Envelope feature, or type them on your screen before using Envelope.

WordPerfect has a very robust set of correspondence templates that make use of the Address Book. Let's first take a look at how the standard letter templates work, and how they access information in the Address Book. Then let's examine some of the limitations and dangers of using the Address book, and suggest a few things that can help you work around these limitations.

The Standard Letter Templates

WordPerfect ships with a set of standard templates for creating letters; all include access to the Address Book. Version 6.1 added a few new letter templates and the Letter Expert, and made a few changes in the way that templates are accessed, but basically the two versions are the same. Let's use one of the standard letter templates from version 6.1 to get an understanding of how this powerful feature works.

1. Choose **F**ile, **N**ew.

   Choose File, Template.

2. Select the letter group in the **G**roup list box at the left side of the New Document dialog box.

   Version 6.0 does not support the Group feature with Templates, so you must skip this step.

3. Select one of the letter templates (for this example use the Letter - Contemporary letterhead template) and choose **S**elect.

   Select Letter2 and choose OK.

The Letter dialog box appears, as shown in figure 9.5. From this dialog box you can choose the style of the letter (by choosing from different styles in the drop-down list button under the Letter Format window); you can select options for including a second-page header, a reference line, and your return address; and you can manually type in the recipient's name, address, and salutation.

Fig. 9.5

The Letter dialog box, showing the Address Book button.

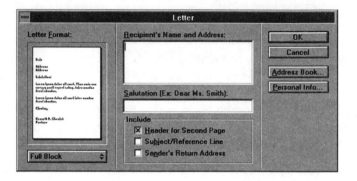

Or, you can access the Address Book to either retrieve an existing address or create and add a new address to the Address Book.

4. Choose the Address Book button at the right side of the dialog box.

The Template Address Book dialog box appears. Because no addresses have been created yet, it will be blank, as shown in figure 9.6.

Fig. 9.6

The Template Address Book dialog box with no entries.

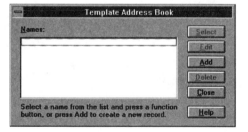

5. Choose Add.

The Edit Address dialog box appears, as shown in figure 9.7.

6. Type in the name, salutation, and other information needed for your letter, then choose OK.

7. The name you just entered should now appear, highlighted, in the Template Address Book dialog box; choose Select.

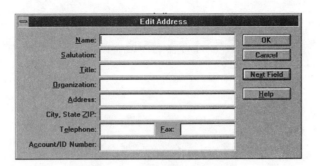

Fig. 9.7
The Edit Address
dialog box.

Note

If you have more than one address, you must highlight the correct one before
choosing **S**elect.

The name, address, and salutation you entered into the Address book
should now appear in the Letter dialog box, as shown in figure 9.8.

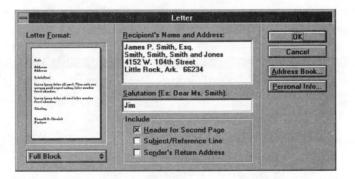

Fig. 9.8
The Letter dialog
box with an
address showing.

8. Choose OK to insert this address into your document.

You now see a message reminding you that the letter formatting has
been completed, and that you can insert a letter closing by choosing
that option from the Insert menu, as shown in figure 9.9.

There is a clever trick in the new Letter templates shipped with
WordPerfect 6.1. Each template includes a custom Menu bar that looks
different from the standard menu bar.

9. Type the body of your letter, leaving the insertion point where you
want the closing to appear.

Fig. 9.9
The Letter
Formatting
Complete
reminder
message.

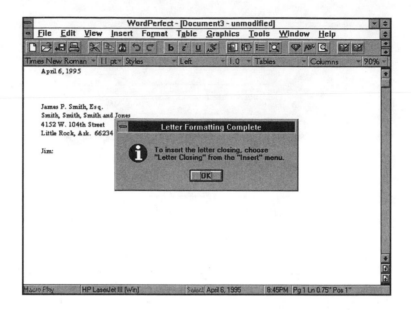

10. To view the special menu bar listing, choose **I**nsert from the menu bar.

    The Letter menu bar is shown in figure 9.10. Note that the Insert menu now includes three special items relating to creating letters.

Fig. 9.10
The special Insert
menu for the
Letter templates.

11. Choose Letter closing.

The Letter Closing dialog box appears, as shown in figure 9.11.

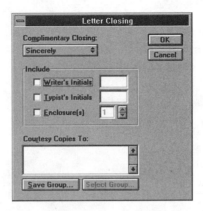

Fig. 9.11
The Letter Closing
dialog box.

12. Choose the appropriate options in the Letter Closing dialog box and
type the name or names of any persons who will receive courtesy copies
of the letter in the box near the bottom of the dialog box.

13. Choose OK.

Your completed letter now appears on your screen, as shown in
figure 9.12.

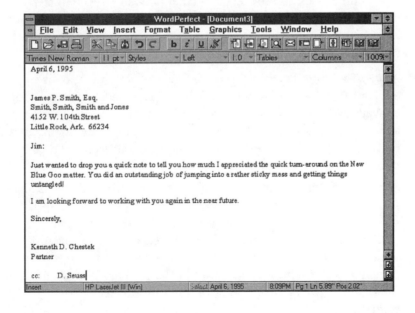

Fig. 9.12
A completed letter
based upon the
Contemporary
letter template.

Using the ADRSBOOK.WCM Macro

You do not need to use a letter template to add or edit items in the Address Book. WordPerfect ships with a macro called ADRSBOOK.WCM which gives you the tools necessary to maintain the Address Book. When you play that macro, you will see the Address Book dialog box shown in figure 9.13; it is very similar to the Template Address Book dialog box that you saw when using the letter template (refer to fig. 9.6).

Fig. 9.13

The Address Book dialog box from the ADDRSBOOK.WCM macro.

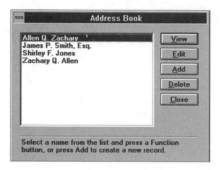

You can add new entries, delete entries, or edit existing entries in the Address Book by choosing the appropriate button at the right side of the dialog box.

Some Limitations of the Address Book Feature

While the Address Book and the templates that provide access to it are very powerful features, there are some hidden limitations inherent in the way this feature works that you should carefully consider before investing a lot of effort into creating a large database of addresses.

- *Address Book sorts names by first name only.* The first limitation is apparent from figure 9.13. Notice that the list of names added in the listing of available addresses is sorted by first name. Thus, "Allen Q. Zachary" appears before "Zachary Q. Allen." If you generate a long list and have problems remembering first names of individuals, this could become a nuisance.

- *Address Book entries are stored in the default template.* This is not as much a limitation as a major caution. The address book entries you specify are stored in your default template (usually STANDARD.WPT unless you specify a different one or have a non-U.S. version of the program). Unfortunately, lots of other things are stored in that file too, so storing a large number of address book entries will cause that file to grow significantly in size, which may slow down the performance of your computer.

More significantly, however, the default template is frequently being queried by the program as you work. It is opened automatically as soon as you launch WordPerfect and is closed when you exit. With all of this access to the file, it is susceptible to "corruption"; that is, rogue data being written to it or key items being deleted from it, making it unusable. Corruption in this file can occur if WordPerfect "crashes," which frankly still occurs from time to time even in the most recent releases of the program. You are therefore at risk of losing your Address Book data if the default template file becomes corrupted.

> **Tip**
>
> For the reasons just explained, it is always a good idea to keep a spare copy of your default template on your hard disk, saved under a different filename. After you have edited the template, or added addresses to the Address Book, exit from WordPerfect, then use File Manager or a DOS command to make a copy of the default template file, saved to a different filename (for example, you might name the copy STANDARD.BAK and place it in the default template directory). This way, if the default template becomes corrupt, you can copy STANDARD.BAK back over to STANDARD.WPT and regain your Address Book entries and other preferences and customization. Be sure that the default template is working properly before making this backup! And remember to periodically update your backup copy as you add Address Book entries and make other changes.

- *Address Book items cannot be easily shared with other computers.* Another side effect of storing Address Book entries in the default template is that it makes it very difficult to share Address Book entries with other users.

If you are working on a network, client workstations may not be able to save Address Book entries. This is because, when the server opens WordPerfect, the default template file is immediately opened, making it a "read only" file to all client workstations. If those stations rely on the server's default template, they will only be able to read Address Book listings from the server's default template; they will not be able to write new entries to it. You can avoid this problem by setting up each client workstation to use a local file as the default template, but then that client loses access to the common Address Book entries on the server.

If you are not electronically networked to other computers but want to "sneakernet" your Address Book files to another stand-alone computer, you would have to carry a copy of your default template by floppy disk to the other computer. *This is a bad idea!* Because the default template carries with it a lot of customization information (beyond Address Book entries) specific to the computer which created it, it may cause problems on the other computer, possibly even preventing WordPerfect from running at all.

There are some solutions to these problems included on the Companion Disk, which are discussed later in the chapter. But first let's take a look at the other address book buried in the Envelope feature.

Addressing Envelopes

WordPerfect also has a powerful feature called Envelope, which you can use to automatically address envelopes. The next example shows you how it works and then examines its limitations too.

You can make an envelope for the letter created in the previous example.

1. With the letter you created on your screen, choose Format, Envelope.

From the **L**ayout menu, choose En**v**elope...

You will see your screen flash briefly as Envelope searches for what it believes to be an address. If it finds text formatted in such a way that it appears to be an address, it will load that text into the Envelope dialog box, as shown in figure 9.14.

Fig. 9.14
The Envelope dialog box with an address selected automatically.

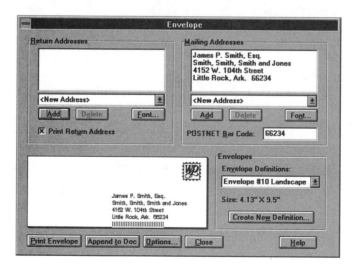

2. If Envelope has correctly located the address (it is usually pretty accurate), all you need to do is choose **P**rint Envelope to immediately send the envelope to the printer, or Append **t**o Doc to append an envelope to the end of the current document. The appended envelope is then printed automatically when you print the full letter.

> **Note**
>
> If Envelope has not correctly identified the address in your document, or if your document uses several addresses and you want to print an address other than the first one found, choose **C**lose to return to your document. Then select the address you want to use and repeat step 1; the text you selected will appear in the **M**ailing Addresses window.

3. To include the address shown in the **M**ailing Addresses window in the Envelope address listing, simply choose the A**d**d button in that group box.

You can also specify standard return addresses, select different envelope forms, and specify other options from the Envelope dialog box.

What if you are trying to print an envelope for the recipient of a carbon copy, or simply need an envelope for a document not created in WordPerfect? Here is where the address list stored with the Envelope feature comes in handy.

1. Open a blank document window.

2. Choose Fo**r**mat, En**v**elope.

From the **L**ayout menu, choose En**v**elope...

Because you started with a blank document, the Envelope dialog box appears with no address appearing in the **M**ailing Addresses window. The insertion point is in that window, however, enabling you to immediately start typing an address.

3. If you have already typed and saved the address you now want to use for the envelope, click on the down arrow at the end of the entry field containing the words <New Address>.

You will see a drop-down list of all of the addresses you have saved to date, again alphabetized by first name, as shown in figure 9.15.

4. Select the address you want to use by clicking it or by using the arrow keys and pressing Enter.

The address you selected is inserted into the **M**ailing Addresses group box, ready for you to use.

Fig. 9.15
Choosing a
preexisting address
from the Envelope
feature.

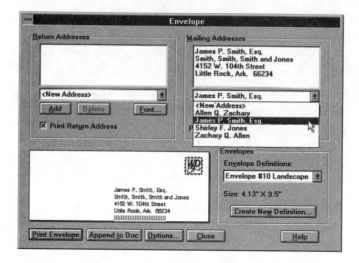

Some Limitations of the Envelope Address List

Like the template Address Book, the Envelope address list has a few limitations too.

- *Envelope cannot read the Address Book.* The chief problem with the Envelope feature is that it does not have access to the addresses stored in the Address Book. The Envelope feature stores its addresses in a configuration file called WPCSET.BIF located by default in your Windows directory. This is a program file that stores a great deal of information about your personal preferences and setup of the WordPerfect program on your computer; its contents cannot be read directly in a WordPerfect editing window.

- *It is awkward to edit pre-existing entries.* There is no direct way to edit an entry on the Envelope address list after you have stored it. If you want to change it, you must delete it, then re-enter and add the corrected entry.

- *Envelope sorts entries by first name.* This is the same limitation as found in the Address Book feature.

- *Envelope entries are stored in a volatile preferences file.* Just as Address Book entries are stored in the default template, along with other personal information and preferences, Envelope addresses are stored in the WPCSET.BIF file, which is also accessed frequently by the program. WPCSET.BIF is even more susceptible to corruption and damage during ordinary use of the program than is STANDARD.WPT, so your Envelope addresses are constantly at risk of loss due to unpredictable problems with that file. The recommendation of keeping a backup copy of STANDARD.WPT handy applies with even greater force when it comes to WPCSET.BIF.

■ *Envelope addresses cannot be shared easily with other computers.* This limitation is also similar to the limitation of Address Book, discussed previously. Sharing a copy of WPCSET.BIF between computers is an even worse idea than sharing a copy of STANDARD.WPT. More than likely WordPerfect will not be able to run, or will "crash" unexpectedly, if you do this.

Maintaining WordPerfect Address Books

There are, fortunately, solutions to these problems; or more accurately, workarounds that can protect your data from damage and which provide a mechanism for exporting address information from one computer to another. These workarounds are contained in macros, some shipped by WordPerfect with the application and others provided on the Companion Disk with this book. These macros read address data from either STANDARD.WPT or WPCSET.BIF and place it into an ordinary WordPerfect document, or take those same documents and write the information back into those two files. You can create backups of your address lists by saving these WordPerfect files, and can safely share just the addresses by moving the address list files from computer to computer.

The macros which perform these tasks are as listed in table 9.1.

Table 9.1 Address List Maintenance Macros		
Macro Name	**Source**	**Function**
ADRS2MRG.WCM	WordPerfect Corp.	Extract addresses from Address Book and store in WP Merge data file
MRG2ADRS.WCM	Companion Disk	Read addresses from WP Merge data file and insert into Address Book
ENV2DOC.WCM	Companion Disk	Extract addresses from Envelope address list and store in WP document file
DOC2ENV.WCM	Companion Disk	Read addreses from WP document file and insert into Envelope address list*

(continues)

Table 9.1	Continued	
Macro Name	**Source**	**Function**
MRG2ENV.WCM	Companion Disk	Converts an Address list created by the MRG2ADRS.WCM macro into a file that DOC2ENV.WCM can use to store the addresses in the Address Book

Requires minor editing to work in Version 6.0a; see instructions in macro file

On the Disk

These macros are useful to maintain backup copies of the two address lists, transfer address lists from the Address Book to the Envelope address list, and to transfer addresses safely from one computer to another.

1. To make a backup copy of the Address Book entries, open a blank document window, then run the macro ADRS2MRG.WCM.

   The macro exports all addresses stored in your STANDARD.WPT and creates a new Merge data file in a blank document window. You can save this new document to your disk and use it as a data file for any form file you create (see Chapter 6, "A Merge Primer").

2. For the purposes of this discussion, name the file created by the macro ADDRESS.DAT.

3. To restore addresses to your Address Book (for example, if you have had to delete your STANDARD.WPT file or if you have changed to a different default directory), simply run the MRG2ADRS.WCM macro.

4. To copy the Address Book listings to a different computer, simply transfer the ADDRESS.DAT file created in step 1 to that computer and run MRG2ADRS.WCM on that computer.

5. To make a backup copy of the entries in the Envelope address list, simply play the macro ENV2DOC.WCM.

   This macro exports all addresses stored in the WPCSET.BIF file for the Envelope feature into a blank document window. Each address is separated on a blank page, as shown in figure 9.16. Notice also that each address is followed by two hard return ([HRt]) codes; this is required so that the Envelope feature can identify the addresses as addresses. You can also save this as a WordPerfect file.

6. For the purposes of this discussion, name this one ENVELOPE.LST.

7. To restore addresses to your Envelope address list (for example, if you have had to delete your WPCSET.BIF file after a crash), simply run the DOC2ENV.WCM macro.

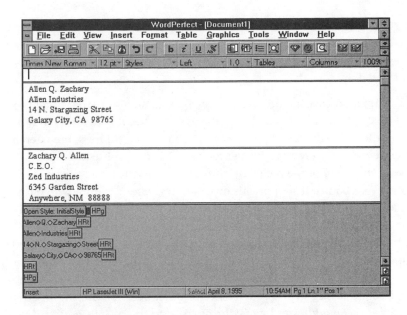

Fig. 9.16
Addresses exported
from the Envelope
address list.

8. To copy the Address Book listings to a different computer, simply transfer the ENVELOPE.LST file created in step 4 to that computer and run DOC2ENV.WCM on that computer.

You can also use these macros to transfer address listings from the Address Book to the Envelope address list, as follows:

1. If you do not already have the Address Book list saved as a Merge data file (see previous example), from a blank document screen play the macro ADRS2MRG.WCM. If you already have the list saved, just open that file.

2. Run the macro MRG2ENV.WCM. This strips out all merge codes and converts the data file into the format needed by DOC2ENV.WCM.

> **Note**
>
> If you want to save the resulting file, be sure to save it with a different file name than the Address Book backup file with which you started. If you save it to the same file name, you will lose all of the merge codes and additional data, such as telephone numbers, salutations, and so on, from your Address Book backup document.

3. Play the macro DOC2ENV.WCM to insert the resulting addresses into your Envelope address list.

An Alternative Solution: LETTRSYS.WCM

If the limitations and inconvenience of the two-list system of storing addresses is too much for you, there is help on the Companion Disk that came with this book.

The Companion Disk includes The Letter System, an alternative system to speed up creation of letters and retrieval of addresses. It is controlled by a macro called LETTRSYS.WCM which fills in the name, address, file reference, and salutation, and creates a header for page 2 and all subsequent pages showing the name of the recipient, the date of the letter, and the page number. As a bonus, it supports its own "address book" feature which captures addresses as you type them the first time, allowing you to store and retrieve them later. After you capture an address, you store it in one of any number of WordPerfect files that you designate. These "address files" can be grouped according to case, file number, or in any other way that makes sense to you. You can then retrieve that address out of any address file almost instantaneously, along with case reference or other personalized information. You can also edit addresses by making changes to the specific address file.

The disk also includes a simple letterhead template, called LETTRSYS.WPT, which starts the LETTRSYS.WCM macro as soon as you use it. This makes it simple to gain access to The Letter System without going through the Macro menu.

This system has certain advantages over the built-in Address Book and Envelope address list systems, as follows:

- Your address lists are stored as ordinary WordPerfect documents, which are easier to share across a network or transfer by floppy disk to different computers.

- Your address list data is not stored in a program file which is susceptible to corruption or damage during ordinary use, or removed during upgrades or reinstallation of the program.

- Addresses can be located in the address files using the WordPerfect Find feature; you are not required to hunt through a list sorted by first name, but can search for any unique part of the address block you are looking for, including the "in re:" fields.

- The address lists are easy to edit and revise.

- You can create multiple addressee addresses and retrieve them quickly.

- You can create groups of related addresses by saving them in separate files, topically organized (for example, one file containing the list of all counsel in one case, another file for a different case, and so on).

Because this macro requires a number of documents to support it, an explanation on how the system works is needed.

Setting Up a Letterhead Template

You probably already have a letterhead form that you use. It can be as simple as a document containing a couple of hard returns that position the insertion point at the correct spot below the names on your printed stationery, or it could be more involved. My own form letterhead actually prints the entire document, including the firm name, address, phone number, and names of the attorneys in the firm. (For more information on setting up letterhead in this way, see Chapter 3, "Tricks with Typography.")

LETTRSYS.WCM inserts the current date from the computer's clock at the very end of your letterhead form, so it is important to be sure that the your letterhead form ends at the exact location where you will want the date to appear. Thus, if you want the date to be centered underneath the printed part of the stationery, be sure to include a [Hd Center on Marg] code at the end of the file. (To get this code, choose **F**ormat, **L**ine, **C**enter.)

Note also that LETTRSYS.WCM inserts three hard returns (creating two blank lines) below the date before inserting the address.

A simple letterhead form is included on the Companion Disk as LETTRSYS.WPT. If you want your own letterhead template to automatically start the LETTRSYS.WCM macro when you use the template, you can simply modify LETTRSYS.WCM using the Edit Template feature (see Chapter 7, "Using Templates" for a discussion of editing template files).

On the Disk

Tip

If you do modify the LETTRSYS.WPT for use as your own letterhead template, it is best to save it to a different filename, so that you can return to a "clean" LETTRSYS.WPT file to start over again if you need to. You may also want to define several different letterheads, for different purposes; simply give each one a different filename, ending in ".WPT", and save them in your default or supplemental template directories.

A Macro to Store and Retrieve Addresses

Now let's take a closer look at the operation of The Letter System.

Using Address Files

The Letter System stores addresses in ordinary WordPerfect documents, referred to as "address files" because all they contain are lists of addresses.

It is not essential, but it is highly useful, to store all of these address files in a single directory, such as C:\WPWIN60\ADDRESS\. It is also very useful to use that directory for nothing but address files.

The Letter System creates, opens up, and adds to these files as it needs to. However, you may want to edit these files from time to time (for example, if a person you want to write to has moved her office), so it is important to understand how these files are set up. Each address is isolated on a single page of the document by using hard page breaks (shown as [HPg] in Reveal Codes). Note that the first address actually appears on page 2 of the document, because the file opens up with a hard page break. LETTRSYS.WCM uses these hard page breaks to distinguish the beginning and end of an address, so it is important not to delete them.

Note

This is the same format used by the ENV2DOC.WCM macro described in the previous section of this chapter. This makes it easy to place addresses from The Letter System address file into your Envelope address list: simply run the DOC2ENV.WCM macro through the desired address list.

The number of address files you create, and the names you give them, are entirely up to you. You may find it useful to create separate address files for each case you are working on, and give the files a name that identifies the case in some way (such as a file number or a descriptive name).

Setting Up LETTRSYS.WCM

The first time you play the LETTRSYS.WCM macro on your computer, you will get a special message asking you to set up the macro. This is because LETTRSYS.WCM needs to know where to find certain things on your computer's hard disk.

After you choose OK, you will see the Edit Setup dialog box shown in figure 9.17. In the text box, type in the path of the directory where you want to store your address files. Be sure that this directory exists on your computer before playing the macro.

If you ever want or need to change this setting, simply play the macro LETTRSYS.WCM and select the Edit Settings option.

Fig. 9.17
Setting up
LETTRSYS.WCM.

Playing The Letter System

Now that you have set up The Letter System to capture address information, you are ready to use it. When you want to create a letter, play the LETTRSYS.WCM macro from a blank document window. Or, use the LETTRSYS.WPT template (or one of your own creation copied from LETTRSYS.WPT); it will start LETTRSYS.WCM automatically.

Whichever way you start LETTRSYS.WCM, you will see the menu screen shown in figure 9.18.

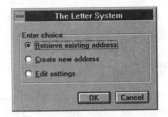

Fig. 9.18
The Letter System
main menu.

Let's assume that you are using LETTRSYS.WCM for the first time, so you have no address files created yet. Select the second option, **C**reate New Address. The Letter System retrieves your letterhead form, and then you will see The Letter System dialog box shown in figure 9.19.

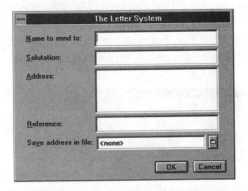

Fig. 9.19
Creating a new
address for a letter
using The Letter
System.

Simply fill in the necessary information in the edit boxes provided. You can provide "reference" information (for example, a case name or other information to identify to the recipient what matter the letter will refer to). If you fill in this field, the letter will be created with a reference line between the address and the salutation; if you leave it blank this line will be skipped.

Note that when the insertion point is in the **A**ddress edit window, the Enter key behaves differently. Instead of accepting all of the information shown in the box, pressing Enter in that window will simply place a hard return there so that you can move to another line of the address. You can even add multiple addressees in this way if you prefer.

If you want to save this address in a new address file, type in the file name you want to use in the entry field marked Sa**v**e in file. It is a good idea to use a name that can be easily recalled, such as a case name or file number. Then choose OK; the address will be written both into your new letter and saved in the address file you specified.

If you already have an address file started and want to save the address to that file, simply fill in the filename for the address file you want to use in the Sa**v**e in file field. If you aren't sure if the address file exists, or if you can't remember its name, click the File icon at the end of that entry field and choose a file from the Select File dialog box which appears.

Assume that you know that you have already written and stored the address you want to use. In this situation, from the initial The Letter System menu screen (refer to fig. 9.18), choose the first option, **R**etrieve existing address.

LETTRSYS.WCM then asks you to designate the address file from which you want to retrieve the address, as shown in figure 9.20. Note that the address directory you specified during setup appears as the default in the dialog box. If you already know the name of the address file, just add it to the end of your default directory in the dialog box and select OK. Or, to search through that directory for the correct file, click the File icon at the end of the entry field to open a directory listing of your address directory. (Note that you can select address files from different directories if you choose.)

Fig. 9.20
Specifying an
address file to use.

LETTRSYS.WCM then opens up the address file you designate. You then see the query screen shown in figure 9.21. Simply type the name, or some unique part of the name, of the person or company to which you are writing and choose OK. (You can even search for a file number or some other identifying information you may have placed in the "In re:" field earlier.)

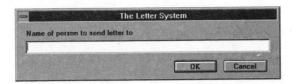

Fig. 9.21
Entering a string to search for.

LETTRSYS.WCM uses the Find feature of WordPerfect to search through the address file and find the name or number you provided. If it finds it, it will show you that match in the address file you specified and ask if you want to use it (see fig. 9.22); respond **Y**es or **N**o as appropriate. (You may need to drag the dialog box out of the way using the mouse if it obscures the address the macro found.)

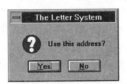

Fig. 9.22
Verifying the address found by The Letter System.

If you answered No, LETTRSYS.WCM will continue the search until it finds the next occurrence of the string you entered. If no match is found, you will see the message screen shown in figure 9.23.

Fig. 9.23
This message appears when an address is not found.

If you respond **Y**es, you will be returned to the query screen shown in figure 9.21 to repeat the process. If you answer **N**o, you will be taken to the new entry screen shown in figure 9.19. You can enter the address information and store it as described previously from that point.

When you have finished using the macro (or your letterhead template has finished "opening" your new letter document), you will have the current date (in text format), an address, a reference field, and a second-page header already prepared. All you need to do at this point is type the body of the letter.

A Macro to Create a Closing

You probably already have a simple macro that types "Very Truly Yours" and adds the name of the letter writer. If your system is used to create letters for several people, there may be a variety of such macros on the system, one for each author. These macros are simple to record and use, and if they work, great!

An "all-in-one" solution is also included on the Companion Disk. It is the macro CLOSINGS.WCM, and can create a variety of different closings for a number of different authors. You can even edit it to add different typist information if your computer is used by more than one person.

> **Note**
>
> This macro serves the same function as the Letter Closing feature of the built-in WordPerfect letter templates, discussed previously.

When you first play the macro, you will see the Insert Signature Block dialog box shown in figure 9.24. You will need to add the closings, author names and titles (if any), and typist information before using the macro.

Fig. 9.24
Setting up the CLOSINGS.WCM macro.

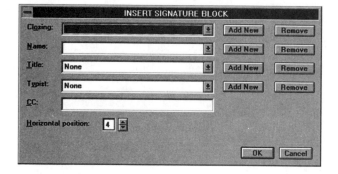

To add any of these elements, select the Add New button next to the element you want to add; you will see the Add Closing dialog box shown in figure 9.25. Type in the closing you want to add and choose OK to return to the Insert Signature Block dialog box; or Choose Add More to save the current closing, but leave the Add Closing dialog box on your screen.

Fig. 9.25
Adding a standard closing to the list for CLOSINGS.WCM.

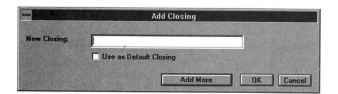

To remove any item, display that item in the Insert Signature Block dialog box and select the corresponding Remove button.

If you want to make an entry the default entry (that is, the one you use the most, which will appear first in the pop-up boxes shown in figure 9.24), click in the checkbox marked Use as Default in figure 9.25.

After you have added all of the author names, titles, closings, and typist information that you need, all you need to do to use this macro is run it at the end of your letter. If you want to use a closing or a name other than the default values, simply select the element you need from the pop-up boxes shown in figure 9.24. When you have selected everything, choose OK to write the closing into your letter.

The macro will, by default, place the closing four inches from the left edge of the paper. If you want to change the horizontal location where the closing will by typed, simply adjust the left margin setting in the box marked **H**orizontal Position near the bottom of the dialog box.

Creating Fax Cover Sheets

The advent of the fax machine has sped up (and in many ways reduced the cost of) communicating between offices. But it has also created a need for one more piece of paper: the fax cover sheet.

Most offices these days have a practice of putting a cover sheet on all outgoing transmissions, indicating the recipient of the transmission, the telephone number to which it was sent, the number of pages sent, and sometimes other information. Many are hand-written, probably because the sender thinks the cover sheet is not important enough to waste time typing it out.

The Companion Disk contains FAXSHEET.WPT, a template which automates the process of creating nice-looking, legible, typewritten cover sheets. It also includes an "on-line phone book" that allows you to create and maintain a list of frequently used fax phone numbers. You will probably find that using this macro is at least as fast as preparing cover sheets by hand, but the end product is much cleaner and professional looking.

On the Disk

Setting Up the Fax Cover Sheet Template

The FAXSHEET.WPT template, when filled out, creates a fax cover sheet that looks like figure 9.26. You can use this form as supplied, or you can customize it to include other information. For example, if you have created a firm letterhead in WordPerfect, you could insert it at the top instead of the simple one provided in the template.

Here is how this template works:

1. Choose **F**ile, **N**ew.

From the File menu, choose **T**emplate...

Fig. 9.26
A filled-in fax
cover sheet.

Jones, Jones, Jones & Smith

456 E. Tenth Street
Anyplace, IA 56502
FAX NUMBER: (813) 555-8520
VOICE NUMBER: (813) 555-5368

The information transmitted by this facsimile is considered attorney-client privileged and confidential and is intended only for the use of the individual or entity named. If the reader of this message is not the intended recipient, or the employee or agent responsible to deliver it to the intended recipient, you should be aware that any dissemination, distribution or copying of this communication is strictly prohibited. If you have received this communication in error, please immediately notify us by telephone, and return the original message to us at the above address via the U.S. Postal Service. Thank you.

FAX COVER SHEET

DATE: November 9, 1995

TO: John W. Smith

of: Smith, Smith, Smith & Jones, P.C.

Fax Number: (813) 555-2354

Your Reference: Hard Rock Cafe transaction

FROM: Kenneth D. Chestek

Our Reference: File no. 141412.103

Pages Sent (including this sheet):   8

Remarks: Enclosed please find a draft copy of the Articles of Agreement for
            execution by your client

2. Find the FAXSHEET.WPT template in the list and choose **O**ptions, then
Edit Template.

The FAXSHEET.WPT file is then opened into a template editing window, as shown in figure 9.27.

As you can see, FAXSHEET.WPT uses bookmarks to identify where specific information should be placed in the final document. There are actually two "series" of bookmarks: one set of numbered bookmarks, enclosing items in angle
brackets (such as the <Organization> field at the very top of the template),
and another series of named bookmarks enclosing items in square brackets
(such as the prompt [Insert recipient name here] in the middle of the template). These "blanks" get filled in different ways.

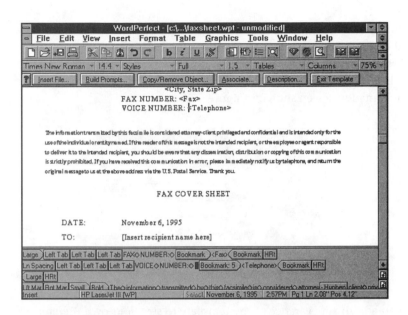

Fig. 9.27
Editing the
FAXSHEET.WPT
template (shown
in Reveal Codes).

The items in angle brackets are filled in automatically from the Personal Information stored in the computer. The first time you used a macro or template requiring an item of Personal Information, you were prompted to fill in information specific to the user of the computer where the macro or template was played. Items like the user's name, his or her organization, telephone and fax numbers, and addresses are stored in Personal Information. Because Personal Information does not change from fax cover sheet to fax cover sheet there is no need to prompt the user to fill in this information.

> **Note**
>
> Because the name of the fax sender is taken from the Personal Information stored on the computer where the template is used, FAXSHEET.WPT as shipped can be used by only the user for whom the computer's personal information is set up; if the form is likely to be used by more than one sender, consider deleting the <Name> marker (and the bookmarks surrounding it) in the FROM: section of the form and replacing it with the actual name of the user. Save the form to a different filename, ending in WPT, where the filename includes the initials of the sender. Create several different copies of the template, with different filenames, for the possible users of the form.

II

Assembling Documents

The information enclosed in square brackets is filled in by a template macro called FILLIN. This macro is associated with the Post New trigger of the FAXSHEET.WPT template, so it is played immediately on starting a new document based on this template. When you use the template, FILLIN will create the information screen shown in figure 9.28.

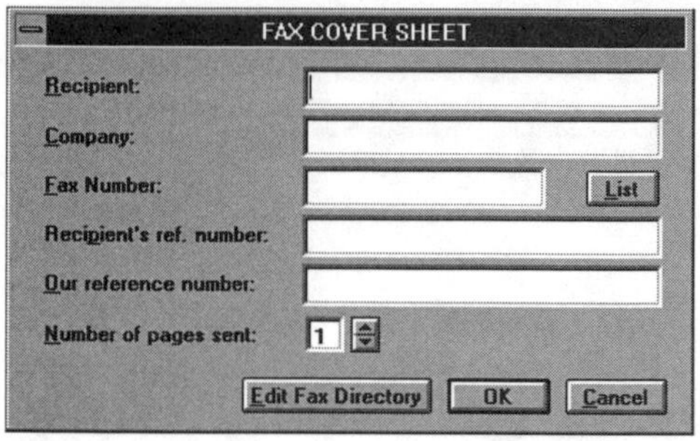

Fig. 9.28
The Fax Cover
Sheet dialog box
from
FAXSHEET.WPT.

You can edit the appearance of the template to suit your own preferences; however, you should be sure to do this with Reveal Codes on to make sure you do not inadvertently move or delete one or more of the bookmark pairs.

3. When you have finished editing the file, choose **E**xit Template from the Template Feature Bar, remembering to save the changes you made.

Using the Fax Cover Sheet Template

All you need to do when using FAXSHEET.WPT is to use the template (from the New dialog box) and fill in the information required in the Fax Cover Sheet dialog box shown in figure 9.28; the FILLIN macro puts that information in the proper location in the finished document.

The **F**ax Number field has a special trick. If you are using FAXSHEET.WPT to create a fax cover sheet for a company or firm for the first time, you will need to enter the company's fax phone number manually in that field. After you do, when you select OK to create the fax cover sheet you will see a message box asking if you want to save the phone number you just entered. Choose Yes to save the listing in your private fax number listing.

The fax number is saved along with the name of the organization where the fax machine is located. The name of the recipient is not saved, however, because you may want to send faxes to more than one person at any organization in your list.

Now, each time you use FAXSHEET.WPT, if you have previously saved a fax number, you can press the **L**ist button to bring up a directory of fax telephone numbers. The list is alphabetized by the name of the organization you entered earlier each time you call it up, so you need not worry about storing the numbers in any particular order.

A sample fax directory listing is shown in figure 9.29. To use this directory, simply use your mouse to highlight the firm name to which the fax will be sent, then click OK. The firm name and the phone number will be inserted into the appropriate fields in the Fax Cover Sheet dialog box shown in figure 9.28. If you cannot find the firm name you are looking for, simply select Cancel in the Fax Number Directory dialog box to return to the Fax Cover Sheet dialog box.

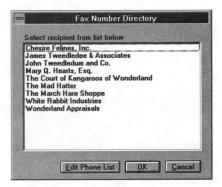

Fig. 9.29
The Fax Number Directory listing of FAXSHEET.WPT.

The fax number listing is stored in a special file, located in your default macros directory, called FAXLIST.BIF. The template creates and edits this file automatically, so there is no need for you to open it or edit it yourself. However, note that when you use the directory feature, the macro must read every listing in this file and insert it into the dialog box. This means that, the more fax numbers you save, the longer it will take to build this dialog box. You may want to limit your directory listing to the 15 or 20 most commonly used phone numbers to save yourself some time using the FAXSHEET.WPT template later on.

Tip

If you want to share a fax directory created on one computer with another computer, simply copy the FAXLIST.BIF file to the default macros directory of the new computer.

Of course, sometimes phone numbers or firm names change, and you will need to edit this listing. You can do this in one of two ways; from the Fax

Cover Sheet dialog box by choosing **E**dit Fax Directory, or by selecting **L**ist from the main dialog box, then choosing **E**dit Phone List. Either method brings you to the Edit Fax Number Directory dialog box shown in figure 9.30. To add a new phone number, select the option, **A**dd entry; to delete or change an existing entry, select **C**hange/delete entry. Respond to the ensuing dialog boxes with the appropriate information to add, delete, or change information.

When you are done adding, deleting, or changing entries, simply press Do**n**e to return to the previous dialog box.

Fig. 9.30

The options to change or add a fax number listing in FAXSHEET.WPT.

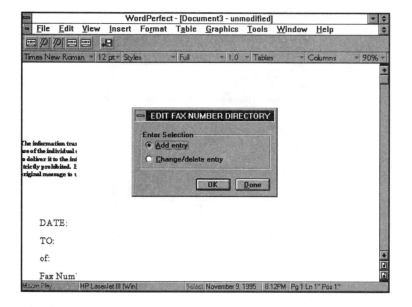

From Here...

A few of the office productivity problems common to most any business were covered in this chapter. The next chapters focus more closely on how to generate documents specifically for a law practice.

You learn how to create the following:

- Documents for a litigation practice
- Documents and settlement statements for a real estate practice
- Letters, complaints, and records for a commercial practice
- Wills, trusts, and other documents for an estate planning practice
- A client management database system

10

Litigation Documents

As any trial lawyer knows, a litigation practice does not involve just courtroom appearances and oral presentations. The road to the courtroom is paved with paper; complaints, answers, motions, briefs, and other pleadings are filed, scrutinized, and ruled upon. Even during trial, lawyers are called on to quickly produce motions in limine, jury instructions, and other written documents.

This chapter is designed to help the trial lawyer create a variety of litigation documents quickly and efficiently. It makes use of the Template feature of WordPerfect, sprinkled with a good measure of macros, to automate as much of the process as can be automated. Several sample templates are provided with a description of how they work. (If you want to edit these templates to suit your own needs, or create new templates that work in the same way, refer to Chapter 7, "Using Templates.")

This chapter looks at the following:

- Several templates to create releases and other litigation-related documents that require no case caption
- A template and macro system to create court pleadings that require case captions
- A menu macro that gives you instant access to the various pleadings and other documents you create for your own personal forms system

Documents Without Captions

There are two basic types of litigation documents: those that require a "caption" (or case name) and those that do not. Because the latter type of document is much simpler, let's start there.

You probably already have a number of form documents that you use in litigation: fee agreements, document requests, form letters seeking medical records, and so on. Chances are the form on your hard disk is the last letter you sent out, on the most recent case you were working on. You typically just retrieve the old letter, change the names and send it back out, hoping that you remembered to change *all* of the things that needed to be changed.

While this method of "filling in the blanks" in a form document can work, it is cumbersome and inefficient, and can lead to confusion if the name-switching isn't finished correctly (for example, did you remember to change the name of the recipient of the letter in the page two header?). Using automated templates can not only speed up the process and increase accuracy, but it can give your documents a "custom-built" look that is difficult to achieve otherwise. Here are two examples of how this can work.

MEDAUTH—A Medical Records Release Form

The first example is fairly simple. The Companion Disk that came with this book includes the file MEDAUTH, which creates the authorization form shown in figure 10.1 to release medical records to an attorney. It is designed so that, when the template is selected, it automatically asks the user for the name of the person who is authorizing the release of his or her records, and the name of the attorney to whom permission is being given to obtain these records.

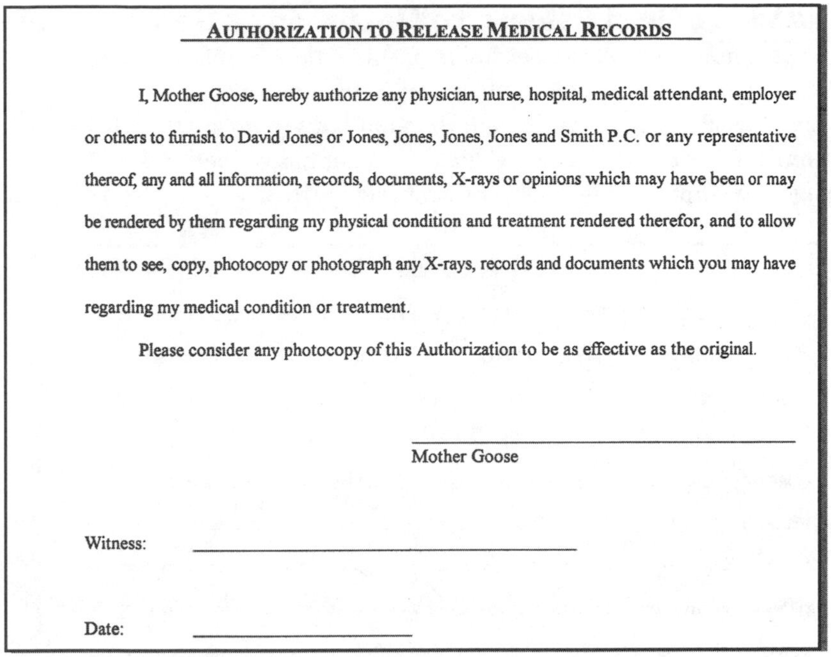

AUTHORIZATION TO RELEASE MEDICAL RECORDS

I, Mother Goose, hereby authorize any physician, nurse, hospital, medical attendant, employer or others to furnish to David Jones or Jones, Jones, Jones, Jones and Smith P.C. or any representative thereof, any and all information, records, documents, X-rays or opinions which may have been or may be rendered by them regarding my physical condition and treatment rendered therefor, and to allow them to see, copy, photocopy or photograph any X-rays, records and documents which you may have regarding my medical condition or treatment.

Please consider any photocopy of this Authorization to be as effective as the original.

Mother Goose

Witness: ____________________

Date: ____________

Fig. 10.1
A sample authorization to release medical records.

The template uses the AutoTemplate feature of WordPerfect to fill in the blanks with the necessary information. For a detailed look at how this template performs its tricks, take a look at Chapter 7, "Using Templates."

When you open this template, you will see the Template Information dialog box shown in figure 10.2. Fill in the name of the person whose medical records you are trying to obtain in the first text box, and the name of the attorney seeking the records in the second text box.

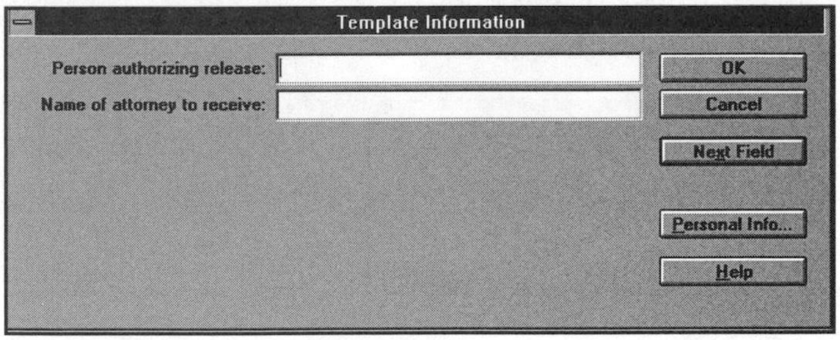

Fig. 10.2
The MEDAUTH template information screen is used to fill in information for the release.

RELEASE—A Final Release to Document a Settlement

A somewhat more complicated example of a litigation template that does not require a caption is RELEASE, which creates a "full and final general release" for a pending lawsuit. (You may want to modify this template slightly to create a similar form to use in cases where no lawsuit has yet been filed.) The first page of a completed release is shown in figure 10.3.

Fig. 10.3
The first page
of a completed
litigation release.

FULL AND FINAL GENERAL RELEASE

KNOW ALL MEN BY THESE PRESENTS, that Mother Goose, in consideration of the sum of One Million Five Hundred Thousand Dollars ($1,500,000), lawful money of the United States of America, to her in hand paid by or on behalf of Jane Doe and Acme Shoe Leather Corporation, the receipt of which is hereby acknowledged, does hereby RELEASE AND FOREVER DISCHARGE and by these presents does for herself, her heirs, successors and assigns, RELEASE AND FOREVER DISCHARGE the said Jane Doe and Acme Shoe Leather Corporation, their heirs, successors, assigns, insurers and all other persons, firms, corporations from any and all liability, claims, causes of action, damages, costs, damages, costs, expenses or demands of any kind whatsoever in law or in equity, which against the said Jane Doe and Acme Shoe Leather Corporation the above named Mother Goose now has or which she may have in the future, or which her heirs, executors, successors, or assigns hereinafter can or may have by reason of any bodily or personal injury, damages to property and the consequences thereof, known or unknown, foreseen or unforeseen, arising or which may arise as a result of or in any way connected with the causes of action set forth in Plaintiffs' Complaint filed in Court of Common Pleas of the County of Rhyme, State of Fantasia, at No. 52451 of 1994.

It is further understood and agreed that the acceptance of this sum is in full accord and satisfaction of a disputed claim and the payment of this sum is not to be construed as an admission of liability and liability is hereby expressly denied.

The parties to this agreement declare that they fully understand the terms of this settlement, that the amount stated herein is the sole consideration for this release and that they have voluntarily accepted the said sum for the purpose of making a full and final compromise and settlement of all claims.

This template is more complicated because it does more. Not only does it require more information, and thus has more "blanks" to fill in, but this template also customizes itself to match the gender and number of parties to the settlement. That is, rather than use the awkward compound pronoun "he/she/they," RELEASE will ask you once for the number and gender of the parties, then use the correct pronoun for each party throughout that document. This gives the finished document a more polished, customized look.

RELEASE uses an embedded macro called FILLIN to fill in the needed information. Because the FILLIN macro embedded in RELEASE is more than four pages long, in the interest of space it is not described here line-by-line. Generally, it works by asking for the information it needs to fill in the blanks, then uses the Replace feature to make the necessary corrections.

But there are some interesting twists in this macro. When you use this template, FILLIN displays the dialog box shown in figure 10.4. Depending on what the user fills in, the macro will know that whether more than one person is giving the release or receiving the payment, or if only one person is giving or receiving, whether that person is male, female, or a corporation; the template will then use gender-specific pronouns and verbs throughout.

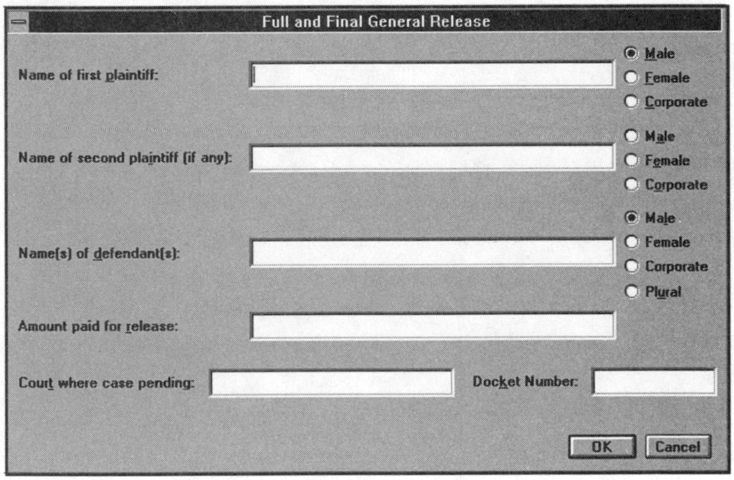

Fig. 10.4
Filling in the blanks in the RELEASE.WPT template.

You can study FILLIN in this template on your own to see how this macro works. For more information on how to create similar "smart" templates, see Chapter 7.

Documents with Captions—Creating Pleadings

The more complicated types of litigation are those that begin with a caption.

Figure 10.5 is a sample legal pleading: a simple Notice of Deposition. It can be broken down into the four component parts that are indicated in the following list.

Fig. 10.5
A sample Notice of Deposition, marking the different elements.

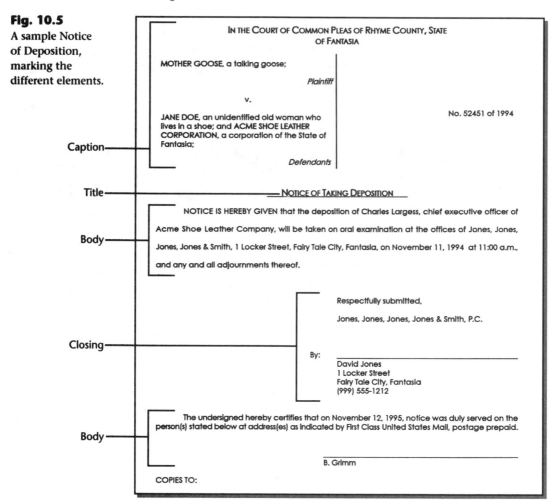

- The caption, including the name of the court in which the pleading is being filed, the names of the parties to the lawsuit, and the docket number.
- The title of the pleading.
- The body of the pleading.
- The closing, including the name of the firm and the address and phone number of the attorney who is signing the pleading.

All of these pieces can be automated to some degree. For example, creating the body of the pleading may be completely automated, such as in the case of a simple fill-in-the-blank notice or other form document; or it may be virtually impossible to automate, as in the case of a responsive pleading or a brief. But even in those cases, there are certain things that you can do to automate the creation of parts of the document.

Creating a Caption with WRITECAP.WCM

One of the toughest parts of creating any pleading is writing the caption. Fiddling with the margins, appearance attributes, tabs, and the like can get tedious.

On the Disk

The Companion Disk includes a complex macro named WRITECAP.WCM to make this job easier for you. (To save space on the disk, the "source code" of this macro has been erased, so you cannot "read" this macro on your screen; it does, however, run correctly.) This macro's job is to insert a case caption at the precise location of the insertion point. All of the templates described in this part of the chapter run WRITECAP.WCM automatically to write or retrieve the case caption; however, you can also play the macro from the Macro menu like any other macro (taking care to position your insertion point exactly where you want the caption to appear *before* playing the macro).

WRITECAP.WCM allows you to write a simple caption, suitable for use in most courts. After you write the caption, you are given the option of storing the caption in a special file (created by the macro) called CAPTIONS.DAT. You can then use WRITECAP.WCM to search through that file, retrieve any caption contained therein, and place it at the top of any new pleading that you want to create.

WRITECAP.WCM allows you to change the appearance of many different parts of the caption, to suit your preferences. For example, you may want the name of the court to appear in larger type, or the names of the parties themselves to be in boldface type. WRITECAP.WCM allows you to select appearance attributes for the following parts of your caption:

II

Assembling Documents

- The name of the court in which the pleading will be filed
- The names of the parties themselves
- The designation of each group of parties (such as "Plaintiffs" or "Appellees")

Figure 10.6 shows a sample caption with those three parts labeled. For each of these three parts, you can specify any combination of Bold, Italic, Large & Small Caps, and Large type size; you can also specify whether the part should appear in all capital letters. You can also specify the style of line (if any) that separates the two "halves" of the caption (the party names on one side and the docket number on the other).

Fig. 10.6
A sample caption, with the elements labeled.

Court Name

Party Name

Party States

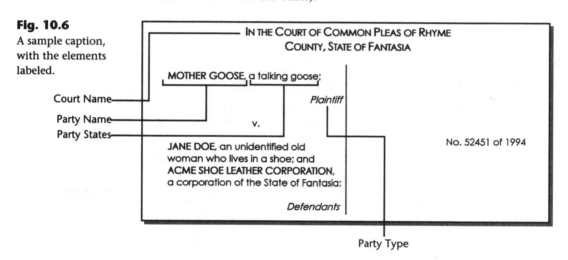

Setting Up WRITECAP.WCM

The first time WRITECAP.WCM is played (either manually by you or automatically through a template), WRITECAP.WCM detects that it has not been set up. You then see the welcoming message shown in figure 10.7. Click OK to clear this message and begin the setup process.

Fig. 10.7
Setting up the WRITECAP.WCM macro.

Setting up WRITECAP involves two basic steps: selecting various options for the appearance of your caption, and identifying the courts in which you practice most frequently. Each step is controlled by a dialog box. To set up WRITECAP.WCM, follow these steps:

1. When you see the dialog box shown in figure 10.7, click OK.

2. In the Set Up Caption Macro Options dialog box (see fig. 10.8) specify the directory in which you want to store your captions data file (to retrieve completed captions from later).

Fig. 10.8
Setting up appearance options for WRITECAP.WCM.

Tip

Click on the file icon at the end of the entry field in that group box to view a list of directories that exist on your computer.

3. In the next group box, specify the appearance attributes that you want to assign to the court name portion of your caption. You can select as many attributes as you like.

4. Next, select the appearance attributes for the party names in the next group box.

5. In like fashion, select appearance attributes for the party designations.

II

Assembling Documents

6. Finally, the last group box contains three pop-up buttons that show various options for the lines which may appear around the left half of the caption (containing the names of the parties). Select the type of lines you prefer, or None if you do not want lines.

7. When you have finished making your selections, choose OK to save your setup.

> **Tip**
>
> You can change these selections at any time by choosing **E**dit, Setup from the main menu of the macro, described in the next section of this chapter.

After the appearance attributes are selected, you need to create a list of courts in which you regularly practice. This is done in the Set Up Caption Macro Court Names dialog box, shown in figure 10.9. This dialog box appears after you finish selecting appearance attributes. WRITECAP.WCM allows you to identify as many as seven courts (four trial courts and three appellate courts) in which you principally appear.

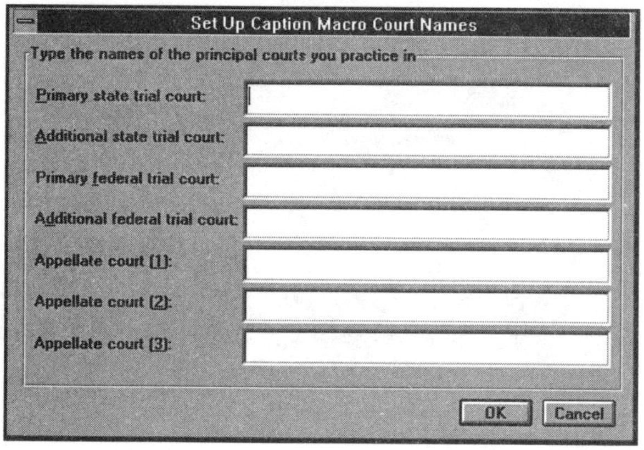

Fig. 10.9
Specifying the courts you most frequently practice in.

8. In the **P**rimary state trial court edit box, enter the name of the state trial court you most frequently appear in.

9. In a similar fashion, enter the names of the other courts you frequently appear in and want to list in the WRITECAP.WCM macro.

> **Note**
>
> Although the dialog box suggests that you specify two state trial courts, two federal trial courts, and three appellate courts, you may use any combination of state and federal court names in these boxes. You should, however, be sure to enter only trial courts in the first four fields, and only appellate courts in the last three fields, because the macro will default to "Appellant" and "Appellee" designations later if you select one of the last three courts.

10. After you have finished entering as many of the courts as you choose to set up, click OK. The caption macro has now been set up.

The WRITECAP.WCM Main Menu

After WRITECAP.WCM has been set up, the first screen you see when the macro is played is the main menu, entitled Create/Retrieve Caption as shown in figure 10.10. It is easy to use.

Fig. 10.10
The WRITECAP.WCM main menu.

1. To create a new caption for a new case, select Create New Caption. This option walks you through the steps of creating a new caption and gives you the option of saving the caption after it is finished.

2. If you know you have already created a caption for the case you are working on and want to retrieve it from the CAPTIONS.DAT file, select Retrieve Existing Caption.

3. If you want to change the setup settings for how the caption will appear, select Edit Setup.

4. Finally, if you want to edit or add to the list of courts you practice in regularly, select Edit Court Names.

5. Click OK to accept your selection.

The operation of each of these options is discussed in more detail in the sections that follow.

Creating a New Caption with WRITECAP.WCM

WRITECAP.WCM writes each new caption in this way: After typing the name of the court where the pleading will be filed, the macro creates a Table consisting of two cells, side-by-side (designated cells A1 and B1). The cells have no lines unless, when you set up the macro, you specified types of lines to place around the caption. If you did specify lines, the type of line you chose is added around cell A1. The macro then inserts all of the party names, using the appearance attributes you select, into cell A1. It then places the docket number, centered between the top and bottom of cell B1.

To create a new caption using WRITECAP.WCM, follow these steps:

1. Select the Create New Caption option from the main menu, then choose OK. The Create New Caption dialog box (shown in fig. 10.11) appears.

Fig. 10.11

Selecting a court name from the Create New Caption dialog box.

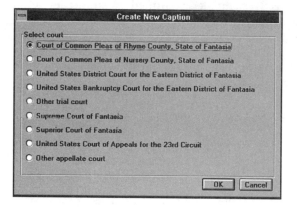

2. Select the court for which the pleading will be created, then choose OK.

   You can use any of the seven "default" courts that you created during the setup process, or select one of the Other radio buttons to create a caption for any other trial or appellate court. (If you select one of the Other buttons, you will be asked to identify the name of the court in a separate dialog box.)

3. Next you need to add the names of the parties to the caption. In the Type of Party to Add dialog box, select one of the listed party types (or select Other if you want to use another designation), then choose OK.

Note

The appearance of this box varies depending on how far along in the caption you encounter it. The first time through it will look like the box shown in figure 10.12; note that the default item is "Plaintiff," ordinarily the first group of parties listed in a caption. The macro will default to "Appellant" if you chose an appellate court in the previous screen.

Fig. 10.12
Selecting a party type to add to a caption.

4. Now enter the name of the first Plaintiff (or other party) in the Name of Plaintiff number 1 dialog box.

   The title of this box will vary, depending on the party designation you chose in the last step and the number of parties of that type you enter. For example, the dialog box to add the first Plaintiff to the caption would is entitled "Get Plaintiff number 1," and looks like the box shown in figure 10.13. As you add Plaintiffs, or other parties, the party type and number change in the title bar so you can keep track of where you are.

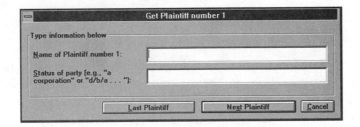

Fig. 10.13
Adding the first Plaintiff to the caption.

5. You can also add a "status" tag to the Plaintiff's name (such as "a Pennsylvania corporation," "Executor of the Estate of," or similar designations) in the second entry field below the Plaintiff's name.

   These status tags, if you use them, will appear in ordinary type immediately after the name of the party.

6. To add another Plaintiff, choose the Next Plaintiff button. The same dialog box reappears with no names in it, but with the number incremented by one.

7. Continue adding Plaintiffs until you have completed that portion of the caption.

8. To move on to the next type of party, choose the **Last** Plaintiff button.

   If you pressed Next Plaintiff by error and don't want to add another Plaintiff, just choose **Last** Plaintiff with no names displayed in the entry field, and the macro will automatically move on to the next type of party.

9. The Type of Party to Add dialog box reappears, but it will look different this time (see fig. 10.14).

Fig. 10.14
Selecting the responding party type for a caption.

Note that the default item in this box is now "Defendant," and that a new button (designated **N**one) now appears at the bottom.

10. If there is no Defendant or Respondent, simply choose **N**one; otherwise, select the designation for the next group of parties and choose OK.

11. Add as many Defendants as you need, in the same manner that you added the names and status of all of the Plaintiffs previously.

12. After you are done with the Defendants, you are given a chance to add Additional Defendants or Intervenors in a similar fashion.

13. After you have added any Additional Defendants (if any), you are asked to specify the docket number for the case. If you are filing a new Complaint and have no docket number yet, just leave this blank.

    After you have finished adding all of the parties, the caption is displayed on your screen underneath a message box asking if you want to save the caption in your captions file.

14. If you want to save the caption in your captions data file, simply answer **Y**es to the Save this Caption? message box.

    If you choose Yes, the caption will be automatically stored in your CAPTIONS.DAT file for later use.

Retrieving an Existing Caption

The second option on the WRITECAP.WCM main menu is to **R**etrieve Existing Caption.

1. To retrieve a caption that you previously wrote and saved, select **R**etrieve Existing Caption from the WRITECAP.WCM main menu, then choose OK.

    When you select this option, WRITECAP.WCM will load the file CAPTIONS.DAT into an empty document window (although you will not see it).

2. Enter in the Retrieve Caption dialog box a name or some other unique string of characters that appears in the caption you are searching for (shown in fig. 10.15) and choose OK.

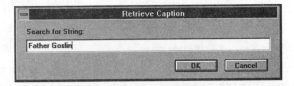

Fig. 10.15
Entering a name to search for in an existing caption.

> **Tip**
>
> The macro uses the Search feature of WordPerfect to look through the captions file. You don't have to type the entire name or string you want to search for, only a sufficient number of unique characters are required.

If WRITECAP.WCM finds that string of characters, it will place the caption containing that string into your document and show it to you, underneath a message box asking you to confirm that this is the caption you want to use.

3. If you answer Yes, WRITECAP.WCM will end.

4. If you answer No, the macro will remove that caption from your document and continue searching for more matches for the same string.

If no matches are found, you will see the message box shown in figure 10.16, which gives you the option to enter a different string to search for.

Fig. 10.16
The Caption Not Found dialog box.

5. To search for a different string of characters, answer Yes to the message box.

You are returned to the Retrieve Caption dialog box, where you can enter a new string as in step 2.

6. If you choose not to search for another string, you will be returned to the WRITECAP.WCM main menu, where you can elect to write a new caption (see the discussion earlier in this chapter in the section "Creating a New Caption with WRITECAP.WCM") or press Escape to end the macro.

Editing the Setup Options

The last two items on the WRITECAP.WCM main menu (refer to fig. 10.10) allow you to edit either the default settings for how your captions appear, or the names of the courts in which you regularly practice. They use the same dialog boxes described in the section "Setting up WRITECAP.WCM" earlier in this chapter.

Editing the CAPTIONS.DAT File

It is not uncommon for a case caption to change as a case progresses; for example, additional defendants are added, or a name changes. It is a simple matter to edit the stored captions so that you can make such corrections once and save them, without redoing the entire caption.

As noted previously, the captions you create using WRITECAP.WCM are stored in a WordPerfect file called CAPTIONS.DAT. It is located in the directory you specified when you first set up the macro.

If you find you need to edit one of the captions stored in this file, simply follow these steps:

1. Open the file CAPTIONS.DAT in WordPerfect.

> **Tip**
>
> If you forget what directory you specified for this file, just play the macro WRITECAP.WCM and select the **E**dit Setup option. The path for the captions file is displayed in the entry field for the first group box.

2. Make the necessary changes to your caption manually.

You will notice, when you open CAPTIONS.DAT, that each caption is stored on a separate page of that document (separated by hard page breaks). This is simply to allow WRITECAP.WCM to quickly retrieve a caption into a pleading. Do not erase any of the hard page breaks while editing CAPTIONS.DAT. (Also, do not erase any bookmarks you may encounter!)

3. Save the file to the disk and close it.

Adding Captions to CAPTIONS.DAT Manually

You may also find that you already have a captions "data bank," or you may want to add captions to the CAPTIONS.DAT file that do not conform to the style of caption created by WRITECAP.WCM. WRITECAP.WCM can search through and find captions in any format; it is not limited to a caption originally written by the macro itself. All you need to do is to add captions manually to the CAPTIONS.DAT file through a simple cut-and-paste operation:

1. Open the CAPTIONS.DAT file in an editing window.

2. Move to the end of the CAPTIONS.DAT file and insert a hard page break (Ctrl+Enter).

> **Tip**
>
> WRITECAP.WCM uses hard page breaks (shown as a [Hpg] code in Reveal Codes) to determine the beginning and ending of captions when copying them into your new pleadings, so it is important to be sure that each caption is separated from every other caption by a hard page code (you get this code by pressing Ctrl+Enter). WRITECAP.WCM can handle multipage captions as long as there is a no hard page code between the several pages of the caption.

3. Place your pleading or your captions data bank into a second document window.

4. Select the text of the caption you want to add to the CAPTIONS.DAT file.

> **Tip**
>
> Be sure to include any formatting codes that are used at the beginning of the caption. You may want to turn on Reveal Codes before selecting the caption text to be sure that you are including all necessary codes.

5. Copy the caption to the capture buffer (choose **E**dit, **C**opy).

6. Switch back to the CAPTIONS.DAT editing window.

7. After verifying that your insertion point is at the bottom of that document and immediately after a hard page code, insert the new caption from the capture buffer using **E**dit, **P**aste.

Creating Closings for Pleadings

On the Disk

You probably already have a macro that types a basic signature line for a pleading. If you are a secretary or paralegal who prepares pleadings for more than one attorney, you may have several macros that do this, one for each of the attorneys for whom you prepare documents. If this system works for you, excellent! But there may be a better way.

The Companion Disk includes a macro called PCLOSING.WCM. This macro can be set up to create signature lines for pleadings for any number of attorneys. Plus, it has been integrated into several of the templates discussed later in this chapter, and can be used in any new templates you create as well.

Setting Up PCLOSING.WCM

PCLOSING.WCM actually relies on a second macro, FIRMNAME.WCM, to obtain the name and address of your law firm. It does this so that other macros on the Companion Disk that also need firm name information can obtain that information by playing the same macro.

The first time you play PCLOSING.WCM (or any other macro that needs to get the name of your firm), FIRMNAME.WCM checks to see if it has been set up yet.

To use PCLOSING.WCM, follow these steps:

1. Play the PCLOSING.WCM macro.

    If you have not yet used PLCLOSING.WCM or any other macro that requires firm name information, the macro FIRMNAME.WCM will be automatically started. You need to set up the name of your firm before continuing.

2. In the Set Up Firm Name and Information dialog box (see fig. 10.17), enter all of the information in the spaces provided; the macro uses this information to write the name and address of the firm into the signature block of your pleading.

Fig. 10.17
Setting up your firm name and address for PCLOSING.WCM.

Set Up Firm Name and Information

Complete firm information below

Firm name:
Address line 1:
Address line 2:
City, State, Zip:
Phone number:

OK   Cancel

After you have set up your firm name information, you will not see this screen again. Instead, the first screen you see when you play PCLOSING.WCM is the Closing for Pleading dialog box shown in figure 10.18.

II

Assembling Documents

Fig. 10.18
The main screen of
PCLOSING.WCM.

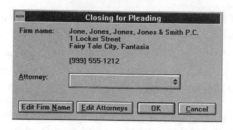

Before using the macro, you must add at least one attorney name to the pop-up list of attorneys (notice it is blank in figure 10.18).

3. In the Closing for Pleading dialog box, choose **E**dit Attorneys.

The Edit/Add Attorney Names dialog box appears, as shown in figure 10.19.

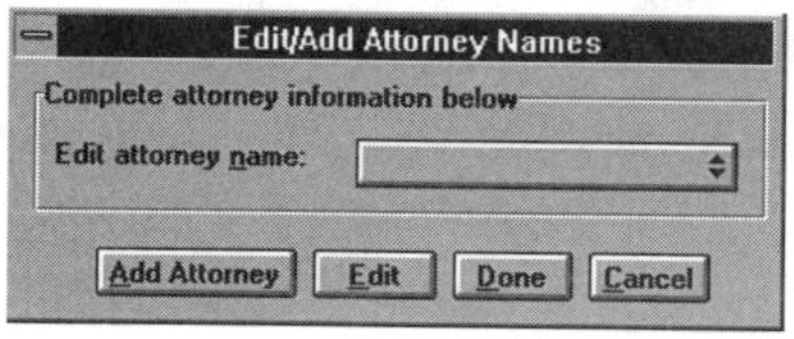

Fig. 10.19
Adding attorney
names in
PCLOSING.WCM.

4. Choose **A**dd Attorney.

5. Type in the name of an attorney in your firm, as you want it to appear in the pleading closing, then choose OK.

6. In the next screen, add an attorney ID number if you want such a number to appear underneath the attorney's name in the final document, then choose OK.

You will be returned to the Edit/Add Attorney Names dialog box. The attorney name you just added is displayed inside the pop-up button.

You can use this macro for any of the attorneys in your office simply by repeating steps 4 through 6 to add their names and identification numbers to the pop-up list.

To edit or delete any attorney name from the list, follow these steps:

1. Play the PCLOSING.WCM macro.

2. In the Closing for Pleadings dialog box, choose **E**dit Attorney.

3. In the Edit/Attorney Names dialog box, select the name of the attorney you want to delete or edit from the Edit Attorney **N**ame pop-up button.

4. Choose **E**dit. The Edit dialog box for the attorney you selected appears as shown in figure 10.20.

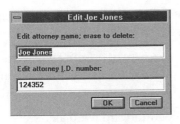

Fig. 10.20
The Edit dialog
box used for
editing an attorney
name.

5. If you want to edit the name or attorney ID number, make the changes in the appropriate text box.

6. If you want to delete the attorney, use the Backspace key to erase the name in the Edit Attorney **N**ame text box.

7. Choose OK to return to the previous dialog box.

To insert a signature block for one of the attorneys in the firm, do this:

1. Put the insertion point where you want the signature block to appear, then play the PCLOSING macro.

2. Click on the pop-up button marked **A**ttorney and move the highlight bar to the name of the attorney who will sign the pleading.

3. Release the mouse button. The name of the attorney you selected should now appear on the pop-up button.

4. Choose OK to create the signature block shown in figure 10.21.

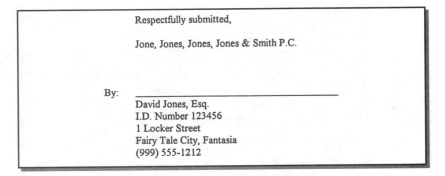

Fig. 10.21
A sample closing
for a pleading.

Creating a Custom Pleading

Now let's take the process one step farther, and examine how you can use templates to automate the creation of pleadings even more.

You can, of course, use the WRITECAP.WCM macro like any other macro; just play it from the Macro menu. But be careful: the macro is designed to place the caption into an existing document. If you play this macro while another document is open in the active window, the caption will be stuffed inside of that document at the exact location of the insertion point.

If you want to avoid the necessity of opening a new document window, and finding and playing the macro, you can use the template NEWPLEAD to automate that process.

NEWPLEAD is a fairly straightforward template. Every time you use this template, a macro called FILLIN is played. (For more information on how this works, see Chapter 7.) FILLIN does two things. First, it plays the WRITECAP.WCM macro to allow you to create a new caption or retrieve a caption you have written previously and stored. The caption is placed in a new document window.

Second, FILLIN looks for a macro called TITLE.WCM. If it finds this macro, it will play it. The TITLE.WCM macro is a macro that prompts the user for the title of the pleading being created. It then inserts the title immediately below the caption, formatted in any way that you choose.

The Companion Disk includes a sample TITLE.WCM macro that writes a pleading title; the text of the macro is shown in figure 10.22. However, if you do not like the way the title created by this macro looks, you can easily create your own TITLE.WCM.

Fig. 10.22
The text of TITLE.WCM (to create a pleading title).

```
 1    Application (A1; "WordPerfect"; Default; "US")
 2    UnderlineTabs (Yes!)
 3    MarginLeft (2.5")
 4    MarginRight (2.5")
 5    AttributeRelativeSize (NormalSize!)
 6    AttributeRelativeSize (Large!)
 7    AttributeAppearanceOn ({Bold!; SmallCaps!})
 8    Justification (Center!)
 9    GETSTRING (title;"Title of pleading";"TITLE.WCM")
10    Type (title)
11    HardReturn
12    Justification (Full!)
13    AttributeAppearanceToggle ({Underline!})
14    FlushRight
15    LineHeight (0.02")
16    HardReturn
17    LineHeight (Auto!)
18    AttributeNormal
19    HardReturn
20    MarginLeft (1.0")
21    MarginRight (1.0")
22    HardReturn
23    LineSpacing (2.0)
```

1. It is easiest to start in a blank document, or at the end of a caption created by WRITECAP.

2. Record a macro. Choose **T**ools, **M**acro, **R**ecord.

3. In the Record Macro dialog box, enter the macro name TITLE.WCM.

4. Record all of the steps to set up the format in which you want your titles to appear.

5. Type a "dummy" title (such as **This is Where the Title Goes**) just to mark the location in the macro where the text of the title will be typed.

6. Chose **T**ools, **M**acro, **R**ecord to end the recording.

7. Open the macro in an editing window.

8. Locate the line in the macro that reads: Type "This is Where the Title Goes" or whatever you typed as the dummy title.

9. Immediately before that line, copy the GETSTRING command shown on line 9 of figure 10.22. Be sure that the command appears on a separate line of the macro.

10. Delete the phrase "This is Where the Title Goes" (also delete the quotation marks) from the Type command and replace it with the single word **title** (without quotation marks). The Type command should now look like line 10 of figure 10.22.

Now your own title macro can be played, formatting your titles in the way you prefer.

Templates for Standard Pleadings

You can also create templates to automate the entire process of creating standard pleadings, such as notices, standard motions, and other documents where you just need to fill in a few blanks. Begin by using the deposition notice shown earlier in this chapter in figure 10.5 to demonstrate how WordPerfect templates can be used to automate the process of creating these kinds of pleadings.

The Notice of Deposition shown in figure 10.5 was created using NOTDEPOS, which is included on the Companion Disk.

Operation of NOTDEPOS

To create a Notice of Deposition using NOTDEPOS, follow these steps.

1. From the New Document dialog box (choose **F**ile, **N**ew), highlight the template described as Notice of deposition to take place in your office and choose **S**elect.

II

Assembling Documents

From the Template dialog box (choose **F**ile, **T**emplate), highlight the NOTDEPOS template and choose OK.

NOTDEPOS.WPT "nests," or automatically plays, the WRITECAP.WCM macro to retrieve a case caption for your notice of deposition.

2. Create a new caption or retrieve an old caption from the menu on your screen (see the discussion of WRITECAP.WCM earlier in this chapter for more information).

After you have created or selected a caption, you will see the Template Information dialog box shown in figure 10.23.

Fig. 10.23
Filling in the information for a notice of deposition.

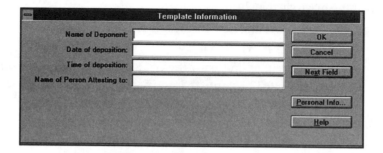

3. Fill in the information requested in the blanks found in the Template Information dialog box.

4. Choose OK to insert the information into the template.

> **Note**
>
> Chances are you will most often be preparing notices for depositions to take place in your own office. For this reason, NOTDEPOS inserts your firm name and office address as the "default" location for the deposition. You can always change this to another location after you have used the template, since the resulting document will be an ordinary word processing file. Or, you can create a new template using a different location, or a blank location, by making a copy of this template and saving it to your template directory with a new filename. Then use the Edit Template feature to make the necessary changes to the new form.

The template will finally "nest" the PCLOSING.WCM macro described earlier in this chapter.

5. Insert the signature block for the attorney who is sending the notice of deposition by selecting his or her name from the PCLOSING.WCM initial screen and choosing OK.

A Macro to Find Your Templates

If you begin to create a number of templates, you will soon discover that finding them in the Templates menu gets to be a problem. You need to scroll through a number of irrelevant files, and all you can see at first is the eight-character filename. When you highlight a template you can see the longer description in the lower portion of the Templates dialog box, but moving the focus of the dialog box from file to file just to read that description can be time-consuming.

The problem is compounded if you use macros like NOTDEPOS.WCM to further automate your templates, because those macros may be mixed in with a long list of other macros, making the job of searching for the one you want even tougher.

The Companion Disk contains a macro, LITMENU.WCM, which is designed to give you a specialized, descriptive listing of all of your litigation template macros. By using this macro, you can view a select list of only those macros that create litigation forms, without wading through the many other macros that may be stored in your macros directory. Plus, rather than just the filename you will see a descriptive phrase for each macro and the template it uses. You can add and delete macros from this list at the press of a button, so as your collection of litigation templates and macros grows you can keep this macro's listing current too.

Setting Up LITMENU.WCM

Like the other macros, LITMENU.WCM needs some basic information before it can operate. Follow these steps:

On the Disk

1. The first time you play this macro, you will see a message advising you that the macro must be set up before using. Choose OK.

2. In the Set Up Litigation Menu Macro Options dialog box (see fig. 10.24) type the full path to the directory where your litigation macros are stored.

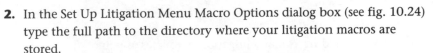
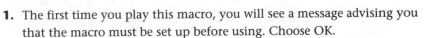
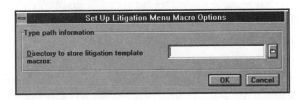

Fig. 10.24
Setting up the LITMENU.WCM macro.

If you cannot remember the path, use the file icon at the end of the entry field to bring up a list of directories on your computer.

You have to add at least one template to the listing before the macro will be useful. Suppose you wanted to add the NOTDEPOS.WCM macro, discussed previously, to your list.

3. In the Add Items to Litigation Menu dialog box (see fig. 10.25) specify the complete path and filename for the template in the entry field labeled **F**ilename of litigation template to add to menu; you can use the file icon at the end of that window to locate templates on your disk. In this example, type **NOTDEPOS.WPT** immediately following the path for your template directory.

Fig. 10.25
Adding templates to the LITMENU.WCM list.

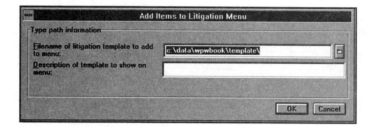

4. In the entry field marked **D**escription of template to show on menu, put a brief description of the template that will be started by the macro. In this example, type Notice of Deposition.

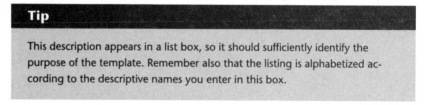

> **Tip**
>
> This description appears in a list box, so it should sufficiently identify the purpose of the template. Remember also that the listing is alphabetized according to the descriptive names you enter in this box.

5. Continue adding as many litigation templates as you prefer.

You can add and delete more templates from the main menu screen later if you need to. The LITMENU.WCM dialog box, completed to include a selection of litigation templates, is shown in figure 10.26.

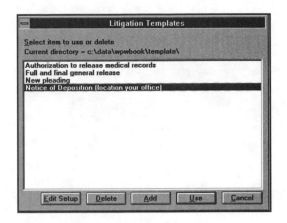

Fig. 10.26
The completed
LITMENU.WCM
listing, showing
various templates.

To use any listed template, play the LITMENU.WCM macro, then select any listed template. Choose **U**se; the macro launches the designated template to complete the document you selected.

You can also choose **A**dd or **D**elete to add or delete new litigation templates to or from the menu listing. If you ever need to change the default directory where you want to store your litigation templates, choose the **E**dit Setup button.

From Here...

This chapter looked at how to use templates to automate the preparation of various types of standard documents for litigation. It also presented a macro that gathers your templates and displays them in a dialog box where you can quickly select the document you want to prepare. You also learned the techniques that make these templates work, so that you can create your own templates and add them to the system.

Some of the techniques described in the upcoming chapters may also be useful to the litigator. For example, the next chapter shows you how to

- Create deeds, mortgages, and other documents
- Create real estate closing settlement statements
- Assemble new documents out of pieces of your standard form documents

II

Assembling Documents

11

Real Estate Documents

A real estate practice, like most areas of legal practice, is also document-intensive. It seems to be getting worse, too; as more and more lending institutions begin trading in mortgages, and more certifications and documents are generated at closings to make the loans more marketable.

A comprehensive treatment of real estate loan documentation is beyond the scope of this book. Instead, this chapter helps you set up your own forms as templates and merge documents, so that it will be simple to prepare all of the documents you need for one transaction.

In this chapter you will:

- Learn how to create a set of form documents to automate the production of all the documents you need for a particular real estate transaction
- Use a macro to set up a custom listing of forms that you can use in your real estate practice
- Use a spreadsheet-like template, included on the Companion Disk, to prepare a standard HUD-1 settlement statement

An Overview of the Real Estate Practice System

The Real Estate Practice System described in this chapter, like the systems to be described in the following chapters, relies on the Merge feature of

WordPerfect to speed the creation of a variety of documents necessary for any real estate transaction. By creating a set of form documents which use a common set of standard fields, you can create a WordPerfect data file for each transaction, then simply merge that data file with whichever forms you need. The data file can also be edited as the transaction moves through your office and information needs to be added or changed.

> **Note**
>
> For more information on setting up Merge data and form files, see Chapter 6, "A Merge Primer."

The Real Estate Practice System also includes REPSMENU.WCM, a single macro which helps you through the process of setting up data files for your real estate closings, and choosing and preparing all of the documents for that closing. Obviously, this system depends on correctly setting up the forms you use in your office. The Companion Disk includes several sample documents for you to study; later in the chapter how to set up your own form documents is described.

It is recommended that you create a separate directory on your hard disk to store the data files you will be using with this system. If you have many forms you may also want to set up a special directory for your real estate forms; however, there is nothing wrong with storing them in any other directory, as long as all of the forms are located in the same directory.

> **Note**
>
> This chapter does not discuss leases. However, because a lease is essentially a contract, the concepts discussed in Chapter 13, "Wills and Estate Planning," regarding preparation of contracts work very nicely for preparation of real estate leases.

The key to a successful Real Estate Practice System is to create data files that contain enough information to correctly fill in any of the forms that are in the system. Obviously, not all of the information is used in any single form; for example, the form to prepare a deed does not need to include how much the mortgage amount is. But if you set up the data file to include a field for the mortgage amount, you will be able to use the same data file for all of the forms. It would be wasteful to have to prepare separate data files for each of the different forms in your system; doing so would be no faster than preparing each document manually.

Thus, before you create a data file to use with your real estate form documents, it is probably best to set up all of your forms first. Having done that, you will be able to come up with a comprehensive list of all of the fields required for your personal system, and you can then set up a real estate data file template that includes all of the needed fields.

Setting Up the Form Documents

The first thing you need to do is establish a list of the documents you want to include in the system. There is no limit to the number of forms you can set up. For example, you may want to include the following forms in your system:

- Individual warranty deed
- Corporate warranty deed
- Fiduciary warranty deed
- Individual special warranty deed
- Corporate special warranty deed
- Fiduciary special warranty deed
- Individual quitclaim deed
- Corporate quitclaim deed
- Fiduciary quitclaim deed
- Note
- Mortgage
- Mortgage satisfaction piece
- Lien waivers (various types)
- Buyers and sellers certificates (various types)
- Attorney's title certificate

Your own practice may require many more types of documents; the system described here is flexible enough to allow you to include any document you may routinely need.

After you have identified the list of documents you want to include in your system, you have to convert each document into a WordPerfect merge form file. Each document must use the same field names where the information is going to be placed. For example, because the buyer on a deed may also be a mortgagor on a mortgage, a single field named "Buyer/mortgagor" will suffice and can be used in both form documents.

For help with setting up merge form files, see Chapter 6, "A Merge Primer."

The following sections look at a few examples of documents that have already been set up as merge form files, ready to be used with the Real Estate Practice System. Look at these files, which are included on the Companion Disk, and model your own forms after them.

A Sample Deed

On the Disk

The first form is a simple warranty deed, from individuals to individuals (see fig. 11.1). It is included on the Companion Disk as WARDEED1.FRM.

Fig. 11.1
The
WARDEED1.FRM
merge file.

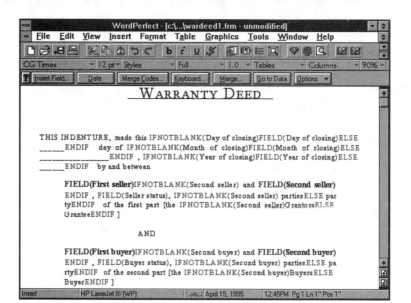

Notice that, throughout the file, there are numerous IF NOT BLANK merge codes. These codes alter the appearance of the finished deed, depending on the contents of certain fields in your data file. The first such codes appear in the introductory paragraph shown in figure 11.1. The first line begins:

```
THIS INDENTURE, made this IF NOT BLANK(Day of closing)FIELD(Day of
closing)ELSE_____ENDIF . . .
```

Translated, this says to WordPerfect: "Type the words 'THIS INDENTURE, made this ' (notice the space after the word 'this'). Then look at the Day of closing field in the data file. If that field has something in it, type that next; otherwise, type a blank line and keep going." The rest of the introductory paragraph then performs the same analysis on the month and year fields.

> **Tip**
>
> Setting up your data file with separate fields for the day, month, and year in this fashion gives you the flexibility to prepare dated or undated deeds, or even change the data file to add a date if needed later. When you first create the data file, you can leave the date fields blank because you won't know the date of the closing. After the closing date is set, you can edit the data file to add the date, or just the month and year, re-merge and reprint the deed.

In many other locations in the WARDEED1.FRM file, notice that the file tests whether there is any information stored in the Second seller and Second buyer fields, then types different things depending on the result. This form uses those fields to determine whether to use singular or plural forms of various nouns, pronouns, and verbs, avoiding the necessity for the form to use awkward constructions like "Grantor(s) has/have...." The finished deed looks cleaner and reads more smoothly as a result.

There is a special problem at the spot where the legal description of the property is to be inserted. The Quick Data Entry feature of WordPerfect makes it easy to insert short words and phrases, but a long legal description, which may require several paragraphs, is extremely difficult to insert into the data file in that way. So the WARDEED1.FRM (and also the MORTGAGE.FRM discussed next) use the DOCUMENT() merge code to insert the legal description. To do this, you have to type the legal description for the property being transferred as a separate document—no heading or title, no extraneous blank lines before or after the description, no formatting of any kind—and save it as an ordinary WordPerfect document. When you prepare the data file for the transaction, all you will need to do is supply the correct path and filename, and that document will be inserted in the proper location in all documents, formatted properly for that document.

> **Tip**
>
> To save yourself some typing later and to make it easy to find your legal descriptions, you may want to create a directory on your computer to store only legal documents. The form documents described later in this chapter use a suggested directory name of C:\WPWIN\DESCRIPS, but you can choose any name you prefer.

Figure 11.2 shows the merge codes used to accomplish this insertion.

Fig. 11.2

Inserting the description into the deed.

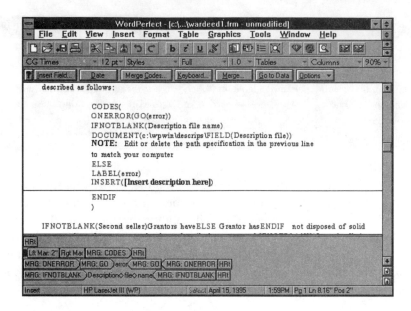

First, notice in the Reveal Codes window that, just before the location where the description is to be inserted, the margins of the document have been changed to 2" on either side. This allows the description to be indented on both sides, even if the description is more than one paragraph long. The margin widths are returned to 1" on both sides after this series of merge codes. (You can edit these margin settings if you prefer.)

The first code after the margin change codes is a CODES() command. This command encloses a series of merge commands which are to be executed, disregarding hard returns, text, and other formatting within the CODES() command. (The function of this command is to make the merge file more readable.)

Next, notice the error trap. WARDEED1.FRM is designed so that, if the user specifies no description file, or an incorrect path, or filename for the description file, the resulting error will not halt the merge. Rather, the merge simply skips to the LABEL(error) command and proceeds from there to place a visual marker instructing the user to insert the description manually; the merge then continues through completion.

If the user has specified a correct description filename in his or her data file, however, the DOCUMENT() command will insert the contents of that file in this location. Note that the file as shipped on the disk suggests that you keep your descriptions in a directory called "c:\wpwin\descrips". You will almost certainly want to change that path to conform to your own drive and directory specifications; or, if you don't want to specify any default location for deed descriptions, delete the path information from the DOCUMENT() command altogether.

> **Note**
>
> When you specify a default directory, you only need to provide the specific filename when you prepare the data files for each transaction. If you specify no default directory, you will have to specify the path and filename for the legal description files for all data files. If you elect to specify a default path, be sure to include the final backslash ("\") at the end of the path specification in the DOCUMENT() command.

You can edit WARDEED1.FRM to conform to any special requirements of your jurisdiction. You can also make additional copies of it for special purposes, to change the warranty of title, or any other change; you can then add each variation of the form to your list of forms that operate with the Real Estate Practice System. Just be sure to use the same field names in each of the forms you create.

A Sample Note and Mortgage

The Companion Disk also includes a sample Note and simple form of accompanying Mortgage, to demonstrate how several documents can be integrated to work from a single data file.

On the Disk

The first page of the MORTGAGE.FRM merge file is shown in figure 11.3. Because the buyers in the deed prepared previously in this chapter are also the mortgagors of the property, notice that the same field names are used (First buyer and Second buyer) in the mortgagor clause; now you don't have to enter the same information in two places in the data file, or create separate data files for the deed and mortgage forms. Note that some new field names not used by the WARDEED1.FRM file were added, including Mortgagee, Mtg. $ (words), and Mtg. $ (nums). The fact that these new fields are included in the common data file is no problem; because you are using named fields, neither form file is thrown off track by the existence of unneeded fields in the data file.

II

Assembling Documents

Fig. 11.3
The first page
of the
MORTGAGE.FRM
file.

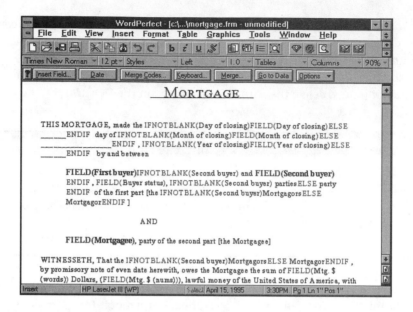

Figure shows WordPerfect window with MORTGAGE.FRM file content:

MORTGAGE

THIS MORTGAGE, made the IFNOTBLANK(Day of closing)FIELD(Day of closing)ELSE
_____ENDIF day of IFNOTBLANK(Month of closing)FIELD(Month of closing)ELSE
_____ENDIF , IFNOTBLANK(Year of closing)FIELD(Year of closing)ELSE
_____ENDIF by and between

FIELD(**First buyer**)IFNOTBLANK(Second buyer) and FIELD(**Second buyer**)
ENDIF , FIELD(Buyer status), IFNOTBLANK(Second buyer) parties ELSE party
ENDIF of the first part [the IFNOTBLANK(Second buyer)Mortgagors ELSE
Mortgagor ENDIF]

AND

FIELD(**Mortgagee**), party of the second part [the Mortgagee]

WITNESSETH, That the IFNOTBLANK(Second buyer)Mortgagors ELSE Mortgagor ENDIF ,
by promissory note of even date herewith, owes the Mortgagee the sum of FIELD(Mtg. $
(words)) Dollars, (FIELD(Mtg. $ (nums))), lawful money of the United States of America, with

---

Note

You may notice that some of the field names used in these forms seem heavily abbreviated. While it is possible to use longer, more descriptive field names, the Quick Data Entry screen is limited in the amount of space devoted to displaying the field names. To squeeze enough important information into the field names, so that enough information appears in the Quick Data Entry screen to allow the user to properly fill in the data, field names short enough to fit within the space allocated on that screen were chosen.

A Sample Title Certificate

Finally, the Companion Disk includes the file CERTITLE.FRM, a form of an attorney's letter certifying title to the property. It uses the same field names as the other form documents in the Real Estate Practice System. It is shown in figure 11.4.

The CERTITLE.FRM points out some of the limitations of this kind of a form system. This form is not completely filled out in the merge process; there is some information which has to be inserted by hand after the REPSMENU.WCM macro has finished playing.

[Your Letterhead Here]

April 18, 1995

FIELD(Lend. atty.)
FIELD(Lend. atty. addr.)

Re: FIELD(First buyer)IFNOTBLANK(Second buyer)
and FIELD(Second buyer)ENDIF
FIELD(Property addr.)

Dear Sirs:

I have examined the indices at the [name of county] County Courthouse with respect to title to the premises listed above and find from my examination good and marketable fee simple title to be vested in FIELD(First seller)IFNOTBLANK(Second seller) and FIELD(Second seller)ENDIF, FIELD(Seller status), by deed dated [date] and recorded in the Office of the Erie County Recorder of Deeds on [date recorded] at Deed Book [Number], Page [page]. I further find said property to be free and clear of all liens and encumbrances except that first mortgage given by the owners to [mortgage holder] dated [mtg date]. All taxes are paid through 19[year].

The above certification does not cover size or dimensions of the lot or location of buildings or improvements thereon, nor liens or assessments not of record. This certification also excepts restrictions, easements and rights-of-way of record. I further certify that I am carrying adequate Lawyer's Protective Insurance.

It has been a pleasure to be of assistance to you, and if I can be of any help in the future, please do not hesitate to contact me.

Very truly yours,

[standard signature block]

Fig. 11.4
The CERTITLE.FRM title certificate letter.

II

Assembling Documents

For example, if you practice in more than one County, you have to manually replace the prompt "[name of County]" in the first paragraph of the form with the name of the County where the property is located. Also, you have to fill in certain recording information based on your findings at the courthouse and elsewhere. You may also have to include specific limitations on the quality of title you find.

While it would theoretically be possible to automate even these additional bits of information by including them in the data file, you may decide against that approach. The title letter is likely to be the only document in your system which needs recording information, for example. Why clutter up the data file with this information when it is just as easy to manually add it to the only document in the system which needs it?

Don't be a slave to automation; remember that sometimes doing a simple task manually is just as fast as attempting to automate it.

Setting Up the Data Documents

So now you've gone through all of your form documents and set them up to use with the Real Estate Practice System. All that is left to do before you can create these documents is to create the data file containing the information to be inserted.

Creating the Form Data File

The simplest way to do this is to create a form data file consisting of nothing but the FIELD NAMES() code. Then, when you want to create a new data file for a new closing, insert the form data file into a blank document window, then use the Quick Data Entry feature to expedite the insertion of information into the right fields.

> **Tip**
>
> Be sure to save your new data files to a name other than the form data filename after you have created them.

To create the form data file, follow these steps:

1. First, look through all of the form files you have created to use with the system, and generate a list of unduplicated field names.

The list of field names used in the four files discussed earlier in this chapter (with a few extras for use in forms not described above) is shown in table 11.1. You may want to include more or fewer fields. Remember, you don't have to put information into each field in every data file; in fact it will probably be the rare case when you are able to fill in every field.

Table 11.1   Suggested Field Names for the REPS System

Field Name	Information Stored
Month of closing	Month of closing (spelled out in full)
Day of closing	Day of closing (ordinal: *e.g.,* 21st, 3rd, etc.)
Year of closing	Year of closing (numeric)
First seller	Full name of first seller
Second seller	Full name of second seller, if any (*e.g.,* name of spouse)
Seller status	Marital status of seller(s)
Seller atty.	Full name of seller's attorney

Field Name	Information stored
Sell. atty. addr.	Address of seller's attorney
First buyer	Full name of first buyer
Second buyer	Full name of second buyer, if any (*e.g.,* name of spouse)
Buyer status	Marital status of buyer(s)
Buyer atty.	Full name of buyer's attorney
Buy. atty. addr.	Address of buyer's attorney
Purchase price	Sale price of the real estate
Property locat.	Municipality where property is located
Property addr.	Street address of property
Description file	Path [optional] and filename for property description file
Mortgagee	Name of lender
Lender atty.	Full name of lender's attorney
Lnd. atty. addr.	Address of lender's attorney
Mtg. $ (words)	Amount of mortgage (written out in words)
Mtg. $ (nums)	Amount of mortgage (expressed as numbers)
Interest rate	Rate of interest of loan
Monthly paymt.	Standard principal and interest monthly payment on mortgage
1st pay. date	Full date of first payment due date
Reg. pmt. date	Day of month when payments are due (ordinal, *e.g.,* "first")

2. Try to organize the field names in some sort of functional order, so that they make sense when they show up in the Quick Data Entry screen. Listing them alphabetically will only confuse you. List them in some logical sequence. Remember that you cannot view the entire list of field names at one time in the Quick Data Entry window.

3. After you have created and organized your list of field names for your system, create a new data file (choose **T**ools, M**e**rge, **D**ata). If you stayed with a document already on your screen, be sure to specify **N**ew Document Window.

4. Insert the field names in the order you listed them in step 2.

5. Choose OK when you have finished typing in all of your field names. The Quick Data Entry dialog box appears (see fig. 11.5).

Fig. 11.5

The Quick Data Entry screen for a Real Estate Practice System data file.

WordPerfect - [Document1 - unmodified]

File   Edit   View   Insert   Format   Table   Graphics   Tools   Window   Help

Quick Data Entry

Record

Mnth of closing

Day of closing

Year of closing

First seller

Second seller

Seller status

Seller atty.

Sell. atty. addr.

Next Field

Previous Field

New Record

Close

Delete Record

Find...

Field Names...

Help

First   Previous   Next   Last

Press Ctrl+Enter to add a new line at the insertion point.

☐ Edit Fields with Functions

Insert   HP LaserJet III (Win)   Select   April 18, 1995   10:03PM   Pg 1 Ln 1" Pos 1"

6. Choose Close without adding any records in the Quick Data Entry dialog box.

7. Save the new data file to disk under any filename that you choose.

The form data file is now ready to use.

Note

An alternative to the "form data file" (which sounds like an oxymoron) is to set up a data file as a Template document, and access it through the New dialog box. However, for no apparent reason, WordPerfect does not recognize the resulting document as a merge file, so you need to take the additional step of opening the Merge menu and instructing WordPerfect to make a data file out of the resulting document. The method described previously avoids that extra step.

On the Disk

The Companion Disk includes a "form data file" called REPSDATA.DA! which includes the field names shown in table 11.1. You can edit the FIELD NAMES() command in this document to suit your needs if you want different field names for your system.

Note

The form documents provided on the Companion Disk (WARDEED1.FRM, MORTGAGE.FRM, PROMNOTE.FRM, and CERTITLE.FRM), all use the same field names as those found in REPSDATA.DA!. If you want to change the field names for your data files, you will have to edit those forms to exactly match the revised field names you select.

Creating Individual Data Files

The last step is to create individual data files for use in particular closings. You can use the "form data file" you created previously to expedite this process considerably.

First, you need to open a copy of your "form data file" into a blank document window. Use the REPSDATA.DA! file from the Companion Disk for this example:

1. Choose **F**ile, **N**ew, **S**elect to create a new blank document.

   Choose **F**ile, **T**emplate, OK to create a new blank document.

2. Choose **I**nsert, **F**ile.

3. Find your form data file (in this example, REPSDATA.DA!) in whichever directory you stored it, then choose **I**nsert to insert that document into the new blank document window.

Tip

By doing this, instead of opening the REPSDATA.DA! file itself, you minimize the chance that you will inadvertently add specific data to your form file and save it, rendering it less useful as a form file.

In version 6.1, WordPerfect automatically recognizes that you are creating a new data file, and the Merge Feature Bar is automatically displayed over your new document.

4. From the Merge feature bar, choose **Q**uick Entry.

   The Quick Data Entry dialog box, shown in figure 11.5 appears, ready for you to enter data.

However, in version 6.0, WordPerfect does immediately recognize the file as a merge data file, so you have to perform the following additional steps:

5. Choose **T**ools menu, **M**erge.

6. Choose **D**ata to specify that you want to set up the active document as a data file.

7. Leave the Use File in Active Window options selected and choose OK.

8. Because the file in the active window already includes a FIELD NAMES() code, choose OK in the Create Data File dialog box without specifying any field names.

You will then be taken to the Quick Data Entry box.

9. Type in as much of the data as you know for the particular closing you are working on.

Do not feel the need to fill in every field; blank fields do not cause a problem for later merge operations. You can press Enter or Tab to move down a field (or use the Next Field button), or press Alt+Tab (or use the Previous Field button) to move up a field in the dialog box; you can also navigate through the fields using the mouse pointer. Remember, you can always return to this data file later and add or change information that you did not have originally, then re-run the merge to create documents with the updated information.

10. When you get to a field, such as one of the address fields, where you need to enter more than one line of information, press Ctrl+Enter to place a [HRt] into the data and move the insertion point to another line within that field.

> **Tip**
>
> You can click the up and down arrows at the end of each entry window to view additional lines of any multiline field.

11. When you have entered all of the information that you have available, choose **C**lose.

12. Save the modifications to the new data file to any disk file that you prefer.

> **Tip**
>
> Consider using a filename, such as the client or file number from your office numbering system, that can be easily identified with the client you are representing in this transaction.

13. Close the document.

If you ever need to go back to the data file for any client and make additions or corrections to the information listed there, it is easiest to use the Quick Data Entry screen again to be sure that information is placed in the right fields. Simply do this:

1. Open the data file.

2. Leaving the insertion point at the top of the data file, choose **Q**uick Entry.

The Quick Data Entry dialog box appears with the information from the first (and only!) record in the data file already in place in the correct fields.

3. Make the necessary changes and choose **C**lose.

4. Save the modifications to the data file.

The REPSMENU.WCM Macro

Finally, to tie the entire Real Estate Practice System together, the Companion Disk includes the macro REPSMENU.WCM. This macro allows you to create a listing of all of the form documents you have set up to work with your own system. You can then choose as many as nine documents at a time from the listing and perform a merge on all of the documents at one time, quickly creating final documents for use at your closing.

On the Disk

> **Caution**
>
> There is a bug in the WordPerfect program, through the first release of version 6.1 dated 11/4/94, which may cause this macro to slow down as you use it more during a WordPerfect session. The problem becomes more acute as you add more documents to the menu system. Your computer may begin to slow down, and if you continue using the macro your computer may hang. If you experience this problem, just exit from WordPerfect and restart the program; this clears the memory used
>
> (continues)

(continued)

by WordPerfect. This problem has finally been fixed by a "patch" released by WordPerfect Corporation in a file called POUPDT.EXE. The file is available from WordPerfect Corporation and for download from the NPOFILES forum on CompuServe. After you obtain the file, run the program POUPDT from the File menu of Program Manager, and the program will automatically update your program files.

Setting Up REPSMENU.WCM

The first time you play REPSMENU.WCM, the macro asks you for some initialization information.

Although it is not necessary to store all of your Real Estate Practice System form documents in a separate directory, and your data files in another separate directory, it is probably a good idea to do so you can easily find the form and data files you need.

1. If you choose to place these documents in separate directories, create the needed directories.

   For example, you may want to create a directory "c:\wpwin60\repsform\" to store your form documents and a directory "c:\wpwin60\repsdata\" to store data files.

2. Place all of the form documents you have created for your system into the directory you want to specify for such form documents.

3. Now play the macro REPSMENU.WCM.

   After an introductory message, you will see the Edit Real Estate Practice Setup dialog box shown in figure 11.6.

Fig. 11.6
Setting up the REPSMENU.WCM macro.

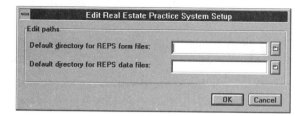

4. Fill in the needed directory information in the dialog box and choose OK.

   You now see the Real Estate Practice System Main Menu dialog box shown in figure 11.7.

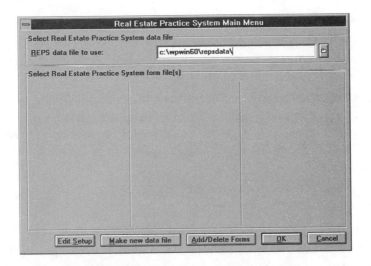

Fig. 11.7
The Real Estate
Practice System
Main Menu.

Note

After you set up the directories in steps 3 and 4, every subsequent time you play this macro you will be taken directly to the main menu screen shown in figure 11.7. If you have to edit the directory information you specified on the first playing of this macro, choose Edit **S**etup from the Real Estate Practice System Main Menu dialog box.

Next, you need to add your forms to the dialog box.

5. Choose **A**dd/Delete Forms.

    The Available Documents dialog box, shown in figure 11.8, appears. Note that the first time this dialog box appears it is empty. This is the screen from which you can add, delete, or edit items on the main menu.

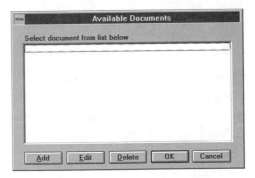

Fig. 11.8
The Available
Documents dialog
box of the Real
Estate Practice
System Main
Menu.

6. Choose **A**dd.

7. In the Add Document dialog box, specify the correct filename for one of your Real Estate Practice System documents, and give it a descriptive title in the second entry window.

   Note that the forms appear in the Main Menu by descriptive name only, and that they appear in the order in which you enter them. Take care to enter these documents in some logical order so that they are easier to locate on the screen later.

8. Choose OK.

9. Repeat steps 6 through 8 for each of the documents you want to add to the menu.

   REPSMENU.WCM can accommodate as many as 45 documents on the listing; however, the more documents you place on the list, the longer the macro takes to retrieve and display the list. How many documents is "too many" is a matter of personal taste, depending on how fast your computer is and how patient you are!

   When you have finished adding documents to the system, the Available Documents dialog box looks something like figure 11.9.

Fig. 11.9
The listing of available documents.

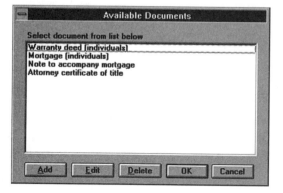

If you want to edit the description of a document in your system, or change its position in the list in the main menu, do the following:

10. Select the item you want to edit by clicking on it, then choose **E**dit.

    The Edit Description dialog box appears, as shown in figure 11.10. You can change the description or increase or decrease the position of the item in your listing from this screen.

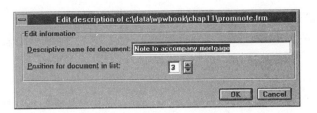

Fig. 11.10
Editing a description and priority of a listed item.

11. Choose OK to accept the changes you have made and return to the Available Documents list.

> **Note**
>
> You cannot edit the path or filename of a document in your system. If you want to change the filename or location of any document, you must delete the old document using the **D**elete button from figure 11.9, then add the new document using the **A**dd button.
>
> If you change the list position of an item from the Edit Description dialog box as shown previously, it may not appear to move in the Available Documents list box. This has to do with the manner in which items are stored in the file RESPMENU.BIF. The item is correctly displayed in the main menu, however.

12. From the Available Documents screen, choose OK to return to the main menu.

    The Real Estate Practice System Main Menu reappears, now showing the documents you have added, as shown in figure 11.11.

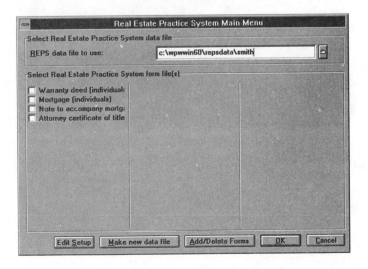

Fig. 11.11
The main menu, showing the documents added.

Creating Documents Using REPSMENU.WCM

After you have finished adding the documents to the menu listing, using REPSMENU.WCM to create documents is a cinch.

1. If the macro is not already running, play REPSMENU.WCM.

2. In the Select Real Estate Practice System data file group box near the top of the main menu, enter the name of the data file to use (use the file icon at the end of the entry window to search through your directories if you cannot remember the filename).

Note

If no data file yet exists, choose the **M**ake new data file button at the bottom of the main menu to expedite the creation of a new data file based upon the default form file REPSDATA.DA! described above. This file should be stored in your default forms directory so that the macro can find it; you can edit its list of field names to suit your needs but you must not change its filename.

---

3. Select as many as nine different documents from the listing of form files by clicking on them (an X appears in the check box by their names).

4. Choose OK to merge each of the form files with the specified data file, thereby creating the chosen documents.

Each new document appears in a separate document window, already filled out and ready to edit or print.

Note

Because WordPerfect allows nine document windows, you can create as many as nine documents at one time using this macro. However, if one or more document windows is not blank when you play this macro, you may not be able to create all nine at once. The macro stops when it runs out of blank document windows and lets you know that it did not finish the assigned task.

Creating the Closing Statement

Finally, the Companion Disk includes the file HUD_1.WPT. This template sets up the standard HUD-1 settlement statement used in many law offices.

This template uses the WordPerfect Table feature to create the form shown in figure 11.12. The document actually includes two separate tables, one for the first page and another for the second; but the two tables are tied together so that, when you enter information in one table, it is automatically inserted where it is needed in the other. Formulas have been included in some places to make automatic calculations of the amounts to be paid at the closing.

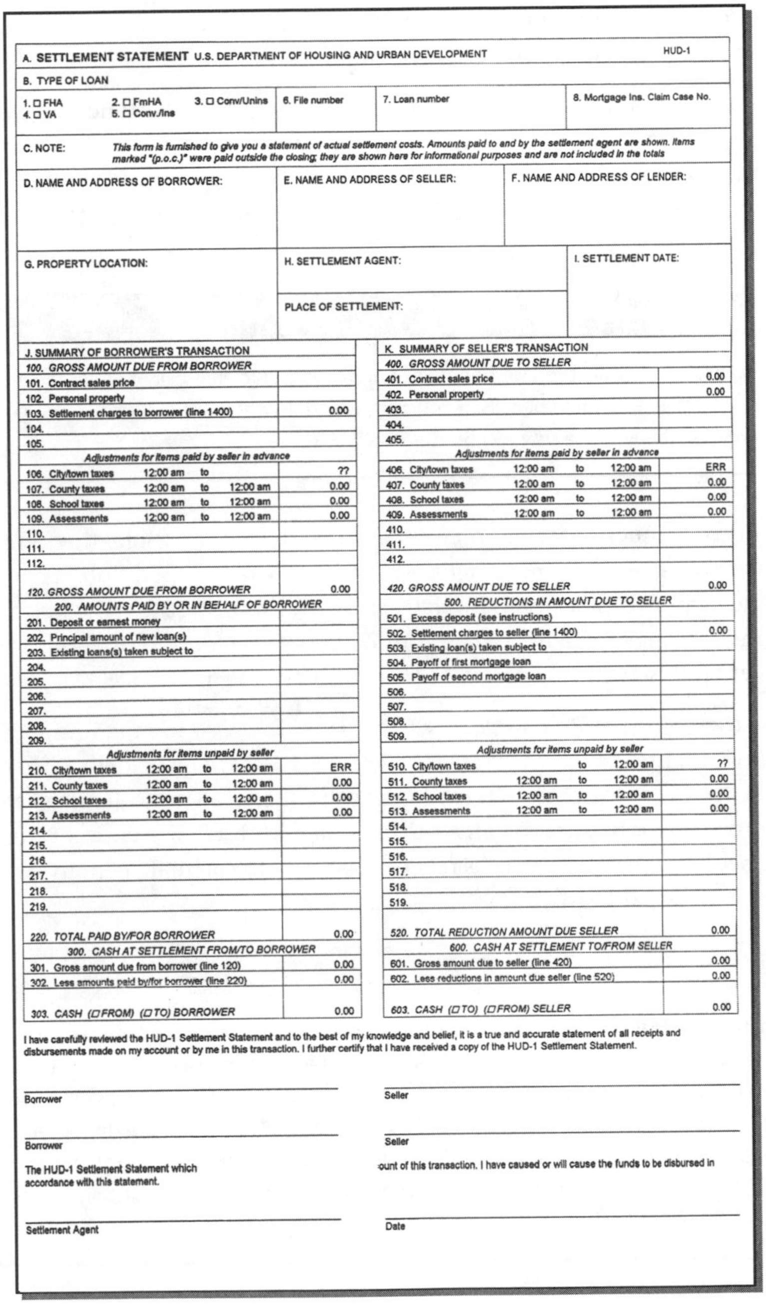

Fig. 11.12
The first page of a HUD-1 settlement statement.

II

Assembling Documents

The form has been set up with numerous "locked cells." That is, cells containing text or formulas have been set up so that the insertion point is locked out. This serves two functions: first, it prevents you from accidentally deleting or erasing a formula; and second, it makes it easy to locate places where you may need to insert information. If you press the Tab key to move the insertion point through the form, it will skip the locked cells and will enter only those cells which may need user input.

The side effect of using locked cells is that you may notice erratic movement of the insertion point if you use the arrow keys on your keyboard to move it around. For example, pressing the down-arrow key may cause the insertion point to jump a dozen or more cells down, if the intervening cells contain text or formulas.

Caution

If you press Tab while the insertion point is in the last unlocked cell of either table, you will get an extra row of cells. If you do this and do not want the extra rows, you can reverse this action easily by choosing **E**dit, **U**ndo.

To squeeze as much information onto a single sheet as possible, the form uses very narrow (1/4") margins on all sides, and legal-sized paper. You may notice that the form does not fit all the way across your screen due to the narrow margins; you may have to change your Zoom setting (choose **V**iew, **Z**oom) to a longer view (say, 80%) to see all of the form on-screen at once.

To use the HUD_1.WPT template, select it from the New menu (Template in Version 6.0). Its descriptive name is "HUD-1 Settlement Statement." Then, insert the needed information in the blank cells; the totals are calculated as you add information. Be sure to enter a closing date in the first section of the form, because several other cells rely on that date to calculate certain amounts to be paid.

Note

Whether the HUD-1 template automatically calculates information as you type it depends on whether you have set up WordPerfect to automatically calculate all tables. If you want to have the template automatically calculate all of the cells as you enter data choose **T**able, **Ca**lculate. In the Automatic Calculation Mode group box of the Calculate dialog box, select the Calculate **D**ocument radio button and choose OK. This updates all tables in any document in your computer automatically when you change data formula cells.

The template automatically handles the pro-ration of real estate taxes based on the date of the closing entered in block I near the top of the form. For the pro-rations to occur, you have to enter the following information:

1. If the taxes were paid by the seller prior to the closing, enter December 31 of the year of the closing in the space provided in line 106 of the form, then enter the total amounts paid by the seller immediately after the message "Paid before closing" on lines 1303 through 1306.

2. If the taxes are unpaid and will be paid at the closing, enter January 1 of the year of the closing in the space provided in line 510, then enter the amount of the taxes being paid in the column marked "Paid from Borrower's Funds at Settlement" on lines 1303 through 1306.

> **Note**
>
> The HUD_1.WPT template prorates taxes based on a 365-day year. The Companion Disk also includes a similar template, HUD_1LP.WPT, which prorates taxes during a leap year.

On the Disk

Also note that, on lines 801 and 802, you can specify the number of "points" (percentage) charged by the lender for the loan origination or discount. Enter the number of percentage points, if any, on those lines; the number you enter is multiplied by the loan amount and filled in the appropriate place.

In version 6.1, the template automatically recalculates as you enter data. In version 6.0, you need to manually calculate the settlement statement after you have finished entering information. Just choose Calculate from the Formula Entry feature bar (choose Table, Formula Bar) when you have finished entering in the data needed for the calculations.

From Here...

In this chapter, you have seen how to set up many form documents to use with a single merge file. By doing this you can generate a large number of documents for a specific real estate closing, simply by merging whichever form file needed with the data file for the closing. A macro which helps to automate the preparation of these documents, as well as a settlement statement template which uses the Tables feature to automatically calculate the amounts to be paid at the closing were also discussed.

II

Assembling Documents

In the next chapter, you will use many of the same techniques to create a complete system of handling a commercial law practice. You will learn how to:

- Create letters, complaints, and reports
- Create data files for each case
- Use a macro to prepare documents for any case
- Keep track of payments made and the current balance due using a macro

12

Commercial Law Practice

Another "form intensive" type of legal practice is commercial law, especially including collections. Law firms that specialize in this field generally have large libraries of form letters, form complaints, and a computerized database system to keep track of payments, add interest, and generate reports.

But what about the smaller firm that does not have a high enough volume of work to invest large amounts of money in specialized software? WordPerfect's Merge feature is sufficiently robust to handle the creation of any of the form letters, complaints, pleadings, and other documents that are needed for this type of practice, but what about keeping track of the financial side of things?

In this chapter, you look at the following:

- How to set up a complete set of form letters and complaints to use with a single data file created for each case, to help speed the preparation of such documents
- A macro that allows you to create a set of documents by choosing them from a listing you create and merging them with the data file for any open case
- A macro to help you keep track of expenses, payments received, interest, and other financial aspects of each individual case

An Overview of the Collections Practice System

Like the Real Estate Practice System described in the prior chapter, the success of the Collections Practice System described in this chapter depends on how you set up your data and form files. The Collections Practice System is similar to the Real Estate Practice System in many ways. It relies on a single data file, generated for every collection case you are handling, to use with any number of form letters, pleadings, and other documents. By using common field names for all of your form documents, you can create the data file once, and create many documents from it.

The Collections Practice System has a new wrinkle, however. The macro that tracks financial transactions in the case (which can be numerous) updates several fields in the data file as payments are made or expenses are recorded. This enables your letters or other documents to show accurate current balances, updated with the most recent payments and expenses. But for this feature to work with the macro supplied on the disk, you must be careful in how you set up your data files.

Creating Form Files

As in the previous chapter, the best place to start in setting up your own library of files for your personal Collections Practice System is to create your form documents. And again, the first thing you will want to do is set up a list of the documents you want to create.

The CPSMENU.WCM macro described later in the chapter will actually maintain two separate lists of documents to use in the Collections Practice System: a list of letters, reports, and other correspondence, and a list of legal pleadings. You should therefore make two separate lists of the kinds of documents you want to include.

A partial list of letters, reports, and other documents to include on your first list might look like this:

- Initial demand letter to debtor
- Second demand letter to debtor
- Final demand (suit notice) to debtor
- Letter to debtor acknowledging partial payment
- Letter to debtor advising of judgment and demanding payment

- Letter to debtor advising of attachment/execution
- Initial letter to forwarder acknowledging receipt of file
- Letter to forwarder advising of contact with debtor
- Letter to forwarder enclosing partial payment from debtor
- Letter to forwarder advising of lack of response from debtor
- Letter to forwarder advising of suit requirements
- Letter to forwarder advising of filing of suit
- Letter to forwarder advising of taking of judgment
- Letter to forwarder requesting authority to issue execution
- Letter to forwarder advising of results of execution

Your list of legal pleadings might include things like this:

- Complaint—goods sold and delivered (specific invoices)
- Complaint—goods sold and delivered (open account)
- Complaint—insurance premiums
- Complaint—services rendered
- Notice of intent to take default judgment
- Motion for default judgment
- Notice of entry of default judgment
- Interrogatories in aid of execution
- Writ of execution
- Writ/notice of garnishment
- Interrogatories to garnishee
- Praecipe/motion for judgment against garnishee

Your own list of documents will obviously be different, and probably much longer, depending on your own practice and the requirements of the jurisdiction where you practice.

There is a specific reason why the CPSMENU.WCM macro maintains correspondence and pleadings in separate lists: it needs to deal with them in different ways. Legal pleadings require a case caption, while correspondence does not. By maintaining separate lists, CPSMENU.WCM knows when to look for a caption and when it need not do so.

But this means also that your correspondence forms and your pleadings have to be set up in slightly different ways.

Setting Up Form Letters

To set up a letter form to use with CPSMENU.WCM, you have to create a WordPerfect Merge form file. You can do this either by typing it as a new file, using the appropriate Merge commands and field names, or you can modify an existing file. For help with creating Merge form files, see Chapter 6, "A Merge Primer."

The Companion Disk includes several examples of letter forms that can be used with the Collections Practice System that you can study for further help. Here is a closer look at some of them:

On the Disk

The simplest of the form documents provided on the Companion Disk is the original demand letter to the debtor. This letter, shown in figure 12.1, is file LDEBTOR1.FRM on the disk.

Fig. 12.1
The initial demand letter to the debtor.

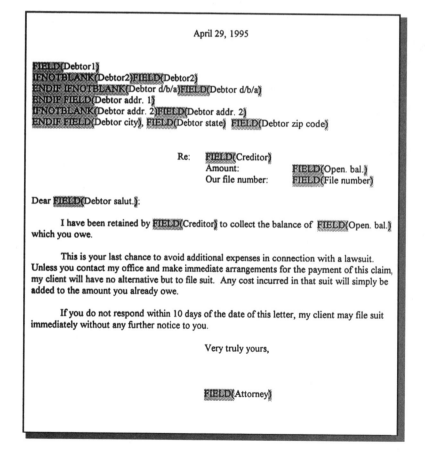

As you can see, this letter makes use of a number of fields to insert customized information. Most are self-explanatory, but several require an explanation.

Notice that, in the address for the letter, the form uses fields named Debtor1 and Debtor2. This allows the Collections Practice System to know whether to use singular or plural word forms in other form files. Your office may frequently handle claims against joint debtors; if so, all you have to do is fill in the Debtor2 field in the data file for any case, and the forms generated by that data file can then use "they" instead of "he" or "she", and so on. (An example of how this is done is shown in the sample Complaint described later in the chapter.)

The form also uses IFNOTBLANK( ) merge codes to avoid printing blank lines if certain fields are not filled in a particular data file.

A very similar type of form file, which creates an acknowledgment letter to the collection agency or law firm which has forwarded the claim to you, is included on the Companion Disk as LFORWRD1.FRM. It is shown in figure 12.2.

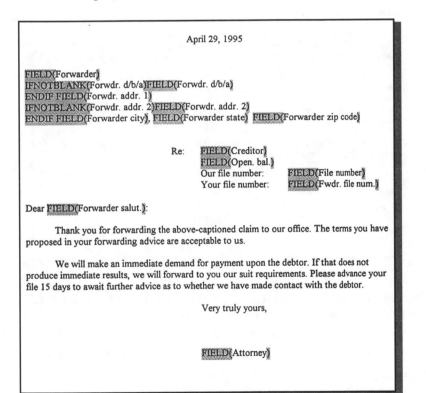

Fig. 12.2
A sample acknowledgment of claim letter.

Finally, the Companion Disk includes the letter LDEBTOR2.FRM, which acknowledges the receipt of a partial payment from the debtor. It is shown in figure 12.3.

Fig. 12.3
A sample letter acknowledging receipt of a partial payment from the debtor.

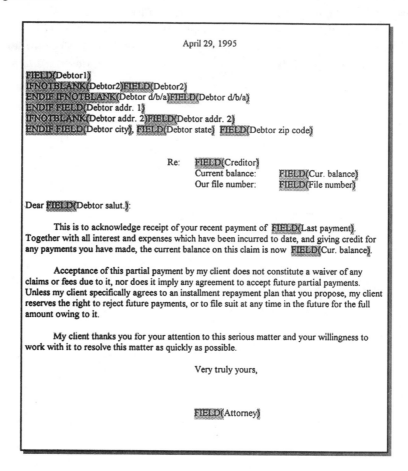

April 29, 1995

FIELD(Debtor1)
IFNOTBLANK(Debtor2)FIELD(Debtor2)
ENDIF IFNOTBLANK(Debtor d/b/a)FIELD(Debtor d/b/a)
ENDIF FIELD(Debtor addr. 1)
IFNOTBLANK(Debtor addr. 2)FIELD(Debtor addr. 2)
ENDIF FIELD(Debtor city), FIELD(Debtor state) FIELD(Debtor zip code)

Re: FIELD(Creditor)
Current balance: FIELD(Cur. balance)
Our file number: FIELD(File number)

Dear FIELD(Debtor salut.):

This is to acknowledge receipt of your recent payment of FIELD(Last payment). Together with all interest and expenses which have been incurred to date, and giving credit for any payments you have made, the current balance on this claim is now FIELD(Cur. balance).

Acceptance of this partial payment by my client does not constitute a waiver of any claims or fees due to it, nor does it imply any agreement to accept future partial payments. Unless my client specifically agrees to an installment repayment plan that you propose, my client reserves the right to reject future payments, or to file suit at any time in the future for the full amount owing to it.

My client thanks you for your attention to this serious matter and your willingness to work with it to resolve this matter as quickly as possible.

Very truly yours,

FIELD(Attorney)

The LDEBTOR2.FRM contains a hidden feature. Notice that, while the LDEBTOR1.FRM used a field named Open. bal. in the reference block to identify the amount of the claim, the LDEBTOR2.FRM file uses a field named Cur. balance. In the body of the letter it also refers to a field named Last payment.

These two fields are maintained automatically by the macro CPSLEDGR.WCM described later in this chapter. As you receive payments from debtors, you can use that macro to record the payments. That macro automatically updates the data file for the case you have received payment on, and includes both the amount of the most recent payment and the updated balance in those two fields. Thus, when you merge this form with the data file, the updated amounts are automatically inserted.

> **Note**
>
> For this automatic updating feature to work, you must remember to use the CPSLEDGR.WCM macro to record the payment before merging the LDEBTOR2.FRM form with the data file.

Setting Up Form Pleadings

The second list of documents you want to prepare for this system is a listing of form Complaints, motions, and other legal pleadings for those claims that go into litigation. You should use the same standard list of field names so that the same data files can be used to prepare your pleadings; however there is a slight difference in the way the CPSMENU.WCM operates.

All pleadings must begin with a case caption. There are several possible approaches to how to handle this problem, including inserting a complex series of Merge commands into the pleading form so that the caption can be generated anew each time the form is used. However, not only is that approach complicated to program, it results in many more entries in the data file, and creates a more complex merge with more potential for errors.

A similar, but simpler, approach is to create the caption and store it as a complete field, by itself, in the data file. In that way, using a single named field in the form file inserts the entire caption with a single command. You may want to consider using this option. Its major drawback is the fact that it is virtually impossible to use the Quick Data Entry feature to create a caption field; you would have to manually enter the caption in the correct field from the main editing screen.

The Collections Practice System described in this chapter takes a third approach. Chapter 10, "Litigation Documents," uses a macro called WRITECAP.WCM to create, store, and retrieve case captions. Because the caption you create for a collections file in this system may eventually be needed to create a more customized document, CPSMENU.WCM uses WRITECAP.WCM to create and store captions. After creating a case caption, CPSMENU.WCM places a special pair of bookmarks in the CAPTIONS.DAT file so that the caption can be quickly found and copied into any pleading created by CPSMENU.WCM.

The implication of this system is that, when you set up your form pleadings for your own Collections Practice System, do not have to worry about the caption. Create the form starting from the title of the pleading; CPSMENU.WCM adds the case caption automatically when you play that macro.

The Companion Disk includes one sample Complaint, shown in figure 12.4. It is a simple complaint for the sale of goods that have been delivered but not fully paid for. It uses some complex merge programming commands to modify itself depending on the contents of the data file.

Fig. 12.4
A sample complaint for the sale of goods.

COMPLAINT-CIVIL ACTION

NOW COMES Plaintiff, FIELD(Creditor), by and through its attorneys, [Firm name] and respectfully represents:

1.　　The Plaintiff, FIELD(Creditor), is a FIELD(Cred. type of bus.) with a principal place of business at FIELD(Creditor city), FIELD(Creditor state).

2.　　The IFNOTBLANK(Debtor2)DefendantsELSE DefendantENDIF, FIELD(Debtor1) IFNOTBLANK(Debtor2) and FIELD(Debtor2)ENDIF, FIELD(Debtor marital status), IFNOTBLANK(Debtor d/b/a)FIELD(Debtor d/b/a), with a principal place of business at ELSE with a residence at ENDIF FIELD(Debtor addr. 1), IFNOTBLANK(Debtor addr. 2)FIELD(Debtor addr. 2), ENDIF FIELD(Debtor city), FIELD(Debtor state) FIELD(Debtor zip code).

3.　　IFNOTBLANK(Date of sale)On or about FIELD(Date of sale), ENDIF FIELD(Creditor), at the oral instance and request of IFNOTBLANK(Debtor2)DefendantsELSE DefendantENDIF, sold, and IFNOTBLANK(Debtor2)DefendantsELSE DefendantENDIF agreed to buy, FIELD(Goods/svcs. sold).

4.　　IFNOTBLANK(Debtor2)DefendantsELSE DefendantENDIF agreed to pay to the Plaintiff the sum of FIELD(Sale price). A true and correct copy of the invoice representing the said contract for sale is attached hereto, made a part hereof, and marked Exhibit A.

IFNOTBLANK(Int. rate)　　5.　　The contract between Plaintiff and IFNOTBLANK(Debtor2) DefendantsELSE DefendantENDIF specified that, if the principal balance were not paid in a timely fashion, the Plaintiff would be entitled to charge interest at the rate of FIELD(Int. rate) per cent per annum on any and all unpaid balances.

ENDIF　　6.　　The IFNOTBLANK(Debtor2)Defendants haveELSE Defendant hasENDIF

Several things should be noted about the use of this form:

■ Note that the form has to be modified in several locations to specify information about your firm. For example, in the introductory paragraph, replace the bracketed prompt "[Firm name]" with the name of your firm; also add your firm name and address in the signature block at the end of the Complaint.

■ In some cases, you may have a contract that specifies an interest rate in the event the goods are not paid for in a timely fashion, while in other cases there may be no such agreement. If no interest rate has been specified in the writings between the customer and the merchant, you can leave the "Int. rate" field blank in the data file, and Paragraph 5, which specifies the contracted rate of interest, is skipped. (The paragraphs after 5 are automatically renumbered if that paragraph is skipped).

■ Paragraph 6 also includes some complex merge commands that determine whether any payments have ever been made by the debtor. It does this by comparing the original sale price first with the original balance submitted to you for collection, and second with the current balance (if any), including any payments made after the file was referred to you. If no payments have been made, the paragraph in the resulting document will note that fact; otherwise it will recite that some payments have been made, but that the balance remains unpaid.

> **Note**
>
> For these comparisons to be made accurately, it is necessary for you to enter a dollar sign in the "Sale price" and "Open bal." fields when you enter information in the data file for the case you are working on. The CPSLEDGR.WCM macro automatically inserts a dollar sign in the "Cur. balance" field as it is periodically updated.

■ Note also that this form periodically tests the contents of the field "Debtor2", using plural word forms if that field has anything entered into it and singular word forms otherwise.

■ In the WHEREFORE clause on page two, if your jurisdiction allows for a "default" interest rate (where no other rate of interest is specified by agreement), you can specify that rate in the IFNOTBLANK structure at the end of that paragraph. The IFNOTBLANK(Int. rate) command tests to see if that field (which should contain the contractual rate of interest, if any) has any contents; if not, the form as shipped makes a demand for six percent interest. You can modify that amount, or delete it entirely, depending on the laws of your jurisdiction.

Creating the Data Files

After you have your form files created, you can create a standard format for the data files that populate the system. Care in this step will save hours later.

Setting Up a Standard Data File

First, you need to create a "form data file" consisting of nothing but the FIELD NAMES( ) code, which contains the list of your standard field names. The process is identical to the process used in Chapter 11 to create a form data file for the Real Estate Practice System; refer to "Creating a Form Data File" in that chapter for more information about how to set up this file.

The Companion Disk includes such a file, called CPSDATA.DA!. Like its Real Estate Practice System counterpart, this file is designed to make use of the Quick Data Entry feature of WordPerfect Merge. The field names (shown in table 12.1) are abbreviated so as to provide enough useful information in that screen to allow the user to properly fill in the data file.

Table 12.1 The Suggested Field Names for the Collections Practice System

Field Name	Information stored
File number	Your office file number
Debtor1	Name of first debtor
Debtor2	Name of second debtor (if any)
Debtor marital status	Relationship of individual debtors (if any)
Debtor d/b/a	Business name of debtor (if any)
Debtor addr. 1	First line of debtor's address
Debtor addr. 2	Second line of debtor's address
Debtor city	City of debtor's address
Debtor state	State of debtor's address
Debtor zip code	Zip code of debtor's address
Debtor salut.	Letter salutation for debtor(s)
Creditor	Name of creditor
Creditor d/b/a	Business name of creditor (if any)
Cred. type of bus.	Type of organization (*e.g.* corporation, partnership) of creditor
Creditor addr. 1	First line of creditor's address
Creditor addr. 2	Second line of creditor's address
Creditor city	City of creditor's address

Field Name	Information stored
Creditor state	State of creditor's address
Creditor zip code	Zip code of creditor's address
Creditor salut.	Letter salutation for creditor
Goods/svcs. sold	Description of goods or services sold
Sale price	Amount of original contract price (sale price)
Open. bal.	Amount forwarded to you for collection
Int. rate	Contracted rate of interest on balance due (if any)
Int. from date	Date from which interest should be calculated
Forwarder	Name of agency or person forwarding claim to you
Forwdr. d/b/a	Business name of forwarder
Forwdr. addr. 1	First line of forwarder's address
Forwdr. addr. 2	Second line of forwarder's address
Forwdr. city	City of forwarder's address
Forwdr. state	State of forwarder's address
Forwdr. zip code	Zip code of forwarder's address
Forwdr. salut.	Letter salutation for forwarder
Fwd. file num.	Forwarder's file number
Attorney	Name of attorney in firm to whom file is assigned
Last payment	Last payment made by debtor [reserved for CPSLEDGR.WCM]
Cur. balance	Current balance owed [reserved for CPSLEDGR.WCM]

On the Disk

Keep in mind that CPSDATA.DA! contains suggested field names only. If you found, when creating your form files earlier in the chapter, that you need more fields, or fewer, or want to use different names, you are free to define the list of field names in any manner you like. You can either edit CPSDATA.DA! to add, delete, or change field names, or you can write your own file from scratch. Just remember that, whatever you settle on, you should be consistent in the use of fields for all of your cases. Also, the CPSMENU.WCM macro described later looks for the CPSDATA.DA! file to help you set up new cases, so whenever you settle on the final list of field names for your office, be sure to save them in a file with that filename.

Figure 12.5 shows the Quick Data Entry dialog box for the CPSDATA.DA! file (as shipped on the Companion Disk) with the first group of fields displayed.

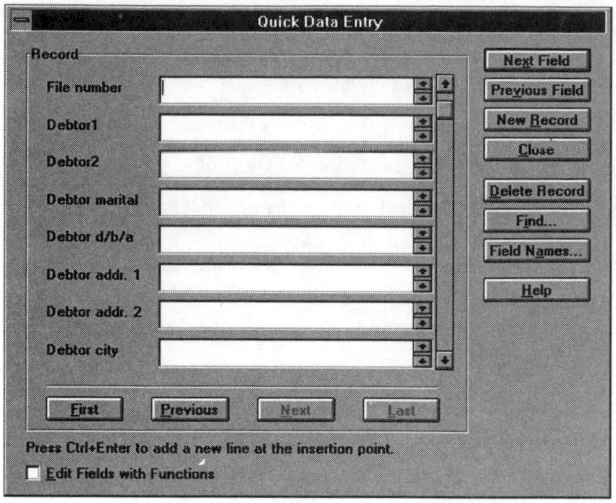

Fig. 12.5

The Quick Data Entry dialog box used for entering data into a Collections Practice System data file.

While many of the fields suggested are self-explanatory, several require clarification:

- The field File number should be a unique file number for the case in your office. You should also use this number to store the data files for each case, and the ledger files that maintain the listing of charges and payments and calculates the current balance due (see the description of those files later in this chapter). Although you can use any characters you want in this field in the data file, when you store the individual data and ledger files you are limited to eight characters, and they must be legal characters for a DOS filename.

  Suppose your standard office numbering system includes numbers and decimal points. If your new collection file is numbered "14,572.101", you can use that number in the File number field of the data file. But when you save the data file to your hard disk, because CPSMENU.WCM will expect the data file to have an extension of DAT, you cannot include any decimal points; nor is the comma a legal character for a DOS filename. You may therefore decide to save your data file with the filename 14572101.DAT and the ledger file for that case to the filename 14572101.LDG. (The CPSDATA.WCM macro described later in this chapter automatically creates and saves the LDG files for you.)

- The fields relating to the creditor are intended to describe the client for whom you are trying to make a collection. The fields relating to the forwarder are intended to contain information about the collection agency or law firm that has forwarded the claim to you. If you have received the case directly from the client, you should repeat the client's information in the fields relating to the forwarder. By doing so, you can use any form letters you create to send to a forwarder to correspond directly with your client.

■ The field Sale price is intended to contain the original contract or sale price at the point of sale. It should always begin with a dollar sign.

■ The field Open. bal. is intended to contain the amount that has been forwarded to you for collection, including any interest added or any payments received by the client prior to forwarding. It should always begin with a dollar sign.

■ You should always leave the Last payment and Cur. balance fields blank when you open up a new file; these fields are intended to keep track of payments received by you, and additional charges or payments re-corded in your office. Both fields will be automatically updated by the macro CPSLEDGR.WCM.

You can use the CPSDATA.DA! file as your "form data file" if you like, or modify it to suit your needs. However, if you decide to modify it (either by adding or deleting fields, or providing different field names), you must be careful of the following:

1. For CPSLEDGR.WCM to work, the last two fields in all data files must be Last payment and Cur. balance, in that order. You can edit, add or delete any fields but those two; they must be the last two fields in the file, in that order.

2. If you decide to change anything, you should do so before creating any individual data files. If you create some data files based on one list of field names, and then change the list and create data files based on a different list of field names, you may be in for some surprises—such as information in the wrong places—when you create documents later on. Try to make all changes before creating your first data file.

3. You must be extremely careful that the field names you use in the "form data file" exactly match the field names you use in the form files. Even an extraneous space in the field name used in the form files can cause the merge not to recognize the field, and leave unwanted blanks in your resulting documents.

Creating Individual Data Files

After you have created the "form data file" (or modified CPSDATA.DA! to suit your needs), creating individual data files to use in the system is easy. Simply make a copy of the "form data file," use the Quick Data Entry feature to insert all of the needed information for the case you are setting up, then save the data file to disk. It is recommended that you create a special directory on your hard drive to store these files; that you use your office file number as the DOS filename; and that you always save the file with a DAT extension, so that CPSMENU.WCM can easily locate and identify the documents.

The CPSMENU.WCM macro also includes an option to assist you in creating data files for new cases, which is discussed in more detail later in this chapter.

For more help on how to create and store individual data files, see the related discussion of this subject in Chapter 11, "Real Estate Documents."

Using the CPSMENU.WCM Macro

The final step in setting up your own personal Collections Practice System is to set up the CPSMENU.WCM macro.

On the Disk

CPSMENU.WCM, like the REPSMENU.WCM macro described in Chapter 11, helps you maintain a list of both your standard correspondence forms and your pleading forms. It can also start the CPSLEDGR.WCM macro to allow you to record disbursements or payments, or to add interest on unpaid amounts. Once set up, it stores this information in two separate files. The list of correspondence forms and other information is stored in a file called CPSMENU.INF; the list of pleading forms is stored in a file called CPSPLEAD.INF. Both files are stored in your default macros directory.

Note

Although these files are editable WordPerfect documents, you should never attempt to edit them manually. They make heavy use of specialized bookmarks, and the entries in the file may be related to other entries in ways that are not immediately obvious. The CPSMENU.WCM macro includes all of the routines you need to edit this file, including the options to add, delete, or change the list position of any item; you should always use CPSMENU.WCM to make any needed changes to this file.

Setting Up CPSMENU.WCM

The first time you play CPSMENU.WCM, you will be asked to provide certain setup information about the directory structure for your computer. You should decide where you want to store your Collections Practice System documents before you play the macro.

You have to specify directories for four different types of documents:

- Your Collections Practice System form documents (you may want to specify a directory that contains all of your form documents, whether they are for the Collections Practice System alone or shared by other form documents)

- Your Collections Practice System data files (this should be a separate directory just for CPS data files)

- Your Collection Practice System ledger files (this should also be a separate directory)

- Your captions data file (this should be the same directory that you specified for that file for use with WRITECAP.WCM, described in Chapter 10)

It is recommended that you use separate directories for the CPS data files and the CPS ledger files (which keep track of costs and payments on individual cases), because both types of files are stored with the same root name (derived from your office file number). Segregating these files into separate directories help avoid confusion.

After you have decided where you want to place the documents, create the necessary directories and play the macro CPSMENU.WCM. After an initial message telling you that you need to set up the macro, you see the Edit Collections Practice System Setup dialog box, shown in figure 12.6.

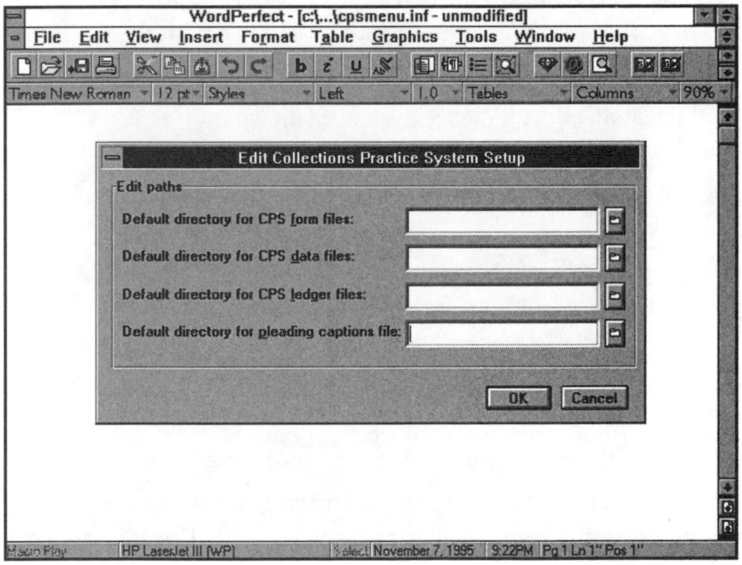

Fig. 12.6
The Edit Collections Practice System Setup dialog box.

Fill in the correct path information; click the file icon at the end of any of the text boxes if you want to search through your directories to find the correct directory name. When all of the information is filled in, choose OK. You are then taken to the Collections Practice System Main Menu, shown in figure 12.7.

Fig. 12.7
The Collections Practice System Main Menu.

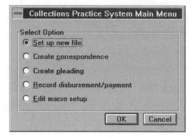

This screen is the first screen you see on subsequent playings of this macro

Editing the Setup

If you ever have to change the directory setting you specified at the initial setup of the macro, simply select the **E**dit macro setup radio button in the Collections Practice System Main Menu and choose OK. You will be returned to the Edit Collections Practice System Setup menu where you can make the necessary changes.

Setting Up Data Documents for Your System

Next, you have to set up one or more data files to use with the Collections Practice System.

1. From the Collections Practice System Main Menu (see fig. 12.7), select **S**et up new file and choose OK.

   You will see the Set Up New Case dialog box shown in figure 12.8.

Fig. 12.8
The Set Up New Case dialog box.

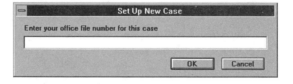

2. Type in the file number for the case in your office and choose OK.

   It is recommended that, for ease of use, you specify your office file number to store information for a particular file. This ensures a unique file number for each data file created by the system and makes it easy to locate the correct data files on your disk.

You then see a message, shown in figure 12.9, telling you that you need to set up a case caption for the claim. CPSMENU.WCM then pauses automatically and runs WRITECAP.WCM to allow you to create a new case caption, or specify an existing caption, to use with the new collection case.

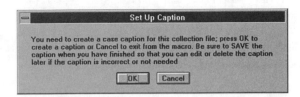

Fig. 12.9
The reminder message advising the user to create a case caption.

3. Create the caption for the collection case, following the prompts generated by WRITECAP.WCM.

4. Be sure to save any new caption that you create while using WRITECAP.WCM, so that the Collections Practice System can find the correct caption when you create pleadings.

For more information on setting up a caption using WRITECAP.WCM, see Chapter 10, "Litigation Documents."

After you have finished creating the caption, CPSMENU.WCM creates a new data file for the case you are setting up. It makes a copy of the file CPSDATA.DA! and stores it under the filename you specified in step 2, then displays the message shown in figure 12.10.

Fig. 12.10

The Finish Setup
dialog box with
instructions on
completing the
creation of a data
file.

5. Choose OK to dismiss the Finish Setup dialog box.

CPSMENU.WCM ends at this point and you are returned to an editing window with your data file displayed, as shown in figure 12.11.

Fig. 12.11

The new data file,
with no data
entered.

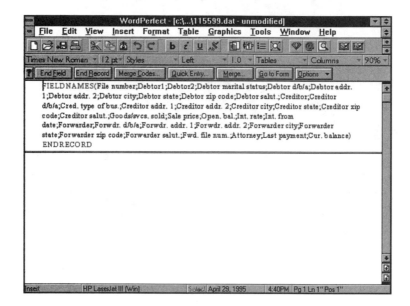

6. Choose **Q**uick Entry from the Merge Feature Bar displayed above the data file.

7. Insert all of the information that you have for the case you are setting up. Use the scroll bar or the Next Field button to display additional field names.

It is not necessary to enter information in every field; in fact it is unlikely that you will have information for every field for every case. You can simply leave blank any field that you have no information for.

When you have finished inserting all of the information, your screen should look something like figure 12.12.

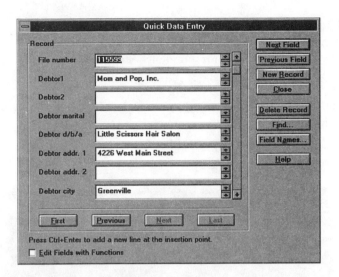

Fig. 12.12
A sample data file
with information
filled in the Quick
Data Entry dialog
box.

8. Choose **C**lose to write the information into the new data file.

9. Answer **Y**es to the question, Save changes to disk?

10. WordPerfect reminds you that a file with that filename already exists on
    the disk; you can answer Yes to indicate that the old file should be over-
    written by the new file with updated information.

Your data file has now been set up; you can exit and close the file normally.

Editing a Data File

You will probably find that, as a case progresses through your office, you may
have to change the date in the data file, or add new information as it is received. You can easily do this by editing the data file for the case.

To edit a data file which has been previously created, open the file normally
in WordPerfect; then choose **Q**uick Entry. You are taken back to the Quick
Data Entry dialog box with the existing data displayed in it. Move to the field
you have to change, and add or change the information, then choose Close
and resave the new data.

If a case proceeds into litigation, you will probably have to edit the caption
you created at the outset to include the docket number assigned after suit
has been filed. To do this, simply retrieve the CAPTIONS.DAT file from the
directory you specified when you set up WRITECAP.WCM, then edit the
caption for the case as needed. For more information about editing the
CAPTIONS.DAT file, see "Editing the CAPTIONS.DAT File" in Chapter 10.

Adding Forms to the Correspondence Menu

Next, you have to add correspondence forms and other documents to the Collections Practice System Correspondence Menu.

1. Play the macro CPSMENU.WCM.

2. From the Collections Practice System Main Menu (refer to fig. 12.7), select Create Correspondence and choose OK.

   The Collections Practice System Correspondence Menu appears, as shown in figure 12.13.

Fig. 12.13
The Collections
Practice System
Correspondence
Menu.

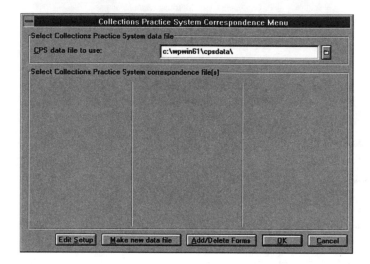

3. Choose Add/Delete Forms.

   The Available Correspondence Documents dialog box appears, as shown in figure 12.14.

Fig. 12.14
The Available
Correspondence
Documents
dialog box.

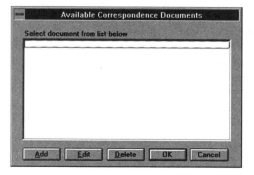

4. Choose **A**dd.

The Add Correspondence Document dialog box appears, as shown in figure 12.15.

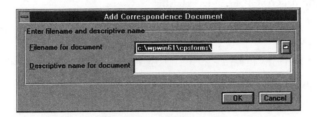

Fig. 12.15
The Add Correspondence Document dialog box.

5. In the **F**ilename for document edit box, type in the DOS filename for the document you are adding. Click on the file icon at the end of that entry window if you want to search the hard disk for the correct filename.

6. Type a descriptive name in the edit box marked **D**escriptive name for document.

> **Note**
>
> To allow a maximum number of correspondence documents to appear on the menu at one time, you are limited to 25 characters in selecting a descriptive name.

7. Choose OK.

You are returned to the Available Correspondence Documents dialog box (see fig. 12.14), where the entry you just made is now displayed.

8. Repeat steps 4 through 7 for each document you want to have appear in the Collections Practice System Correspondence Menu.

9. When you have added all documents, choose OK to return to the correspondence menu.

Editing the List of Correspondence Documents

If you have to edit the description of any document, or change its priority in the correspondence menu, choose **E**dit from the Available Correspondence Documents dialog box (refer to fig. 12.14) and make the necessary changes in the dialog box that appears. To change the filename of any entry, you must use the **D**elete button in the Available Correspondence Documents dialog box; then **A**dd the corrected item.

II

Assembling Documents

Creating Documents Using the Correspondence Menu

Finally, you are ready to create correspondence documents!

1. Play the macro CPSMENU.WCM.

2. From the Collections Practice System Main Menu, choose Create **C**orrespondence.

   The Collections Practice System Correspondence Menu appears.

3. Enter the file number for the file you are working on (this should correspond to the data file) in the edit box marked CPS data file to use:.

   You can click the file icon at the end of that edit box to search your disk for the proper filename.

4. Select as many as nine letters that you want to create in the Select Collections Practice System correspondence file(s) group box.

Note

You can create only as many new documents as you have available document windows when you start the macro. If, when you play the macro, you have four documents open, there are only five available document windows, so only five documents can be created at one time. If you select more documents than you have available document windows, the macro will create as many as it can until all nine document windows are filled, and will then stop with a message advising you that it was unable to complete the documents you selected.

At this point, your screen will look something like figure 12.16.

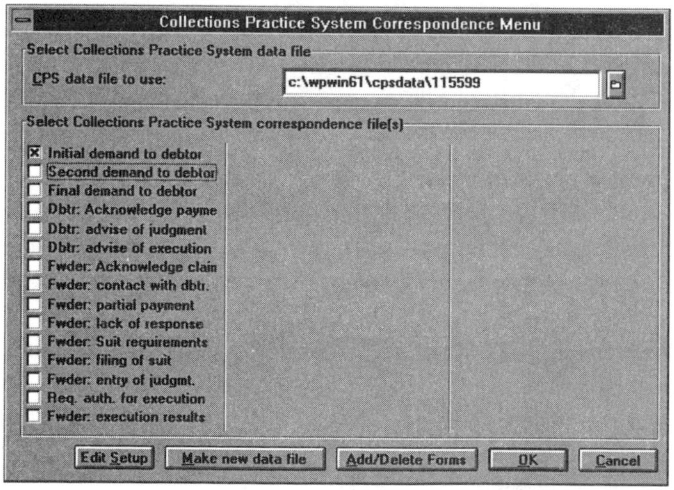

Fig. 12.16

A sample listing of correspondence using CPSMENU.WCM.

5. Choose OK.

The macro then creates the documents you selected (or as many of them as will fit in the available document windows).

6. Edit, print or save the documents created as necessary.

Adding Pleadings to the Pleadings Menu

As mentioned earlier, CPSMENU.WCM maintains a separate listing of litigation documents. This is done to increase the number of forms that can be handled by the system, but also because pleading documents require the extra step of retrieving a caption, as discussed above.

The process of adding pleadings to the Collections Practice System Pleading Menu is identical to the process of adding correspondence documents described above. Simply play the CPSMENU.WCM macro, select the Create Pleading option, and proceed in exactly the same manner as described above.

Creating Pleadings

Likewise, creating pleadings works in exactly the same manner as creating correspondence. Select the pleading or pleadings you want to create from the Collections Practice System Pleading Menu, specify the data file, and choose OK. Notice that the macro first retrieves the case caption from the CAPTIONS.DAT file before proceeding to add the body of the pleading.

Tracking Payments with CPSLEDGR.WCM

The Collections Practice System described in this chapter also includes a useful macro and form document for keeping track of expenses and payments relating to your files, as well as adding interest as time progresses.

The macro that operates this feature is called CPSLEDGR.WCM. You can play this macro either right from the disk, or by choosing Record disbursement/payment from the Collections Practice System Main Menu.

CPSLEDGR.WCM creates a "ledger sheet" that shows the original balance forwarded to you for collection. As you use it, you can add expenses (costs) and interest to the balance, and record payments made, leaving you with a running total of the current balance owed. The current balance owed is then written into the related data file for the case, so that the various forms you have set up can refer to the most current balance owing from time to time.

Modifying and Using the Ledger Form

On the Disk

The ledger form document is included on the Companion Disk as the file COLLEDGR.FRM, shown in figure 12.17. It is a WordPerfect merge form file.

Fig. 12.17
The
COLLEDGR.FRM
form file.

		ACCOUNT HISTORY		

Debtor: FIELD(Debtor1) File open date: DATE

Creditor: FIELD(Creditor) Interest from: FIELD(Int. from date)

Our file: FIELD(File number) Interest rate: IFNOTBLANK(Int. rate) FIELD(Int. rate)ELSE 6 ENDIF

Original amt: FIELD(Sale price)

Date	Item	Expense	Payment	Balance
DATE	Beginning balance	FIELD(Open. bal.)		$0.00

The bulk of the form is a WordPerfect Table (although cells A1 through E4 have no lines surrounding them). The CPSLEDGR.WCM macro creates an individual case ledger for every case by merging the COLLEDGR.FRM file with the data file for the individual case, and then stores the individual ledger file in the directory you specified for ledger files in the original setup of the CPSMENU.WCM macro. Some basic identifying information is included at the top of the ledger document, as well as the date the ledger file was opened, the date interest should be taken from, and the contractual interest rate (if any) specified in the data file.

The "Interest rate" cell provides an option for you. Take a look at the merge codes in cell E3: IFNOTBLANK(Int. rate) FIELD(Int. rate) ELSE 6 ENDIF. This says, "If there is a contractual rate of interest specified in the Int. rate field of the data file, type that rate here; otherwise, type 6 percent." This form is based on Pennsylvania law which specifies a "default" rate of 6 percent per annum interest where the parties have not contracted for a different rate. If your jurisdiction specifies a different "default" rate, you can delete the "6" in cell E3 and replace it with whatever rate your jurisdiction provides for. Or, if you prefer not to add interest through this form, you can specify "0" instead of "6".

This is probably the only modification you have to make to the COLLEDGR.FRM document. CPSLEDGR.WCM handles all of the data entry and recalculation of the amount due for each of the individual ledger documents created.

The individual ledger documents are stored as ordinary WordPerfect files in the ledgers directory. You can retrieve and/or print the ledger document for any case whenever you need to review the history of payments and/or costs added to a particular file.

Using CPSLEDGR.WCM

Using CPSLEDGR.WCM to keep track of payments and disbursements is easy.

1. Play CPSLEDGR.WCM (or choose Record disbursement/payment from the Collections Practice System Main Menu).

   The CPS Ledger Maintenance Menu appears (see fig. 12.18).

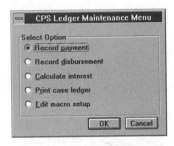

Fig. 12.18
The CPS Ledger Maintenance Menu.

2. Select one of the first four options, depending on whether you want to record a payment from a debtor, record a disbursement or cost incurred by your office, add interest on the file, or simply print a case ledger, then choose OK.

   Regardless of which of the four options you choose, you are asked to specify a ledger file to update, as shown in figure 12.19.

Fig. 12.19
The CPS Ledger Maintenance Menu to select a ledger file to update.

If it has been more than a month since the ledger file you specified has been updated, you will be asked whether you want to add interest to the balance due, as shown in figure 12.20.

Fig. 12.20
You have the option of adding interest to a ledger file.

II

Assembling Documents

3. Choose **Y**es or **N**o as you prefer.

If you selected the Record payment option from the menu, you will see the Enter Payment dialog box shown in figure 12.21.

Fig. 12.21
The Enter
Payment dialog
box used to record
payments.

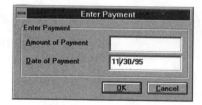

4. Enter the amount of the payment in the **A**mount of Payment edit box.

5. Adjust the date if necessary.

6. Choose OK.

If you selected the Record disbursement option from the menu, you will see the Enter Disbursement dialog box shown in figure 12.22.

Fig. 12.22
The Enter
Disbursement
dialog box to
record a disburse-
ment to a file.

7. Type a brief description of the disbursement in the **T**ype of Disbursement edit box.

8. Enter the amount of the disbursement in the **A**mount of Disbursement edit box.

9. Adjust the date if necessary.

10. Choose OK.

If you chose any of the first three options from the menu, after you have recorded the payment, the disbursement or updated the interest, you will see the Print/Save Ledger File Options dialog box shown in figure 12.23.

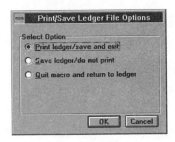

Fig. 12.23
The Print/Save Ledger File Options dialog box.

11. Select the desired option and choose OK.

Choosing the last option, Quit macro and return to ledger, ends the macro with your ledger document on your screen, ready to review, edit, print, or save. The other options save and/or print the ledger file, then loop back and ask if you want to continue with another file. Answer Yes or No as appropriate.

From Here...

This chapter presented a sophisticated system to help generate a variety of documents needed to maintain a commercial law practice.

In Chapter 13, you learn about ways to speed production of documents in an estate planning practice. Specifically, you learn:

■ How to create a will form document

■ How to use a macro to assemble new wills from a form document

■ How to create trust instruments

13

Wills and Estate Planning

An estate planning practice is another type of practice in which a good set of form documents can save you lots of time (and money). If you practice in this area, you probably already have a good set of forms that you cut and paste from freely. If you are old enough to remember the days of practicing law before computers, you are probably thankful that the word processor has taken the drudgery out of customizing these forms for each individual client.

But are you getting the most productivity out of your forms and out of your computer? Are there ways you can not only produce wills, trust agreements, and other estate planning documents faster, but obtain a better end product as a result?

This chapter looks at some ways to get the most out of WordPerfect:

- Setting up a will form that can be easily customized for individual clients
- Creating an inter vivos trust agreement
- Using a macro to quickly generate customized documents

But remember: this is not a forms book! The Companion Disk contains two sample documents that show you examples of how you can set documents to make them easy to customize for individual cases; instructions are provided in this chapter and elsewhere in the book to allow you to set up your own documents to work just like these. The two sample documents provided on the disk are not complete and will have to be reviewed and modified to conform to the legal requirements of the jurisdiction in which you practice.

Preparing a Will

In chapter 8, "Document Assembly," you learned about different methods by which new documents can be assembled from bits and pieces of other documents. The example used in that chapter was that of preparing a will, hypothetically called WILL.FRM. That chapter also described the operation of two macros, DOCSETUP.WCM which helped you to identify discrete "segments" of WILL.FRM file, and DOCBILDR.WCM which helped you quickly select those pieces that you wanted to include in your new document.

The hypothetical WILL.FRM becomes two real files in this chapter. The Companion Disk includes HWILL.FRM and WWILL.FRM, which help you prepare wills for (respectively) a husband and a wife. These files are already set up for you to modify and use with the DOCBILDR.WCM macro described in chapter 8. Instructions on how to modify and use the file are included in this chapter.

The *x*WILL.FRM files actually combine several techniques for document-building. As shipped on the disk, it includes a number of WordPerfect Merge codes. When you use DOCBILDR.WCM to select the segments you want, those merge codes are carried into the new document. All you have to do to finish the new, customized form is to merge the new document with a data file containing all of the information needed for the case you are working on. And, like the merge files described in the previous two chapters, a single data file can be devised that will correctly supply information to any of the forms in this chapter.

The Data File

Let's look at the data file that contains the client information needed to complete the will.

The Companion Disk includes the file ESTATEPL.DA!, a WordPerfect Merge form file consisting of just a FIELDNAMES() command. The field names included in that command, and a brief description of their use, are listed in table 13.1.

Table 13.1 Suggested Field Names for Estate Planning Forms	
Field Name	**Information stored**
Husband	Name of male testator/settlor
Wife	Name of female testator/settlor
Children	Names of children of testator(s)/settlor(s)

Field Name	Information stored
Town	Town of residence of testator/settlor
County	County of residence of testator/settlor
State	State of residence of testator/settlor
Executor	Name of executor/executrix of will
Subst. exec.	Name of substitute executor/executrix of will
Representative	Type of executor (*i.e.*, executor, executrix, co-executors, etc.)
Guardian	Name of guardian(s) of minor children
Subst. guard.	Name of substitute guardian(s) of minor children
Trust name	Name of trust (testamentary or inter vivos) in instrument
Trustee	Name of trustee
Addr. of tr'ee	Address of trustee
Subst. trustee	Name of substitute trustee
Will contractor	Name of other party to contractual will

It does not matter where on your disk you store this document, as long as you know where to look for it. You may want to store it in the directory you use to store form documents.

Most of these fields are self-explanatory, but a few require some explanation. Remember that you don't have to fill in every item in a data file, and in fact it is unlikely that you will fill in every blank in very many cases.

- Despite its name, the "husband" field is for a male testator or trust settlor, regardless of whether he is married or single. The HWILL.FRM will form on the Companion Disk determines whether the testator is married depending on whether the "wife" field is blank.

- Similarly, the "wife" field is for use by any female testator or settlor regardless of whether she is married; the WWILL.FRM file checks the contents of the "husband" field to determine whether the testator is married.

- The "executor" field should contain the name or names of the executor, executrix or co-executors; the "representative" field should contain either the word "executor", "executrix", or "co-executors", depending on who has been named in the "executor" field.

To use the ESTATEPL.DA! file to set up data files for use with any of the forms provided on the disk, do the following:

1. Open a blank document window.

2. Choose **I**nsert, **F**ile.

3. In the Insert File dialog box, locate the directory containing the ESTATEPL.DA! file and select that file in the Filename: window.

4. Choose **I**nsert.

   A copy of the ESTATEPL.DA! file is then opened into a new, unnamed document window, as shown in figure 13.1.

Fig. 13.1
The FIELD NAMES code, used to create a new form file for a will.

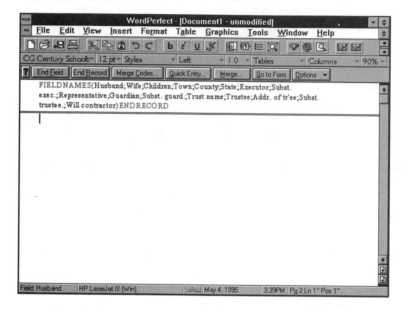

5. From the Merge Feature Bar, choose **Q**uick Entry.

   The Quick Data Entry dialog box appears, as shown in figure 13.2.

6. Insert all the information you have in the appropriate fields in the Quick Data Entry dialog box.

7. When you have finished entering data, choose **C**lose.

8. To be safe, answer **Y**es to the question, `Save the changes to disk?`

9. Specify a filename and save the new data file.

Tip

It is recommended that you get in the habit of using this method to start a new data file, so that you do not inadvertently overwrite or damage the ESTATEPL.DA! file.

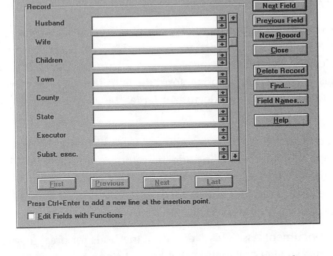

Fig. 13.2
Entering data
through the Quick
Data Entry dialog
box.

It also makes no difference where you store your data file, as long as you can find the file easily. Consider creating a special directory to store data files for use with these forms, using either the name of the person making the will or your office file number for easy reference.

The new data file can be used with any of the form documents provided on the Companion Disk, or any other form files you create which use the same field names. You can add or delete fields to or from the ESTATEPL.DA! file if you need a different list of fields in your practice.

Setting Up a Form File

Creating form files to use with the ESTATEPL.DA! form is easy. All you have to do is retrieve your form documents and replace the "blanks" with FIELD() codes, using the same field names specified in ESTATEPL.DA! (or any different names that you may select).

> **Note**
>
> If you use field names other than those set up in the ESTATEPL.DA! form file, you must be consistent in the way you use the field names in every form file you create. The field names must exactly match in all forms, not only in form (spelling and capitalization) but in substance too (the field names must stand for the same information in every document).

For help with creating a WordPerfect Merge file out of your existing files, see chapter 6, "A Merge Primer."

You have two options at this point. The simplest option is to create a series of stand-alone, complete documents, ready to merge with the various data files you create for each client. Creating a finished document using this method is easy: you just merge the appropriate form file with the data file you created using ESTATEPL.DA! and your document (at least a good first draft) is ready to print.

The second option is to create a "combined" form file, containing segments of information which you may include or exclude at your leisure. This larger document may contain alternative paragraphs that contradict each other, so you won't be able to use it as a form by itself; you will need a method to sort through the document and select the alternatives you need.

Chapter 8, "Document Assembly," discussed methods for breaking form documents into smaller "segments" that could be combined in different ways to produce customized documents very easily. Two macros were discussed in that chapter: DOCSETUP.WCM, which helps you mark different segments and create a list of segments for each document you set up; and DOCBILDR.WCM, which helps you pick and choose from among those segments to create new, custom-built documents.

If you want to take advantage of the DOCBILDR.WCM system of forms management, you can use DOCSETUP.WCM to run through each of the forms you set up as discussed previously and mark different segments that you may want to individually select later. For more help on how to use this macro, refer to chapter 8.

Using HWILL.FRM and WWILL.FRM

Now let's take a closer look at how to create a custom document from a document set up for the DOCBILDR.WCM system. The HWILL.FRM and WWILL.FRM documents on the Companion Disk are already set up to be used with that macro.

Installing and Modifying DOCBILDR.INF

Before you use these forms, however, make sure that the file DOCBILDR.INF, included on the Companion Disk, has been placed in your default macros directory. As noted elsewhere, several of the macros in this book create files with an INF extension. An INF file is a file that contains certain custom settings and preferences for documents, paths, and directories, and other information needed for proper operation of the macro; saving this information in a disk file allows the macro to remember this information from session to session. But INF files are highly structured and full of hidden codes and tricks; chances are very good that, if you attempt to edit one of these files, you may inadvertently delete a bookmark or a code or rearrange something so that the macro which uses the file will not operate properly. Therefore, *you should not attempt to edit any INF file from the main editing window of WordPerfect.* Any modifications needed should be made by choosing the appropriate options from the macro which created the INF file. Also, if a macro that uses an INF file stops unexpectedly, you may see an INF file still open; you should simply close this document without saving it.

The DOCBILDR.INF file is the only INF file supplied on the Companion Disk, because it is needed to support the operation of the three forms discussed in this chapter. One of the bits of information DOCBILDR.WCM needs is the location of the form files you have set up. As shipped on the disk, DOCBILDR.INF contains path information specific to the author's computer, therefore it will not work on your computer until you edit the file. This can, and should, be done by playing the macro, as follows:

1. Play the macro DOCBILDR.WCM.

2. If you played the macro with a document on-screen, you will first see a message asking if you want to insert segments into the active document window; answer **N**o.

You should now see the Available Documents window, which serves as the main menu for DOCBILDR.WCM, as shown in figure 13.3.

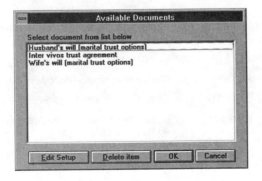

Fig. 13.3
The Available Documents dialog box of DOCBILDR.WCM.

3. Choose **E**dit Setup.

The Edit Setup dialog box appears, as shown in figure 13.4.

On the Disk

II

Assembling Documents

Fig. 13.4
The Edit Setup
dialog box from
DOCBILDR.WCM.

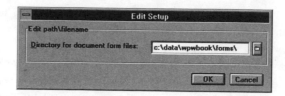

4. Type in the correct path for the directory where you want to store your form documents to use with the DOCBILDR.WCM macro, then choose OK.

5. Choose Cancel from the Available Documents dialog box to exit from the macro. Your new path is saved on disk when the macro ends.

Editing the Will Forms

As noted, the HWILL.FRM and WWILL.FRM documents are already set up to be used with DOCBILDR.WCM. They are parallel and virtually identical documents, one designed for use by a male testator and the other for a female testator.

Both have the same segments defined. The segments in these files, and a brief explanation of their use, are listed in table 13.2.

Table 13.2 Available segments in the xWILL.FRM files

Segment Name	Information stored
Introduction/kin/authorization	Heading, name of testator, identification of next of kin and authorization to pay debts
Specific bequests	Introduction to specific bequests (details to be filled in after assembly)
Resid. clause: intro	Standard introduction to residuary clause
Resid. clause: simple	Option one: residue directly to family members
Resid. clause: std. marital tr	Option two: residue into a marital trust
Resid. clause: A/B marital tr.	Option three: residue into A/B marital trusts for estate tax avoidance
Resid. clause: I.V. pour-over	Option four: residue poured over into pre-existing inter vivos trust
Resid. clause: std. testmt. tr	Option five: residue into testamentary trust
Resid. clause: spendthrift tr.	Option six: residue into testamentary trust with spendthrift protections
Executor: family member	Option one: family member(s) appointed as executor(s)
Executor: corp. trustee	Option two: bank or trust company appointed executor

Segment Name	Information stored
Appointment of guardian	Appointment of guardian of minor children
Admin. powers: standard	Option one: standard administrative powers to executor
Admin. powers: limited	Option two: limited administrative powers to executor
Admin. powers: corp. trustee	Option three: administrative powers for corporate executor
Presumption: simul. deaths	Option one: presumption that husband survived wife if order of deaths undeterminable
Presumption: 30-day required	Option two: requirement that beneficiary survive testator by 30 days before taking
Misc.: heading	Heading for article containing Miscellaneous matters
Misc.: standard definitions	General definitions
Misc.: retention of counsel	Direction to retain law firm as counsel
Misc.: governing law	Direction as to law governing will
Misc.: will revocable	Option one: Recitation that will is not pursuant to contract and therefore revocable
Misc.: will by contract	Option two: Recitation that will is pursuant to contract and therefore irrevocable
Misc.: number and gender	Inclusiveness of pronouns
Signature page	Standard signature page

The segments are listed in table 13.2 in the order they appear in the DOCBILDR.WCM macro later in this chapter. They have not been inserted randomly, but in the sequence typically found in a will. This is so that, when you use DOCBILDR.WCM to assemble your document, the segments will be placed in the most logical order, avoiding the need for significant editing.

Before using either of the *x*WILL.FRM documents, you will have to edit them to include certain information, or to add your preferred language. For example, due to the constantly changing tax laws and with the understanding that every lawyer or law firm has a different "standard" will, I have not tried to provide a complete marital deduction trust provision in these forms. You will have to complete the various paragraphs of Article IV, dealing with the residue of the estate, before using the form. Likewise, you will have to complete the various optional articles for administrative powers for the executor and fill in the state where you practice in the "governing law" paragraph under Miscellaneous Provisions.

Optionally, you may want to add information to the general Definitions section under Miscellaneous Provisions, or change other parts of this form to suit your needs.

You can edit either form, but you must do so carefully. Recall that DOCBILDR.WCM identifies "segments" of a form document by looking for paired bookmarks. These bookmarks are positioned throughout the *x*WILL.FRM documents, and *must not be disturbed*. If you inadvertently omit or move one of the bookmarks, or insert text outside of the pair of bookmarks, DOCBILDR.WCM will not work correctly.

For example, suppose you want to edit the HWILL.FRM document to include an A/B marital trust to minimize federal estate taxes. Do this:

1. Open the HWILL.FRM file into a new document window.

2. Turn on Reveal Codes (choose **V**iew, Reveal **C**odes).

> **Tip**
>
> When editing any document which has been set up for use with DOCBILDR.WCM, it is a good idea to do so with Reveal Codes turned on so that you can easily see where the bookmarks are located. This helps you avoid accidentally moving or deleting them.

3. Move the insertion point to the location where the A/B trust provisions will be inserted.

   At this point, your screen should look something like figure 13.5.

Fig. 13.5
The HWILL.FRM file, shown in Reveal Codes.

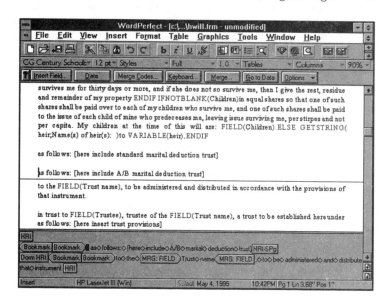

Notice that, in figure 13.5, the prompt to "include A/B marital deduction trust" is placed between two bookmarks, visible in the Reveal Codes window. If you move the insertion point to the left of either bookmark, the bookmark code in Reveal Codes will expand to reveal that the bookmark pair is named "DocBuild5", because it is the fifth segment in the form.

4. Type or paste your firm's standard A/B marital deduction trust language in at that location, making certain that all of the text (even if it is several pages long!) remains inside the DocBuild5 bookmark pair.

Make all of your corrections or additions to this form document in the same way, then save the document to disk

Note

Editing the xWILL.FRM files is useful to make minor changes to the forms; however, if you want to add more segments, or delete existing ones, or make other major changes to the form, you will be better off deleting the form from the Available Documents main menu screen (refer to fig. 13.3), then using DOCSETUP to redefine your segments. After you redefine the segments, you can use the Add button of the Available Documents screen to reinstall the form. For more information on adding and deleting forms from the DOCBILDR.WCM system, see Chapter 8.

Creating a New Will

It has taken a long time to get to the act of creating a new will. Setting up a will form (or any good form system) takes some thought and time on the front end. But the benefits of the system are now to be realized: creating customized wills are a snap once the form is fully prepared. The time savings in future operations should more than make up for the care you took in getting the system set up in the beginning.

Creating a custom will using the xWILL.FRM forms is a two-step process. First, you must select the clauses or paragraphs to include in the finished will. Then you have to merge the custom form with a data file to "fill in the blanks". Both tasks can be accomplished in a matter of minutes.

Suppose you want to create a will for a husband and wife. Follow these steps:

1. Create the data file for the clients (see the discussion of how to do this earlier in this chapter).

2. Save the new data file to disk and exit from the document.

In this example, save the data file to SMITH.DAT in whatever directory you find convenient. (It is a good idea to use the file extension DAT to identify a Merge data file, so the Merge feature can help you quickly locate the correct file.)

3. Next, create the husband's will. Play the macro DOCBILDR.WCM.

4. From the Available Documents dialog box (refer to fig. 13.3), select Husband's will (marital trust options) and choose OK.

   A listing of the available segments (the 25 items listed in table 13.2) is displayed, with a check box next to each one.

5. Select the items you want to include in this will. (Note that some options are mutually exclusive.)

   After you have selected the segments, your screen will look something like figure 13.6.

Fig. 13.6

The Available Segments dialog box, showing various segments to include in a will.

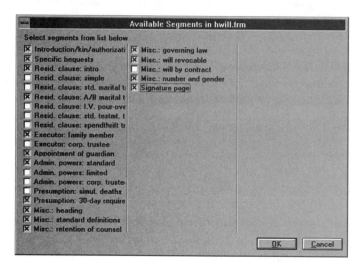

6. Choose OK.

   The macro then retrieves each of the segments you selected from the form document and places them into a new document window, in the order listed in figure 13.6.

7. Finally, merge the assembled document with the appropriate data file (in our hypothetical, SMITH.DAT) to fill in the appropriate names and other information into the "blanks".

> **Note**
>
> Notice that, in the "simple" residuary clause of both forms, if your data file contains neither the name of a spouse nor the names of any kids, the merge process will pause and ask you to specify the heir or heirs who will take the residue. This is handled by the GETSTRING merge command in that paragraph.

You should now have a completed will, or a very nearly completed will, ready to print, save, and share with the client. You may, of course, have to fill in some additional information by hand after the merge is completed; for example, if your client want to make some specific bequests, you have to include that segment when you run DOCBILDR.WCM and then go back to the document created to type in the specific bequests.

Repeat the process for the wife's will (you can use the same SMITH.DAT file for the appropriate information to insert into her will).

A Sample Trust Agreement

The other form document listed in the DOCBILDR.WCM main menu (and included on the Companion Disk as file INTERVIV.FRM) is an inter vivos trust declaration, intended for use by either individuals or a husband and wife. It includes optional paragraphs to make the children of the marriage the immediate beneficiaries, or to give the settlor's spouse a life estate in the income of the trust with the remainder to pass to the children of the marriage.

On the Disk

The Data File

The INTERVIV.FRM document is also a Merge form file. It uses the same field names as the *x*WILL.FRM documents described in the previous section of this chapter. You can create individual data files, based on the ESTATEPL.DA! file, by following the instructions found in the preceding section of this chapter.

Using INTERVIV.FRM

Likewise, using INTERVIV.FRM to create individual trust declarations is identical to the process described previously for the *x*WILL.FRM documents. All you have to do is run DOCBILDR.WCM, select the segments you want to include in your customized trust agreement, and then merge the assembled document with a data file to "fill in the blanks."

A listing of the segments defined in INTERVIV.FRM, and their function, is shown in table 13.3.

II

Assembling Documents

Table 13.3 Available segments in INTERVIV.FRM	
Segment Name	**Information stored**
Introduction	Title and introduction
Designation of trust estate	Identification of trust assets
Distributions (title only)	Title for Article II regarding distribution of income
Distrib. to children	Option one: income payable to minor children
Distrib. to spouse	Option two: life estate to spouse
Distrib./death of a benefcry.	Distribution upon the death of any beneficiary
Invasion of principal	Standards for invasion of principal
Term.: age 18	Option one: trust terminates when children attain age 18
Term.: age 21	Option two: trust terminates when children attain age 21
Term.: age 30	Option three: trust terminates when children attain age 30
Term.: to kids after life estate	Option four: to children after death of spouse
Term.: to others after life estate	Option five: to others after death of spouse
Premature death of beneficiary	Failure of trust on death of beneficiary before distribution
Prem. death all beneficiaries	Failure of trust on death of all beneficiaries
Trustee powers: general	General powers of trustee
Trustee powers: investments	Trustee: power to invest
Trustee powers: management	Trustee: power to manage assets
Trustee powers: borrowing	Trustee: power to borrow money
Trustee powers: allocations	Trustee: allocation of receipts between principal and interest
Trustee powers: taxes/expenses	Trustee: taxes and expenses as charge against trust estate
Trustee powers: limitations	Trustee: limitations on powers
Trustee duties: general	Duties: general
Relations with trustee	Authority of trustee
Limitations on Trustee liab.	Standard of conduct for trustee
No compensation (ind. trustee)	Option one: no compensation for family member trustee

Segment Name	Information stored
Compensation (corp. trustee)	Option two: compensation for institutional trustee
Administrative powers (genrl.)	Payment of taxes and expenses of trust
Spendthrift provision	Spendthrift trust provision
Payments to minors	Payment of income due to minors
Payments to incompetents	Payment of income due to incompetent persons
Successor trustee (cotrustees)	Option one: replacement of co-trustees
Successor trstee (ind. trstee)	Option two: replacement of individual trustee
Powers of successor trustee	Succession of replacement trustee to rights and duties
Construction: applicable law	Construction of trust in accordance with state law
Severability	Severability of clauses of trust instrument
Number and gender	Interpretation of pronouns and word forms
Notices	Notices pursuant to trust agreement
Signature block	Settlor(s) signature(s)
Acknowledgment	Acknowledgement of settlor(s) signature(s)
Appendix A heading page	Title page for Appendix A (identification of initial trust estate)

Like the *x*WILL.FRM files described earlier in this chapter, you will undoubtedly want to edit this form prior to using it, to conform to any special requirements of your jurisdiction or your own personal tastes. If you can make minor changes without changing the identified segments, feel free to edit this document (again taking care not to disturb the location of any of the bookmark pairs). If, however, you have to add segments or make major revisions, you have to delete this form from the DOCBILDR.WCM main menu as described previously, make your changes or additions, then run DOCSETUP.WCM to replace and redefine the segments.

You might use INTERVIV.FRM as a starting point to get some ideas on how to set up your own documents.

II

Assembling Documents

From Here...

This concludes the discussion of methods to create documents for substantive practice areas. Even if you do not practice extensively in one of the practice areas discussed in the past several chapters, many of the same techniques, macros, and forms can be used by you in your practice, whatever it may be.

Chapter 14, "Client/Case Management," describes a client management system, running entirely within WordPerfect, which allows you to do the following:

- Maintain a database of current and retired clients and matters
- Prepare form letters and mailings to your clients
- Generate management reports for your firm
- Quickly prepare daily time sheets to record the hours you work on a matter

14

Client/Case Management

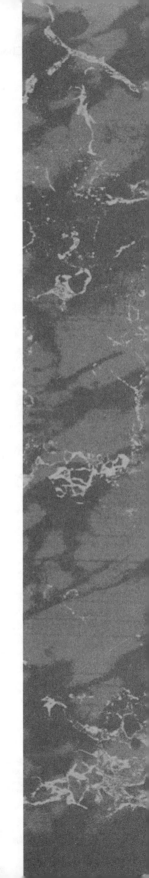

Up to this point, Part II of this book has discussed ways in which to make production of your substantive work product—documents prepared for clients, courts, and other lawyers rather than for internal firm use—more efficient. But there is a "business" side to the practice of law as well, and WordPerfect also includes many tools that can help you there.

This chapter looks at a Client Management System which helps you maintain a listing of your current and retired cases. The "database" is stored as a WordPerfect data file, so that you can generate any sort of report you may need simply by creating a WordPerfect form file to merge with the data file. Or, you can use one of the several form files supplied on the Companion Disk.

You can set up a database for your entire firm, or just a practice group within the firm, or even for a single lawyer. The system allows you to categorize cases by type and can be used to check for conflicts of interest, statute of limitations deadlines, and other items.

Another common problem for lawyers is recording hours spent on a matter. The Client Management System also includes a macro and a form document to record time entries on an individual timesheet. This macro refers to the Client Management System files to get a listing of currently open cases and the billing rates established for each. You can run the macro from the Client Management System or by itself; the daily timesheets created can then be printed and submitted to the billing department of your firm for entry into your billing system. (WordPerfect is powerful enough that you can take these timesheets and create your own billing program to generate individual client bills on bill forms you create, if you so choose.)

In this chapter, you learn how to:

- Set up and maintain a database of current and retired clients and matters
- Prepare form letters to send to all clients or selected clients, using the Merge feature
- Create a wide variety of management reports, either those supplied on the Companion Disk or new reports designed by you
- Use a macro to prepare time sheet entries and automatically look up client file numbers and billing rates

An Overview of the Client Management System

Like the practice systems described in earlier chapters, the Client Management System described in this chapter is not intended to be a comprehensive set of form documents (or in this case, management reports). Rather, the forms and macros provided on the Companion Disk are the tools that you can use to craft your own set of form documents and reports, to suit your own needs and preferences. The reports and forms which are provided on the disk are intended as samples only; you can modify any of them to suit your needs or get ideas from them to create your own set of forms.

The Client Management System is, however, a bit more structured than several of the practice systems described in the preceding chapters. While those systems all allowed you to create your own list of fields to suit the needs of your own form documents, the Client Management System macros are much more tightly integrated with the database. If you want to add fields to the Client Management System, the macro which automates the system will not be able to read from or write to those new fields.

However, the system does include a wide range of fields that should suit most any need you have.

The concept of the Client Management System is simple: You store information about all of your cases in a single WordPerfect data file (named CMSDATA.DAT), then use a series of WordPerfect form files to extract the information you need from that file using the Merge feature. The information can be a few fields from a single record, or numerous fields from selected records, or even all fields from all records. All you have to do is write the form file which retrieves the information (much as you would write a query or a report for use with a traditional database program).

For more help on using Merge, see Chapter 6, "A Merge Primer."

The Data File Structure

To make full use of the Client Management System, you have to understand the "database structure"; that is, the use of the various fields contained in the data file.

The field names defined for the Client Management System are all contained in the file CMSDATA.DA! on the Companion Disk. This file consists simply of a FIELDNAMES() merge command containing all of the named fields. You can use that file to start your own database. Or, simply run the CMSDBASE.WCM macro described later in this chapter; that macro makes a copy of the CMSDATA.DA! file and starts a client database for you automatically.

The field names available in CMSDATA.DA! are listed in table 14.1. Most are self-explanatory, but several require an additional explanation.

On the Disk

II

Assembling Documents

Table 14.1   Field Names for the Client Management System

Field Name	Information stored
Client title	Mr., Mrs., Ms., Dr., etc.
Clt. first name	First name of client
Clt. m. initial	Middle initial of client
Clt. last name	Last name of client
Spse. first name	First name of client's spouse
Spse. m. initial	Middle initial of client's spouse
Spse. last name	Last name of client's spouse
Company name	Business name (if business client)
Contact person	Contact person at business location
Salutation	Salutation for letters to client
Clt. addr. 1	First line of client address
Clt. addr. 2	Second line of client address
Clt. city	City of client address
Clt. state	State of client address
Clt. zip	Zip code of client address
Clt. home phone	Client home phone number
Clt. work phone	Client work phone number
Clt. fax number	Client fax number

(continues)

Table 14.1 Continued	
Field Name	**Information stored**
Opponent	Name of opposing party if contested matter
Matter type	Code to define type of matter
Matter name	Descriptive name of matter
File open date	Date file opened in your office
Date of injury	Date of injury
Alert date	Deadline or future action date
Comment	Notes, tickler information or other free-form data
Our file num.	File number of file in your office
Clt. file num.	File number of matter in client's office
Atty. Name	Attorney in your office handling matter
Active/retired	Code to indicate if matter is active or retired

- Like the practice systems described in prior chapters, it is unlikely that you will have enough information to fill in every field in each record (case) you create. If you use the Quick Data Entry feature or the CMSDBASE.WCM macro to fill information into your database, you need not worry about leaving blank fields; the data you do enter will be placed in the correct "slot" for each record.

- The Matter type field allows you to specify a code or word to describe the practice field or area that the case or file involves. The use of this field is optional; it is designed to allow you another "hook" by which to screen or sort files to generate reports about specific types of cases. For example, if you want to send a letter only to firm clients for whom you have done wills, you can write a form file that skips all records except those where the "Matter type" field contains your code for wills. You can generate your own list of matter type codes.

- If you use CMSDBASE.WCM to add new records to the database, the Matter name field will be used by the timesheet macro as part of a descriptive name to help you pick the correct file from a listing of active files.

- The Date of injury field, while obviously designed for a personal injury case, can be used for any other relevant date (for example, the date Articles of Agreement were signed in a real estate sale file).

- The Alert date field is designed to help you keep track of upcoming deadlines. You could, for example, use it as a tickler system: by simply revising that record to adjust the date forward, you could create a form file which retrieves all records where the date in this field exceeds today's date to obtain a list of files which need work. Or you may want to record the date on which the statute of limitations for a personal injury case expires.

■ The Comment field allows you to attach a short note to any record in the file. You may want to use this to contain tickler entries in conjunction with the Alert date field; that is, as you edit the file to change the tickler date, you can edit the comment to indicate what task should be performed on the specified date. Or you can use it for any other information which you may want to incorporate into any of your forms.

■ The Our file num. field is the only field required by the CMSDBASE.WCM macro. For simplicity, you should use your office file number here. You are not limited to legal characters for a DOS filename; any string of characters that you may use to name files in your office will work.

■ The Atty. Name field should contain the full name of the attorney in your office handling the file. (The CMSDBASE.WCM provides you with a pop-up list of attorneys in your firm to help you insert this information quickly into new file records.)

■ The Active/retired file is designed to allow you to maintain a complete record of all files handled by the firm, including closed matters, while keeping a separate listing of active files. It should contain only the uppercase letter "A" for active files and the uppercase letter "R" for retired matters. The CMSDBASE.WCM macro automatically updates this field as you retire files.

II

Assembling Documents

Note

Besides these 29 named fields, CMSDBASE.WCM creates two more "hidden" fields, containing a code to define which of any defined fee structures you want to set up for each file. This information is stored as binary information rather than as a merge field to make it easier for the timesheet macro described later to quickly "look up" that information. See the discussion of CMSDBASE.WCM and TIMESHEE.WCM later in this chapter.

As you study the list of fields shown in table 14.1, you note that the basic client information has been broken into many separate fields. Rather than a single field for the name of the client, for example, there are four fields: the title (for example, Mr., Ms., Dr., and so on), the first name, a middle initial, and last name. The address field has separate fields for the street address, city, state, and ZIP code. This is done to permit maximum flexibility in creating form documents. For example, you may want to produce an alphabetical listing of clients, sorted by last name; by designing a merge form file which retrieves the last name before the first name, then sorting the resulting list, you can do this easily. Or, you may want to select records for a particular merge based upon the content of the zip code field. By separating all of these bits of information into separate fields, you are able to fine-tune your form files much more easily.

Entering Data Manually

You can add data to your Client Management System database in two ways. First, you can use the Quick Data Entry feature to add records to your database file manually; or you can use the CMSDBASE.WCM macro described in "Automating the Client Management System" later in this chapter.

Note

If you plan to use the timesheet macro described in this chapter, you should enter new files into your system using the CMSDBASE.WCM macro, because this will also gather information about billing rates that can be accessed by the timesheet macro.

Now let's add records to the database manually first; this will help you understand what the CMSDBASE.WCM macro is doing.

Note

You can maintain several separate lists of clients (for example, one for each practice group in your firm) by creating more than one data file, saving each to different filenames. You can then manually merge any of your form documents with any of the data files you create. However, you cannot use the CMSDBASE.WCM macro to automatically maintain the client list, because that macro only works with a client data file named CMSDATA.DAT.

If you have not run CMSDBASE.WCM and are entering your first file to the system, you have to create a database file. The easiest way to do this is to base your database file on the CMSDATA.DA! file included on the disk. Follow these steps:

1. Open a new blank document window.
2. Choose **I**nsert, **Fi**le.

3. In the Insert File dialog box, locate the file CMSDATA.DA! in whatever directory you have placed it, then choose **I**nsert.

4. Answer **Y**es to the prompt, Insert file into current document?

   A copy (unnamed) of that file is placed in your document window, as shown in figure 14.1.

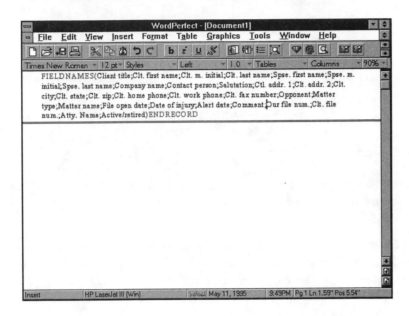

Fig. 14.1
The FIELD NAMES code used to create a new data file.

5. Choose **T**ools, **M**erge.

6. In the Merge dialog box, choose **D**ata to indicate that you want to set up the file as a Merge data file.

7. In the Create Merge File dialog box, leave the option **U**se File in Active Window option selected and choose OK.

8. Because the field names are already set up, click OK in the Create Data File dialog box without entering any field names.

   You are taken directly to the Quick Data Entry screen for the new data file, as shown in figure 14.2.

9. Enter data in as many of the fields as you have information for. You will have to press Tab, Next Field or use the mouse pointer to scroll the list down to get to additional fields which do not appear in the initial listing of available fields.

10. When you have entered all information, choose **C**lose.

11. Answer **Y**es to the prompt, Save the changes to disk?

Fig. 14.2

The Quick Data Entry dialog box to enter data in the new data file.

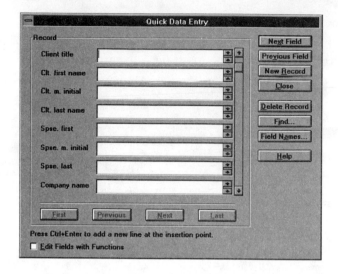

12. You are prompted to supply a filename. Because the CMSDBASE.WCM macro is looking for a file called CMSDATA.DAT, use that name and put the file in whatever directory you want to use.

Your Client Management System data file has now been created and is available to add more client records. You can continue to add records using the Quick Data Entry screen shown in figure 14.2, or you can use the CMSDBASE.WCM data entry screen shown in "Creating a New Case Record" later in this chapter.

Creating Form Files

The heart of the Client Management System is the collection of form files which extract information from the database. Because the database contains a good deal of information, broken into many separate fields, you can get quite creative in how you extract information.

Your form files can be relatively simple (for example, a form letter to send to all clients of the firm, or selected clients based on the content of one or more fields), or more complex (such as a form to find a specific file and prepare a report for just that one file). A good working knowledge of the Merge feature and the Merge codes available for form files is very helpful in creating custom forms. Chapter 6, "A Merge Primer," gives you a start; Appendixes A, B, and C of the WordPerfect for Windows 6.1 program manual (Appendixes H, I, and J in the manual for version 6.0) provide more detailed information on the use of those codes, merge variables, and expressions.

You can also study the form files included on the Companion Disk, and discussed later in this chapter, for more ideas on how to create useful form files that query the client database.

A Sampling of Form Files

The Companion Disk includes seven sample form files, which pull information out of the Client Management System date file through the WordPerfect Merge feature. You can use these form files as provided on the disk, or modify them to suit your needs.

The following sections look at these forms, starting with the simplest forms and working up to some fairly sophisticated forms.

CLNTLIST.FRM

The first form included on the disk, CLNTLIST.FRM, is a fairly straightforward file which generates a listing of all clients.

To use this form, merge it with the CMSDBASE.DAT file which contains your client information. The resulting document looks something like figure 14.3.

On the Disk

CLIENT DIRECTORY
Prepared on October 12, 1995

Client Name, Address, Phone	Matter	File number
Jayleen J. Smith 42154 Bayview Street Sacramento, CA 98765 Home phone: (999) 555-1212 Work phone: (999) 555-2121 Fax number: (999) 555-1122	Incorporation of business	67425.101
Nancy M. Rooney 2351 East Ridge Blvd. Atlanta, GA 23456 Home phone: (999) 555-3333 Work phone: (999) 555-3344	Purchase of office building	543245a
George's Widgets, Inc. 100 Highpoint Tower Building Sacramento, CA 98765 Work phone: (999) 555-2211 Fax number: (999) 555-1111	Copyright infringement	54125.901

Fig. 14.3
A sample client directory using CLNTLIST.FRM.

Note that the client listings appear in the order that they appear in your database. If you want an alphabetical or other listing, you will either have to rearrange the records in your database or sort the directory list after it has been produced.

CLNTLETR.FRM

Another relatively straightforward form is CLNTLETR.FRM, which produces the address block for a letter to your client.

The form is shown in figure 14.4. Notice that it is set up to begin the letter several inches down the page, to allow the use of preprinted stationery. You may have to edit the form to position the DATE merge code in the correct location for your stationery.

Fig. 14.4
The CLNTLETR.FRM form file.

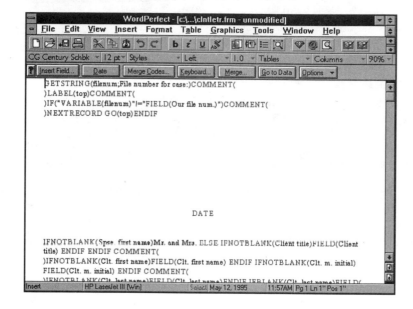

The merge codes at the very top of the document are important. The first command, GETSTRING(filenum;File number for case:), causes a prompt box (shown in fig. 14.5) to appear as soon as you perform the merge. This allows the user to specify which client (identified by his or her file number) to send a letter to.

Fig. 14.5
The GETSTRING prompt when using CLNTLETR.FRM.

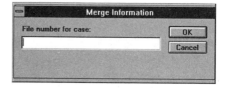

The next several merge commands compare the user's entry (stored in the merge variable filenum with the contents of the FIELD(Our file num.) in each record in the CMSDBASE.DAT file. If WordPerfect finds no match, the

NEXTRECORD command moves the merge to the next record, and the comparison is made again.

If a match is found, however, the remainder of the form is processed for that record, and the address block is created. The very last code in the file is a QUIT merge code, so that as soon as a matching record is found, the address block is generated and the merge halts, avoiding a pointless search through the remainder of the data file.

You can modify this form to create "standard text" letters as well (for example, a standard cover letter to send with a monthly invoice); simply add the standard text you want to include, making use of any additional FIELD() codes which may be relevant (such as the FIELD(Atty. Name) to insert the name of the attorney handling the file in the signature block). Remember to save your modification to a different filename so that you do not overwrite this file; you may want to use this file as the basis for a number of standard letters.

You can copy just the merge codes at the beginning of the document to add to any form you create where you want to generate just one document.

ATTYCLNT.FRM
CLNTLETR.FRM is designed to select a single record out of the client database. There may be times, however, when you want to select a group of records from the database. The ATTYCLNT.FRM file is an example of how this can be accomplished.

The ATTYCLNT.FRM file produces a report of which files a named attorney is responsible for. The form is shown in figure 14.6.

On the Disk

Like CLNTLETR.FRM, ATTYCLNT.FRM begins with a GETSTRING() command which asks the user for the name of the attorney for whom the list should be prepared. The merge then goes through the entire client database and compares the user's response (stored in the merge variable "respatty) with the contents of the FIELD(Atty. Name). If a match is found, the client name, matter name, matter type, and file number for the matching record are inserted in the appropriate columns. If no match is found, the NEXTRECORD command moves the pointer to the next record in the data file and the merge is directed back to the top of the loop which makes the comparison.

CASETYPE.FRM
A similar form, CASETYPE.FRM, generates a listing of cases by matter code (see fig. 14.7). It performs the same type of comparison, this time between the user's input and the contents of the FIELD(Matter type).

On the Disk

Fig. 14.6
The
ATTYCLNT.FRM
file.

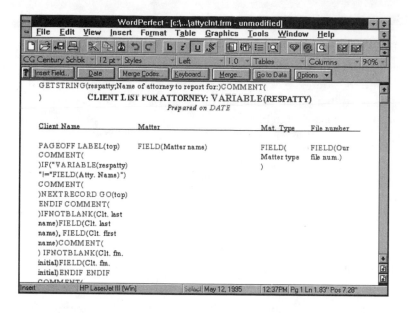

Fig. 14.7
The
CASETYPE.FRM
file.

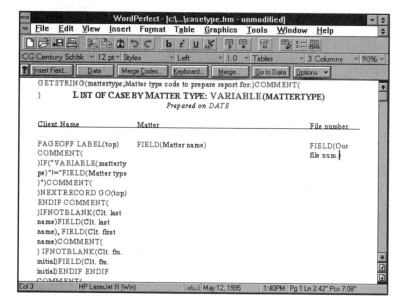

For this form to be useful, you have to define a standard set of codes for different areas of your practice. You must then take care to enter the correct codes when you add clients to the client database.

> **Note**
>
> When Merge performs the comparison, it is case-sensitive. For example, if your code for a real estate case is "RE", and you type "re" in the box asking what code to search for, the form will not report any case where the "Matter type" is "RE". For this reason you may decide to use numeric rather than alphabetic codes.

CHKCONFL.FRM

A slightly more involved form is CHKCONFL.FRM, which searches through your client database and selects records for clients which the firm has represented in the past. You can use this either to check for potential conflicts of interest or simply to quickly find a file number that you have forgotten.

On the Disk

The form is shown in figure 14.8.

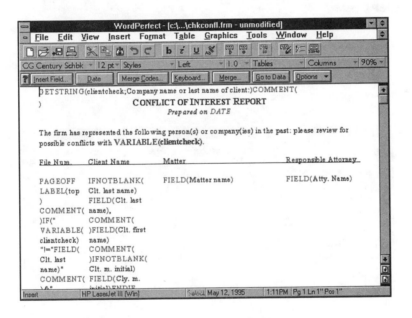

Fig. 14.8
The CHKCONFL.FRM form.

This form goes one step beyond the several form files discussed previously: it simultaneously checks two different fields for matches. The GETSTRING() command at the top of the document asks the user for a company name or client last name, and stores the information in the merge variable checkclient. Now look at the IF command found in the first column of figure 14.7. Stripped of formatting, that command reads as follows:

```
IF("VARIABLE(checkclient)"!="FIELD(Clt. last
name)"&"VARIABLE(checkclient)"!="FIELD(Company name)")
```

This somewhat complicated "expression" compares the contents of the user's response, the VARIABLE(checkclient), with both the FIELD(Clt. last name) and the FIELD(Company name). If neither matches (that is, the firm has never represented anybody with that last name or company name before), the record is skipped. If either field matches, appropriate information about the matching record is placed in the report form, in four columns.

Note

For this form to find a potential match, either the client last name or the company name field in the record must match the user's input *exactly*. Case counts! If you tell the form to search for "smith", it will not find instances where the last name is "Smith."

CASEREPT.FRM

The CASEREPT.FRM file demonstrates how a merge file can screen user input, rejecting input which does not meet certain criteria. This form generates a listing of either all of the active cases in the database, or the closed or retired cases. Take a look at the merge codes at the top of that file, shown in figure 14.9, to see how this works.

Fig. 14.9
The
CASEREPT.FRM
file.

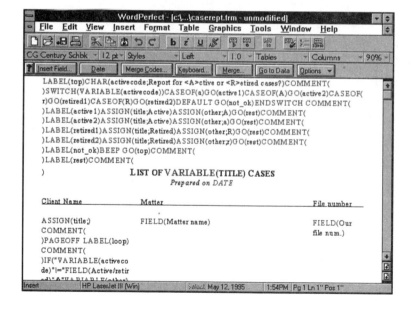

Initially, instead of using a GETSTRING() command to get the user's input, this form uses the CHAR() merge command, which restricts a user's input to a single character. The advantage of this command is that the input box is dismissed as soon as the user types any character, so that the user does not have to press Enter.

Because you are looking for either an "A" or an "R" in the "Active/retired" field of the client database, you have to further restrict the user to allow only one of those two characters to start the merge. This is accomplished by the SWITCH/ENDSWITCH structure beginning on the second line of the file. This command compares the user's input (stored in the merge variable activecode) against four possible matches: "a", "A", "r", and "R". If no match is found, the DEFAULT command sends the macro to the LABEL(not_ok). There, the computer is told to beep once and return to the top of the loop to ask for another character. The only way out of this loop is to press either an upper- or lower-case "A" or "R".

Once an "A" or an "R" is stored in the merge variable activecode, that variable is compared to the contents of the FIELD(Active/retired). Matching records are reported in columnar format as shown in figure 14.9.

TICKLER.FRM

The last sample form, TICKLER.FRM, is fairly complex, but useful. It helps you maintain a tickler system or list of upcoming deadlines, using the Alert date and Comment fields of your database.

On the Disk

Because this merge file is more involved than the previous ones, the entire file is reproduced as figure 14.10.

> **Note**
>
> The line numbers shown in figure 14.10 are for reference only; they are not included in the file on the Companion Disk.

To use the TICKLER.FRM, you must enter information in your client database in the Alert date and Comment fields. Put a deadline or completion date in the Alert date field and a notation in the Comment field as to what the deadline or completion date is. (You can edit and update those fields easily over time using CMSDBASE.WCM, described later in this chapter.)

When you merge TICKLER.FRM with the client database, the form compares the contents of the Alert date field with the current date (taken from your computer's internal clock). If the Alert date field contains a date after the current date, that record will be selected and reported on this form. However, making this comparison accurately requires that the two dates be converted into identical formats so they can be compared.

Fig. 14.10
The TICKLER.FRM file.

```
1   CODES(
2   ASSIGN(curyear;SYSTEM(DateYear))
3   ASSIGN(curyear;"SUBSTR("VARIABLE(curyear)";3;2)")
4   ASSIGN(curmonth;SYSTEM(DateMonth))
5   ASSIGN(curmonthlen;STRLEN(VARIABLE(curmonth)))
6   IF(VARIABLE(curmonthlen)=1)
7        ASSIGN(curmonth;"0VARIABLE(curmonth)")
8   ENDIF
9   ASSIGN(curday;SYSTEM(DateDay))
10  ASSIGN(curdaylen;STRLEN(VARIABLE(curday)))
11  IF(VARIABLE(curdaylen)=1)
12       ASSIGN(curday;"0VARIABLE(curday)")
13  ENDIF
14  ASSIGN(curdate;"VARIABLE(curyear)VARIABLE(curmonth)VARIABLE(curday)")
15  GO(startfile)
16  LABEL(getfiledate)
17       ASSIGN(alertdate;"FIELD(Alert date)")
18       ASSIGN(alertdatelen;STRLEN("FIELD(Alert date)"))
19       ASSIGN(year;"SUBSTR("FIELD(Alert date)";VARIABLE(alertdatelen)-1;2)")
20       ASSIGN(monthday;"SUBSTR("FIELD(Alert date)";1;VARIABLE(alertdatelen)-3)")
21       ASSIGN(slashpos;STRPOS("VARIABLE(monthday)";/))
22       ASSIGN(monthdaylen;STRLEN("VARIABLE(monthday)"))
23       ASSIGN(month;"SUBSTR("VARIABLE(monthday)";1;VARIABLE(slashpos)-1)")
24       ASSIGN(monthlen;STRLEN("VARIABLE(month)"))
25       IF(VARIABLE(monthlen)=1)
26           ASSIGN(month;"0VARIABLE(month)")
27       ENDIF
28       ASSIGN(day;"SUBSTR("VARIABLE(monthday)";VARIABLE(slashpos)+1;
29           VARIABLE(monthdaylen)-VARIABLE(slashpos))")
30       ASSIGN(daylen;STRLEN("VARIABLE(day)"))
31       IF(VARIABLE(daylen)=1)
32           ASSIGN(day;"0VARIABLE(day)")
33       ENDIF
34       ASSIGN(newdate;"VARIABLE(year)VARIABLE(month)VARIABLE(day)")
35  RETURN
36  )LABEL(startfile)                  UPCOMING DEADLINES
37                                    Prepared on DATE
38
39       Client Name             Matter          Deadline        Item
40  PAGEOFF LABEL(top)       FIELD(Matter name)           FIELD(Alert FIELD(Comment)
41  COMMENT(                                              date)
42  )CALL(getfiledate)
43  COMMENT(
44  )IF(VARIABLE(curdate)>
45  VARIABLE(newdate))
46  COMMENT(
47  )NEXTRECORD GO(top)
48  ENDIF COMMENT(
49  )IFNOTBLANK(Clt. last
50  name)FIELD(Clt. last name),
51  FIELD(Clt. first name)
52  COMMENT(
53  )ELSE FIELD(Company name
54  )ENDIF COMMENT(
55  )
56  NEXTRECORD GO(top)
```

Lines 2 through 14 get the current date from the computer's system clock, using the system variables DateYear, DateDay, and DateMonth. The year, day, and month are converted into a two-digit version. For example, line three takes the last two digits of the year and assigns them to the merge variable curyear. Lines 4 through 8 determine the current month, and, if it is a single-digit month, line 7 adds a leading zero to it. Lines 9 through 13 perform the same operation for the current day.

Line 14 then strings these items together, in the format YYMMDD. Thus, January 1, 1996 is stored in the merge variable curdate as 960101.

Lines 17 through 34 dissect the date found in the Alert date field of each record, but notice that this operation is not performed immediately. As soon as the merge has formatted the current date, line 15 sends the merge directly to line 36, bypassing the codes which analyze the Alert date field. The merge then proceeds to create the heading and columns used in the report.

When the merge reaches line 42, it is sent temporarily back to the LABEL(getfiledate), which begins back on line 16. Now the codes which analyze the contents of the FIELD(Alert date) are performed, and the results are again stored in the merge variable newdate in the format YYMMDD.

After this analysis is completed, line 35 returns the merge to where it left off, on line 43. Because the variables curdate and newdate have now been stored in identical 6-digit formats, they can be accurately compared. This is done on lines 44 through 45. If the curdate is after the newdate, no deadline is indicated so the macro skips to the next record and repeats the process. Otherwise (that is, if a future deadline is found), the merge inserts the client name, matter name, deadline date, and the comment explaining what the deadline is into the four columns of the report form.

Generating Reports

Now that you have set up both your database file and your form files, generating reports is as easy. All you have to do is to use the Merge feature to merge whichever form file you want with the database file. All of the "smarts" for gathering information have been stored in the form files; you simply have to perform the merge and print the resulting output.

The beauty of this system is that you can add form files at any time you like, even a form that you may only use once.

Automating the Client Management System

Setting up the form documents may take some time at first, although you may find it is easier than it looks. But after that task is completed, it does not have to be repeated.

Not so with the data file, however. Your client database is an ever-changing thing. You are always opening and closing files, and you have to constantly modify the CMSDBASE.DAT file to reflect new clients, retire old clients, and make other changes.

The Companion Disk provides help, in the form of two macros. CMSDBASE.WCM helps you create and maintain your client database file; TIMESHEE.WCM helps you keep track of billable hours spent on the open files in your database. The two macros work together, but either can be played independently of the other.

Using CMSDBASE.WCM

On the Disk

The main macro in the Client Management System is CMSDBASE.WCM. This macro automates the chore of maintaining your client database file. By using this macro exclusively to edit the client database, you can ensure that all corrections are made accurately.

The CMSDBASE.WCM macro also provides a link to TIMESHEE.WCM. When you set up cases for CMSDBASE.WCM, the macro also creates a listing that can be used to quickly retrieve billing rate information to include on a daily timesheet, as discussed later in the chapter.

Setting Up CMSDBASE.WCM

The first time you play CMSDBASE.WCM, you have to provide some setup information about your computer's directory structure, your firm's attorneys, and your standard billing rate structures. This information is stored in two files, created by the macro: CMSDBASE.INF and CMSRATES.BIF. Both of these files are located in your default macros directory.

Note

After you set up CMSDBASE.WCM on one computer in your office, if you want to transfer the basic setup information to another computer you can transfer the CMSDBASE.INF and CMSRATES.BIF files to the other computer. If the directory structure is different on the two computers, you can use the Edit Macro Setup feature from the Client Management System Main Menu to adjust that information on the second computer.

The first time you play CMSDBASE.WCM, you will see the CMSDBASE.WCM Setup dialog box shown in figure 14.11.

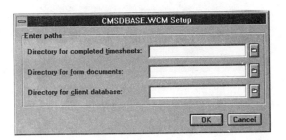

Fig. 14.11
Setting up the
directories for
CMSDBASE.WCM.

You have to enter three pieces of information in this dialog box. (Each editing window has a filename select button at the end of the entry field to allow you to easily search through your directories).

- You must enter where you want to store your completed timesheets. This information is used exclusively by the TIMESHEE.WCM macro, so if you do not intend to use that macro it does not matter much what directory you specify here. If you do plan on using TIMESHEE.WCM, however, it is best to specify a separate directory (perhaps called "\TIMESHEE") to store completed timesheets.

- In the Directory for form documents window, enter the directory where you want to store the various form documents used by the Client Management System. These include a form timesheet, a form data file, and a Merge form file used to extract information from the client data file to enable the macro to edit that information. These files can be stored in your general forms or template directory.

- In the Directory for client database window, specify the location where you want to store your client database file (CMSDATA.DAT). If you created such a file manually as described previously, place that directory name in this window; otherwise specify a directory that makes logical sense to you.

After you have entered all of this information, choose OK to dismiss the CMSDBASE.WCM Setup dialog box. You will then see the Edit/Add Attorneys dialog box shown in figure 14.12.

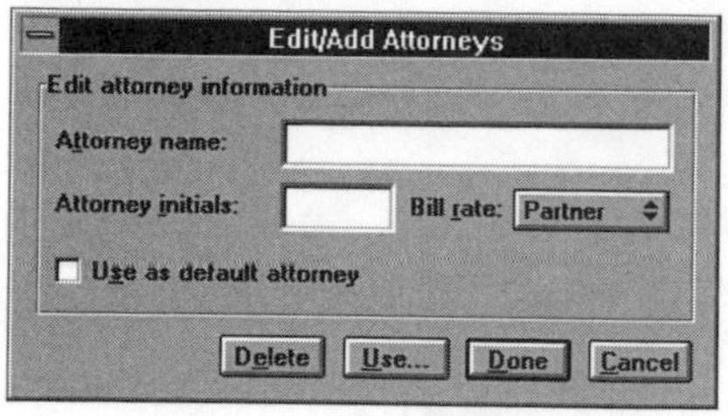

Fig. 14.12
Creating the list
of attorneys in
the firm.

To set up the list of attorneys in your firm (or at least the attorneys in the group that will be using this system), do the following:

1. In the Attorney name: window, type in the full name of a timekeeper (whether an attorney or a paralegal) as you want it to appear in your finished documents.

> **Note**
>
> To give yourself greatest flexibility in using the Atty. Name field in your form documents, you should probably not type in "Esq." in this dialog box. You can include that designation in the form files directly after the FIELD(Atty. Name) code where appropriate, and leave it out in other forms as you want.

2. Type in the initials for that timekeeper in the Attorney initials window. (This information is used to store timesheets if you use the TIMESHEE.WCM macro, so be sure that each timekeeper has a unique set of initials.)

3. Use the pop-up button marked Bill Rate to specify whether the time-keeper should be billed at Partner, Associate, or Paralegal rates.

4. You can specify which timekeeper's name pops up first in the CMSDBASE.WCM and TIMESHEE.WCM initial menus by selecting the Use as default attorney checkbox near the bottom of the dialog box. The most recently selected "default" attorney appears first in both main menus.

5. When you have entered all of the information for the first timekeeper, choose Done. That information is stored in the CPSDBASE.INF file.

6. You will then see a dialog box asking if you want to add another attorney. Select Yes or No as appropriate, and repeat the process for each timekeeper you want to add.

7. If you want to edit the information for a timekeeper previously entered, choose Use from the Edit/Add Attorneys dialog box, then select the

name of the timekeeper you want to edit from the pop-up button which appears. That name is returned to the Edit/Add Attorneys dialog box where you can edit the initials, billing rate, or specify the time-keeper as the default attorney.

8. If you want to delete an attorney from the listing, repeat step 7 to select that attorney's name and return it to the Edit/Add Attorneys dialog box. Then choose Delete and respond **Y**es to the ensuing confirmation message.

After you have finished entering the attorneys as described here, you will see the Edit/Add Billing Rates dialog box as shown in figure 14.13. This dialog box is asking you to specify one or more "rate structures" to use with the Client Management System. While this information is mostly used by the TIMESHEE.WCM macro, it is probably a good idea to establish a set of rate structures for your firm or practice group and save the information with each client you set up.

Fig. 14.13
The Edit/Add
Billing Rates
dialog box.

A rate structure consists of a set of three billing rates: one each for partners, associates, and paralegals who may work on a particular file. By specifying a rate structure for each file and a bill rate for each attorney, the TIMESHEE.WCM macro can immediately determine the correct billing rate for each attorney on each case in your office. To create a rate structure, choose **A**dd in the Edit/Add Billing Rates dialog box; the Add Rate Number 1 dialog box appears as shown in figure 14.14.

Fill in the appropriate rates for partners, associates, and paralegals, then choose OK. The macro then loops to allow you to add additional rate structures, if you choose. If you do not want to enter any additional rate structures, answer "No" to the prompt, and you will be taken to the Client Management System Main Menu.

To edit any of the directories, attorney, or rate information you just entered, you can select the appropriate option from the Client Management System Main Menu to return to the setup screens just described.

Fig. 14.14
Adding a rate
structure.

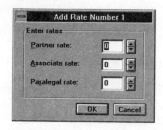

Creating a New Case Record

After you have set up CMSDBASE.WCM, the first screen you see when you
play the macro is the Client Management System Main Menu, shown in
figure 14.15.

Fig. 14.15
The Client
Management
System Main Menu.

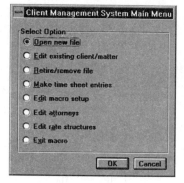

To add a new case to the Client Management System database, select the first
option, Open **n**ew file, and choose OK. The Open New Case dialog box appears, as shown in figure 14.16.

This screen includes entry fields for all of the named fields contained in the
Client Management System database, which was described previously. All
you have to do is enter information into as many of the fields for which you
have information, then choose OK to write the information into your
CMSDATA.DAT file. (The macro automatically creates that file, based on the
CMSDATA.DA! form file, if you have not created a client database file manually as described previously.)

For a discussion of the available fields and their intended uses, see table 14.1
and the corresponding discussion earlier in the chapter.

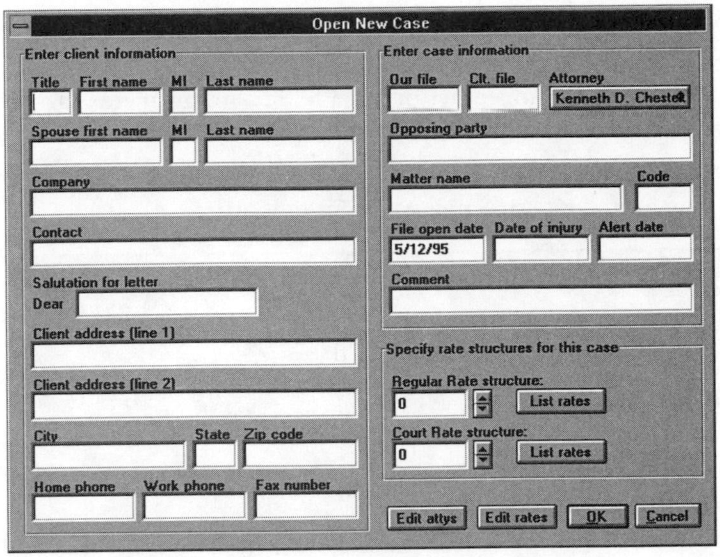

Fig. 14.16
Opening a new
file in the Client
Management
System database.

There are a few new wrinkles with this screen, however:

■ The only field in the Open New Case dialog box that is required is the Our file field, in which you specify your office file number. Any other field can be left blank if you so choose.

■ The Attorney pop-up button near the upper-right corner of the dialog box initially displays the attorney you have specified as the default attorney during the set-up phase. You can change the name for any record by clicking on that button and selecting a different attorney from the pop-up list which appears; this saves you having to type the name of the attorney.

■ The File open date field defaults to the current date, but you can change that to any date you prefer.

> **Note**
>
> You can leave any of the three available date fields blank if you prefer; but if you fill in any of them, the macro will test the input to be sure you have entered it in the correct MM/DD/YY format.

■ The group box in the lower right side of the dialog box allows you to specify two separate hourly rate structures for each case: one for non-court (regular) hours, and another for court time. This information is used by the TIMESHEE.WCM macro. If you do not use separate hourly rates for court time, simply specify the same rate for both.

- For fixed-fee, contingent fee or other billing arrangements that do not depend on the hourly rate, you can leave the rate structures as "0".

- To look up the rate structures you defined earlier, press the List rates button for the rate structure you want to look up.

Note

The rate structure information is not stored as a field in the CMSDATA.DAT file, but as binary information in the CMSRATES.BIF file to make it readily accessible to the TIMESHEE.WCM macro.

Editing Existing Cases

You can also use CMSDBASE.WCM to edit existing entries in your client database. You may have to do this to update client information, add or change an alert date, and/or a comment for a tickler system, or for any other reason.

On the Disk

This feature of the macro relies on a form file, CMSDATA.FRM, included on the Companion Disk. This file locates the record you want to edit, reads all of the contents into variables so that CMSDBASE.WCM can display the contents of the record, then quits without actually typing any text into the editing window. If you merge this file manually with the CMSDATA.DAT file, it will appear to do nothing.

To edit any active case, choose Edit existing client/matter from the Client Management System Main Menu (refer to fig. 14.15). You then see the Defined Cases/Matters list box shown in figure 14.17.

Select the case you want to edit by clicking it, then choose OK. The Edit Case Data dialog box, with the information from the selected case already filled in, appears, as shown in figure 14.18.

Make the necessary changes and choose OK to save the updated information.

Retiring or Deleting Cases

Deleting or retiring an active case is even easier. Choose Retire/remove file from the Client Management System Main Menu (refer to fig. 14.15), then select the case you want to retire or delete from the Defined Cases/matters list box (see fig. 14.17). You then see a confirmation dialog box, shown in figure 14.19, giving you two options.

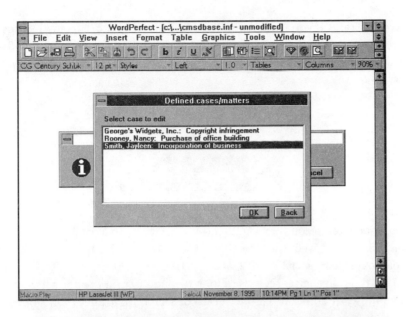

Fig. 14.17
Selecting an active
case to edit.

Fig. 14.18
Editing an
active case.

II

Assembling Documents

If you choose the first option, Mark the file as retired only, the record will
remain in your CMSDATA.DAT file, but the "Active/retired" field will be
changed to include an "R" (for retired) instead of an "A" (for active). If you
choose this option, you will still be able to send letters or extract other client
information about former clients or retired matters, because all of the client
and matter information will remain in the database. (You can design forms to

skip retired cases if you like by simply telling the Merge to skip any records where the "Active/retired" field contains an "R". For an example of how to do this, see the CASEREPT.FRM document on the Companion Disk, or study figure 14.9.)

Fig. 14.19
The options to retire or remove a case from the active client database.

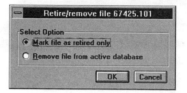

If you choose the second option, Remove file from active database, the entire record will be removed from the CMSDATA.DAT file. This helps keep your client database file to a smaller size, and speeds up the operation of some forms (because they have fewer records to look through to find the correct one), but you will lose the ability to send letters to or search for former clients or retired matters.

Using TIMESHEE.WCM

The other macro of the Client Management System is TIMESHEE.WCM, which helps you keep track of your daily activities.

Most law firms use specialized billing programs to generate bills from a computer. But getting the time spent on a case recorded and into a format that the billing department can use can be troublesome. Most software packages do not allow direct entry of time from an attorney's work station; such packages generally rely, for control reasons, on a single user or group of users to enter time in the format required by the billing software.

The path that the timesheet entries take to get from the attorney's desk to the billing department varies widely from firm to firm, and often within each firm. Some attorneys use handwritten entries on preprinted forms; others dictate time entries to their secretary or the typing pool; still others have timekeeping programs on their computers which generate hard copy to send to the billing department.

TIMESHEE.WCM falls into the final category. It generates a daily timesheet showing the case worked on, a description of the work done, the time spent on the case, the billing rate, and the value of the work performed. The billing rate is automatically retrieved from the CMSRATES.BIF file and the calculations are performed automatically; the macro also has a look-up function to allow the user to view a summary list of the active cases and select the right one, without knowing the precise file number. The timesheet generated can be then sent to the billing department for input into the main billing system.

Note

The WordPerfect Tables feature is powerful enough to be able to generate professional-looking bills comparable or superior to anything created by the dedicated billing systems. It is theoretically possible to create a complete billing program running entirely within WordPerfect. Such a system could read and automatically post the timesheets created by TIMESHEE.WCM to individual client bills, which could then be edited and printed as ordinary WordPerfect documents.

Setting Up TIMESHEE.WCM

TIMESHEE.WCM is designed so that it can either work as an adjunct to CMSDBASE.WCM, or as a stand-alone system.

If you choose to use TIMESHEE.WCM in conjunction with CMSDBASE.WCM, you need not do anything special to set it up. TIMESHEE.WCM uses the same initialization files as CMSDBASE.WCM, so that when you set up the CMSDBASE.WCM macro, the information stored there will also allow TIMESHEE.WCM to work.

When you choose to use TIMESHEE.WCM without CMSDBASE.WCM, or if you happen to run TIMESHEE.WCM before CMSDBASE.WCM, you are asked to provide certain set-up information the first time you play TIMESHEE.WCM. The set-up routine is identical to the set-up of CMSDBASE.WCM, described previously; refer to the section "Setting Up CMSDBASE.WCM" for more information about setting up the Client Management System.

One additional note is important here: One of the items you have to specify during the set-up phase of either macro is a directory where form documents are stored. TIMESHEE.WCM uses a file called TIMESHEE.FRM, supplied on the Companion Disk, as a template for all daily timesheets that it creates. Make sure that this file is located in the directory you specify for form documents during the set-up of this macro.

On the Disk

It is also recommended that, during the set-up, you specify a separate directory in which to store the completed daily timesheets. This allows you to quickly find and identify those documents later.

II

Assembling Documents

An Overview of the TIMESHEE.WCM System

If you are using TIMESHEE.WCM in conjunction with CMSDATA.WCM, you have the option of starting TIMESHEE.WCM by simply choosing the Make timesheet entries option of the Client Management System Main Menu (refer to fig. 14.15). Whether you use the two macros together or just use TIMESHEE.WCM alone, you can also start the macro simply by playing it from the Macro menu.

> **Tip**
>
> Consider assigning the TIMESHEE.WCM macro to a hot key or as a Toolbar or Menu Bar item for easy access; see chapter 1, "Making WordPerfect Work the Way You Do," for help with doing this.

Either way, every time you play TIMESHEE.WCM after it has been set up, the first screen you see is the TimeSheet Entries dialog box shown in figure 14.20. This dialog box serves as the control panel for TIMESHEE.WCM.

Fig. 14.20
The TimeSheet
Entries dialog box.

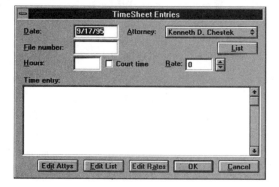

Making a timesheet entry with this dialog box is pretty straightforward, but a lot is happening in the background that is not immediately obvious. You have to understand a little bit about how the macro operates and how it stores completed timesheets.

Notice that the first two pieces of information requested by the TimeSheet Entries dialog box are the date and the attorney. The date field defaults to the current system date, but you can change this to any valid date (the macro checks your input for correct formatting of the date). In this way you can make timesheet entries for prior days if you were away from the office or otherwise unable to make the timesheet entries simultaneously with the work performed.

The attorney pop-up button also defaults to the default attorney you specified in the set-up phase. You can select a different attorney to make a timesheet entry for simply by clicking that button and choosing a name from the list of timekeepers which pops up.

TIMESHEE.WCM then takes those two bits of information and looks for the daily timesheet for that timekeeper. It does so by combining the date and the attorney name into a seven- or eight-digit filename. The first four digits are the month and day for the time being entered, and the last three or four digits are the initials of the timekeeper selected. For example, the timesheet for Kenneth D. Chestek for September 17 is stored in the timesheets directory under the filename 0917KDC (with no extension).

If TIMESHEE.WCM does not find such a timesheet when you first enter time for a specific day and attorney, TIMESHEE.WCM automatically creates that timesheet and store it in the directory you specified for timesheet entries. Subsequent timesheet entries for that attorney on that day are added to the same timesheet, with a running total of time and dollar value for the day maintained.

Note

If you have a timesheet for a particular date from a prior year already in your timesheet directory, TIMESHEE.WCM will add new time to the old timesheet. Thus, you may end up with a timesheet showing hours worked on September 17, 1994 and September 17, 1995 on the same sheet. You should therefore take care to periodically remove old timesheets from your timesheet directory.

Making the TimeSheet Entry

After you have specified the date and the attorney for whom the entry is being made, you have to specify the file number for the file on which work is being recorded. If you know that number, you can just type it in the **F**ile Number edit window near the top of the dialog box. If you do not know it, you can look it up by choosing the **L**ist button to the right of the **F**ile Number edit window. A listing of your active cases will pop up, as shown in figure 14.21.

Fig. 14.21
The list of active cases in your client database.

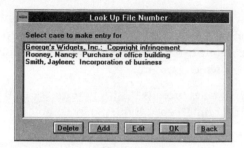

When you select a case from the list box and choose OK, that file number and case description is returned to the TimeSheet Entries dialog box, along with the billing rate you defined for that file when you created it.

> **Note**
>
> This dialog box is similar to the list box generated by CMSDBASE.WCM, shown in figure 14.17. Notice, however, that it contains more buttons at the bottom. These buttons allow you to edit the client list directly from TIMESHEE.WCM, without returning to CMSDBASE.WCM (see discussion later in this chapter). This feature also allows you to use TIMESHEE.WCM as a stand-alone macro without CMSDBASE.WCM.

When you select a case from the list box and choose OK, that file number and case description is returned to the TimeSheet Entries dialog box, along with the billing rate you defined for that file when you created it.

> **Note**
>
> If you select the Court time checkbox *before* choosing List, the macro will retrieve the predefined court rate, rather than the regular rate, to the Rate entry field in the TimeSheet Entries dialog box.

All you have to do now is fill in the number of hours worked and a description of the work performed. When you have completed this, your screen looks something like figure 14.22.

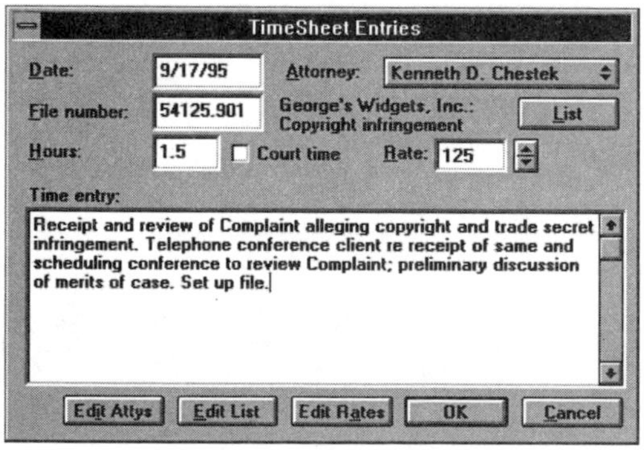

Fig. 14.22
A sample time entry, ready to post to the timesheet.

When you choose OK, the timesheet entry will be posted to the correct timesheet, stored under the filename by the method described previously. You will then see a confirmation message, shown in figure 14.23, asking if you want to make another time entry. If you choose **Y**es, the macro will loop back to the TimeSheet Entries dialog box so you can make another entry, either for the same day and same attorney, a different day and a different attorney, or any combination thereof. If you choose **N**o, the macro will end.

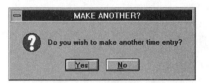

Fig. 14.23
The option to make an additional timesheet entry.

A sample completed timesheet, in the format set up by TIMESHEE.FRM, is shown in figure 14.24.

Fig. 14.24
A sample completed timesheet.

TIMESHEET ENTRIES

DATE: 9/17/95
ATTY: KDC

File	Description	Hrs.	Rate	Value
54125.901	Receipt and review of Complaint alleging copyright and trade secret infringement. Telephone conference client re receipt of same and scheduling conference to review Complaint; preliminary discussion of merits of case. Set up file.	1.50	$125	$187.50
543245a	Review of Articles of Agreement, subtenant leases, mortgage documents and other paperwork regarding proposed transfer of building. Telephone conference city zoning and building inspection offices seeking certifications required for closing.	1.30	$125	$162.50
67425.101	Conference client, co-owner and co-owner's counsel re buy-sell agreements, issues relating to guarantys and limitation of liabilities, new bank loan to finance corporate expansion and miscellaneous matters. Initial preparation of draft Agreement between parties, buy-sell agreement and necessary corporate minutes to reflect same.	3.70	$125	$462.50
				$0.00
TOTALS		6.50		$812.50

II

Assembling Documents

Editing the Client list

If you are using TIMESHEE.WCM in conjunction with the CMSDBASE.WCM macro, the best way to update the client list is by adding, retiring, or deleting clients from the Client Management System Main Menu. This not only updates the file number and billing rate look-up feature of TIMESHEE.WCM, it also maintains a complete and accurate database with all relevant client information.

If, however, you are using TIMESHEE.WCM as a stand-alone macro, and are not using the CMSDBASE.WCM macro, you can still edit the look-up features in TIMESHEE.WCM. There are several ways of doing this.

From the TimeSheet Entries dialog box (refer to fig. 14.20), you can choose any of three buttons to edit, respectively, the list of attorneys in the firm, the case list, or the defined rate structures. The attorney list and rate structure buttons take you to the same editing screens you saw when you initially set up the Client Management System, described earlier in this chapter.

Choosing Edit List from the TimeSheet Entries dialog box takes you to the Edit Case List dialog box, which is functionally identical to the Look Up File Number dialog box shown in figure 14.21. From that box, you can choose buttons to add a new case to the list, delete a selected case from the list, or edit a selected case that currently appears on the list.

However, adding or editing cases does not work the same way as in CPSDBASE.WCM, because TIMESHEE.WCM only needs a few pieces of information. You are asked to enter the full screen of client information as in figure 14.16. Suppose, for example, you want to edit an existing case (even one that you set up with CMSDBASE.WCM). You will see a screen similar to figure 14.25.

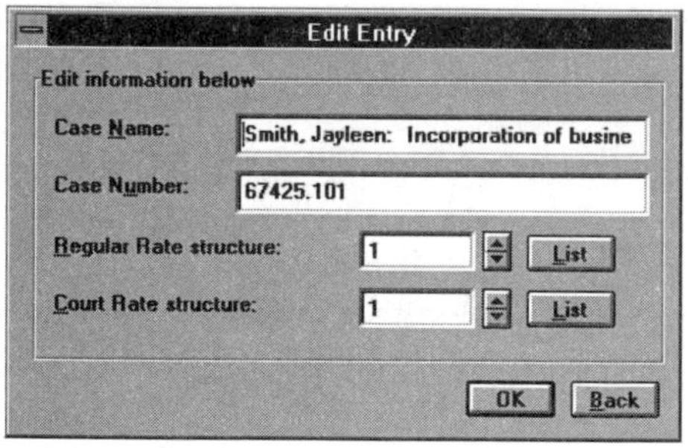

Fig. 14.25

Editing a case listing for TIMESHEE.WCM.

Any changes you make to the information shown in this screen are *not* recorded in the CMSDATA.DAT file; rather, they are stored in the initialization files CMSDBASE.INF and CMSRATES.BIF. These changes will appear in the look-up boxes in both TIMESHEE.WCM and CMSDBASE.WCM in future sessions, however.

> **Tip**
>
> You can use this feature to make quick adjustments to the billing rate structure without running CMSDBASE.WCM if you like, or to make adjustments in the screen listing of a particular case without affecting the entry in the CMSDATA.DAT database itself.

Conclusion

In this chapter, you learned about a Client Management System to help you maintain an accurate listing of your current clients. You learned how to write form files to extract information from that database, and saw how two macros on the Companion Disk can help you maintain the database and help you keep track of the hours you spend working on different cases in your office.

This book has covered a lot of ground in relatively few pages. It is not designed to be the "answer of all answers" to your law office word-processing needs. Hopefully, you have gained an understanding of some of the more useful features of WordPerfect for Windows, and learned some tricks that you can put to immediate use in your office.

I also hope that you can take away from this book some useful ideas about ways in which you can make the production of documents more painless and efficient. There are many ways to solve most word-processing problems. Hopefully, this book has suggested several (or many!) which you find useful. The only way to find out if these suggestions work for you is to jump in and try them out. You may be surprised at how easy things really can be!

What's on the Disk

The Companion Disk included with the book contains numerous files, including macros, templates, and other form documents. The use of each of these files is described in the body of the book.

Installing the Files

The files included on the disk are in compressed format, and they must be installed using the installation program provided on the disk. To install the files:

1. Put the Companion Disk in your computer's floppy drive. (For the purpose of these instructions, we are assuming your floppy drive is drive A. If the appropriate floppy drive is B or another designation, use that designation in step 3 below.)

2. From the Windows Program Manager, choose **File**, **R**un.

3. In the Command Line text box, type **a:\install** and click OK.

4. Optional: Specify the drive where you want the program to install the files to.

5. After the files are unzipped, click OK and then click **C**lose.

The files are installed to the designated directories described below.

Default Directories for the Files

To prevent one of the files on the Companion Disk from accidentally overwriting a macro or file with the same filename that already exists on your hard drive, the installation program will create a new directory,

C:\WPWINLAW, and several subdirectories below that. (If you specified a drive other than C: in step 4 above, the directory will be placed in the drive you specified.)

The directory structure created by the installation program, and the kinds of files stored in each directory, will look like this:

C:\WPWINLAW   Root directory; no files

    \MACROS   All macro files (.WCM extensions)

        \TEMPLATE   All template files (.WPT extensions)

           \MISC   Various other files (.FRM, .DA!, .INF extensions)

Using the Files

The operation and use of all macros and files is described in the body of the book. However, to use the files effectively, you need to set up your WordPerfect preferences so that the program can locate the files.

Several of the macros "nest" (or play) other macros. For this to happen, all of the macros in the C:\WPWINLAW\MACROS directory must be in either the main or supplemental macro directory defined in your computer's preference settings. You can do this either by copying all of the macros in that directory to your main macros directory, or by specifying C:\WPWINLAW\MACROS as the Supplemental Macros Directory.

Likewise, the Template files must be located in either the main or Additional template directories. Again, you can do this by copying all of those files to your Main Template Directory or by specifying C:\WPWINLAW\TEMPLATE as your Additional Template Directory.

To specify these directories as your Supplemental Macros Directory and Additional Template Directory, do this:

1. From the **E**dit menu, choose P**r**eferences.

   Or, from the **F**ile menu, choose P**r**eferences.

2. Choose **F**ile.

3. In the File Preferences dialog box which appears, select **M**acros.

4. In the S**u**pplemental Macro Directory text box, type **C:\WPWINLAW\MACROS** (or whatever drive you specified when the macros were first installed).

5. In the File Preferences dialog box, now choose **T**emplates.

6. In the Additional Directory text box, type **C:\WPWINLAW\TEMPLATE** (again, change the drive letter if you have installed the files to a drive other than C:).

7. Choose OK to close the File Preferences dialog box.

8. Choose Close to close the Preferences dialog box and store the new directories with your preferences.

If you had previously set up a Supplemental Macro Directory or an Additional Template Directory, you can always return to your prior choices using the steps listed above.

> **Tip**
>
> Once you become comfortable with the macros and templates on the disk, consider moving those files to your primary macro or template directories.

List of Files

Following is a complete listing of all of the files found on the Companion Disk, by chapter in which they are discussed. The operation of each of these macros and files is described in the chapter listed.

Chapter 1, "Making WordPerfect Work the Way You Do"

 FOOTER.WCM

Chapter 2, "Outline, Numbers, and More"

 PARANUM.WCM

 BRIEF.WPT

Chapter 3, "Tricks with Typography"

 HEADER.WCM

 NAMEFOOT.WCM

Chapter 4, "Footnotes, Tables, and Compare"

 MAKETOA.WCM

 CASECITE.WCM

 CONSTCIT.WCM

 STATCITE.WCM

 OTHERCIT.WCM

Chapter 5, "Automating with Macros"

BRFMENU.WCM

Chapter 8, "Document Assembly"

DOCSETUP.WCM

DOCBILDR.WCM

Chapter 9, "Correspondence Systems"

MEMO.WCM

PHONEMSG.WCM

MRG2ADRS.WCM

ENV2DOC.WCM

DOC2ENV.WCM

MRG2ENV.WCM

LETRMAKR.WCM

LETRMAKR.WPT

CLOSINGS.WCM

FAXSHEET.WPT

Chapter 10, "Litigation Documents"

MEDAUTH.WPT

RELEASE.WPT

WRITECAP.WCM

PCLOSING.WCM

FIRMNAME.WCM

NEWPLEAD.WPT

TITLE.WCM

NOTDEPOS.WPT

LITMENU.WCM

Chapter 11, "Real Estate Documents"

WARDEED1.FRM

MORTGAGE.FRM

PROMNOTE.FRM

CERTITLE.FRM

REPSDATA.DA!

REPSMENU.WCM

HUD_1.WPT

HUD_1LP.WPT

Chapter 12, "Commercial Law Practice"

LDEBTOR1.FRM

LFORWRD.FRM

LFORWRD1.FRM

LDEBTOR2.FRM

COMPLT1.FRM

CPSDATA.DA!

CPSMENU.WCM

CPSLEDGR.WCM

COLLEDGR.FRM

Chapter 13, "Wills and Estate Planning"

HWILL.FRM

WWILL.FRM

ESTATEPL.DA!

DOCBILDR.INF

INTERVIV.FRM

Chapter 14, "Client/Case Management"

CMSDATA.DA!

CLNTLIST.FRM

CLNTLETR.FRM

ATTYCLNT.FRM

CASETYPE.FRM

CHKCONFL.FRM

CASEREPT.FRM

CMSDATA.FRM

TICKLER.FRM

TIMESHEE.FRM

CMSDBASE.WCM

TIMESHEE.WCM

Index

Symbols

Complete and Return this Card
for a *FREE* Computer Book Catalog

Thank you for purchasing this book! You have purchased a superior computer book written expressly for your needs. To continue to provide the kind of up-to-date, pertinent coverage you've come to expect from us, we need to hear from you. Please take a minute to complete and return this self-addressed, postage-paid form. In return, we'll send you a free catalog of all our computer books on topics ranging from word processing to programming and the internet.

Mrs. ☐ Ms. ☐ Dr. ☐

me (first) [ ] (M.I.) ☐ (last) [ ]

dress [ ]

[ ]

y [ ] State [ ] Zip [ ]

one [ ] Fax [ ]

mpany Name [ ]

nail address [ ]

Please check at least (3) influencing factors for purchasing this book.

nt or back cover information on book .... ☐
ecial approach to the content .... ☐
mpleteness of content .... ☐
thor's reputation .... ☐
olisher's reputation .... ☐
ok cover design or layout .... ☐
lex or table of contents of book .... ☐
ce of book .... ☐
ecial effects, graphics, illustrations .... ☐
ner (Please specify): _____ ☐

How did you first learn about this book?

w in Macmillan Computer Publishing catalog .... ☐
commended by store personnel .... ☐
w the book on bookshelf at store .... ☐
commended by a friend .... ☐
ceived advertisement in the mail .... ☐
w an advertisement in: _____ ☐
ad book review in: _____ ☐
ner (Please specify): _____ ☐

How many computer books have you purchased in the last six months?

is book only .... ☐   3 to 5 books .... ☐
ooks .... ☐   More than 5 .... ☐

4. Where did you purchase this book?

Bookstore .... ☐
Computer Store .... ☐
Consumer Electronics Store .... ☐
Department Store .... ☐
Office Club .... ☐
Warehouse Club .... ☐
Mail Order .... ☐
Direct from Publisher .... ☐
Internet site .... ☐
Other (Please specify): _____ ☐

5. How long have you been using a computer?

☐ Less than 6 months   ☐ 6 months to a year
☐ 1 to 3 years   ☐ More than 3 years

6. What is your level of experience with personal computers and with the subject of this book?

	With PCs	With subject of book
New	☐	☐
Casual	☐	☐
Accomplished	☐	☐
Expert	☐	☐

Source Code ISBN: 0-7897-0613-x

7. Which of the following best describes your job title?

- Administrative Assistant ☐
- Coordinator ☐
- Manager/Supervisor ☐
- Director ☐
- Vice President ☐
- President/CEO/COO ☐
- Lawyer/Doctor/Medical Professional ☐
- Teacher/Educator/Trainer ☐
- Engineer/Technician ☐
- Consultant ☐
- Not employed/Student/Retired ☐
- Other (Please specify): _____ ☐

8. Which of the following best describes the area of the company your job title falls under?

- Accounting ☐
- Engineering ☐
- Manufacturing ☐
- Operations ☐
- Marketing ☐
- Sales ☐
- Other (Please specify): _____ ☐

9. What is your age?

- Under 20 ☐
- 21-29 ☐
- 30-39 ☐
- 40-49 ☐
- 50-59 ☐
- 60-over ☐

10. Are you:

- Male ☐
- Female ☐

11. Which computer publications do you read regularly? (Please list)

_____
_____
_____
_____
_____
_____
_____
_____
_____
_____
_____

Comments: _____
_____
_____

Fold here and scotch-tape to mail.